GERMANTOWN PRESBYTERIAN CHURCH
2363 Germantown Road
Germantown, Tennessee

CHRISTIAN RELIGIOUS EDUCATION

CHRISTIAN RELIGIOUS EDUCATION

Sharing Our Story and Vision

THOMAS H. GROOME

HARPER & ROW, PUBLISHERS

SAN FRANCISCO

Cambridge
Hagerstown
Philadelphia
San Francisco

1817

London
Mexico City
São Paulo
Sydney

Designed by Jim Mennick

Library of Congress Cataloging in Publication Data

Groome, Thomas H
CHRISTIAN RELIGIOUS EDUCATION.

Bibliography: p. 279
Includes index.
1. Christian education. I. Title.
BV1471.2.G687   207   80-7755
ISBN 0–06–063491–X

---

81 82 83 84 10 9 8 7 6 5 4 3 2

To the memory of my parents,
Terence P. Groome and Margaret Flood Groome,
who together told me both Story and Vision

Contents

Preface

IN SEPTEMBER 1966 I walked into a "religion" class for the first time as teacher. The setting was a Catholic boys' high school, and some thirty-five juniors awaited me there. I was a third-year theologian in a seminary nearby, and they were my "ministerial practicum" for the year. The course, entitled simply Religion III, was scheduled to meet three times each week for forty-five minutes. A few days earlier the person in charge of the religion program gave me a text book with a comment that sounded slightly apologetic. He said in effect that, given my extensive theological background, he was sure I would not need the text; however, the topics suggested by the chapter headings were the material to be covered in junior year.

I, too, assumed that I had to do little more than draw upon my new-found theological wisdom, which, because it was so limited, seemed extensive at the time. The weekend before the class began I prepared three fine lectures for delivery and sallied forth that first Monday morning with the enthusiasm that belongs only to a neophyte. And on that Monday morning I had my own first "great awakening" as a religious educator. At least that is how I now describe from a distance what happened, but at the time it seemed more like a catastrophe. By the end of my third lecture I knew only one thing with certainty—I was using the wrong approach.

The beginnings of my metanoia (and it was a change of heart) were caused by a number of factors, but especially by the students' very obvious and nearly total lack of interest in the fine lectures I had prepared. In a mood akin to desperation, fraught with insecurity, I abandoned my lecture notes. Not knowing what to do next, I decided that I should talk to the students about my quandary, tell them my problem, and indicate that it would also be their problem since we were assigned to each other for the remainder of the school year.

Somewhat humbled, on the second Monday morning I asked for their advice as to how we should spend our time together in Religion III. Their reaction was like a damburst. They had never been asked that question in religion before, and they certainly took the opportunity to voice their opinions. Over the following weeks we continued to talk and listen to each other. Gradually a pattern began to emerge. They developed a list of religious topics and life issues of interest to them that became our curriculum. Following some discussion of each one in small groups and in the total group, I would then respond, explaining my understanding of the Christian tradition in regard to each life issue or matter of faith which they had raised (I even used some of my old lecture notes). But even after my presentation of "the answers" to their questions, the case was seldom accepted as closed. The questioning and reflection went on. My first reaction was to stifle or reprimand their continuing skepticism. But on second thought I knew I could not do so, although their apparent lack of faith in my answers continued to worry me. Now I wrestled with whether or not I was really doing my job. By the end of the year I found that we had in fact talked about much of the curriculum outlined in the text book. But this had happened in the midst of a great deal of dialogue, discussion, debate, open disagreement, and common struggle. We had also become friends, and I at least had come to know better the little I knew.

Before long the course was much talked about within the school. One teacher asked if he could sit in to observe. At the end of the class he seemed enthusiastic about what he had witnessed and asked me, "What are you doing in this class?" To my amazement, I could not tell him. I assumed I knew what I was doing since I was (or we were) doing it, but when asked the question point-blank, I could not give an adequate response. I spent the next few days in self-questioning, and some doubt. I met him again and explained, "Well, I'm not shoving religion down their throats any more." He replied, "Yes, but what *are* you doing?" Again, I could not name our activity, neither for him nor for myself.

In one way or another, at all age levels and in a variety of settings, I have been "doing" Christian religious education ever since that September, and I am still trying to answer my first observer's question. His question and my efforts to answer it led me to other questions that seem equally foundational and at least as important. The answers I have given to them have shaped and given form to my own educational praxis,[1] just as my praxis has shaped how I answer them.

What follows is a reflection on my own praxis as a religious educator over the years and on the praxis of many fine religious educators I have observed or with whom I have worked. I hasten to add that I also have turned to and been greatly informed by pedagogical, philosophical, theological, psychological, and sociological literature and research, as will be evident, I trust, from what follows. That "scholarly quest" led up to my doctoral work in religion and education and continues to the present. Whatever clarity and insight I offer here have arisen from the mutual enrichment of theory and praxis, both my own and those of other educators.

Long since that first September I have become convinced, in head and heart, that there are no easy answers to the questions posed by the task of religious education. To do religious education well is a most difficult challenge. It is certainly an enterprise in which, to use Dietrich Bonhoeffer's term, there is no "cheap grace." Like many others, I have spent my time over the past years on the array of bandwagons that have come through promising easy solutions, only to be disillusioned again and again. When Alfred North Whitehead wrote "I merely utter the warning that education is a difficult problem, to be solved by no one simple formula,"[2] he was stating a truism, but one whose truth we are often reluctant to face. We continue to search for the right technique or "how to do it," hoping that such will be on the next bandwagon. But it will not be there. There is no sure and simple technique. Anyone who appears to offer as much is immediately deserving of our skepticism.

On the other hand, from my research and experience I have become equally convinced that there are a number of foundational questions which undergird the whole enterprise of education, including Christian religious education. While these questions and the ways we answer them form the bedrock of our enterprise, in practice they are typically treated as taken-for-granted assumptions that usually remain at a subconscious level in our educational decision making. But if we are to give our practice intentionality (in other words, if it is truly to be a praxis), and if we are to give it form in a manner likely to promote our intentions, then these issues must be posed as foundational and abiding questions. At the intersection of theory and practice each would-be Christian religious educator must consciously answer these questions for himself or herself, and our sponsoring communities must answer for themselves. The degree of critical consciousness and intentionality we have about them will shape our praxis of religious education.

My own religious tradition is the Christian one, and more immediately the Catholic expression of it. Because my religious education has been done from within the Christian tradition and community of faith, I choose the title *Christian Religious Education* for what I reflect on here. I am deeply concerned with other expressions of religious education, and indeed with education of any kind. I hope my reflections can strike resonant notes in the hearts of religious educators from other traditions, especially from the Jewish tradition. But I know that any possibility of the universal must always be grounded in the particular, and I recognize that the only religious education I know sufficiently to share reflections on is the one I know from my own praxis.

The What are you doing? question posed by my observer remains first here. That first question then gives rise to five other foundational questions. Because of the years of praxis and theoretical research in the interim, I am in a slightly better position to respond to them now. The six questions, which can be characterized by their interrogative pronouns—what, why, where, how, when, and who—constitute the six parts of the book:

Part I, The Nature of Christian Religious Education (the What)
Part II, The Purpose of Christian Religious Education (the Why)
Part III, The Context of Christian Religious Education (the Where)
Part IV, An Approach to Christian Religious Education: Shared Praxis (a How)
Part V, Readiness for Christian Religious Education by Shared Praxis (the When)
Part VI, The Copartners in Christian Religious Education (the Who)

Readers already familiar with my attempts to use and articulate what I call a shared praxis approach to Christian religious education may wonder how that is included in this work. I describe it in Part IV. The fact that it takes up four chapters and about one-third of the book indicates the importance I attach to this part of my presentation. However, this work is not intended exclusively as an argument for or an explanation of a shared praxis approach to Christian religious education. True, the responses I pose to the other foundational questions lead me to answer the "how" question with such an approach, just as my own experience with shared praxis shapes how I answer the other foundational questions. I hope my use of that approach can inform other educators, but I am not arguing that all Christian religious educators should use a shared praxis approach and as I use it. I am arguing, however, that each of us must come consciously to realize and intend what we are doing as Christian religious educators, why we are doing it, the social context in which our educating takes place, the "readiness" of our copartners for our educational approach, and their and our identity in that partnership.

The very least of my intentions is that the responses I propose here to these six foundational issues be taken as a final word for either myself or my readers. I state them strongly because I am convinced of their value. They have made sense to me and to other Christian educators. But not only are they not *the* last word, they are not even *my* last word. My very commitment to the truth that is in these responses requires that my positions continue to develop and expand.

And other religious educators must bring their own selves and praxis to answer these basic questions. By responding to them together, we will explain the hope that is in us (1 Pet. 3:15) and keep that hope alive.

This book is intended for any religious educator who is interested in raising and reflecting on such foundational issues. Some familiarity with the literature and practice of religious education is presumed. For this reason people professionally trained in the field may have a slight advantage in reading it, but I believe that nonprofessionals may also benefit from what is presented here. In an attempt to speak to both audiences I take little for granted by way of previous professional training; on the other hand, I often only recognize in passing or relegate to footnotes debates and issues that may be of more interest to specialists in particular disciplines. (The possible exception is Chapter Eight, in which I outline my philosophical roots for a praxis way of knowing in Christian religious education.) However, the work invites self-reflection on the part of any reader and thus often calls for pause, wrestling with ideas, struggle, and decision making—in other words, some hard work. Given the challenge and difficulty of our task, we cannot expect to fulfill it with less.

The very journey to maturity of faith itself demands a struggle and a certain "wrestling." To come to religious identity requires that we wrestle, like Jacob of old, with ourselves, with our past, with our present, with our future, and even with our God (see Gen. 32:23–33). The educational process that attempts to sponsor people toward maturity of faith can be expected to entail a similar kind of struggle. Our wrestling must be at the level of the foundational issues and questions posed by the enterprise itself. Our ways of responding will vary from one point on our pilgrimage to another, but the issues are abiding. Our responses should be informed not only by our own experience and insights, but also by the insights of the generations of educators who have gone before us, even as we hope our efforts will be worthy of inheritance by those who come after us. Only by holding our past traditions, our present opportunities, and our future possibilities in fruitful tension can we fulfill our responsibility as educators in our time and be faithful to "the truth handed down." But holding them in a fruitful tension requires that we do our own share of wrestling. That will continue until the coming of God's reign in its fullness.

The note format used throughout the book is as follows. In the interest of conserving space, the complete publication details of all works cited are given only in the Bibliography at the end of the book. In the notes at the end of each chapter only the author's surname and the title of the work are cited. When a frequently cited work has a lengthy title, an abbreviated form of the title is used. Thus, for example, Alfred North Whitehead, *The Aims of Education and Other*

Essays (New York: The Free Press, 1929), p. 14, is cited simply as Whitehead, *Aims,* p. 14. The notes for each Prologue are at the end of the chapter that follows it. The scripture quotations are taken from the New American Bible.

I have attempted throughout to use inclusive language. Thus I prefer the slightly cumbersome he or she, his or her, etc., to so-called generic terms and hope that we will soon have a more aesthetic but inclusive language to talk about ourselves. However, since many of the works cited were written before we were so conscious of exclusive language, when quoting other authors, I allow their statements to stand as printed in the original, rather than taking it upon myself to "correct" their language.

My pleasant duty now is to express a deep sense of gratitude to a host of people who have helped and supported me in bringing this work to publication. Most notably, I am indebted to my colleagues in the Institute of Religious Education and Pastoral Ministry at Boston College. The Institute has a "spirit" that is rare in academia; I have experienced here the blessing of working with colleagues who are also friends. Our constant and open dialogue has greatly shaped my positions, and they contributed by reading large sections of the manuscript in its formative stages. Thus, to Richard P. McBrien (who first urged me to write this book), Padraic O'Hare, Mary C. Boys, and Claire E. Lowery, each in his or her own way a steadfast source of encouragement, help, and advice, I am deeply grateful. Other colleagues in the department of theology, Boston College, have also given generously of their time in reading different parts of the manuscript that pertained to their expertise. I am especially indebted to Professors Theodore Steeman, Frederick G. Lawrence, Pheme Perkins, Margaret Gorman, Lisa Sowle Cahill, and James W. Fowler (now at Emory University, Atlanta). Sr. Maryann Confoy, for whom I served as doctoral advisor, also read and commented on the manuscript. Professor Dwayne Huebner, my friend and former advisor at Columbia University, read most of the first draft and, as so often in the past, offered insightful criticisms as well as support and encouragement.

Joseph De Martino has been my student assistant over the past year, and his meticulous care in checking and double-checking every quotation, footnote, and biblical reference leaves me much in his debt. Professor Elizabeth White of the English department, Boston College, read the first and roughest draft of the manuscript and attempted to put my Celtic style into less loquacious English. Nancy Witting also read the entire manuscript and gave editorial advice. My editor at Harper & Row, John Loudon, has been generous with his editorial assistance and encouragement, especially during the "last mile," which indeed seemed the longest. I am also grateful to my typist Cheri Sheaff, who, among other things, mastered the nigh-impossible task of reading my handwriting.

And there were some other special helpers. My brother and sister-in-law, Bernard and Dorine Dwyer Groome, have supported and believed in what I am doing as only family can. In many ways I wrote this book for their son Brian, my godson, and for all the other two-year-olds who someday may benefit from what is here. My dear friend and colleague Sharon Parks lent insight and nuance to many of my ideas, while her encouragement and support have saved the manuscript on a number of occasions when it hovered dangerously close to my trashcan. Philip J. King, professor of Old Testament at Boston College, has been an example as a senior scholar, a sponsor, and a true friend.

Finally, I owe more than I will ever know to a host of other people, too many to mention. I am referring especially to the people who have been with me in courses, workshops, seminars, and symposia where many of the ideas here have been shared. From my fourth-grade C.C.D. class to my graduate students at Boston College; from Newfoundland, Canada, to Queensland, Australia, I have learned much from the reactions, objections, and perceptions of many people.

To all of these people I am deeply grateful. They have contributed more than they know, or might want to own, to what is here. I alone accept responsibility for its limitations.

THOMAS H. GROOME

Boston College
Thanksgiving, 1979

NOTES

1. The term *praxis* will occur many times throughout this work. Chapter Eight will deal with it at length. For now let it be understood as "reflective action," that is, a practice that is informed by theoretical reflection, or, conversely, a theoretical reflection that is informed by practice. I use it here in preference to the more common word *practice* because the latter term very often has the connotation of a skill or a technique, or of something that is done as the application of theory and is thus, in fact, dichotomized from theory. The term *praxis* attempts to keep theory and practice together as dual and mutually enriching moments of the same intentional human activity.
2. Whitehead, *Aims,* p. 36.

THE NATURE OF
CHRISTIAN RELIGIOUS
EDUCATION

Prologue

IT IS difficult to name what is actually done in the act of educating. Although the enterprise has a recognizable history that spans at least three millennia, when we raise the question, What are we doing when we educate? there is little consensus about the nature of the activity itself. A more abstract question, such as What is education? might be more easily answered. But education is not an ahistorical abstraction. It is a human activity. "Education" as such does not exist, there is only what people do and want to do in its name, and that is the heart of the matter.

There may be a reluctance on our part as educators to face this foundational question. What are we doing? when asked seriously calls for an examination of conscience we might prefer to avoid. But surely it is one of the most fundamental questions to any human enterprise. For educators a clear consciousness (and conscience) about the nature of our activity is necessary if we are to do in fact what we intend to do. Part I is an attempt to describe—to name—the nature of educational activity, and, more particularly, the nature of religious education within the Christian faith community.

In recent years the growing awareness among religious educators of the need for clarity about the nature of our educational activity has expressed itself in a concerted effort to define our terms, which in turn has led to "the language debate."[1] Are we doing religious education, or religious instruction, or education in religion? If we are educating in the Christian faith tradition, then should we call our activity Christian (or even more specifically Catholic, or Baptist, or Presbyterian, etc.) education, or Church education, or catechesis? All such terms and many more are in current usage in the Christian Church. But are they all equally descriptive? Can they be used interchangeably, or is there a difference in the activities described by the different terms?

I will express some caveats about the language debate. It would be foolish, however, to dismiss it as a mere exercise in semantics. I share Heidegger's conviction that "language is the house of Being."[2] Language names the world within which we reside and thus establishes both its limits and its horizons. We create it, but language in turn shapes our consciousness and either expands or maintains the parameters of our lives. For this reason there is a constant concern throughout this book for the language we use to name our world and a search for language capable of promoting a Christian religious education that is emancipatory. The debate about terms in religious education is, in fact, a debate about the nature of the activity itself. Thus the attempt to name the nature of Christian religious education activity will conclude (Chapter Two) with a "coming to terms." But first it is necessary to look at the nature of education in time.

Education in Time

THREE ASSUMPTIONS AND CONCERNS OF
EDUCATORS OVER TIME

Education is as old as human consciousness. Small wonder, then, that many of the great philosophers and thinkers of history have given their time and attention to it. Plato, Aristotle, Augustine, Alcuin, Aquinas, Erasmus, Luther, Calvin, Comenius, Locke, Rousseau, Kant, Pestalozzi, Hegel, Herbart, Marx, Whitehead, and Dewey all have membership in education's pantheon. And yet, like all great human questions and enterprises, it has eluded anything like a universally accepted definition or description.

The etymology of the word offers a significant clue to the nature of the activity itself. The English word comes from the Latin *ducare* (and its cognate *ducere*), meaning "to lead," and the prefix *e*, meaning "out." At its root meaning, then, education is an activity of "leading out."

Three dimensions or points of emphasis can be discerned in "leading out": 1) a point from which, 2) a present process, and 3) a future toward which the leading out is done. In this sense, education has an "already," a "being realized," and a "not yet" dimension to it. While these three dimensions should never be separated in practice, they can be distinguished for the sake of analysis.

The "already" dimension is expressive of either what the learner already knows or what the educator knows and the learner has the inner capacity to consciously appropriate. The image of a sculptor who "educes" a statue from a piece of marble may help to clarify this dimension. The figure was already in the marble potentially. The sculptor knows what the shape of it ought to be and educes out the possibility which the marble already possessed within itself. (This image should not be pushed too far in an educational context or it leads to total passivity on the students' part.)

The second dimension, a "present process being realized," emphasizes not what is there already, but what is being discovered by the learner as it comes to meet him or her from beyond present limitations. In this dimension knowledge is more to be met and discovered in the experience of the journey than to be awakened or formed by someone who already knows the design of it.

When these two emphases are placed together, they give rise to a tension that has characterized the debate about the process of knowing at least since Plato and Aristotle. Is knowledge promoted by guiding the self-discovery of the learner from present experience, or is it attained by awakening the dormant potential of the person for what is already known. Plato took the latter view, arguing that knowledge is already in the soul as sight is in the eye.[3] The inner spark only needs to be fanned and guided to be brought to conscious possession. On the other hand, Aristotle argued that "nothing is ever in the mind that was not first in the senses." Since the senses gather their data from the outside and take it inward, for Aristotle the knowing process has its origin in sense experience and not, as Plato claimed, by the awakening of what was already within us. Paradoxically, both positions are true, and educational activity must reflect the truth in each of them.

The third dimension, "not yetness," refers to the point toward which the leading out is done. To lead out is an activity directed toward the future, toward a horizon beyond one's present limits and not yet realized. Since our future is open, there can never be an end to the human possibility for knowledge. This future dimension is a transcendent aspect of educational activity; it enables people to transcend what they are to become what they are not yet, but potentially can be. In their own way, both of the first two dimensions of educational activity share this future emphasis. To consciously appropriate what was already there in potency, or to discover through present experience what was not previously known are both movements toward a "new" future.

These three emphases discernible in the word *education*—the already, the present experienced process, and the movement toward a new future—are evident throughout the historical practice of education. In fact, they constitute three fundamental assumptions about the nature of all educational activity, which in turn give rise to three concerns that cause us to educate. The three assumptions, and their corresponding concerns, correlate with our traditional words for talking about time—past, present, and future. But, to sound a caveat that I return to below, we educators must be extremely cautious in our understanding of time. While we may use our traditional words to talk about time, it is imperative for

our educational activity that we not understand past, present, and future as separated from each other in the old linear sense. If time is thus misunderstood as
three separate times, then educational activity tends to emphasize one and neglect the other two to the detriment of the whole enterprise.

THE ASSUMPTION AND CONCERN FOR THE "PAST"

One of the basic assumptions from which educational activity arises is that
the people who were here before us learned from their experience. This assumption gives rise to a concern that we preserve what is "already" known in
the heritage of the human family. This is what Dewey called "the funded capital of civilization."[4] Part of the task of education is to ensure that our "funded
capital" is conserved and made available to people in the present. Without it our
present is impoverished and our future diminished. And while we can appropriate it only in our own present experience, this knowledge comes to us out of the
past of our people, the fruits of their experience and experimentation. In other
words, it is more inherited by us from the community we join than discovered
from our own experience.

In the context of educational activity, the funded capital of civilization is
typically organized into traditions of knowledge and disciplines of learning. For
example, there is a tradition and discipline of engineering developed by the past
experience and experimentation of the engineering community. The educator's
task is to make that tradition available to present and future generations of engi-
neers. Without such conservation and transmission each generation would have
to reinvent the wheel. Thus, we are motivated to educate so that out of the past
heritage of our people we may build a present and future for ourselves and our
students.

There is an obvious wisdom and validity in this assumption about and concern for knowledge already known. When it is given primacy in educational decisions, the curriculum is drawn mainly from the disciplines of knowledge.
Pedagogically it tends to express itself in a deductive or didactic form of teaching
that takes the content of the disciplines as its starting point. Undoubtedly deductive teaching in the disciplines of learning can be a most appropriate and rich
form of educational activity. However, when carried to an extreme (and such is
often, though not inevitably, the case[5]), undue emphasis on what is "already"
known leads to what Paulo Freire calls "the 'banking' concept of education"[6]
and the assumption that education is simply a matter of depositing information
in passive receptacles. But as Whitehead well wrote, "It must never be forgotten
that education is not a process of packing articles in a trunk."[7] Attention to
what is already known will always be an essential emphasis of educational activity, but it cannot be allowed to hold sway without balance.

THE ASSUMPTION AND CONCERN FOR THE "PRESENT"

The section on time below argues that the "present" is the only time that actually exists for us, and within the present reside the heritage of the past and the possibility of the future. Long before such an existentialist understanding of time was current, however, educational activity demonstrated an assumption about the present and a concern for its role in human knowing. The reason for such attention to the present can be stated simply. The time of immediate engagement in life is the present. We are not "now" in the past, nor "now" in the future. Therefore, knowledge as a human possibility must be appropriated by a present process. Even when educators emphasize the heritage of knowledge already known as the starting point for educational activity, the wiser ones recognize that to truly appropriate such knowledge as their own, students must enter into a present active encounter with that heritage. Without such a present active process (in one sense a rediscovering), students are reduced to passivity, and memorization rather than cognition takes place. A contemporary expression of this insight can be found in Piaget's insistence that to truly understand anything, even what was previously known, requires that we "reinvent" it in the sense of coming to see its truth for ourselves.[8] In consequence, Piaget claims, all cognition must be grounded in a present active/reflective process.

But beyond this, present experience is not merely a means of actively learning what was already known by people before us. From present experience we come to know what may not have been known before, or not known in the same way. Since cognition springs from present active experience, the present is a source of knowledge in its own right; it has a possibility for new knowledge that must be respected and promoted. The present does not merely appropriate and rediscover what was already known; it adds to the heritage of knowledge.

This concern for the present is an expression of the creative dimension of educational activity. If the present is allowed to do no more than inherit the past, then creativity is stifled and the consequence is more domesticating than educating. True education can never settle for sameness. It is to be a leading out rather than a standing still.

As concern for the heritage of knowledge already known is often proposed as the primary variable to be considered in making curriculum decisions, so too concern for the present experience and interests of students is frequently proposed as the primary consideration. Pedagogically, beginning the educational activity with the lived experience of the students rather than with the content of the disciplines of knowledge, tends to lead to inductive or "discovery" models of teaching.

Such an approach to educational activity is certainly appropriate and valid. But here again there is danger of an imbalance. When too much emphasis is placed on the present experience and interests of the students, the past heritage can easily be forgotten and responsibility for the future ignored. Then the present (and the people within it) becomes a prisoner of itself, captured in an ahistorical cage of "now," deprived of its past and disowning its future.

THE ASSUMPTION AND CONCERN FOR THE "FUTURE"

As noted, in all educational activity there is a "not yet" dimension, a leading out toward a knowing not yet realized. The future is open, not only for the students, but also for the educators. The assumption underlying this dimension of educational activity is that if we are to have a usable future, we must educate toward it. The concern to which this assumption gives rise is typically posed as a concern for the students' future, but it is also, in fact, a concern by educators for the future of the whole community. We educate to ensure that all of us can have a future. When this concern is properly expressed in educational activity, then the future is seen as arising from the heritage of the past and the creativity of the present but with a newness beyond either past or present.

Attention to this future dimension of education can be traced historically to when people first began to wonder about the nature of education. In *The Republic* Plato makes it clear that one's vision for the learner's future is what most determines how one educates.[9] In contemporary education a similar concern is always evident in the work of John Dewey. "The educator by the very nature of his work is obliged to see his present work in terms of what it accomplishes, or fails to accomplish, for a future whose objects are linked with those of the present."[10] Dwayne Huebner makes this concern for the future possibility of the person and the community central to his understanding of education.[11] To Paulo Freire concern for the future is the utopian dimension of education. By this he means that education must not allow people to settle for what *is* already, but lead them instead to build a better world. He insists that "the Utopian character of our education theory and practice is as permanent as education itself."[12]

Following the thinking of Freire, concern for a new future that is a transformation of the present and its past is a vital and necessary emphasis of educational activity. However, concern for the future as a transforming force has rarely been adequately realized over the history of educational activity. It has been subsumed instead by the self-perpetuating interest of the societies and other agencies promoting education. Often it has been reduced to a concern by the group for its self-maintenance. In fact, this "maintaining" attitude toward the future is still the typical interest motivating rulers, leaders, and governments to promote education in the first place.

In educational decisions the predominance of this societal concern for the future has led to a school of thought, especially evident in the "curriculum debate,"[13] that students ought to learn what society needs them to know. The primary variable to be considered in choosing what to teach is not the experience of the learners or the content of the disciplines, but the needs of society. In other words, educators should teach what society needs its citizens to know if they are to function effectively within it.

To be sure, concern for its continuation is a necessary interest for any group, and education must prepare people to cope and function effectively within society. But if the future dimension of educational activity is coopted totally by concern to maintain and fit people into present society, the consequence is more domesticating than educative. It leads to personal and social stagnation rather than growth and transformation. Such is a betrayal of the future dimension of educational activity; it denies the creativity of the present with the possibility of a new future within it.

The Assumptions and Concerns in History

Throughout the history of education concern for the future has been the most constant of the three assumptions and concerns I have discussed. It has motivated social agencies to promote educational activity in the first place.[14] Meanwhile, in decisions on the substance of the curriculum and the educational approach to be used, concern for the past and present (or in current educational literature, for the "disciplines of knowledge" and the "present experience of the students") have vied for predominance. This is especially evident in educational debates since Comenius (1592–1670).

In the seventeenth century Comenius was arguing for an inductive method of teaching "under the guidance of nature" that begins with the native abilities and experiences of the students.[15] On the other hand, Augustus Hermann Francke (1663–1727), the chief theoretician of the Prussian education system, which became a model for all of Europe, was arguing for education in "accurate and vivid knowledge" to be imparted by strictly disciplined instruction.[16]

Later in the eighteenth century and at the beginning of the nineteenth, Johann Pestalozzi (1746–1827) and his student Friedrich Froebel (1782–1852) argued for a pupil-centered, experiential approach.[17] Their contemporary and perhaps more influential colleague Johann Herbart (1776–1841), however, favored an approach centered in the subject matter of the disciplines.[18]

John Dewey (1859–1952) perceived the lines of the debate. Ever the enemy of dichotomies, he argued for a synthesis between the disciplines of knowledge and present experiential learning. At first glance it appears as if Dewey came down on one side of the argument. Education, for Dewey, must always be grounded in present experiential activity. He described it as "that reconstruction or reorganization of experience which adds to the meaning of experience, and which increases ability to direct the course of subsequent experience."[19] But Dewey never argued that education should be limited within the confines of "present experience." On the contrary, he claimed that by the "method of intelligence" experience must be so organized as to lead the students back into the disciplines of knowledge which have arisen from the similar experience of the race over its past history. For the students to inherit the "funded capital of civilization," educators must "reinstate into experience the subject matter of the studies, or branches of learning."[20] In other words, educators must enable their students to have the experiences that gave rise to the branches of learning in the first place. In this way present experience and knowledge organized into the disciplines could be brought together.

Although this basic philosophy was evident in one of Dewey's earliest and best known works, "My Pedagogic Creed" (1897), some forty years later his desired synthesis had not been effected in the schools, his best efforts in the interim notwithstanding. In 1938 he reproached educators for persisting in their "either/or" mentality, then being expressed in the opposition between traditional and progressive education. In his *Kappa Delta Pi* lectures Dewey articulated the age-old polarity. The traditional approach held that "the subject matter of education consists of bodies of information and of skills that have been worked out in the past; therefore, the chief business of the schools is to transmit them to the new generation." On the other hand, he listed the differences between the traditional approach and the "common principles amid the variety of progressive schools now existing" as follows:

To imposition from above is opposed expression and cultivation of individuality;
to external discipline is opposed free activity;
to learning from texts and teachers, learning through experience;
to acquisition of isolated skills and techniques by drill, is opposed acquisition of them
  as means of attaining ends which make direct vital appeal;
to preparation for a more or less remote future is opposed making the most of the opportunities of present life;
to static aims and materials is opposed acquaintance with a changing world.

Dewey faulted both approaches. He argued again that, although "the educator cannot start with knowledge already organized and proceed to ladle it out in doses," yet neither should beginning with experience be allowed to imprison the learners in an isolated present that forgets the past and ignores the future. "Every experience both takes up something from those which have gone before, and modifies in some way the quality of those which come after."[21]

Dewey's call for a synthesis has continued to be more honored in the breach than in the observance. Ole Sand points out that the student-centered experiential approach of the 1930s and 1940s was replaced in the late 1950s and 1960s by a return to the disciplines of learning.[22] A similar polarity of positions can be discerned in the recent history of Christian religious education.[23]

It would seem then, that while the assumptions and concerns expressed in educational activity can be summarized around the three traditional words for naming time, like time itself they have often been trichotomized so that educators have argued for the primacy of one over the others to the point of imbalance. It is my contention that in educational activity of any kind our assumptions about and concern for the future must be consciously articulated, not in the interest of maintaining the present and its past in the future, but in the interest of transformation and creation of a new future out of the present and its past. Then, rather than overemphasizing knowledge already known or discovery through present experience, the educator's task is to hold past, present, and future in a fruitful tension with each other. I contend further that the trichotomizing of educational activity to the point where the concerns are treated as separate, or to where one is overemphasized to the point of imbalance, arises from a misunderstanding of the nature of time. To hold all three concerns in a fruitful tension calls for a reconceptualizing of the nature of time, away from our typical linear understanding. Such a shift is proposed by existentialist philosophy. It remains to be reflected in our educational activity.

PILGRIMS IN TIME

IN TIME

The poet William Butler Yeats wrote, "Many times man lives and dies/Between his two eternities."[24] Out of eternity we have come by our birth, and back to eternity we return by our death. Between the two eternities we live "in time." But how to name and talk about this time is a challenge that has bedeviled philosophers since they first began to reflect upon the nature of it.[25]

Until recently our Western mentality has tended to accept Aristotle's explanation of time as a measure of motion along an imaginary line.[26] This linear conception typically thinks of past, present, and future as three distinct "times" separated from each other. But if the linear understanding is pushed to its logical conclusion, it robs the present of its existence and thus deprives people in the present of their historicity. Any given point on the line of time can be subdivided so minutely into past and future that the present disappears into "nontime" between them. As a result, we are robbed of "our time," and time becomes objectified outside ourselves, something that merely flows by us unperturbed.

More recently a different understanding of time has been advanced by existentialist philosophers, most notably Kierkegaard and Heidegger. In the disarray and disagreements of opinion among existentialists there is consensus at least in rejecting the linear and objectified notion of time. They have heralded a new consciousness about the subjective nature of time, and their position will inform the one I offer below. But the beginnings of an alternative to the linear notion of time can be found in St. Augustine (354–430), sometimes referred to as one of the first existentialists.[27]

In Book Eleven of *The Confessions* Augustine rejects the linear concept of time with its separation of past, present, and future. He argues instead that the three divisions are no more than three aspects of the same reality, "that all past time is driven back by the future, that all the future is consequent on the past, and all past and future are created and take their course from that which is ever present. . . . If future and past times exist . . . they are there neither as future nor as past, but as present. For if they are in that place as future things, they are not yet there, and if they are in that place as past things, they are no longer there. Therefore, wherever they are, and whatever they are, they do not exist except as present things."[28] For Augustine, then, past, present, and future do not exist as three distinct times but only as aspects of the one time, time present. He admits that in everyday speech and because of our imperfect language, we may need to use three different terms, but we can do so only if we intend them to mean "the present of things past, the present of things present, and the present of things future."[29]

If time is objectified to being a "thing" outside of us, as the linear notion seems to do, then we have lost "our time." If time is apart from us, then we are apart from time and are robbed of our historicity. But the truth is that we are radically rooted in time, living out our lives between the two eternities, with a beginning and a destiny. In other words, we are historical beings. Heidegger argues in *Being and Time* that we live authentically only insofar as we live out our historicity in face of the dread of our destiny, the end of our time in death. Thus, far from being an objectified reality outside of us, time for me, or for any individual, is what I live within; it is "my time," "our time." By our very nature, or as the philosophers would say, ontologically, we are beings in time. Time is the ground of our *being*. Without it, we would not *be*.[30]

As I live out my temporality, radically rooted in historical time, I cannot separate what I have been from what I am, nor these from what I will become. I am who I am because of my past; my past is in my present. I will be who I will be because of my present and the past that is in it. My past, in fact, is not past at all—it is with me in my present. My future is not simply "not yet"—it is already finding form in and shaping my present. My past and future *are* for me only insofar as they are in my present.[31] Thus in my temporality, "my (our) time" is the present, and there resides within that present the consequences of the past and the possibilities of the future.[32]

Concomitant with this existential notion of time the awareness has emerged that we are capable of taking and shaping time. We are not helpless pawns fatefully determined by the inevitable flow of history.[33] We live in history and are shaped by it. But we can also be shapers of it. We cannot totally control it, but neither should history totally determine us.

The awareness that we can be shapers of history gained ground in human consciousness after the Industrial Revolution. With the advent and expansion of industrialization people became aware that they could take and shape material things, giving them form and potential uses they would not have without human intervention. Gradually the consciousness emerged that if we can take and shape material things, then we can also take and shape "time," and thus influence the course of history.

When this existentialist understanding of time is taken seriously, educational activity must attend to all time—the present, its past, and its future. And as time should not be divided in three, so too, in educational activity, the disciplines of learning, the present experience of the learners, and care for our common future are not three opponents that vie for supremacy. Instead, they are three essential aspects of the same reality. For educating with concern for human temporality all three sources must be equally attended to and held in fruitful tension with each other.

Huebner recognizes that if the shift in our understanding of time is to be reflected in educational activity, then a new language and imagery is called for to move us away from the age-old trichotomy. He proposes the language of "pilgrimage."[34] I find his language shift helpful for a number of reasons, but since our primary interest in this work is Christian religious education, it seems especially appropriate. It is language and imagery integral to the Jewish and Christian traditions.

PILGRIMS

The Hebrew scriptures propose an understanding of time and history that finds apt expression in the imagery of a pilgrim people. Such imagery, however, is not exclusive to the Hebrew scriptures. Poets and philosophers often speak of life as a journey and the human family as pilgrims.

We are a pilgrim people in time, coming down through history, moving ever forward toward our "end time." Along the way we develop and devise ways of being in time, with systems and artifacts to support us in being together. But the ongoingness of the pilgrimage is not something automatic, as if driven by a mechanistic source outside us. It is not a conveyor belt carrying us forward even as we stand still. There is a pilgrimage only because there are pilgrims. Any one place on the pilgrimage is possible only because of who and what went before it. Pilgrims can be where they are only because of where pilgrims before them have been, and they will be where they will be because of where they are now.

It is imperative that the past of the pilgrims' progress be intentionally carried forward into the present as we work into our future. Without it we cannot know who we are, why we are here, or where we can go. Without a common past to live out of we become aimless and wandering individuals instead of a pilgrim people.[35] Thus the past of our people, with its stories, discoveries, customs, myths, symbols, rituals, artifacts, systems, institutions, skills, and so forth are precisely why we can have the present we can have and out of it shape our future. To the extent that they are remembered and made available to the present, we can have a human and intelligible present. And if our journey is to be an ongoing pilgrimage, then the future, while coming to meet us out of our present and its past, cannot be simply a repetition of them. By human creativity it must be given its own newness, or else the pilgrim progress is stagnated.

The language and imagery of pilgrimage, then, express well the understanding of time and temporality I propose above. As educators carry on intentional education with "pilgrims in time," all three assumptions and concerns of that activity are essential, as all three aspects of time are expressions of "our time." The educators' role is to ensure that the heritage of the past pilgrimage not be lost, but intentionally remembered and made available to the present. And it is equally their role to maintain the ongoingness of the pilgrimage, seeing to it that both the present and its past are a creative and transforming activity toward an open future.

THE POLITICAL NATURE OF EDUCATING PILGRIMS IN TIME

Educational activity with pilgrims in time is a political activity. I understand political activity to be any deliberate and structured intervention in people's lives which attempts to influence how they live their lives in society. To be rooted in time is to be in relationship with other people who share that time. We live out our temporality in a historical community. If education is to address us in our temporality, then it must address us in a historical community and attempt to influence us in the way we live out our time in community. If education pretends to be a private or nonpolitical enterprise, it is treating us as beings "out of time," rather than "in time." But such a pretense is just that—a pretention. Educational activity cannot be confined to some private sphere. As a deliberate and structured intervention in people's lives, education in time is eminently political.

When I point to the political nature of educational activity, I am certainly not offering a new insight. Plato and Aristotle talked of education only within the realm of politics. Both saw education as a political activity that serves to maintain the state,[36] and their position has been repeated by a long line of educators and politicians after them. More recently, John Dewey posed education as a source of social reconstruction rather than maintenance, but as such it is also a political activity.[37] Today Paulo Freire gives renewed emphasis to the political nature of all education, seeing the authentic political task of educators as enabling people to deal critically and creatively with their social reality, rather than simply fitting them into it. Freire claims that education more often does the latter, but whatever it does, it is never politically neutral.[38] Thus although these diverse thinkers, spanning more than two millennia, disagree on the political purposes of education, none of them doubts the political nature of educational activity itself.

The political dimension of education is highlighted further by looking specifically at the curriculum question. Using the imagery of pilgrims in time, the curriculum question becomes a question of what stories, myths, symbols, and the like from the past we intentionally recall and make available to the present, and out of those what shape do we propose for the future. From the past of any people there is a variety of traditions, and any number of biases and slants can be given them by the educators who make them available. The educator must make a number of choices. Which tradition will be presented as primary? Will it be used to legitimate present social arrangements or to call them in question? Will it be used to socialize people into the "given" world or to enable them to deal critically and creatively with the present? These are political questions, and the decisions have political implications.

The political consequences of curriculum decision making are immediately evident in the example of history as a school subject. The history taught in our American schools is predominantly a white, male, middle-class (and often Northern[39]) American history. The history of black America, red America, poor America, and women's America is rarely taught. Such choosing and excluding has the effect of promoting a world view and value system likely to maintain present cultural arrangements and social structures. History cannot be taught without proposing a world view and value system. The point is that choosing which ones to propose is a political choice.

The political implications of curriculum choices are often less obvious than in the case of history, but they are no less real. At first glance the simple primary readers, designed only to teach reading, do not appear to be political. But on closer examination the traditional readers in both text and illustrations have tended to present sex-role stereotypes and typically portray the consumer life as the good life. This is the "hidden curriculum," of which even those who write the readers are often unaware. The point is that in all educational activity choices are made about the past to be conserved and the future to be proposed. These are political choices, and the activity arising from them is a political activity.

Integral to recognizing the political nature of what educators do is to see educational activity as an exercise of power. Power is a given of the educational context. By intervening as educators in other people's lives to influence how they live in society, we are exercising power. It is easy to hide this power dimension from ourselves.[40] But rather than leaving it hidden, or naively denying its existence, the educator must make conscious choices about how to use this power. In

Freire's terms it can be used either as "power over" or as "power with."[41] In other words, educators can use their power to control and dominate students or to free and empower them.

If educators are to use their power as "power with" students, then their educational activity must maintain a fruitful tension between conservation and creativity. Without conservation of what was known and created by pilgrims before us our present is impoverished and our future diminished. But without a creative and liberating dimension transformation and newness are stifled, and the future is doomed to be a repetition of the past. The educator must intentionally make the past heritage available as the basis upon which people in the present can shape a new future. If this dialectic between conservation and creativity is maintained, then the educators will be using their power as "power with" their students. And perhaps at its core educational activity is a way of "being with" students. We are fellow and sister pilgrims alongside them, of whom they ask the way. As we point ahead of them, we also point ahead of ourselves.

NOTES

1. The "language debate" about what to call the enterprise first surfaced among Protestant religious educators in the United States. John Westerhoff's collection of essays *Who Are We?*, from the journal *Religious Education*, indicates that the debate first emerged as one aspect of the confrontation in religious education between liberal and neo-orthodox theology (see Westerhoff, *Who Are We?*). The liberals favored the term *religious education*, and the neo-orthodox preferred *Christian* or *church education*. In more recent years the debate has been joined by Catholic theorists, who, among other things, have brought the terms *catechesis* and *catechetics* into the discussion (see, for example, McBrien, "Toward an American Catechesis"; Moran, "Two Languages of Religious Education"; and for a collection of opinions, O'Hare, *Foundations*).
2. Heidegger, *On the Way to Language*, p. 63.
3. See Plato, *Republic* (Book VII, 517C–519C), pp. 316–317.
4. Dewey, "Creed," p. 19.
5. I frequently call attention throughout to the work of Bruce Joyce and Marsha Weil on models of teaching. Joyce and Weil have done teachers an invaluable service by drawing together from pedagogical, psychological, and sociological literature a host of teaching models (see Joyce and Weil, *Models of Teaching*). In subsequently published works they offer detailed directives on how to develop skills in using nine of the models (see Weil and Joyce, *Information Processing Models of Teaching* and *Social Models of Teaching*; and Weil et al., *Personal Models of Teaching*).

   Joyce and Weil offer a series of deductive models of teaching which are designed deliberately to prevent passivity in the learners and to avoid "banking education." One such model I have used and found particularly helpful and active is the "advance organizer model," which they draw from the writings of David Ausubel (see Weil and Joyce, *Information Processing Models of Teaching*, pp. 197–275).
6. Freire, *Oppressed*, pp. 58ff.
7. Whitehead, *Aims*, p. 33.
8. See Piaget, *Invent*.
9. See Plato's whole discussion of the Cave in *Republic* (Book VII, 514A–540E), pp. 312–341.
10. Dewey, *Experience and Education*, p. 76.
11. See Huebner, "Curriculum as Concern for Man's Temporality," pp. 237–249.
12. Freire, *Cultural Action for Freedom*, p. 20.
13. It is frequently pointed out that the "curriculum debate" since the turn of this century has re-

volved around three main points of emphasis: the disciplines, the students, and the society. Emphasis on any one of these variables has given rise to three distinct schools of curriculum theory—those who emphasize beginning with the disciplines of learning; those who emphasize beginning with the aptitudes, interests, and experiences of the learners; and those who say that curriculum decisions should be based primarily on the needs of society (see Bellack, "History of Curriculum Thought and Practice"; Sand, "Curriculum Change").

But, as indicated by our discussion thus far, this debate is about far more than curriculum. At root it is a debate about the nature of educational activity.

14. Both Plato and Aristotle realized that education is essential for the future of the State. Charlemagne, the first ruler in the Western world to decree universal education, saw it as necessary for pacifying his unruly empire. Jefferson insisted that the new Republic could not survive as a democracy without an educated populace. And in a less worthy way totalitarian regimes inevitably turn to "education" (as indoctrination) for their survival.

15. See Comenius, *The Great Didactic.* Later Rousseau (1712-1778) in *Emile* argued even more forcefully for an educational process grounded totally in the natural dispositions and interests of the student.

16. See Francke, *Memoirs of Augustus Hermann Francke.*

17. See Pestalozzi, *How Gertrude Teaches Her Children*; Froebel, *The Education of Man.*

18. See Herbart, *The Science of Education.*

19. Dewey, *Democracy,* pp. 89-90.

20. Dewey, "The Child and the Curriculum," in *Dewey on Education,* p. 104.

21. See Dewey, *Experience and Education,* pp. 17-35, 82.

22. See Sand, "Curriculum Change."

23. The polarity of positions in Christian religious education will be set out in detail in Chapter Seven.

24. From William Butler Yeats, "Under Ben Bulben," in *The Collected Poems of W.B. Yeats,* p. 341.

25. To catch a flavor of the complexity of the discussion, see *The Encyclopedia of Philosophy,* "Time," by J. J. C. Smart, 8:126-134.

26. See, especially, Aristotle's *Physics,* Book VI, 231A20-231B18. There Aristotle uses the image of a continuous line to talk about both time and motion. He argues that "it is plain that everything continuous is divisible into divisibles that are infinitely divisible," and adds, "The same reasoning applies equally to magnitude, to time, and to motion" (Aristotle, *Physics,* in *The Basic Works of Aristotle* [Book VI, 231B15-231B18], p. 317).

27. See *The Encyclopedia of Philosophy,* "Existentialism," by Alasdar MacIntyre, 3:147-154.

28. Augustine, *Confessions,* pp. 285, 291.

29. Augustine, *Confessions,* p. 293.

30. Dwayne Huebner, whose thinking on the nature of human temporality and its implications for educational activity has greatly influenced my own position, writes, "In fact, man can be defined by his temporality. The problems of change and continuity, conditioned and unconditioned, necessity and freedom, or of fixation and creativity are essentially problems of man's temporality" (Huebner, "Curriculum as Concern for Man's Temporality," p. 241).

31. Huebner explains this well when he writes, "Human life is not futural; nor is it past, but, rather, a present made up of a past and future brought into the moment. From his finite temporality, man has constructed his scientific view of time as something objective and beyond himself, in which he lives. The point is that man is temporal; or if you wish, historical. There is no such "thing" as a past or a future. They exist only through man's existence as a temporal being" "Man's Temporality," p. 244.

32. The thinking of Gabriel Moran on temporality has also influenced my position here. On this point Moran writes, "The unity of time is the present and that there are within the present two dimensions of time, the past and future" (Moran, *The Present Revelation,* p. 119).

33. Moran explains, "Time considered as linear provides a past that is simply there, fatefully limiting where we are now; it also provides a future that simply is not here yet, distracting us by the thought of what may or may not happen. By contrast, time as humanly and organically understood frees us from the bondage of any fate and allows us to live as free men" (*The Present Revelation,* p. 127).

34. For example, "Education points to the search for communities by groups of people on pilgrimage, working the land with their tools, building the structures that house them from the elements, caring for those who are pushed into their presence, reshaping their life together, and

telling and retelling the stories of where they have been and where they seem to be going" (Huebner, "Toward a Remaking of Curricular Language," p. 52).

35. H. Richard Niebuhr states this well when he writes, "Where common memory is lacking, where men do not share in the same past there can be no real community, and where community is to be formed common memory must be created" (Niebuhr, *The Meaning of Revelation*, p. 84).

36. Burnet says, "Neither Plato nor Aristotle would ever have dreamt of discussing education as a science by itself. . . . The theory of education is treated by Plato and Aristotle as a part of politics . . ." (Burnet, *Aristotle on Education*, p. 131).

   A central theme of Plato's Republic is that all people must be prepared to do in the *polis* what they are best suited to do, and education is to prepare them for their role. Then, " 'The philosophers must become kings in our cities,' . . . or those who are now called kings and potentates must learn to seek wisdom like true and genuine philosophers, and so political power and intellectual wisdom will be joined in one" (Plato, *Republic*, Book V, 472C–474A), p. 273.

   Aristotle is equally clear about the interest of the society in education. He writes, "No one will doubt that the legislator should direct his attention above all to the education of youth; for the neglect of education does harm to the constitution. The citizen should be moulded to suit the form of government under which he lives." He adds, "And since the whole city has one end, it is manifest that education should be one and the same for all, and that it should be public, and not private—not as at present, when every one looks after his own children separately, and gives them separate instruction of the sort which he thinks best; the training in things which are of common interest should be the same for all. Neither must we suppose that any one of the citizens belongs to himself, for they all belong to the state, and are each of them a part of the state, and the care of each part is inseparable from the care of the whole" (Aristotle, *Politics*. In *The Basic Works of Aristotle* [Book VIII, Ch. 1, 1–30], p. 1305).

37. In "My Pedagogic Creed" Dewey expressed this well when he said, "I believe that education is a regulation of the process of coming to share in the social consciousness; and that the adjustment of individual activity on the basis of this social consciousness is the only sure method of social reconstruction" (p. 30).

38. Richard Shaull, in the Foreword to Freire's *Pedagogy of the Oppressed*, summarizes this dimension of Freire's position: "There is no such thing as a neutral educational process. Education either functions as an instrument which is used to facilitate the integration of the younger generation into the logic of the present system and bring about conformity to it, or it becomes 'the practice of freedom,' the means by which men and women deal critically and creatively with reality and discover how to participate in the transformation of their world" (Shaull, "Foreword," in Freire, *Oppressed*, p. 15).

39. For the sake of some critical perspective it is well to remember that history is always written by the victors, by those who survived or triumphed in its struggles. One can only wonder how differently accounts of the same incidents would read if native Americans had won the "Indian War" or the South had won the Civil War. To begin with, the present heroes and scoundrels would have to change places.

40. Huebner warns, "We can easily teach the new being to accept our standards, concealing from ourselves the power that we exercise over another in the act of teaching" (Huebner, "Toward a Remaking of Curricular Language," p. 38).

41. See Freire, *Oppressed*, pp. 126 ff.

2

A Coming to Terms

EDUCATION

As I noted in the Prologue, there is little agreement about the precise nature of educational activity. Small wonder then that there is nothing like a universally agreed upon definition of the enterprise. Actually, for such a complex activity there never could be anything like one precise and exhaustive description. There are, of course, a myriad of definitions available, some well known and others less so. Our primary criterion for evaluating them should not be so much whether they are true or false as whether they are more or less useful; that is, whether they make evident essential aspects of the enterprise and thus enable us to do it more effectively. I use that criterion here to draw insights from two of the more well-established statements. Then I draw upon their insights, coupled with the reflections offered in Chapter One, to formulate a useful description of educational activity.

Lawrence Cremin defines education as "the deliberate, systematic, and sustained effort to transmit, evoke, or acquire knowledge, attitudes, values, skills, or sensibilities, as well as any outcomes of that effort."[1] One strength of his definition is its emphasis on education as a "deliberate, systematic and sustained" activity. In this view education always requires intentionality. It is often glibly asserted that all experience is educational.[2] But this is not automatically true. Some experiences are miseducational and others are not educational at all because we do not attend deliberately and intentionally to what they could possibly teach us. Many people have had long years of experience in a particular endeavor and yet seem to know relatively little about it. On the other hand, people with far less experience in the same area may know far more about it. The difference is in whether or not the people "reconstructed" (Dewey's word) their experience. For the educator to consistently promote such reconstruction requires a deliberate, systematic, and sustained effort.

Another strength of Cremin's definition is that it directs educational activity toward the total person, one's "knowledge, attitudes, values, skills or sensibilities." Our understanding of education has been greatly impoverished by limiting it to a narrow intellectualism, an affair of the mind alone. But from the ancient Greek pedagogues, who stressed a healthy mind, a healthy body, and the cultivation of the virtues, down to our present, the better educational theorists have all emphasized that good education must be cognitive, affective, and behavioral.

Also useful is Alfred North Whitehead's definition: "Education is the guidance of the individual towards a comprehension of the art of life; and by the art of life I mean the most complete achievement of varied activity expressing the potentialities of that living creature in the face of its actual environment."[3] Like Cremin, Whitehead emphasizes that education requires a holistic approach to the person that attends to the whole "art of life." A second strength is its emphasis on the "potentialities" of the students in the context of their social environment.

Drawing on these definitions and on the ideas expressed in Chapter One, I name the nature of education activity as *a political activity with pilgrims in time that deliberately and intentionally attends with people to our present, to the past heritage it embodies, and to the future possibility it holds for the total person and community.* As a political activity *with* pilgrims in time, education should empower them to critically reclaim their past so that they can work creatively through their present into their future. The constant human quest is toward the realization of our possibilities. The education we undertake together should empower us as individuals and as a pilgrim people along that journey. Insofar as education aims constantly to move us beyond our present limits toward realization of our full possibilities, one can say that all education, at least implicitly, is a reach for the transcendent.

RELIGIOUS EDUCATION

If indeed all education is ultimately a reaching for transcendence and an expression of that human quest, then all good education can be called religious.[4] There is a profound truth in Whitehead's often quoted words, "We can be content with no less than the old summary of educational ideal which has been current at any time from the dawn of our civilisation. The essence of education is that it be religious."[5] Here Whitehead is placing himself in a long and ancient tradition that includes, among others, Augustine, Alcuin, Erasmus, Comenius, and Herbart. Although this notion is fundamentally true, however, there is danger of religious imperialism if it is pushed too far. Many fine educators in mathematics, social science, art, and so on would never assume nor agree that they engage in "religious education." It is not precise and scarcely fair either to them or to the specificity of what religious educators do to settle for saying that religious education is synonymous with all education. There is a specificity to religious education that gives it its own distinctive function in relation to education in general.

To clarify how the adjective *religious* qualifies the noun *education*, some understanding is necessary of the noun from which the adjective comes, namely, *religion*. With the noun *religion* we again confront the limitation of language in stating comprehensively and exactly what we mean. The more realistic people who have attempted to define religion have realized this. John Macquarrie writes, "Religion assumes such a variety of forms that attempts to give a succinct definition covering them all have usuallly turned out to be unsatisfactory,"[6] and David Tracy acknowledges, "There is no universally agreed upon single definition for the human phenomenon called 'religion.'"[7] Wilfred Cantwell Smith suggests that the word *religion* be dropped entirely because it is "confusing, unnecessary and distorting."[8] The great variety of definitions is due either to the different traditions of religion or to the different academic disciplines that would-be definers bring to discussion of "religion." People from different traditions of religion will tend to define it from their own experience. And the anthropologists, psychologists, sociologists or other scientists who might study this human phenomenon will define it from their specific interests. Knowing full well that the following definition is also so influenced, I understand religion as *the human quest for the transcendent in which one's relationship with an ultimate ground of being*[9] *is brought to consciousness and somehow given expression.*

Given this understanding of religion, *religious education activity is a deliberate attending to the transcendent dimension of life by which a conscious relationship to an ultimate ground of being is promoted and enabled to come to expression.* Religious education focuses specific attention on empowering people in their quest for a transcendent and ultimate ground of being. It leads people to consciousness of what is found, relationship with it, and expression of that relationship. Any educational endeavor that attempts to do this is and should be called religious education. It may draw upon one particular tradition to inform the quest and promote the relationship, or it may draw from a cross-section of religions (for instance, a course investigating a number of world religions from a faith perspective), or from no particular tradition (for instance, a course investigating the religious dimensions of modern literature). Moran is correct when he says, "The proper name of the field is religious education."[10]

Religious education is a rich term. By its adjective it points to its specificity, and by its noun it retains its commonality with all education, an important bond to maintain. So often religious educators are greatly concerned about what takes place within our own religious communities but seem to show little concern for the quality of education taking place in the broader community and in the many public agencies that educate (schools, television, radio, newspapers, advertising, government agencies, armed services, and so on). Religious educators share with other educators a common responsibility for the quality of all education taking place in our society.

And maintaining the bond is also of benefit to our own specific task. As long as we realize that education is much broader than schooling, that good education needs to be a holistic approach to the total person—cognitive, affective, and behavioral—then naming our activity as *education* provides us a rich tradition with an enormous body of literature and research.[11]

When in practice, however, a community educates out of a particular tradition of religious faith, that tradition and community will alter the educational dynamic in both its process and its content. If religious education is done on behalf of, or, in Moran's language, "from within"[12] a particular community of religious faith, it and its tradition will lend its own specificity to the educational enterprise and distinguish it further within the activity of religious education in general.

CHRISTIAN RELIGIOUS EDUCATION

Hans Gadamer, among others, makes the point that although there is always a subjective dimension to language, it must also attempt to describe objective reality with some accuracy. In regard to my present historical situation in a community of Christian faith, for example, that community constantly poses itself the questions of how and when to prepare people for the Christian sacraments of initiation. Those are educational and religious educational questions. But there is a specificity to the task of Christian initiation and to the educational activity devised to fulfill that task. Therefore, a more descriptive term is needed to name such religious education activity.

Religion may be talked about in general as if it were an ahistorical phenomenon, but in reality religion finds expression in specific historical manifestations. As Richard McBrien remarks, "There is literally no such thing as religion as such. There are specific religions which participate, to one degree or another, in the general definition of religion."[13] What exists in the historical context is a great variety of religious traditions by which human beings have pursued the transcendent and have come to various ways of understanding and expressing the relationship with their ultimate ground of being, whoever or whatever that may be. The term *religious education* accurately describes the general investigation of the religious dimension of life and the common human quest for a transcendent ground of being. But if a religious community uses its specific tradition to sponsor people in their transcendent quest, if a certain relationship with a transcendent ground of being is advocated, and a particular symbol system offered for expressing that relationship in the community, then that educational activity should be specifically identified with that tradition. For this reason I claim that when religious education is done by and from within a Christian community, the most descriptive term to name it is *Christian religious education*.

Having said as much, there are problems that remain. If a solution to the "language problem" was so simple, the debate about what to call the enterprise would not have gone on so long. To begin with, the term *Christian religious education* is cumbersome and not very aesthetic. It sounds like a piling up of words. Thus for the sake of a smoother sentence structure, and when the community doing the educating is obvious, I will often use instead *religious education*.

At first sight a more obvious solution might be to simply drop the adjective *religious* and call the educating activity of a Christian community *Christian education*. There is evidence, however, that *Christian education* can have a pejorative connotation, especially for people who have come through the Sunday school tradition of some Protestant churches. Moran claims that in Protestantism "Christian education" is generally understood as the activity by which "officials of a church indoctrinate children to obey an official church."[14] Moran may be overstating the case. I am confident a time is coming when the emancipatory possibilities of Christianity will be realized more faithfully, and then the term *Christian education* will have no such oppressive overtones.[15] However, since a primary concern throughout this work is to find a language that can enable all traditions of the Christian Church to do religious education in an emancipatory manner, I am willing, for now, to avoid the term *Christian education* as a general practice.

Another objection is that the adjective *Christian* is not sufficiently specific. There is Roman Catholic, Presbyterian, Baptist, and so forth religious education, and often subdivisions within them, too. However, to become unduly specific could promote a narrow sectarianism in what ought to be a common enterprise. With the emergence of a strong ecumenical movement, the Christian Church should be sufficiently at one to at least permit our educational efforts to be named by the generic term *Christian religious education*. The term can serve to remind us further that we are all called to a universal Christian Church. In this a basic unity is both affirmed and proposed as a vision. Meanwhile, the richness of the various traditions of Christianity is not being denied. Rather, it will emerge inevitably in the context of the faith community in which the religious education is being done.

Although the term *Christian religious education* has its inadequacies, it also has some important advantages. By putting the adjective *Christian* before *religious education*, we Christians remind ourselves that we do not own the enterprise but are only one expression of it. Given our history of imperialism in the West, that is an important reminder. Then, the term *religious education* after the word *Christian* reminds us that the quest for the transcendent is far broader than our own community and tradition. While our educational work begins "at home," it should never promote the notion that home is the only place to encounter the transcendent. A true grounding in the particular should create openness to the universal. The term *religious education*, even as we prefix it with the adjective *Christian*, reminds us of our common quest and bond with all religious educators, regardless of their particular religious community. It is especially important that we affirm our bond with Jewish religious educators. But there is also the possibility of affirming solidarity and mutuality with Buddhist, Moslem, and other religious educators. It thus reminds us that all pilgrims toward God have a common bond which transcends our differences along the way.

Christian religious education, like all education, is a complex enterprise, and no description of it will ever be exhaustive. Statements of its purpose, context, and so on will come later; here I am attempting to name only the nature of this activity as it is carried on in an historical context. Christian religious education is *a political activity with pilgrims in time that deliberately and intentionally attends with them to the activity of God in our present, to the Story of the Christian faith community, and to the Vision of God's Kingdom, the seeds of which are already among us.*

In that description the specificity of what Christian religious educators do derives from the Christian communities' Story, with its primordial expression in Jesus Christ, and the Vision of God's completed Kingdom to which the Story gives rise.[16] But perhaps the most important point for attention is my claim that Christian religious education participates in the political nature of education in general. If few educators advert to the political nature of their educating, Christian religious educators are even more reluctant to recognize the political implications of our activity. The standard argument for refusing to admit such implications arises from the classical (Greek) distinction between the secular and the religious, and more recently from the Enlightenment distinction between the citizen and the individual (Rousseau). When these distinctions are accepted as accurate "religion" is confined to the private sector, and thus religious educators are to intervene in the lives of individuals to influence them only in "spiritual" matters, not in social ones.

But the dichotomies at the base of this argument are false. Any kind of educational activity, either immediately or ultimately, influences people in how they live their lives in society. Educational activity of any kind can never have only "private" consequences, since the individual and the citizen are the same person. Nor can a Christian spirituality ever be "private." Far from denying the spiritual task of Christian religious education, I will later argue at length for its importance. If religious educators promote a spirituality that ignores responsibility for the world, they are not promoting a Christian spirituality (nor a Jewish one either). The heart of a Christian spirituality must flow from the heart of the Christian vocation which is to lead a life of *agape*—loving God by loving our neighbor. Love of neighbor is essentially antithetical to a privatized spirituality. Thus Christian religious education, precisely by proposing a spirituality which is Christian, is being political, that is, intervening in people's lives to influence them in how they live out their temporality in social relationships.

When Christian religious educators dichotomize the spiritual/religious from the social/political, we fall into a false dichotomy. Even if a religious community should set itself the task of confining its educational activity to the "spiritual" in a narrow private sense, it is actually performing a political act, but it is the politics of silence, of nonengagement. By what we reclaim from our past heritage or propose for our future, by what we ignore from our past and refuse for our future, Christian religious educators are being political. We have no choice about whether or not Christian education will have political implications. It is inevitably political and our choice is about the direction in which we should shape the future of society by our present engagement as Christians within it.[17]

There remains one other key word that is often used in talking about Christian religious education. It, too, points to a particular activity that would seem to be essential to the nature of the enterprise. It is the word *catechesis*.

CATECHESIS

In paying attention to this word, I am obviously in dialogue with my own Catholic background. *Catechesis* is an ancient Christian word, but in later years it came to be used almost exclusively by Roman Catholics. In recent times, however, it is being used more frequently by Protestant educators as well.[18]

The word *catechesis* comes from the Greek verb *katēchein*, which means "to resound," "to echo," or "to hand down." Thus the etymology of the word implies an oral instruction. It is used in the New Testament as an oral instruction in which a very simple explanation (one step beyond the kerygma) was given to the people, as milk rather than solid food is given to small children (see Heb. 5:12–14; 1 Cor. 3:1–3). The message was to be taught and spoken accurately (Acts 18:25). This understanding of catechesis as "oral reechoing" continued in the early church, where it was understood as a verbal exhortation to live a moral life.[19]

The term continued to be used down through the history of the Christian Church, by Augustine, Alcuin, Aquinas, and others, always to designate an oral instruction. After the Reformation, however, it seems to have become an exclusively Catholic word, though even in Catholicism its use was not that widespread. The work of the Vienna and Munich catechetical schools at the beginning of this century reintroduced it as a common word among Catholic educators.[20] But throughout its varied history the constant tradition is to understand *catechesis* with its earliest meaning of oral instruction. The Fathers of the Second Vatican Council use catechesis in this sense by invariably speaking of it as instruction and placing it within the "ministry of the word."[21] Attempts have been made to expand the word *catechesis* to mean more than an oral reechoing or handing down. Berard Marthaler, for example, understands the term "as a process whereby individuals are initiated and socialized in the church community."[22] And John Westerhoff proposes a meaning for the word so broad that it describes the whole process of Christian becoming.[23]

What Marthaler and Westerhoff describe is a whole process that might be better named Christian socialization or enculturation. To call that catechesis is asking the word to carry much more meaning than it is capable of conveying. It is not useful, and scarcely accurate, to redefine the word with a meaning so far removed from its etymological roots or its scriptural, early Church, or historical usage.

Even if catechesis could be so broadly redefined, there is a great disadvantage in doing so. It fails to name and thus severs the Christian educational enterprise from its commonality with education and religious education. If this happens, then from what discipline does one draw to empower the activity? How does one do catechesis, or train other people to do it, or build programs to effect it? If we use the term *catechesis* to name the total enterprise of sponsoring people toward Christian faith, then it is difficult to know where to begin or how to prepare oneself to be a catechist. The word *catechesis* is such a "Church word" that the tendency will be (and often is) to draw upon only the "sacred sciences," and especially theology and scripture studies. If the same enterprise is called *Christian religious education*, however, then the word *Christian* calls for the activity to be informed by theology and scripture studies. But the name also points to another very obvious source—the science of education (and thus to the many other sciences which inform education) to draw from to empower the activity.

For these reasons, then, it is both more accurate and wiser to continue using the word *catechesis* with its consistent historical meaning. Then catechesis becomes, or rather remains, the activity of reechoing or retelling the story of Christian faith that has been handed down. Catechesis is thus situated as a specifically instructional activity within the broader enterprise of Christian religious education.

TWO CAVEATS ON "COMING TO TERMS"

My intention in this chapter was to name the nature of educational activity, especially when that is carried on from within the Christian faith community. My attitude toward the question of terminology is still an open one. It ought to be so. Language is always inadequate and thus can always be improved upon. As Michael Polanyi says, "We can know more than we can tell."[24] But while we appreciate the importance of the search for linguistic clarity and consensus, the debate should be accompanied by two caveats.

First, let us avoid an idealist assumption that all our problems will be solved and our task completed if we can only find "the right words." To paraphrase Marx, naming the world is still only preliminary to changing it. As we search for the right words, we must also get on with our educational task and not allow the controversy about terms to immobilize us. Otherwise we are involved in mere verbalism. Again to quote Polanyi, "By concentrating attention on his fingers, a pianist can temporarily paralyze his movement."[25]

Secondly, let us resist the temptation to insist that everyone else use his or her language under penalty of excommunication from the community of discourse. That would be an oppressive stance and an attempt to "own" the enterprise. If our position on terms is so hardened that it represses and stifles dialogue, then the very purpose of language is defeated. In such an important enterprise, disagreement about terms must never be allowed to prevent dialogue about our common concern, even though we may need to move beyond the diversity of terms to get at the tacit knowing which nobody's language can ever completely disclose.

NOTES

1. Cremin, *Traditions of American Education,* p. 134.
2. People who so claim often cite John Dewey as their mentor. But Dewey never said as much. On the contrary, he went to great pains to emphasize that experience is not inevitably educational; its educational value depends on what the individual does with the experience. If experience is to be educational, then, for Dewey, it must be "reconstructed." See Dewey's definition of education already cited in Chapter One.
3. Whitehead, *Aims,* p. 39.
4. See Phenix, *Education and the Worship of God* for a fascinating exposition of how all the main disciplines of learning are grounded in faith and are expressions of the human reach for the transcendent.
5. Whitehead, *Aims,* p. 14.
6. Macquarrie, *Principles of Christian Theology,* p. 149.
7. Tracy, *Blessed Rage for Order,* p. 92.
8. W. C. Smith, *The Meaning and End of Religion,* p. 50.
9. While the definition is my own, the phrase *ultimate ground of being* is obviously from Tillich (see, for example, Tillich, *Systematic Theology,* 2, especially pp. 5–6).
10. Moran, "Religious Education Toward America," p. 481.

11. In this statement I am reacting negatively to a noticeable trend in recent writings to call our enterprise anything that does not include the word *education,* e.g., catechesis, youth ministry, evangelization, and so on. One likely explanation for this trend is that it arises from a widespread criticism of the schooling paradigm (see Westerhoff, *Will Our Children Have Faith?*). Our disenchantment with schooling seems to make us reluctant to call what we do *education.* But that is to make the false assumption that education and schooling are synonymous. While we may rightly critique our overinvestment in the schooling paradigm (though I believe Westerhoff tends to overstate his case), let us not assume that what we do is anything but education. Or rather, let us see to it that what we do as religious education is at least good education. I believe this point has important implications, especially for how we train religious educators.

12. See Moran, "Two Languages of Religious Education," p. 7.

13. McBrien, "Toward an American Catechesis," p. 171.

14. Moran, *Religious Body,* p. 150.

15. This criticism of the term *Christian education* is part of a broader criticism of Christianity as a whole. Both traditional Marxists and Freudians, among others, would claim that the very use of Christian language militates against the promotion of liberation and human freedom. They see Christianity as inherently either oppressive or repressive. They would seem to have some strong historical evidence on their side. But this criticism is rapidly becoming a largely dated nineteenth-century one.

It overlooks the Roman Catholic response to such criticism, beginning in the 1890s with *Rerum Novarum* and increasing with the great social encyclicals ever since. It overlooks the Protestant response, also begun in the late 1800s with the Social Gospel movement and continuing down through such people as Reinhold Niebuhr and Paul Tillich into the present day. It overlooks the whole development of "critical" and "dialectical" theology over the past twenty-five years (for example the work of Rahner, Lonergan, Moltmann, Metz, Pannenberg, Schillebeeckx, Ruether, Baum, Tracy, Gutierrez, and the theologians of the liberation motif) in which it has been rediscovered that Christianity must be a criticism rather than a legitimation of oppressive social systems and cultural arrangements. It especially overlooks the courage and heroic witness of Christians in the Third and Fourth Worlds, where frequently the only voice of opposition to oppressive regimes comes from the Christian churches. But obviously there is still much work to be done. The criticism of the term *Christian education* points us toward a broader task—to reclaim in consciousness and in reality that Christianity is a social critique and a call to human freedom; that it is a travesty of the essential meaning of the Christ event when it is used to promote or legitimate oppressive enterprises, and especially educational ones. Then the term *Christian education* will be taken to mean the enabling of people to live freely and humanly by interpreting and living their lives through the paschal event of Jesus Christ in history.

16. The terms *Story* and *Vision* will be explained in detail in Chapter Nine. Briefly, I use them as symbols to refer to the whole faith tradition of the Christian people, however it is embodied or expressed, and to the lived response the Story invites as it points to the fulfillment of God's reign.

17. Part of our difficulty in recognizing the political nature of all education stems from an impoverished notion of the meaning of politics. For many it is a pejorative word ("dirty politics") that conjures up no more than images of party politics, smoke-filled rooms, running for elected office. But, as suggested by my description in Chapter One, that is only one limited understanding of political activity.

18. John Westerhoff writes, "I suggest that Protestants and Roman Catholics unite in identifying our educational ministry in the Church as 'catechesis,' and direct our attention to the nature of catechesis" ("A Call to Catechesis," p. 354).

19. "Catechesis, an oral teaching in the primitive Church, signified usually a moral instruction" (*New Catholic Encyclopedia,* "Catechesis: Early Christian," by Francis Xavier Murphy, 3:208).

20. It is interesting to note that Catholic Church authorities looked upon it with some suspicion after the publishing of Fr. Josef Jungmann's *Die Frohbotschaft und Unsere Glaubensverkundigung* in 1936 (later translated into English as *The Good News: Yesterday and Today*).

21. See *Dogmatic Constitution on Divine Revelation,* in Abbott, *Documents,* p. 127.

22. Marthaler, "Toward a Revisionist Model in Catechetics," p. 459.

23. See Westerhoff, "Risking an Answer: A Conclusion," in *Who Are We?*, pp. 264–277.

24. Polanyi, *The Tacit Dimension,* p. 4.

25. Ibid., p. 18.

THE PURPOSE OF CHRISTIAN RELIGIOUS EDUCATION

Prologue

NONE OF the six foundational questions about Christian religious education being raised in this work is easily answered. The question of purpose, however, may well be the most difficult of all. Why *do* Christian religious education? That question invites an even deeper level of reflection than the previous question about the nature of the activity. It primarily invites *self*-reflection by each would-be Christian educator, because Christian religious education as such does not have a purpose. The educators are the ones with the purpose, and it is our corporate intentions and hopes that can be posed as the general purpose of the endeavor. It seems beyond question that our purpose must be consciously chosen and constantly recalled to both shape and evaluate our practice.

When we look at ourselves and each other as Christian religious educators, we can discern a myriad of purposes (and cross-purposes) in our activity, some quite noble and worthy and some quite mixed. Intentions can vary in shade as many times as there are Christian religious educators. These individual purposes can and must be discerned by each person looking into his or her own activity. But I contend that the Christian faith tradition itself suggests a purpose for educating in it, and such is the common purpose to which we can aspire. Part II attempts to articulate this common purpose.

By *purpose* I mean the *telos,* the end toward which we carry on Christian religious education. To pose the question with the language of Part I, Toward what end are Christian religious educators to do their leading out? I will describe here more a vision of what our purpose might be than a report of what it typically appears to be in present practice. I propose it not just to criticize present practice, but also to call us forward. And even as I propose such a vision, I know that the proposer is more invited to it than an example of it.

In one sense, our common purpose can be stated very simply, and perhaps should be so stated at the outset lest it be lost from sight along the way. The purpose of Christian religious education is to enable people to live as Christians, that is, to live lives of Christian faith. This would seem to be its purpose since the Christian community first began to educate.[1] What in fact is expected of a Christian and how such a lifestyle is to be promoted has taken different expressions at different times. But lived Christian faith seems to have been the purpose of Christian religious education since Christians first responded to the mandate of Jesus, "Go you therefore, teach. . . ."

Having stated that purpose, we have actually posed another question— What is the purpose of being Christian? That question must be answered before we can understand what a life of Christian faith is or ought to be for our time. Chapter Three will attempt to answer that question, and the answer will constitute the ultimate purpose, I sometimes call it the *metapurpose*, of Christian religious education; in other words, the overarching framework and end toward which our more immediate educational purpose is directed and within which it can be best understood.

The Kingdom of God in Jesus Christ is proposed as our ultimate purpose. Chapter Four deals with the meaning of Christian faith as lived in response to that Kingdom, and Chapter Five reflects on the consequence and condition of living Christian faith toward the Kingdom, namely, human freedom.

3

Education for the Kingdom of God

AT DIFFERENT times in our history different answers have been given to the question Why be a Christian? I have posed this question many times to groups of Christians in adult education situations. The typical answer offered is To save my soul, or some variation of that theme. There is validity and truth in such a statement of purpose. Christianity offers people the grace and hope of eternal salvation through Jesus Christ, and such a hope will always be integral to our purpose in being Christian. But there is a strong consensus in contemporary theology that to understand the purpose of being Christian exclusively in such an individualized and "otherworldly" manner is an impoverished and inaccurate understanding of the salvation made possible by Jesus Christ.[2] Thus we must search for an ultimate purpose and a symbol to express it that is far more than "saving my soul."

I suggest that our metapurpose as Christian religious educators is to lead people out to the Kingdom of God[3] in Jesus Christ. I offer three arguments to support this suggestion. First, in the Hebrew scriptures the vision of God's Kingdom is posed as God's own vision and intention for all people and creation. Second, it is in continuity with and within that Hebrew tradition that Jesus proclaims his Good News. Jesus, whom Christians know as the Christ, lived his life and preached his gospel for the Kingdom of God. Such was his purpose. It should also be the purpose of those who would educate in his name. Third, while the Kingdom of God as the central theme of Christian preaching suffered a demise in the early Church, it has become central again in contemporary theology. Although there is a great divergence of opinion among scripture scholars and theologians today about the meaning of the Kingdom of God, there is also a basic agreement that it is the central theme of the gospels and that Christian living must be in response to that Kingdom. Christian religious education has the purpose of promoting such a response.[4]

The books which have been written on the Kingdom of God fill many shelves. I do not intend to offer a systematic theology of the Kingdom nor a detailed treatment of the many contemporary schools of eschatology.[5] Rather, I bring the hermeneutic of a Christian religious educator to investigate the meaning of the symbol. Thus I draw on the literature only insofar as it is necessary to answer the questions What does the symbol *Kingdom of God* mean for the actual living of the Christian life? and What are its implications for the way we educate people to such a lifestyle? I briefly survey the meaning of the Kingdom of God in the Hebrew scriptures, in the life and preaching of Jesus, and in contemporary theology. At the end of the chapter I present a "composite view" that indicates how I use the phrase *Kingdom of God* throughout the remainder of this work.

THE KINGDOM OF GOD IN THE HEBREW SCRIPTURES

The symbol *Kingdom of God* is rooted deeply in Hebrew consciousness. It seems to be a composite of a Hebrew tradition and a tradition prevalent among neighboring peoples.[6] It means both the actual rule and sovereignty of God in the world as its creator and sustainer, and the universal goal of that divine rule at the completion of history. For the Israelites Kingdom of God is not primarily territory ruled over, nor, on the other hand, is it an abstract concept. Rather, it is a symbol which refers to the concrete activity of God in history establishing God's sovereignty. Norman Perrin writes of the Hebrew understanding, "It is . . . important to recognize that Kingdom of God is a *symbol,* and that, further, its natural function is *to evoke a myth.*"[7] The myth it evokes is "the myth of a God who created the world and was continually active in that world on behalf of his people. . . ."[8] For the Hebrew it is God in God's supreme sovereignty who directs the world and history, unfolding there God's vision for all creation.[9] Time and history are not a meaningless sequence of events without direction, but rather the expression of God's intention for creation, in the midst of which God is constantly and effectively active. The biblical authors often use poetic language, the language of imagination, to describe the Kingdom, but understand it as a concrete reality, what God is doing or will do. By the power of God the Kingdom is being realized, not simply imagined.

As a symbol for the Israelites, the Kingdom of God points to God's everlasting and complete dominion over all creation (Exod. 15:18; Ps. 145:13); heaven

(Ps. 11:4), earth (Ps. 47:3), and all people (Jer. 10:7–10). "The Lord has established his throne in heaven, and his kingdom rules over all" (Ps. 103:19). But the Psalmist's reference to a throne in heaven does not mean that God's reign is only an otherworldly reality. Schnackenburg writes, "The notion of a purely transcendent kingship of Yahweh, limited to the heavenly realm, was quite foreign to Israel."[10] Thus the Israelites could pray, "O God, my King from of old, you doer of saving deeds on earth" (Ps. 74:12).

For the Israelites the Kingdom of God is already a reality in that it is Yahweh who rules all things and people. And yet the final completion of the Kingdom is still to come. It is promised and God is active on its behalf. Therefore it is already being realized and will be realized completely. But it is not an authoritarian rule by a capricious God. It is instead a caring and trustworthy God intervening in history to transform the present order and bring creation to fullness and completion. In the triumph of God's vision for creation, "Nature is wholly and wondrously transformed, the serenity of Paradise is renewed"[11] (see Isa. 35:1–10).

Completion of the Kingdom will mean the fulfillment of all the authentic yearnings of the human heart and the needs of humankind. God wills to love God's people, God wills justice and peace, completion and wholeness, unity and happiness, fullness and plenty, joy and victory, an end to human suffering. As the prophet Isaiah describes it,

> On this mountain the Lord of hosts will provide for all peoples
> A feast of rich food and choice wines, juicy, rich food and pure, choice wines.
> On this mountain he will destroy the veil that veils all peoples,
> The web that is woven over all nations;
> He will destroy death forever.
> The Lord God will wipe away the tears from all faces. (Isa. 25:6–8)

While the Kingdom is promised as the fulfillment of human needs and yearnings, the themes of peace and justice are given constant and central emphasis throughout the Old Testament. Swords will be beaten into ploughshares, and spears into pruning hooks. The nations shall not do battle nor prepare for war again (see Isa. 2:4). God's justice is to be revealed (Ps. 98:1–2) and finally established. God is a God who wills righteousness for all people. As Pannenberg puts it, "The Kingdom of God, according to the Old Testament, is expected in the form of establishing law and justice in the society of man."[12] Thus the Israelite could trust in God, for it is the Lord who

> secures justice for the oppressed,
> gives food to the hungry.
> The Lord sets captives free;
> the Lord gives sight to the blind.

The Lord raises up those that were bowed down;
the Lord loves the just.
The Lord protects strangers;
the fatherless and the widow he sustains,
but the way of the wicked he thwarts.
The Lord shall reign forever;
your God, O Zion, through all generations. Alleluia.
(Ps. 146:7–10)

God's vision for all creation, then, is that it will come perfectly under God's reign, which is to be a Kingdom of peace and justice, wholeness and completion, happiness and freedom. This reign comes and is to come as a gift by the mighty power of God. It is God who effects it. It is God who saves.[13]

But what does this Kingdom expect of the people by way of response? Because God has entered into a covenant with Israel, Yahweh reigns over them in a special way (Judg. 8:23; 1 Sam. 8:7; Exod. 19:6), and they have the duty of total obedience to God's will. Since the Kingdom is God's will for creation and the people, if the Israelites are to live their covenant relationship with God, they must live their lives according to God's intentions. What Yahweh expects as an "acceptable offering" is

releasing those bound unjustly,
untying the thongs of the yoke;
Setting free the oppressed,
breaking every yoke;
Sharing your bread with the hungry,
sheltering the oppressed and the homeless;
Clothing the naked when you see them,
and not turning your back on your own. (Isa. 58:6–7)

Thus what Yahweh expects of them is what Yahweh wills for them.

JESUS AND THE KINGDOM OF GOD

In contemporary Christian theology Christology seems to be the primary focus of attention.[14] It is frequently remarked that if the Catholic Church were to hold a General Council today, then just as ecclesiology was the central concern of Vatican II, Christology would be the focus at Vatican III.[15]

There has also emerged in this outpouring of literature a shift in perspective for understanding Jesus, a shift from a "Christology from above" to a "Christology from below." A Christology from above, typical of much traditional Christology, emphasizes the divine nature of Christ and God's initiative in coming into the world in Jesus. The decisive event for such a Christology is the Incarnation. A Christology from below, on the other hand, emphasizes the human nature and life of Jesus. The starting point for investigation of the Jesus event is not the divine initiative of the eternal *Logos*, but the earthly life of Jesus of Nazareth. This emphasis brings a present understanding of the human condition to bear on the investigation of what the historical Jesus did and said and thus arrives at an understanding of who he was. As a result, the decisive events for a Christology from below are the public life, death, and resurrection of Jesus, who came to be recognized as the Christ.

On one central point there is a strong consensus of opinion evident, especially among proponents of a Christology from below, although it is shared by many who continue to favor a Christology from above and also by those who attempt to strike a middle ground. The consensus can be summarized thus: *The central theme in the preaching and life of Jesus was the Kingdom of God.*[16]

The theologians are on good scriptural grounds. A similar consensus seems to have emerged among contemporary scholars of the New Testament.[17] Gustaf Aulén reviews the results of the past two hundred years of critical scripture scholarship and its attempt to separate the words and sayings of the historical Jesus from the accretions of the faith community, concluding that what remains with certainty as the preaching of the historical Jesus is the Kingdom of God. "The kingdom of God—in Matthew the 'kingdom of heaven'—is the word above all other words in Jesus' proclamation. It is the central content of 'the gospel' which he preaches."[18]

Even a cursory glance at the text of the Synoptic Gospels will reveal the frequency with which Jesus speaks about the Kingdom.[19] There is scarcely a page without some reference to God's reign, the Kingdom of God, the reign of heaven, and so on. When Mark recounts the first appearance of Jesus, he writes, "After John's arrest, Jesus appeared in Galilee proclaiming the good news of God: 'This is the time of fulfillment. The reign of God is at hand! Reform your lives and believe in the gospel' " (Mark 1:14–15). From that opening announcement the Kingdom was Jesus' constant reference and central theme.

Norman Perrin indicates that "as Kingdom of God is the central symbol of the message of Jesus, so is the parable the most characteristic literary form of that message."[20] The literary form of parable was ideal for explaining the Kingdom in concrete terms.[21] Consistency with the traditional Hebrew understanding always marked Jesus' understanding and use of the symbol. He took the tradition to a point where it had not been before, but he never disrupted the continuity with his Hebrew heritage. For Jesus the symbol Kingdom of God means what it meant for his family before him: God's will being done and all creation being brought to wholeness and completion.[22]

The continuity is evident in the fact that for Jesus, too, the Kingdom of God is a dynamic and concrete reality, pointing to God's saving action in the midst of history. By the active power of God the Kingdom is the embodiment, the effecting, the complete realization of God's will. Aulén writes, "Everywhere it is a question of a happening; the dynamic character of the Hebrew expression for the kingdom of God radiates everywhere, an expression which cannot be rendered satisfactorily in translation; everywhere it is a question of how the reign of God makes itself known in what happens."[23] Second, continuity is evident in Jesus' preaching that the reign of God is to be universal (Matt. 8:11; Luke 13:29). Third, Jesus is consistent with the dominant Jewish tradition when he speaks of the Kingdom as both present and future, both the present effective sovereignty of God over creation and the final realization of that reign at the end of time. In fact, he causes the "alreadyness" and the "not-yetness" of the Kingdom to stand out in even bolder relief. He said that it was present and pointed to himself and his work as its effective agent. "But if it is by the finger of God that I cast out devils, then the reign of God is upon you" (Luke 11:20). There Jesus is doing what he frequently does, pointing to his conquest of Satan and the powers of evil as a sign that the Kingdom has already come. On the other hand, he undoubtedly proclaimed a Kingdom to be fully realized only in the future and taught his people to pray for its coming[24] (Matt. 6:10; Luke 11:2). Occasionally he appears to talk of the Kingdom as both present and future in the same statement.[25] "Once, on being asked by the Pharisees when the reign of God would come, he replied, 'You cannot tell by careful watching when the reign of God will come. Neither is it a matter of reporting that it is 'here' or 'there.' The reign of God is already in your midst' " (Luke 17:20–21).

However, in his preaching of the Kingdom Jesus goes beyond his Hebrew tradition in one significant way: *He considers the Kingdom to have already and definitively arrived and points to his own person, his work and ministry, as its effective agent.* In him God is active to bring about the definitive arrival of the Kingdom. Thus not only does he preach the Kingdom, but he ties its coming to his own person and ministry.[26] He points to his miracles as physical, visible signs of the Kingdom's arrival. When John in prison sent messengers to ask him "Are you 'He who is to come' or do we look for another?' In reply, Jesus said to them: 'Go back and report to John what you hear and see: the blind recover their sight, cripples walk, lepers are cured, the deaf hear, dead men are raised to life, and the poor have the good news preached to them' " (Matt. 11:3–5). His forgiveness of sins and expelling of demons is a sign that the powers of evil have been conquered.[27] Like other prophets before him, Jesus proclaims the Kingdom and lives his own life in response to it. But unlike any of the earlier prophets, he points to himself as the effective instrument by which God is active in history on behalf of the salvation of God's people.

There is a second dimension to Jesus' preaching of the Kingdom which cannot be called "new," but is a radicalizing of what was taught before him—namely, how he preached the love commandment as the supreme law of the

Kingdom. Jesus' preaching of the double comandment to love God and one's neighbor is in continuity with Jewish tradition, especially the Wisdom literature.[28] He made the radical dimension of this law of the Kingdom more obvious, however. First, he insisted that one cannot love God without loving one's neighbor, and second, he removed all limits to who is "my neighbor." To the Jewish tradition neighbor tended to mean fellow-Jew. Jesus expanded neighbor to mean all people, even one's enemies.[29] Thus he radicalized the law of the Kingdom by making it clearer that it is not "love of God *and* love of neighbor," but "love of God *by* love of neighbor,"[30] with no limits to "neighbor."

What then, as Jesus taught, are the implications of being called to the Kingdom already and to the promise of its final completion at the end time? From Jesus' whole ministry it is clear that the only fitting response to the Kingdom in him is a *metanoia*, a "change of heart." His announcing of the Kingdom is a call to live the will of God, and since God wills to love all people, this requires our conversion to the neighbor. Such is what Schillebeeckx calls the "praxis of the kingdom of God," a *metanoia* that causes us "faithfully to manifest its coming in a consistent way of living."[31] Jesus' proclamation of the Kingdom is a proclamation of how human life ought to be lived. As the Kingdom is a manifestation of God's love for us, we manifest the Kingdom by loving God in our neighbor. When Jesus calls people to fellowship with him, he is calling them to service in the world. "To live in the fellowship of Jesus is to be called as his fellow worker in the service of men. . . ."[32] Members of the Kingdom are not objects acted upon by God's activity, but subjects called to respond to God's Kingdom by living their lives in partnership for each other. Thus Jesus preached the Kingdom as a symbol of both hope and command. Hope, because it is the promise and assurance of God's saving activity that will finally bring all things within God's sovereign will. But God's activity calls for our activity in response. Thus it is also a command—a call to obey God's will, which in turn demands conversion to the neighbor whom God wills us to love.

The Kingdom as symbol of hope and command leads to a related question concerning Jesus' preaching of the Kingdom. If the Kingdom is coming to its fullness by the grace and power of God, what then is the role of our human response in its ongoing coming? As we will note below, this issue is much debated in contemporary theology and has relevance for how we understand our purpose in Christian religious education. Nowhere is it recorded that Jesus ever said "Go build the Kingdom." But he did say that we are to seek it first (Matt. 6:33) and to be like good soil which brings forth much fruit (Matt. 13:4–23); that the Kingdom is like an invaluable treasure or a pearl of great price to be sought above all other things (Matt. 13:44–46). In other words, although Jesus proclaimed the Kingdom as a gift coming by the grace and power of God, he also demanded of its members an active response according to the values of the Kingdom within time and history.[33] *Jesus could not have said more.* As noted in Chapter One, the awareness that we are capable of contributing to and shaping the course of our future did not emerge in human consciousness until quite recently, probably with the Industrial Revolution. To expect the historical Jesus to have had such a consciousness is to fall into a docetist denial of his humanity.[34]

If the centrality of the Kingdom in Jesus' preaching is so obvious, why then do I belabor the point here? The reason is that the Kingdom of God lost its centrality in the preaching of the Church. Further, when it was referred to in religous education, Matthew's phrase *Kingdom of heaven* was favored, and the meaning proposed for it was exclusively otherworldly. Apparently, a shift in emphasis first emerged in the early Church from preaching what Jesus preached to preaching Jesus as the Christ, Messiah and Lord. Schnackenburg summarizes the shift in emphasis:

> When the apostles took over the preaching and mission of their master, we might have expected that after his death they would have proclaimed the coming reign of God, which had already showed itself, as their central theme. What we actually find is an astonishing change, at least at first hearing. God's reign recedes into the background of the apostolic preaching until it is scarcely noticeable. A second theme occupies the stage, the gospel of Jesus, Messiah and Lord.[35]

This shift is evident in the summaries of the apostolic preaching given in Acts. Except for a triple mention of the Kingdom in the Pauline kerygma to the Gentiles (Acts 14:22; 19:8; 28:23), the centrality of Jesus' preaching of the Kingdom is absent from the preaching of the apostolic Church. For example, in the summary of the kerygma as reported in Acts 13:16–41 it is the risen Christ who is presented as the center of the preaching. And in the kerygma preached by the Church since those apostolic times the Kingdom of God has not occupied a central place. Schnackenburg contends it is "not that the Church forgets Jesus' gospel of the future kingdom of God: but the gospel of Jesus, Messiah and Lord, comes into the foreground."[36] Moltmann insists that the Church's preaching of Jesus as the Christ "cannot lead to a narrowing down of Jesus' preaching of the kingdom, for the church's proclamation of Christ is in essence the gospel of the kingdom. . . ."[37] In point of fact, however, throughout history the Church's preaching of Jesus as Messiah and Lord has been allowed to overshadow, and to contain only implicitly, the Kingdom of God as Jesus preached it.

One of the most fruitful developments in contemporary theology, then, is the insistence that the Kingdom of God is central to our understanding of the Christian faith, and it cannot be reduced to meaning only a "place for souls later on." Clearly this is a reclaiming of the earliest tradition, rather than a new accretion. The development can be stated thus: *There is an essential link between preach-*

ing Jesus Christ as Lord and Savior and preaching the Kingdom of God, so that
to preach Jesus as the Christ requires that we preach what Jesus preached—the
Kingdom. In consequence, the symbol Kingdom of God must be recentered in
our understanding of what it means to live a Christian life and thus, given our
interests here, be understood as the symbol of our primary purpose in Christian
religious education.

THE KINGDOM OF GOD IN CONTEMPORARY CHRISTIAN THEOLOGY

The recentering of Jesus' preaching of the Kingdom in our understanding of
Christian faith has been an evolving process over the past two hundred years.[38]
Over the past twenty-five years the "hope" and "political" theologians have
been most influential in bringing the symbol back into central focus and have
built their theological constructs around this eschatalogical dimension of the
Christian message. More recently still, theologians of a liberation motif (Third
and Fourth World, feminist, and minority theologies) also place the Kingdom at
the center of their reflections. Their stance is more radical than that of the political and hope theologians because they insist that Christian theology must
arise out of a context of active participation in society on behalf of the values of
God's Kingdom. But placing central emphasis on the Kingdom of God is not exclusive to the "hope," "political," and "liberation" theologies. In fact, the whole
broad spectrum of critical theology, within which most "middle of the road"
theologians today can be placed, is informed by a new awareness of the centrality of the Kingdom of God to Christian faith and to the meaning of being a
Christian. This shift has been augmented by the emergence of the "Christology
from below" referred to earlier. When the starting point for Christological reflection is the life, work, and preaching of the historical Jesus, then the centrality of the Kingdom in his ministry becomes obvious and calls us clearly to make
it central in preaching what he preached.

Pastoral Implications of the Kingdom of God

Our primary question as Christian religious educators concerns the pastoral
implications of Jesus' preaching of God's Kingdom for Christian faith today; in
other words, what Kingdom of God means for people who attempt to live lives
of Christian faith in our contemporary world. It is almost two thousand years
since Jesus preached the imminence of the Kingdom. Our understanding of the
Kingdom must be faithful to Jesus' understanding, but we need to reinterpret
the symbol and its meaning for our lives in light of contemporary experience
and consciousness.

The process of reinterpretation has given rise to various schools of eschatology, but there is a centrist position on which most contemporary theologians could agree. To set this view out in bold relief, it will be helpful to see how it has developed from the eschatologies posed before it.

Richard P. McBrien, who makes eschatology the foundation of his theology of the Church, offers a comprehensive overview of the positions in the recent debate.[39] He divides the debate chronologically into five schools of thought.

1. "Consistent, consequent, futurist or thorough-going eschatology" (Schweitzer, Weiss, Werner, Buri). In this view the Kingdom is not something "within the grasp of man" but "breaks into the human situation as a mighty, unexpected and apocalyptic act of God." Here the Kingdom is totally in the *future*. We have nothing to do but await its coming. We can neither foster nor retard it.

2. "Realized eschatology" (C. H. Dodd). In this position the Kingdom is already realized. "According to Dodd, the Kingdom of God had already fully arrived in Jesus Christ . . . and we are confronted here and now with the challenge of accepting or rejecting it." This gives a *past*-oriented character to the Kingdom. We must simply keep the memory of it alive, and "the future has nothing essential to tell us."

3. "Existentialist eschatology." This reflects the thinking of the great scripture scholar and theologian Rudolph Bultmann. From an existentialist perspective God's self-revealing is to be realized "in the present, again and again and again." The Kingdom of God points to the possibility of authentic human existence in the *present*. But it becomes a present reality only in the preaching of the Word and through its transforming power.

4. "Salvation history eschatology." For this school of thought the Kingdom has *already* broken into history definitively and effectively in Jesus Christ. Yet while the decisive battle has been won, the war is not yet over. The perfection of the Kingdom lies in the *future*. In the interim our *present* is not to be spent merely waiting. Rather "the post-biblical period has something essential to contribute to the growth and extension and celebration of this Kingdom."

5. "Proleptic eschatology." This school of thought is very similar to salvation history eschatology. It differs from it in its emphasis on the newness of the future Kingdom, but it, too, emphasizes past, present, and future. "Rooted in the past (in the Resurrection of Jesus, especially), anticipated in the present, and yet to be created as something really new in the future, the Kingdom of God is radically and thoroughly historical in character."[40]

McBrien claims correctly that the majority of contemporary commentators can be situated in either the fourth or fifth schools of thought. Since these positions are very closely related they form a consensus position: that the Kingdom has already come definitively in Jesus Christ; it will come completely and with newness at the end of time; but its working out is an intrahistorical reality and our present time has something vital to contribute to its final perfection.[41]

Even within this consensus view there are questions which remain debated. An important question for our pastoral and educational interest (raised earlier in regard to Jesus' preaching of the Kingdom) is, To what extent does present time and history contribute to the coming of the final Kingdom? That the Kingdom demands a response from our present is agreed upon by all. But some theologians talk about us as "cocreators" of the Kingdom with God.[42] Other theologians reject this, insisting that although we have a contribution to make, it is overstating the human part to call us cocreators.

The view I favor on this question is similar to the centrist position taken by the Second Vatican Council, which states clearly in *Constitution on the Church in the Modern World* that the call of the Christian is "to make ready the material" of the Kingdom (Art. 38), and that the "fruits" of our efforts will endure in the final Kingdom (Art. 39).

> For after we have obeyed the Lord, and in His Spirit nurtured on earth the values of human dignity, brotherhood and freedom, and indeed all the good fruits of our nature and enterprise, we will find them again, but freed of stain, burnished and transfigured. This will be so when Christ hands over to the Father a kingdom eternal and universal: "A kingdom of truth and life, of holiness and grace, of justice, love, and peace."[43]

Thus while we can never claim to build the Kingdom by our own human efforts, yet those same efforts on behalf of human dignity, justice, freedom, and the like will bear fruit in the end. The Kingdom is a gift that comes by the grace of God. But the grace comes to us in our present to enable us to live lives that make the Kingdom present even now. By such lives we help prepare the "material" for its final realization. God is working out the Kingdom within our history, but not without the human activity that constitutes this history. Rahner, commenting on these passages from Vatican II, says that while the final Kingdom will be a "radical transformation" of history, it will not be an obliteration of it.[44] The fruits of our efforts within history will remain.

In the faith of Christians, Jesus Christ, the crucified and resurrected one, is the definitive and effective agent of God's Kingdom. The Kingdom comes to us in our present as a responsibility and as a promise. As promise, it is our sure hope that good will finally triumph over evil, and life over death. In this it is a consolation and comfort. But the Kingdom also comes to us as a radical responsibility and a critique of our present response as individuals, as Church, and as human community. Our new-found awareness of God's intrahistorical working out of the Kingdom poses, in a more compelling way, the intrahistorical responsibilities Christian faith places upon us. The "privatizing" of the Gospel, which led to an "excessively individualistic interpretation of the Christian message" and a system of "each man for himself,"[45] can be rectified when we place the Kingdom of God at the center of our understanding and educating in the Christian faith. The vision of the completed Kingdom returns to critique our present way of being together because in it the future and present are inextricably interwoven. God's action at the end of history and within history are inseparable, as God's time is one time. The imminence of the Kingdom means that the present is not independent of the future, but rather the future has "an imperative claim upon the present, alerting all men to the urgency and exclusiveness of seeking first the Kingdom of God."[46] Thus God's action within history on behalf of the Kingdom at once demands our response and critiques our efforts. McBrien is correct when he says that "all reality is subordinated to, and measured against, the promised future, the fully realized Kingdom."[47]

The pastoral implications of the Kingdom as understood in contemporary theology can now be outlined by summarizing the responsibilities placed on us as individuals, on us as a faith community that forms the Christian Church, and on us as members of social/political structures.

Personal Implications.   All would-be Christians are invited in a specific manner to accept Jesus Christ as their Lord and Savior. To do this means to accept the demands of membership in the Kingdom of God as preached by Jesus. As he invited decision in his own time, so he invites decision in our time: to seek first the Kingdom of God as he modeled and preached it. This is a constant call to continuing conversion and repentance. "This is the time of fulfillment. The reign of God is at hand! Reform your lives and believe in the gospel!" (Mark 1:15). The Kingdom must always begin in the hearts of its members. Without such a conversion it cannot be embodied in social realities. This conversion is to be a constant turning toward God by turning toward our neighbor. Above all other demands the Kingdom places on us the radical mandate of love as preached by Jesus.

Implications for the Church.[48]   The nature and mission of the Church must be understood in light of God's Kingdom in Jesus Christ. To be faithful to the teaching of Jesus, the Church must exist for the sake of the Kingdom.[49] Thus *the Church is to be a community of those who confess Jesus Christ as Lord and Savior, who ratify that faith by baptism, and who manifest the Kingdom of God as preached by Jesus, by proclaiming in word, celebrating in sacrament, and living in deed the Kingdom already and the Kingdom promised.*

My statement is, of course, more a description of what the Church ought to be than of what it is presently. But such will always be the case when the Church is described this side of the completed Kingdom. As the Church strives to exist faithfully for the Kingdom, it has a threefold mission that can be summarized best under three traditional headings of *kerygma, koinonia,* and *diakonia. Kerygma* is the mission of preaching in word and celebrating in sacrament the message and memory of the risen Christ, in whom salvation rests. To preach his message is to preach the Kingdom of God. To celebrate his memory is to remember the effective promise of the Kingdom for which he stands. *Koinonia* is the task of becoming a community of authentic fellowship, a community of faith, hope, and love. Only by embodying within itself the truth of its own message can the Church be a credible sign of the Kingdom in the midst of the world. *Diakonia* calls the Church to the mission of service. It must be a community that makes the Kingdom present now and prepares the material for its final completion by a life of loving service to the whole human family.

Those age-old notes of the Church's mission must be reinterpreted with the consciousness of our time as we attempt to be Church for the sake of the Kingdom. In consequence, our understanding of that mission must be expanded far beyond how we have typically understood it, at least in our recent history. The Church's purpose is not to be what Gutierrez calls a "salvation club" that "guarantees heaven" in the sense of an individualistic and totally otherworldy salvation.[50] Rather, it is to be a sacrament (an efficacious sign that causes to happen what it signifies) of the Kingdom in the midst of history. And the values of the Kingdom point to profoundly social as well as personal and spiritual realities. Kasper notes that "Jesus' message of the coming of the kingdom of God must be seen in the context of mankind's search for peace, freedom, justice and life."[51] If, then, the Church is to be an effective sign of the Kingdom in the midst of such a human search, it will have to preach those values of the Kingdom. But preaching alone will not be enough. To be a credible sign of the Kingdom, it will have to embody within its own structures the values it preaches. Further, it will have to harness its ministry and whole way of being in the world toward helping to create social/political/economic structures that are capable of promoting the values of the Kingdom. Structures which obviate the realization of the Kingdom, or, as is often the case, promote its opposite, must be opposed. Therefore, when Christians join together as Church, the conversion which began in their individual hearts must express itself in a community effort to change such oppressive structures and create alternatives more likely to "prepare the material" of the final Kingdom. This points inevitably toward the political role of the Church in the world.

Talk of a political role for the Church typically evokes a negative reaction. It is often heard, at least in our culture, as a call to run a *Christian* candidate for the presidency or to form an overtly Christian Church political party. There are good historical reasons to be wary of such an approach. But such politics are only one expression, and sometimes a rather impoverished one, of political activity. As indicated in Chapter One, politics is any use of power that deliberately and structurally intervenes to influence how people live their lives in society. With that understanding of politics the Church is inevitably involved in the politics of its social context. People who object to a political role for the Church assume that there is a choice—to be or not to be politically involved. But there is no choice between political involvement or noninvolvement for the Church. By its very being as a social institution in the world, by what it teaches, preaches, and gives witness to, the Church is inevitably political. If the Church makes a concerted attempt not to participate in the political realities and, claiming to be above them, takes a position of silence, it has by that very silence taken a political stance. For example, to remain silent in the face of situations and practices that are antithetical to the Kingdom is to take a political stance of tacit permission and is thus to be unfaithful to the very purpose and mission of the Church. The Church *can* choose, however, to what end it wishes to direct its political influence. Its politics must be for the Kingdom of God.

Implications for Society.   When the Kingdom of God is seen as beginning and as being worked out by God with human cooperation within history, and not just as a spiritual symbol referring only to an otherworldly reality, then it functions as a judgment upon our social, political, and economic structures and upon our cultural arrangements. This does not mean that people who are attempting to respond to God's Kingdom in Jesus Christ should become only negative or ungrateful critics of what we already have. There are signs of the Kingdom already among us, and they are often reflected in social/political structures. For these we must be grateful. But we can never settle for what we have, nor for what our neighbors—near and far—in this global village have, until God's Kingdom is fully realized. While there are signs of the Kingdom already among us, there are social, political, economic, and cultural realities that actively prevent the values of the Kingdom from being promoted. Racism, sexism, oppression, and discrimination of any kind and on any basis; uncontrolled capitalism; atheistic communism; totalitarian regimes; rampant consumerism; and so on all stand condemned in light of the Kingdom of God. As the Second Vatican Council, in its *Pastoral Constitution on the Church in the Modern World* put it so well, "With respect to the fundamental rights of the person, every type of discrimination, whether social or cultural, whether based on sex, race, color, social condition, language or religion, is to be overcome and eradicated as contrary to God's intent."[52]

Thus the social implication of the Kingdom for us as individuals, as a Christian community, and as members of a larger social order, is that we contribute our part, within our own context, to promote the justice, peace, and freedom for all that is the promise of God's Kingdom. The struggle to develop structures capable of promoting the values of the Kingdom is not an option to be left to those with explicitly political inclinations. There are, of course, differences in ability and opportunity to get involved in structural reform. But all Christians who choose to live their lives according to God's intentions, the Kingdom, share in this social responsibility.[53]

A CONSENSUS VIEW OF THE KINGDOM AS ULTIMATE PURPOSE FOR CHRISTIAN RELIGIOUS EDUCATION

In summary, the Kingdom of God is God's intention for creation. It is the central theme and purpose in the preaching and life of Jesus, the Christ. Therefore, when an educational activity is intended to sponsor people toward Christian faith, the overarching purpose (the ultimate, or metapurpose) of such education is the Kingdom of God in Jesus Christ. This conviction will be central to the remainder of this work.

Like any symbol, it has unique connotations for each individual. The truth in Perrin's claim that the Kingdom is a "tensive symbol" (that is, its meaning can never be exhausted; see note 7) must be remembered and its unique meaning for each person affirmed. But in the midst of the various schools of thought and questions remaining a consensus view of the Kingdom can be outlined. I propose the following twelve statements as elements of this consensus. Together they constitute what I intend to evoke with the symbol Kingdom of God when I use it hereafter as the metapurpose that guides the praxis of Christian religious education.

1. The Kingdom of God is a symbol that represents the active presence of God in power *over, in,* and at the *end* of history. This is so because God's sovereignty as creator and sustainer is *over* all things, the completion of God's vision for creation will be realized only at the *end* of history, but meanwhile God is active *in* the midst of history to bring about the fullness of God's reign.

2. Cognizant of the limitations of our language and aware that all time is an aspect of the "same time," we can talk about the Kingdom of God as past, present, and future. It is *past* in that it has already come definitively in Jesus Christ; *future* in that its fullness is "not yet," and its completion will have a radical newness to it; *present* in that there are signs of it already among us, and it is existentially realized when God's will is done in our time.

3. The Kingdom of God is a divine gift. It has come and is coming by the grace and power of God. Though we have our part to play, it cannot be constructed by human effort alone. Because it is God's gift to us, we can afford to live our present with happiness, with joy, with peace. We can celebrate God's gift of the Kingdom already and the Kingdom promised

because there are signs of it among us, and its final coming does not depend entirely on us.

4. In Christian faith God's gift of the Kingdom and the power by which it has come and is coming were incarnated in Jesus, the crucified and risen Christ. God's intervention in Jesus is the definitive activity of God on behalf of the Kingdom. Thus the dying and rising of Jesus Christ is the source of power by which the Kingdom is possible to us. In this sense we can speak, as Paul speaks, about "the Kingdom of Christ and of God" (Eph. 5:5).

5. As Christians, we are called through Jesus Christ to a relationship with God and each other as members of God's Kingdom. But this possibility, now held open to us, demands a lived response—a response of obedience to God's will after the model of Jesus and his preaching. While the Kingdom is a gift and an invitation, it is also a task and a *responsibility*.

6. God has willed to love all people, and thus God's will for all people is that they be loved. Therefore, the primary mandate to be obeyed by respondents to God's Kingdom is that we love God and our neighbor in response to God's love for us. In the Kingdom as preached and lived by Jesus this mandate does not require two different loves, one vertical and the other horizontal. It calls for one radical love of God through love of neighbor as ourselves.

7. The Kingdom of God invites a response of constant conversion, *metanoia*. That inner conversion must turn us outward toward God in our neighbor. This love requires, in turn, that as individuals we strive to live justly and for justice, peacefully and for peace, equally and for equality; that we live by and to promote the values of the Kingdom, God's will for the world.

8. Our conversion requires that we strive to live sinless lives as individuals, but it also demands that we oppose and struggle against all the social and cultural expressions of sin in our world.

9. Stating the positive dimension of the previous point, the promise of the Kingdom in Jesus Christ is of a redeemed people in a redeemed society and universe. Therefore, we must struggle to create social political/economic structures and cultural arrangements that are capable of promoting the values of the Kingdom.

10. As a Christian community, the Church's mission is to be a sacrament of the Kingdom, which means an efficacious sign of it. It does this by empowering people to respond, through God's grace, to God's will in the present, critiquing what is not of the Kingdom, and ever holding out the hope of final completion. The Church is to exist for the sake of the Kingdom and never for its own sake.

11. The fruits of our living such a response to God's intentions for creation are a manifestation of the Kingdom in the midst of history, and the fruits of our present efforts will remain in the completed Kingdom. The awareness that we can be shapers of history adds urgency to the demand that, by the grace of God, we take and shape our present in the direction of the Kingdom.

12. For Christians the Kingdom of God and the Lordship of the risen Christ must stand together at the heart of our preaching and educating. Undoubtedly, to preach Christ as Lord and Savior is implicitly to preach the Kingdom of God. But the Kingdom cannot be treated only as a message implicit in our kerygma. Both themes, Christ as Lord and Savior and the Kingdom as preached by Jesus, must be constantly and intentionally present in our proclamation and education. Without both our kerygma is incomplete.

NOTES

1. See, for example, *The Didache*, the earliest catechetical instruction outside the canon of scripture. *The Didache* makes it clear that Christianity is a call to a "way of life," a life lived according to the example of Jesus and his teachings (*The Didache*, 6:3–25).

2. The answer offered by Hans Küng to the question Why be a Christian? is an interesting example of a contemporary statement. While I have reservations about Küng's statement because of an inadequate emphasis on the social responsibility of the Christian and the social dimension of salvation, his position certainly gives a flavor of the shift that has come in response to this basic question. At the end of his lengthy work *On Being a Christian* Küng asks again the question the book is written to answer: Why should one be a Christian? and offers "a brief recapitulatory formula" in reply:

    By following Jesus Christ
    man in the world of today
    can truly humanly live, act, suffer and die:
    in happiness and unhappiness, life and death,
    sustained by God and helpful to men. (p. 602)

3. There are many problems with using the term *Kingdom of God* here, and I have debated long before deciding to use it. To begin with, the English word *kingdom* conjures up the image of a particular territory ruled over by a sovereign. Such is not the primary sense of the Hebrew *malkuth Yahweh* nor of the Greek *basileia tou theou*, both of which suggest a more active state of reigning than of a place ruled over. In light of this Stanley and Brown suggest "Perhaps 'rule' or 'kingship' would be a better translation than 'kingdom'" (*The Jerome Biblical Commentary*, "Aspects of New Testament Thought: The Kingdom of God," by David M. Stanley and Raymond E. Brown, 2:783). The New American Bible usually translates it as "reign of God." However, *reign of God* seems to place the exclusive emphasis on God, whereas *Kingdom of God*, while retaining the emphasis of God's sovereignty, implies more of a relationship between people within a social and political arrangement in which the citizens have certain rights and responsibilities. In addition, *Kingdom of God* remains the term most often used in both theological and scriptural literature today, and since I am in dialogue with and draw extensively from that literature, it seems more appropriate to continue using *Kingdom of God*, emphasizing that I intend it as an active state of ruling rather than as a static and localized reality.

    A second problem with *Kingdom of God*, often cited as an argument against its use, is that it has little pastoral appeal for people today since the political entity of kingdom is foreign to most contemporary experience. This was one reason the great religious educator George Albert Coe rejected the term in favor of "democracy of God" (see Coe, *What Is Christian Education,* p. 54). However, I see an advantage in the very fact that it is a somewhat outmoded political arrangement in the contemporary world. While it clearly contains a social and political dimension, it is also open to reinterpretation without being inevitably identified, by association of ideas, with any particular nation state.

Perhaps its greatest disadvantage is that it can have unfortunate sexist overtones. When I use the term, I certainly do not intend any sexist implications. However, in this regard, as yet there seems to be no alternative term that remains faithful to what the sources imply by the symbol. Kingdom/Queendom borders on the ludicrous. Thus I settle for using the term, aware of its limitation, anxious to avoid its unfortunate overtones, and welcoming people who might appropriate my work to use what they may consider to be a more adequate term.

4. To propose the Kingdom of God as our ultimate purpose has practical educational advantages, too, which will be apparent below. Most important, because of the obvious social and intrahistorical dimension of the Kingdom, talking about it as our ultimate purpose should help prevent us from educating to a privatized kind of Christianity that looks only to a reward in heaven. I will later draw heavily upon it in recommending an approach that brings us as Christians to accept our intrahistorical responsibilities to live a redemption/salvation that is both social and intrahistorical rather than only individual and extrahistorical.

5. The word *eschatology* comes from the Greek words *eschaton,* meaning "end time," and *logos,* here meaning "treatise." In traditional dogmatic theology eschatology referred to doctrines about the "last things" (death, judgment, heaven, hell, resurrection of the dead) but it was seen as "a kind of appendix not too closely related to the central themes" (Gutierrez, *A Theology of Liberation,* p. 162). However, with the contemporary awareness that the Kingdom of God is the central theme of Jesus' preaching, this has changed. Eschatology is now seen as the central theme from which the other themes take their meaning. Edward Schillebeeckx claims that despite its basic truth, the traditional view of eschatology is "theologically speaking, inadequate." In proposing an expanded meaning of eschatology, he writes "*Eschata* means 'last things, extremities'; everything that has to do with the ultimate, deepest but therefore final meaning of human life is called 'eschatological'; therefore not just the *postmundane* but also whatever concerns the *definitive* meaning of life as well as the 'last days,' the end of the age—and indeed as the time of salvation . . . the emphasis always lies on the aspect of 'what is definitely decisive,' what will become publicly evident only 'in the end' and after death, but is already at issue in the present and is being decided in it" (Schillebeeckx, *Jesus,* pp.742–743).

6. "The divine kingship is an idea common to all the religions of the ancient East" (*Dictionary of Biblical Theology,* "Kingdom," p. 292). However, the Israelites saw the kingship of Yahweh as a critique of the imperial divine kingship attributed to the rulers of Egypt, Babylon, etc.

7. Perrin, *Jesus and the Language of the Kingdom,* p. 5. Perrin also makes an important point when he refers to the Kingdom of God as a "tensive symbol" (p. 31). Here he is distinguishing it from a "steno-symbol." "A symbol can have a one-to-one relationship to that which it represents . . . in which case it is . . . a 'steno-symbol,' or it can have a set of meanings that can neither be exhausted nor adequately expressed by any one referent, in which case it is a 'tensive symbol'" (p. 30). Because the Kingdom of God is a tensive symbol, it has a richness to it that is inexhaustible. Or, to state it another way, the reality of the Kingdom will always be more than the symbol suggests at any particular time or in any particular context.

8. Perrin, *Language of the Kingdom,* p. 22.

9. See Schnackenburg, *God's Rule and Kingdom,* p. 20.

10. Ibid., p. 19.

11. Ibid., p. 35.

12. Pannenberg, *Theology and the Kingdom of God,* p. 79.

13. McKenzie writes, "The multiple developments of the idea of salvation are best summed up, if they can be summed up at all, in the idea of the reign (kingdom) of Yahweh . . ." (*The Jerome Biblical Commentary,* "Aspects of Old Testament Thought: Relations Between God and Israel," by John. L. McKenzie, 2:761).

14. Some of the better known works on Christology now in English are for example, Pannenberg, *Jesus—God and Man*; Schoonenberg, *The Christ*; Moltmann, *The Crucified God*; Kasper, *Jesus the Christ*; Boff, *Jesus Christ Liberator*; Sobrino, *Christology at the Crossroads*; Schillebeeckx, *Jesus.* While Küng's *On Being a Christian* is about the purpose of Christian faith in general, some 250 pages are a discussion of Christology.

15. See the remarks of O'Collins in *What Are They Saying About Jesus,* p. 30.

16. The centrality of the Kingdom of God in the preaching of Jesus is a primary motif in all of the works cited in note 14. A few sample statements will make this point. Küng writes, "This term [Kingdom of God] is at the center of his proclamation, but is never defined" (*On Being a Christian*, p. 214). Schillebeeckx writes, "The Kingdom of God is Jesus' central message, with the emphasis at once on its coming and on its coming close" (*Jesus*, p. 140). And Sobrino notes, "The most certain historical datum about Jesus' life is that the concept which dominated his preaching, the reality which gave meaningfulness to all his activity, was 'the kingdom of God'" (*Christology at the Crossroads*, p. 41).

17. For example, Perrin writes, "The whole message of Jesus focuses upon the Kingdom of God" (*Language of the Kingdom*, p. 1). And Reginald Fuller notes, "It is generally accepted that the focal point of Jesus' message was the inbreaking of the kingdom of God" ("The Double Commandment of Love," *Essays on the Love Commandment*, p. 51).

18. Aulén, *Jesus*, p. 100.

19. The term *Kingdom of God* is mentioned only twice in John's Gospel. However, it is mentioned 14 times in Mark and 31 times in Luke. Matthew mentions it 3 times, favoring instead the term *kingdom of heaven*, which he uses 30 times. However, heaven in Matthew is being used as a reverential synonym for God. (See *The Jerome Biblical Commentary*, "Aspects of New Testament Thought: The Kingdom of God," by David M. Stanley and Raymond E. Brown, 2:782.)

20. Perrin, *Jesus and the Language of the Kingdom*, p. 79.

21. John Dominic Crossan offers a very insightful analysis of Jesus' use of parables. Crossan contends that the power of the parable is in its ability to subvert one's expected meaning and to expose the limits of a taken-for-granted world. He writes, "Parables give God room. . . . They are stories which shatter the deep structure of our accepted world and thereby render clear and evident to us the relativity of story itself. They remove our defences and make us vulnerable to God. It is only in such experiences that God can touch us, and only in such moments does the kingdom of God arrive" (*The Dark Interval*, pp. 121–122).

22. Hans Küng has a lengthy but very helpful summary of Jesus' notion of the Kingdom:

    It will be a kingdom where, in accordance with Jesus' prayer, God's name is truly hallowed, his will is done on earth, men will have everything in abundance, all sin will be forgiven and all evil overcome.

    It will be a kingdom where, in accordance with Jesus' promises, the poor, the hungry, those who weep and those who are downtrodden will finally come into their own; where pain, suffering and death will have an end.

    It will be a kingdom that cannot be described, but only made known in metaphors: as the new covenant, the seed springing up, the ripe harvest, the great banquet, the royal feast.

    It will therefore be a kingdom—wholly as the prophets foretold—of absolute righteousness, of unsurpassable freedom, of dauntless love, of universal reconciliation, of everlasting peace. In this sense therefore it will be the time of salvation, of fulfillment, of consummation, of God's presence: the absolute future. (*On Being a Christian*, p. 215)

23. Aulén, *Jesus*, p. 143.

24. Schnackenburg writes, "The prayer which Jesus taught them shows what is the ultimate issue: that God's reign may come, his holy will prevail on earth and all opposition to God's dominion be overcome" (*God's Rule and Kingdom*, p. 108).

25. Jesus' proclamation of an imminent Kingdom and of a Kingdom in the future, coupled with the historical fact that the completed Kingdom obviously did not come in his time nor in the two thousand years since, at first sight poses a problem for which theologians offer a variety of explanations. Walter Kasper's explanation is particularly helpful. He contends that the key to the apparent discrepancy lies in the biblical notion of time (very similar to the understanding I propose in Chapter One). In this understanding present and future are no more than two aspects of the same time. As a result, "Jesus' message of the Kingdom that is now and in the future becomes more intelligible. What is being said is that now is the time for the coming of God's Kingdom: that is, the present is modified by the fact that the coming of the Kingdom has begun and faces men with a choice. The Kingdom, in other words, is the power which controls the future. It is now forcing a choice, and in this way is active in the present and totally determines it" (*Jesus the Christ*, p. 77). Schillebeeckx favors a similar solution. He writes, "God's rule and the kingdom of God are thus two aspects of one and the same thing. God's dominion points to the dynamic here-and-now character of God's exercise of control; the kingdom of God refers more to the definitive state of 'final good' to which God's saving activity is directed. Thus present and future are essentially interrelated" (*Jesus*, p. 141).

26. See Aulén, *Jesus,* pp. 101 ff.

27. Sobrino writes: "Both his miracles and his forgiveness of sins are primarily signs of the arrival of the kingdom of God. They are signs of liberation, and only in that context can they help to shed light on the person of Jesus" (*Christology at the Crossroads,* p. 48).

28. See Fuller, "The Double Commandment of Love," pp. 41–56.

29. See Schottroff, "Non-Violence and the Love of One's Enemies," *Essays on The Love Commandment,* esp. pp. 10–11.

30. Aulén explains, "But even though Jesus made references to what had earlier been the general rule in Israel, it nevertheless was a revolution when he radically and consistently claimed that obedience to God's will must be realized in care for one's fellow man—with all the stress upon the human level" (*Jesus,* pp. 138–139).

31. Schillebeeckx, *Jesus,* p. 154.

32. Aulén, *Jesus,* p. 144.

33. Kasper remarks, "The coming of the Kingdom of God is, then, the revelation that God is God in love, but this does not imply quietism on the human side" (*Jesus the Christ,* p. 81).

34. The docetist heresy in the early Church denied the humanity of Jesus Christ, saying that he only appeared to be a human person.

35. Schnackenburg, *God's Rule and Kingdom,* p. 259.

36. Ibid., p. 352.

37. Moltmann, *The Church in the Power of the Spirit,* p. 82.

38. In America the reemergence of the Kingdom at the center of Christian faith can be traced back to the Puritan divines and in Europe to Kant and Schleiermacher. It was given significant impetus in this country by the Social Gospel movement, led by Walter Rauschenbusch (1861–1918). The Kingdom of God was the central theme of his preaching and teaching. For Rauschenbusch God is active in history in the social struggle for peace and justice, and Christians are to participate with God in the struggle to create God's Kingdom. We can share with God in the creation of God's Kingdom, or we can resist and retard its progress (see his *Christianity and the Social Crisis*).

   The Social Gospel movement, however, had its most severe critics in commentators who felt that the human role in the building of the Kingdom was being overstated or who preferred to continue thinking of the Kingdom as otherworldly. Some scripture scholars of the late nineteenth century, notably Weiss and Schweitzer, took such a traditional view. Their position constituted a reaction against the liberalism of Kant and Ritschl, and critiqued the naivete of the Social Gospel people. They claimed that the Kingdom of God cannot be influenced by human participation or history and would come about only by the power of God. Weiss conceived of the Kingdom of God as "the breaking out of an overpowering divine storm which erupts into history to destroy and to renew . . . and which man can neither further nor influence. . . . The disciples were to pray for the coming of the kingdom, but man could do nothing to establish it . . ." (quoted in Perrin, *Jesus and the Language of the Kingdom,* p. 67).

   Weiss and his colleagues were making a valid point in emphasizing that the Kingdom is God's gift. But when the criticism of the activist emphasis of the Social Gospel movement is overstated, as it was, then we are robbed of our historicity, and our present seems to have no significance for the Kingdom. Conversely, the Kingdom can have little significance for our present time. The insight of the Social Gospel movement that the Kingdom demands a radical response from the present rather than a passive waiting needed to be retained. It is retained, though better nuanced, in contemporary theology.

39. Georgia Harkness also has a useful categorization of eschatological schools but does not take sufficient account, I believe, of more current opinion. Harkness has four divisions: 1) the apocalyptic eschatology of Weiss and Schweitzer, 2) the prophetic eschatology of Rauschenbusch and DeWolf, 3) the realized eschatology of Dodd, and 4) the Kingdom as an "existential decision" associated with Bultmann and his disciples (see Harkness, *Understanding the Kingdom of God,* pp. 32–51). Schnackenburg divides the positions into seven schools of thought (See *God's Rule and Kingdom,* pp. 115–116), but his classification, too, is now somewhat dated (written in 1963).

40. See McBrien, *Quest,* pp. 14–21.

41. McBrien's overview was written in 1970. Theologians have subsequently reiterated the newness of the coming Kingdom but have further clarified and radicalized our understanding of the demands which the Kingdom makes on our present.

   I also add a caution to this consensus position. Christians must be realistic and far from smug in their claim that the Kingdom has already come *in Jesus Christ*. Indeed, we claim in our faith that Jesus Christ was and is the definitive action by God on behalf of the Kingdom. In him we see God's unbreakable promise that the Kingdom will come to perfection. But God is also faithful to God's promises to Israel. (For some sobering thoughts that might prevent Christians from being glib in our claims for the Kingdom's arrival see Idinopulos, "Christianity and the Holocaust," pp. 257–67.) When we look at the pain, suffering, and sin in our world, we must face reality and know that in a definite sense the promise is yet to be fulfilled. Our faith in Jesus Christ as the definitive agent of the Kingdom must never be allowed to lead to Christian quietism, exclusivism, or imperialism. While the Kingdom is in Christ, there are more than Christians in the Kingdom, and the materials for its completion are being prepared by all of God's people.

42. See, for example, Alves, *A Theology of Human Hope*.
43. Abbott, *Documents*, p. 237.
44. See Rahner, "Christianity and the New Earth."
45. Baum, *Religion and Alienation*, p. 196.
46. Pannenberg, *Theology and the Kingdom of God*, p. 54.
47. McBrien, *The Remaking of the Church*, p. 76.
48. In this section on the Church I am strongly influenced by the ecclesiology of Richard P. McBrien (see, especially, *Quest*, Ch. 4).
49. The Church is not the Kingdom. This important distinction has not always been made. Much traditional Christian theology saw the Church and Kingdom as synonymous: to belong to the Kingdom required membership in the Church. Outside of that Church community the salvation of the Kingdom was not available. In Moltmann's words, "Through the triumphalism it maintained and practised for centuries, the church has set itself up as the kingdom of God on earth in absolute form" (*The Church in the Power of the Spirit*, p. 136). For Roman Catholics the Second Vatican Council finally and clearly made this distinction between the Church and the Kingdom (see "Dogmatic Constitution on the Church," Art. 5, Abbott, *Documents*, pp. 17–18). Maintaining a distinction between the Church and the Kingdom can help Church members realize that the bounds of the Kingdom are not the bounds of the Church, and that other peoples of other faiths also prepare the "materials" for its final completion. Distinguishing between the Church and the Kingdom reminds us, too, that our commitment is to that of which the Church is to be an effective sign rather than to the Church for its own sake.
50. See Gutierrez, *A Theology of Liberation*, p. 255. Gutierrez offers a strong but significant critique of the actual political implications this understanding of the Church has had in a Latin American context.
51. Kasper, *Jesus the Christ*, p. 73.
52. Abbott, *Documents*, pp. 227–228.
53. As Pannenberg explains, "Justice and love are relevant not only to the individual but, primarily, to the structures of human interaction. Obviously, then, the Kingdom of God is pointedly political" (*Theology and the Kingdom of God*, p. 80).

4

For Christian Faith

FROM ITS beginning the Christian community has perceived the purpose of
its educational efforts as the promoting of lived Christian faith. Such will be the
immediate purpose of our educating in any age. This is not to claim that the
Christian community or its educators can "give" faith to anyone. Faith is always the gift of God. As Jesus says in the Fourth Gospel, "No one can come to
me unless the Father who sent me draws him" (John 6:44). And Paul wrote to
the Ephesians that we have salvation by faith in Christ, but "this is not your
own doing, it is God's gift" (Eph. 2:8).

However, while faith is God's gift, and it is the Spirit who gives the increase, this does not obviate or make superfluous the preaching and educational
responsibility of the Christian community. On the contrary, if one's faith response to God's grace is to become and remain explicitly Christian, then the
Christian community must share its lived faith, making accessible the tradition
of faith embodied in the community.[1] New members must be introduced to it
and old ones supported in their journey toward mature faith and ever greater
faithfulness. The same Paul who told the Ephesians that faith is God's gift
wrote to the Romans: "But how shall they call on him in whom they have not
believed? And how can they believe unless they have heard of him? And how
can they hear unless there is someone to preach? . . . Faith, then, comes through
hearing, and what is heard is the word of Christ" (Rom. 10:14–17).

Informed by our discussion of the Kingdom in Chapter Three, Christian
faith is a life lived in response to the Kingdom of God in Jesus Christ. But what
is this manner of living to be? What is the mode and style of it? In this way

Christian religious educators must pose and answer the faith question because it is toward Christian faith as a lived reality that we must do our leading out.

My intention in this chapter, then, is not to write a systematic theology of faith, but to describe the dimensions of Christian faith as a lived reality. For this reason I deal in some detail with the work of James W. Fowler on faith development. Fowler's work might not be as relevant for a systematic theology of faith, but it is of pressing interest to Christian educators and to their concern for sponsoring people toward lived Christian faith. Having advocated an understanding of Christian faith as an existential developmental reality, I attempt in the final section to give a comprehensive description of Christian faith and the educational task it poses when it is named as the immediate purpose of Christian religious education.

CHRISTIAN FAITH IN THREE DIMENSIONS

My claim is that Christian faith as a lived reality has three essential and constitutive dimensions: it is 1) a belief conviction, 2) a trusting relationship, and 3) a lived life of agape. Given that we are speaking here specifically of *Christian* faith, and of this faith as lived, these three dimensions find expression in three activities: 1) faith as believing, 2) faith as trusting, and 3) faith as doing. I argue further that when we propose Christian faith as the purpose of religious education, then all three dimensions and activities must be promoted.[3]

FAITH AS BELIEVING

In the Western mentality faith and belief are often taken to be synonymous. At our Christian worship when we are invited to profess our faith, we begin with "I believe in . . ." even though it would be equally appropriate to begin with "I commit myself to . . ." or "I trust in. . . ." Wilfred Cantwell Smith argues that "monstrous confusion" has arisen from the prevalent notion that "belief is identical with faith."[4] I agree. Christian faith is certainly more than belief, especially when "belief" is reduced by our post-Enlightenment mentality to an intellectual assent to statements of belief.

But while Christian faith is more than belief, there is certainly a belief dimension to it as it finds embodiment in the lives of people. David Tracy describes a *belief* as a symbol which explicates "a particular historical, moral, or cognitive claim involved in a particular 'faith' stance."[5] That Christianity makes certain historical, moral, and cognitive claims and proposes them to people as a way of making meaning in their lives is beyond doubt. The *activity* of Christian faith, therefore, requires, in part, a firm conviction about the truths proposed as essential beliefs of the Christian faith. Insofar as these beliefs are personally appropriated, understood, and accepted by the Christian, there is therefore a cognitive, or what Dulles calls an "intellectualist," dimension to Christian faith.

In recent times emphasis on this dimension of Christian faith activity is typically identified with Roman Catholicism. However, it long predates the Reformation period. St. Augustine (354–430), who is claimed as a mentor both by those who emphasize faith as believing and by those who emphasize faith as trusting, provided the classic expression of the "illuminist" doctrine of faith. Heavily influenced by Plato's epistemology and building on the position of many of the Church Fathers before him, Augustine understood faith as an a priori divine illumination within a person's soul. The "light of faith" is first lit by God's grace within a person, and one comes to know and assent to what one knows to be true by the grace of that inner illumination.[6] This grace "within" acts upon the person's will and, without violating the freedom of the individual, disposes the will to assent to the truth of what is presented to the intellect.[7]

Since the willingness to assent is prior to what is presented to the intellect, for Augustine belief has its origin primarily in the will. However, while the will to believe is prior to understanding, understanding is to follow from believing. He wrote, "For understanding is the reward of faith. Therefore do not seek to understand in order to believe, but believe that thou mayest understand."[8] Thus the illuminist position of Augustine also has a strong intellectualist component to it. Believing by the light of God's grace is to lead to understanding of what is believed. Understanding comes by the power of the intellect guided by revelation and the Church's teaching.

This cognitive dimension of faith activity is expanded by Thomas Aquinas who, while attempting to retain the illuminist position of Augustine, situated the act of believing more obviously in the intellect. That the wise man from Aquino saw faith as the gift of God's grace working "within" is beyond question. He wrote, "Therefore faith, as regards the assent which is the chief act of faith, is from God moving man inwardly by grace."[9] But it is also true that he situated the act of believing in the intellect: "Now, to believe is immediately an act of the intellect, because the object of that act is 'the true,' which pertains properly to the intellect. Consequently faith, which is the proper principle of that act, must needs reside in the intellect."[10] In his passion for the "middle way," Aquinas attempted to combine both the illuminist understanding of faith and the intellectual assent approach. "Now the act of believing is an act of the intellect assenting to the divine truth at the command of the will moved by the grace of God. . . ."[11]

It would appear, however, that his interpreters were not always so wise. The intellectualist position came to overshadow the illuminist understanding to the point that faith became synonymous with belief, and belief was reduced to intellectual assent to officially stated doctrines. In popular Catholic consciousness faith came to mean giving intellectual assent to the teaching of the official *magisterium*. Dulles summarizes this well: "From the Counter Reformation until the present generation, Catholics have generally looked upon faith as a submission of the mind to the teaching of the Church."[12]

Sources of that popular understanding can be found in the documents of the Council of Trent (1545–1563),[13] and later in the documents of the First Vatican Council (1869–1871). In its *Constitution on Faith,* Chapter Three, Vatican I speaks of faith as "a supernatural virtue" by which "with the inspiration and help of God's grace, we believe that what he has revealed is true. . . ." It insists that the "assent of faith is by no means a blind impulse" but "by divine and Catholic faith everything must be believed that is contained in the written word of God or in tradition, and that is proposed by the Church as a divinely revealed object of belief either in a solemn decree or in her ordinary, universal teaching."[14] In these statements Vatican I drew upon both the illuminist and the intellectualist understandings of faith. For our survey here the important point to note is that it equated faith with belief and belief with intellectual assent to what the Church proposes as divinely revealed. In light of the Council's definition of papal infallibility the corollary of this position is that what the *magisterium* of the Church proposes for assent must be accepted unquestioningly.

According to Wilfred Cantwell Smith, the tendency to make faith synonymous with belief and to reduce belief to intellectual assent is not exclusive to Roman Catholicism, but is typical of our Western mentality in general. Smith traces the roots of this tendency to the influence of Greek philosophy[15] and sees it augmented by the rationalism of the post-Enlightenment era.[16] He rejects the equation of faith with belief (understood as intellectual assent) to the point where it is not at all obvious that belief is at least one activity of being in faith. I prefer the position that there is a profound truth in the tradition which emphasizes the rational conviction dimension of faith as long as it is not proposed as a complete description of Christian faith. Thus before criticizing this intellectualist understanding of Christian faith, it is important first to affirm its truth.

To begin, the inner illumination emphasis is a necessary reminder that faith is always God's gift, arising at its base from divine grace working within. Second, rational conviction is necessarily a part of Christian faith. Because we are rational beings, there is always a rational dimension to our faith activity. Christianity is founded on divine revelation, and the reflection of the Christian people on that revelation has given rise over history to a body of doctrines and statements of belief. We need to know and assent to them with conviction if we are to draw upon them to make meaning in our lives. Further, it must be possible to demonstrate the truth that is in them in a reasoned manner. Thus Christian faith as a lived reality will always include an activity of believing, even when "believing" is understood in a very intellectual and cognitive way.

When Christians assemble as a community for liturgical worship, one aspect of their activity is symbolizing and celebrating what they believe. It is entirely appropriate, therefore, to "profess our faith" and begin with "I believe. . . ." Even as we symbolize our beliefs in liturgical celebration, that act becomes a prayer of petition for an increase of conviction. Thus the communal liturgy is both to symbolize and express what we believe, and to pray for a strengthened conviction about what we believe.

The criticism of equating faith with belief, however, arises precisely from the unduly intellectualist consequences of such an equation. If faith and belief are made synonymous, then faith is seen as an affair of the head, and the affective and behavioral dimensions of Christian faith are either overlooked or made secondary. By dwelling on Christian faith as "trusting" and as "doing," I am attempting to correct such an unduly cognitivist understanding of Christian faith, and this correction has great importance for religious education.[17] But there is another important criticism to be made here before moving on to the trusting and doing dimensions.

Neither the illuminist nor the intellectualist understanding of Christian faith alone necessarily promotes active engagement in the world in response to the Kingdom of God, which, I have argued, is the essence of Christian faith activity.[18] Of the illuminist approach to faith Dulles writes: "Thus the pursuit of the life of faith, seen in illuminist and contemplative perspectives, turns the mind away from social and economic problems."[19] This tends to dichotomize, as Augustine did, the "two cities." The scholastics after Aquinas further intellectualized faith and increased the dichotomy between one's faith and one's way of living by seeing faith as a virtue of the intellect and charity as a virtue of the will. In such an understanding a person could have faith without having charity, could believe in the Kingdom of God without responding to it.[20] But Christian faith, in light of the Kingdom, is precisely the lived response one *makes* to the Kingdom. Part of the difficulty is that when faith is understood as belief and intellectual assent is posed as the starting point, then it is difficult to translate belief into action. As Dulles notes wisely, "The propositions of faith, which are generally statements of a highly speculative and abstract character, are difficult to translate into concrete programs of action."[21] Thus to see Christian faith only as belief in the sense of rational assent to official doctrines tends to increase the split between faith and daily life. And, in the words of the Second Vatican Council's *Pastoral Constitution on the Church in the Modern World* (par. 43), "This split between the faith which many profess and their daily lives deserves to be counted among the more serious errors of our age."[22]

Christian faith, then, is always a gift of God's grace. It arises from an inner illumination which disposes a person to believe. By the same grace of God and the power of our own intellect the disposition to believe finds expression in stated beliefs about which we come to conviction and to which we give our assent. But that intellectual account cannot be taken as a complete description of Christian faith. Christian faith is at least belief, but it must also be more than belief if it is to be a lived reality.

FAITH AS TRUSTING

The English word *faith* comes from the Latin *fidere*, meaning "to trust." Thus in its very root being in faith implies an activity of trusting. As the "believing" activity of Christian faith points primarily to a cognitive act, the trusting activity is primarily affective. It is the fiducial dimension of being in faith.

This fiducial/affective dimension of Christian faith takes the form of a relationship of trust and confidence in a personal God who saves in Jesus Christ. And the trust finds expression in loyalty, love, and attachment. Because God is faithful, we can commit ourselves with confidence and trust.

This notion of trust in God's promises is a prominent feature in the Old Testament understanding of faith.[23] In the Synoptic Gospels faith and trust are practically synonymous. As Mark has Jesus explain, if a person "trusts in God" then "faith" can move mountains (Mark 11:22–23). For Paul a person appropriates the consequences of the Christ event by faith. This faith is expressed by a commitment of the total person to a trusting relationship with God in Jesus Christ (see Rom. 4:18–25; Gal. 3:6–9).

As the intellectualist dimension is given some predominance in Roman Catholicism, the fiducial dimension of Christian faith is found more obviously in the Protestant tradition of the Christian Church. Martin Luther, reacting against the unduly intellectualist emphasis of the Scholastics and their doctrine of justification by "good works," insisted on justification by faith alone and understood faith as a trusting reliance on the redemptive work of Christ. In his own words, "Faith is a living and unshakeable confidence, a belief in the grace of God so assured that a man would die a thousand deaths for its sake."[24] While Luther insisted that faith is "a living, creative, active, powerful thing" that "cannot do other than good at all times,"[25] yet for him good works were not decisive.[26]

Emphasis on the fiducial dimension of Christian faith bespeaks a truth that must never be overlooked or taken for granted. The call to God's Kingdom is an invitation to a relationship of unbounded trust in the faithfulness of God and in the power of God's saving grace. Realization of God's power to rule, our dependence on that power, and God's faithfulness to us, leads to trust, awe, wonder, reverence, adoration, gratitude, and petition on our part.

We express these feelings in prayer, both personal and communal. In this sense prayer is the dialogical dimension of our relationship with God in Christ, and without dialogue no relationship can survive. As the liturgical symbols express and celebrate our trusting relationship with God, they also become sources of increased trust, especially as they are celebrated in a supporting community. But our trusting activity must also find expression and be embodied in how we live out our day-to-day existence as "pilgrims in time." Our confidence and trust in God leads us to realize and remember that the Kingdom *is* a gift, and in a definitive sense it has already come in Jesus Christ. Salvation has been won for us. Because the Kingdom is already and its final coming is reliably promised, we can afford to live our present with joy, with peace, with happiness. Jesus came that we might have life and have it to the full (John 10:10). He came that his joy might be ours and our joy might be complete (John 15:11). His announcement of the Kingdom is Good News. We can depend on God and thus live our lives as a redeemed people, celebrating the signs of the Kingdom already among us.

But if emphasis on this dimension of Christian faith activity is valid, overemphasis is distorting. Our trusting relationship with a God who saves in Jesus Christ cannot be allowed to reduce or make superfluous human initiative and responsibility. Excessive emphasis on faith as trust and deemphasis of good works, led, in Dulles' words, to "equally sharp antitheses between Gospel and law, between the heavenly and the earthly kingdoms." As a result, it was easier to understand salvation exclusively in "individualistic and other-worldly terms."[27] But when Christian faith is seen as a response to the Kingdom, then no matter how boldly we trust, our relationship with God must also find expression in a life lived by the mandate of the Kingdom, the mandate to love God *by* loving our neighbor. Without such living, faith is dead (see James 2:20).

Twentieth-century Protestant theologians have undoubtedly offered a corrective to the extreme Lutheran position. Bonhoeffer, in *The Cost of Discipleship*, argued for the "costly grace" that requires "single-minded obedience" and against the "cheap grace" to which an overstatement of the fiducial position can lead. For Bonhoeffer faith and obedience cannot be separated because "faith is only real when there is obedience, never without it, and faith only becomes faith in the act of obedience."[28] For Barth faith is a response to the faithfulness of God after the model of Christ, who was obedient even unto death. Tillich insisted that for Christian faith to be consistent with biblical faith, it must include three dimensions similar to the three for which I argue here. He wrote:

Faith, in the biblical view, is an act of the whole personality. Will, knowledge, and emotion participate in it. It is an act of self-surrender, of obedience, of assent. Each of these elements must be present. Emotional surrender without assent and obedience would by-pass the personal center. It would be a compulsion and not a decision. Intellectual assent without emotional participation distorts religious existence into a nonpersonal, cognitive act. Obedience of the will without assent and emotion leads into depersonalizing slavery.[29]

What Tillich refers to as "obedience" of the will I prefer to make more explicitly performative, calling it the activity of "faith as doing."

FAITH AS DOING

In Matthew's Gospel Jesus explains that professing "Lord, Lord" is not sufficient for admission to the Kingdom. The will of God must also be done (Matt. 7:21). Christian faith as a response to the Kingdom of God in Christ must include a doing of God's will. More specifically, the doing is to find embodiment in a lived life of agape—loving God by loving one's neighbor as oneself.

This call to a life of loving engagement in the world is so crucial to the Christian tradition that we can easily take it for granted or cease to notice its centrality. But it is the heart of the matter. Not all of the great traditions of religious faith call for such a faith response. However, the Christian (and Jewish) response is never for one's own sake alone, but also for the sake of the world and that God's will might be done there. Even in the most strict expressions of its contemplative tradition, Christian faith can never be withdrawal from the world for one's own personal holiness alone; even the life of contemplative prayer is entered for the sake of the world and for the advancement of God's Kingdom within it.

It has been common for theologians to distinguish faith from charity. But if the two can be distinguished for the sake of analysis, they cannot be separated in the life of a person. As Aquinas explained, faith and loving action exist together as necessarily as matter and form (see note 20). It is certainly possible to "know the good" without doing it. But that is precisely what Christians call sin, which is the opposite of lived Christian faith (and my attempt here is to describe Christian faith as an existential reality). Lived Christian faith demands a doing of what is known.

The faith and the doing belong together simultaneously. Or, to state it another way, the faith is in the doing. Thus it is not, as is typically assumed, a matter of first having faith, which then leads to engagement in the world in response to the Kingdom. The faith is in the response, and without the response there is no Christian faith. There is only what Jean Paul Sartre would call "bad faith."[30] In our search for a language to talk about faith we may well speak of believing and trusting as leading to overt doing for the "other." But the reverse is equally true and should also be stated. Our life of agape leads to believing and trusting, with a constant dialectical relationship between what is known and what is done.[31] To paraphrase an old saying, "Only I do it, I would never believe it."

In Chapter Seven I will take up in some detail the topic of biblical "knowing" and what it means "to know the Lord." Here it is relevant to anticipate the conclusions of that discussion. In the biblical understanding of what it means "to know the Lord" there is a "knowing about," there is an "entering into trusting relationship with," but there must also be "a doing of God's will." God is not "known" unless God's will is done, and it is only in the doing that God is truly known. To be in Christian faith is to know the Lord in this sense of a threefold activity. It is because Jesus did the will of God perfectly that he could claim to know the Father best. It is because of his obedience that he can be our model of faith.

By the gospel criterion of faith the response to the seed of the word is to be measured by the fruit it brings forth (see Matt. 13:3-9). When Jesus is explaining to Nicodemus that the "light came into the world," he says, "He who acts in truth comes into the light" (John 3:21). For Paul Christian faith is a response, by the grace of God, of the total person to Jesus Christ. It requires an assent and a trusting relationship with God in Jesus, but it also requires "obedient faith in the gospel of Christ" (2 Cor. 9:13; see also Rom. 1:5; 15:18; 16:26; and 2 Thess. 1:8-12). Far from being an antinomian[32] as some "slanderously" accused (see Rom. 3:8), Paul insisted that faith must express itself through loving service (Gal. 5:6). But perhaps it was James' classic statement that put this idea most forcefully:

> My brothers, what good is it to profess faith without practicing it? Such faith has no power to save one, has it? If a brother or sister has nothing to wear and no food for the day, and you say to them, 'Goodbye and good luck! Keep warm and well-fed,' but do not meet their bodily needs, what good is that? So it is with the faith that does nothing in practice. It is thoroughly lifeless. To such a person one might say, 'You have faith and I have works—is that it?' Show me your faith without works, and I will show you the faith that underlies my works. . . . You must perceive that a person is justified by his works and not by faith alone. . . . Be assured, then, that faith without works is as dead as a body without breath. (James 2:14-18, 24, 26)

Dulles credits the Latin American liberation theologians with enabling us to see again the centrality of the performative dimension of Christian faith. After a historical overview of what he calls the intellectualist and the fiducial approaches to understanding Christian faith, he writes, "The dialectical interweaving of contemplation and praxis in the liberation theology of faith seems to me to be a definite advance over all the theories previously considered."[33] The theologians of liberation make their starting point for theological reflection the historical praxis of people within time and society. Their reflection on praxis in the light of the Gospel is always for the sake of further praxis. Inevitably, then, they emphasize the doing dimension of faith and claim that Christian faith is Christian praxis. Thus they understand the primary question for Christian theology as What must we do? rather than What must we believe?—in other words, a quest for orthopraxis more than for orthodoxy.

One need not, however, take one's theological stance within the theologies of the liberation motif to claim that Christian faith must be incarnated in Christian praxis as a life of loving service. Any brand of Christian theology which takes the Kingdom as central to the meaning of Christianity must see lived Christian faith as both arising from and leading to obedient response to God's intentions for the world.

When the Christian community assembles to offer common worship, it is symbolizing and gathering together there an offering of lives of Christian *praxis*. Conversely, there flows from that liturgical activity a renewed commitment to live lives of Christian service. Thus liturgy is both an expression and a source of Christian faith in all three of its activities.

But, as with the believing and trusting dimensions, neither is it correct to allow this performative dimension to stand alone as a total description of Christian faith. To overemphasize it to the point where the other two dimensions are excluded or made secondary is an imbalance. To begin with, purely functional Christian faith is likely to become mindless activism, and the activism may well be short-lived. As "doers of the word," we must inform our doing by a reflected-upon and convinced belief. Secondly, faith as doing needs the grounding of a trusting relationship with God who saves in Jesus Christ. Without such a relationship and felt dependence we fall either into pelagianism, in which we think we can save ourselves by our own efforts, or into despair when we see how far short our own efforts fall. Our responsibility to be doers of the word must never lead us to assume that we can build the Kingdom alone. And our anxiety about what remains to be done must not allow us to miss out on the signs of the Kingdom already among us. If we fail to celebrate our present, or if we measure ourselves purely on the "results" of our own efforts, then we will be reduced again to the anxiety of an unredeemed people.

Thus lived Christian faith has at least three essential activities: believing, trusting, and doing. While they can be distinguished for the sake of clarity, they cannot be separated in the life of the Christian community as if any one of them could exist alone or have priority over the others. Undoubtedly, there are times and circumstances when one dimension will receive more apparent emphasis than the others. And there are individual Christians who by disposition tend to take their life stance more within one dimension or another (for instance, the professional theologian, the contemplative, the social activist). But as a lived reality, the faith life of the community, and to some extent the faith life of every

Christian, must include all three activities. The religious education which takes Christian faith as its purpose must be designed to intentionally promote this *faith in three dimensions.*

FAITH DEVELOPMENT

The pioneering work of James W. Fowler on faith development holds much promise for informing the enterprise of Christian religious education. An overview of his work is introduced here for two reasons. First, while he deals with faith as a human universal, his findings will further illuminate what was said above about Christian faith. Second, when our purpose of Christian faith is expanded to include all three dimensions, then the educator's task is far more than to teach the "content" of the faith tradition. Our task is to nurture people, with the help of God's grace, in their ability to *be* in faith. Being and becoming a person in Christian faith is a process of formation and maturation. It is a human developmental process and thus Fowler's description of life's faith journey can inform our educational practice.

Drawing upon his own research and the findings of other developmental and social psychologists, Fowler outlines the process and stages people *may* pass through (there is nothing inevitable about it) on their way toward faith maturity. Religious educators must avoid a naive use of Fowler's work as we must avoid a naive use of the social sciences in general. There are dangerous pitfalls in talking of human development as a series of clearly delineated stages. The mystery of human life and becoming can never be captured totally in any easy outline of "stages."[34] As I caution about Piaget's work in Chapter Eleven, what is offered as tentatively descriptive must not be taken by educators as definitively prescriptive. Fowler himself advises such caution and is carefully nuanced and tentative in his claims. He offers his findings as provisional, warning that the stages of faith development are not to be reified nor lead to a "pigeon hole mentality." They can be a useful "lens or filter system" for viewing the process of faith development, but they can also "blur and obscure."[35]

Having offered such caution, however, I am convinced that Fowler's work can fruitfully inform both our designing and our implementing of religious education practice. Vatican II, in its *Constitution on the Church in the Modern World* (Art. 21), talks about "the witness of a living and mature faith. . . ."[36] The *General Catechetical Directory* of Roman Catholicism speaks about "maturity of faith" as the goal of all catechesis. It counsels that "the life of faith passes through various stages, just as does man's existence while he is attaining maturity and taking on the duties of his life."[37] When we attempt to sponsor people toward Christian faith, it is vital that we understand the nature and dynamic of that maturing process. Christian faith as a lived reality has specific characteristics which distinguish it from the faith response of other religious traditions or from faith as a human universal. But coming to Christian faith, and the stages in development thereto, is surely similar to the faith pilgrimage of all people. Awareness of the human developmental process to being in faith can inform our educational efforts and help to fashion our response to the different age levels we work with.

FOCAL THEMES IN FOWLER'S THESIS

Fowler, like other developmental psychologists, can trace his genesis to the insight of Immanuel Kant that the human activity of knowing the world is shaped primarily by what the individual brings to that process. But what Kant saw as innate categories Fowler sees as "developing abilities" that develop through predictable "stages." Before I set out the stages, it will be helpful to summarize some focal themes in his understanding and investigation of faith.

A Structuralist Approach. Fowler approaches the investigation of faith from a structuralist perspective, focusing on "the underlying structures or operations of human thought and belief,"[38] that is, on the laws and patterned process of the human ability for faith activity.

It was Jean Piaget who first argued that a person's thinking develops not only in its content, but also in what he described as the inner operational structures by which the person thinks. A person's ability for cognition develops in interaction with the environment through recognizable patterns or stages. Piaget has spent his life researching and studying this inner maturing process, which he named "cognitive development." Lawrence Kohlberg, informed by Piaget's work, hypothesized that a person's ability to make moral decisions also develops through recognizable and sequential stages. Kohlberg developed sophisticated tests to investigate his hypothesis and found that we progress not only in the content of our moral decision making, but also in our inner patterned ability to make moral decisions.

Fowler, informed by the other developmentalists and carrying out his own independent research, posited that a person's way of being in faith also develops through recognizable and sequential stages. Thus a child's faith differs from an adult's not just in its content, but also in the inner patterned structure of operation by which the child has faith.[39]

Faith as Primary. Faith, for Fowler, is the foundational core of a person, the fundamental disposition that colors and shapes everything that comes after it. Thus it is the primary focus, the basic disposition or orientation to being in the world by which the person makes, maintains, or transforms human meaning. Arising from one's "structural core," faith is the primary orientation of a person's existence.[40]

Faith as Active Knowing. Fowler understands faith not as a static state or possession, but as an activity of knowing, construing, and interpreting experience. By this activity we "make meaning" out of our lives.[41] Faith is an active participatory knowing process, and the knowing is in the activity. He writes, "At the outset, then, we need to begin to think of faith as a way of knowing, of construing, or of interpreting experience. In short, we need to begin thinking of faith as a verb."[42]

Faith as Relational.   For Fowler "faith is an irreducibly relational phenomenon."[43] First the relationship is between ourselves and the everyday world and other people. In this sense faith is bipolar and is always social or interpersonal. But it is also "one's sense of relatedness to the ultimate conditions and depths of existence."[44] These form a third pole of a triad, and thus faith is a triadic or tripolar relationship. Because this triadic relationship is key to Fowler's understanding of faith activity, the third pole requires some further explanation.

Each person has what Fowler calls an "ultimate environment" which he or she composes and struggles to maintain. By ultimate environment I understand him to mean the outer horizon or framework of one's world within which and in relation to which a person makes meaning out of life. Within that ultimate environment there are "centers of value" to which we commit ourselves and in return feel the promise of being valued and sustained. For our context these terms are more understandable when Fowler speaks about them in theological language: "It is time to make clear that my ecological metaphor 'ultimate environment,' if translated into Jewish or Christian terms, would be called 'Kingdom of God' or as Teilhard de Chardin expresses it, 'the Divine Milieu.' "[45] In that case "the center of value" would be the God of Jewish and Christian revelation. In terms of Christianity, then, faith is a triadic relationship among ourselves, our neighbor, and God as revealed in Jesus Christ.

In his research Fowler has discovered that the person's relationship with any one pole of the triad colors the relationship with the other pole. Thus our relationship with the everyday world and with other people shapes and is shaped by our relationship with the centers of value in our ultimate environment and our relationship with our ultimate environment shapes and is shaped by our relationship with the everyday world and other people.

Faith as Both Rational and "Passional."   Since faith is an active knowing of the world and a way of being related to the world, there is both a cognitive and an affective dimension to faith activity. Fowler explains that faith "is a knowing or construing in which 'cognition' (the "rational") is inextricably intertwined with 'affectivity' or 'valuing' (the "passional")."[46]

The passional dimension is the affective emotional aspect that arises from faith as a mode of being in relationship. It includes loving, caring, valuing, and it can also include "awe, dread and fear."[47] This affective dimension carries with it the integral component of commitment. "To 'have faith' is to be related to someone or something in such a way that our heart is invested, our caring is committed, our hope is focused on the other."[48] Thus for Fowler faith is an affair of the head and of the heart; it is both rational and passional.[49]

Faith as a Human Universal.   Fowler claims that faith is a "human universal," whether people "claim to be 'believers' or 'religious' or not."[50] To be in the world as a human being and to choose to continue to participate in it is a faith activity. Universal faith is differentiated into various expressions by the differences in how we perceive our "ultimate environments" and the different "centers of value" within those environments. Religion, as an organized phenomenon, is a community's way of giving expression to the faith relationships held in common.[51] As such, religion can provide models of and for the constructing activity of faith. However, "Faith may be, but is not necessarily 'religious' in the sense of being informed by the creeds, liturgy, ethics, and esthetics of a religious tradition."[52] Religion expresses, informs, and perhaps increases faith. But faith is broader than any organized expression of it. It is a human universal.

STAGES OF FAITH DEVELOPMENT

Fowler's research indicates that six distinctive and recognizable stages can be discerned in the developing human capacity for faith activity. Each stage is its own structural whole, but the stages are related to each other hierarchically and sequentially: they develop in an ascending order (one to two to three, etc.), and each stage incorporates, while adding to, the previous stage. The transition from one to another can be protracted and painful, requiring "relinquishment and reconstruction." A new stage emerges when a person becomes consciously aware of the limitations of the present stage and, while affirming the truth in it, moves beyond its limits.[53] Fowler insists, however, that each stage has its own integrity. Stage four is not "more faithful" than stage three; rather, it is a more developed and mature expression of faith than stage three.[54]

Fowler outlines seven different "structural competencies," or specific human abilities, that shape the activity of faith at each particular stage: form of logic, form of world coherence, ability for role taking, locus of authority, bounds of social awareness, form of moral judgment, and role of symbols.[55] A detailed description of each competency at every stage is beyond the scope of this work. Instead I offer a brief overview of each stage as Fowler outlines them.

Stage One: Intuitive/Projective Faith.   This is the faith of the person from approximately four to eight years old, by which meaning is made and trust established intuitively and by imitation. Knowing is primarily by intuition, and faith is formed by imitation of the moods, example, and actions of the *visible* human faith of significant others, primarily parents. Affectivity dominates. Knowing and feeling are fused. The locus of authority is in parents and in primary adults.

The child begins to discover a reality beyond everyday experience and therein encounters the limits of life, such as death, limits of knowledge and power, and so on. But trust is grounded in the parents and other primary adults, and the world is known by intuitively projecting meaning in imitation of those adults (thus the name of the stage, intuitive/projective).

Stage one is a time of unrestrained fantasy and imagination when long-lasting images and feelings (both positive and negative) are formed. Fact and fantasy are not yet differentiated. In consequence, symbols are taken literally and God is thought of in anthropomorphic, magical terms (for instance, God is an old man with a beard who can do anything). There is an awakening of memory and self-consciousness, and the capacity to take the role of another (empathy) is beginning, but only in a very rudimentary form.

Stage Two: Mythic/Literal.   This stage occurs approximately between the ages of seven or eight and eleven or twelve years. It is an affiliative faith stage in which the person comes more consciously to join and belong to his or her immediate group, or faith community. The person now comes, with some enthusiasm, to learn "the lore, the language and the legends" of the particular community and to appropriate them as one's own. This can happen because there is now a greater awareness of the differentiation between the self and the collective of immediate others.

The way of making meaning is now more linear and narrative rather than episodic as in stage one. One's ultimate environment is conceptualized in those stories and myths which are taken literally (thus the stage's name, mythic/literal). Life is as it appears to be. Reasoning and thought beyond intuition are now possible, but thinking is still in concrete sensory terms, with little abstraction possible. The child is beginning to differentiate the natural from the supernatural, but God continues to be understood largely in anthropomorphic terms.

At this stage, then, faith is a "joining" faith—the person consciously joins the immediate social group, takes on its stories, symbols, myths and doctrines, and understands them literally. The word of significant elders dominates over that of peers. There is an increase in the ability for empathy, but it is only for those "like us," that is, for members of the immediate group.

Stage Three: Synthetic/Conventional.   This stage usually begins at eleven or twelve years as the person's experience is extended beyond the family and primary social group. It can last long into adulthood, and for some it becomes a permanent home. A stage three faith interprets, relates to, and makes meaning out of life according to the directions and criteria of what "they say," in other words, according to popular convention. It is a "conventional" or "conformist" stage in that it is anxious to respond faithfully to the expectations and judgments of significant others. As yet the person is without a sufficient grasp of his or her own identity to make autonomous judgments from an independent perspective.

Stage three is an advance beyond stage two in that a person consciously experiences a division of life into different segments or "theaters of action." Now there are many "theys" impinging on the person's way of knowing and relating to the world—family, school, work, church, peers (and subgroups within peers), leisure ethos, organizations, and the like. Each of these segments of life is likely to provide a variety of different perspectives, expectations, and ways of making meaning. They inevitably come into conflict. How then does the stage three person, dependent on authority in each theater of action, reach equilibrium and synthesis? Fowler claims that synthesis is reached either by subordinating the different authorities under what the person perceives to be the one highest authority, or by "compartmentalization." The latter occurs when one tends to make meaning and interpret the world differently depending on the group one is with. On specifically religious questions there is a strong tendency to rely on institutional authority.

In stage three, then, there is an increase of trust in one's own judgment over stage two, but it is used only to choose between authorities and does not involve personal initiative in solving dissonance among authorities. Faith is still not self-chosen but continues to be "conventional," with the confirming authority localized outside the person. There is a synthesis, but it is not a personal autonomous synthesis. Rather it is a choosing and a balancing of the various conventional expectations of the person's various worlds (thus the title synthetic/conventional). There is an awareness of the faith perspectives of others, but the tendency is toward either prejudice or assimilation of other perspectives into one's own. ("They are like us, really!")

Stage Four: Individuating/Reflexive. This stage does not usually begin before age seventeen or eighteen. For a significant number it emerges only in the mid-thirties and forties, and many adults never achieve it. The transition from stage three to stage four is particularly crucial for the continuation of the faith journey. Here the conventional synthesis of stage three begins to collapse because of a lack of congruence between the self and the various conventional expectations of one's different "groups." The transition to stage four comes when we can no longer tolerate being a "different person" when we are with different groups, or when we realize that we cannot hand the making of our meaning over to even the highest authority. Now the responsibility for synthesis and making meaning shifts from relying on conventional authority(ies) to taking personal responsibility for commitments, lifestyle, beliefs, and attitudes. As a result there is now a qualitatively different degree of autonomy, beyond stage three. One's way of knowing and relating to the world, one's identity and world view, are more personally chosen and self-consciously differentiated from the attitudes and expectations of others. In fact, they become acknowledged factors in one's way of interpreting, judging, and reacting to experience.

Even as one achieves a more autonomous faith, there is at stage four a new-found awareness of the paradoxes and polarities of life. Decisions about life's ambiguities and polar tensions can no longer be avoided as they were at stage three. Fowler lists some of those polar tensions as "individual v. community; particular v. universal; relative v. absolute; self-fulfillment v. service to others; autonomy v. heteronomy; feeling v. thinking; subjectivity v. objectivity."[56] One's faith activity now attempts to handle these tensions and maintain equilibrium between them. However, the tendency at stage four, particularly in its early formulation, is to collapse the tension to favor either side. The person is likely to take an "either/or" approach to such questions and paradoxes. Rather than the polarities being held in a fruitful tension, they become collapsed into either relativism or absolutism. This is also evident in regard to perspectives other than one's own; the tendency is still to overassimilate rather than to genuinely recognize them in a dialogical fashion.

It is not unusual for a stage four person to join a strong ideologically grounded community that offers ready-made answers to the ambiguities and paradoxes of life. But at least the joining is based on a more self-chosen commitment. Stage four, then, is a new ability to stand alone, and one's class or group is reflectively chosen rather than simply accepted or received, as at stage three (thus the name individuating/reflexive).

Stage Five: Conjunctive Faith.[57]   In stage five of faith activity, unusual much before mid-life, the paradoxes that were previously dealt with by some strategy of tension reduction are now embraced, and affirmed, and the tension is incorporated into one's way of "being in faith." In everyday language, life is no longer seen in terms of either/or, but there is a willingness to live with its ambiguities and many shades of grey. This is certainly not a return to relativism and ambivalence. On the contrary, there is a new quality of autonomous commitment to one's own position, while respecting and being genuinely open to the truth in positions other than one's own. As such, it is not relativism but a recognition that one's own position is not the final fullness of truth. This requires a genuine openness to others and a willingness to enter into dialogue with them even at the risk of changing one's own way of making meaning and relating to the world. One's own system is seen as porous and incomplete even in the midst of strong commitment to it. Particulars are valued but only because they hold the possibility of the universal. One's symbols are looked to and affirmed, but also "seen through" to the possibility beyond them.[58]

Stage five faith involves a reappropriation of past patterns of commitment and ways of making meaning. But this is not a regressing. It is, instead, a reclaiming of "old truths" in a new way, personally affirming the truth that was in them, drawing strength from them but refusing their limitations. If stage three was dependent and stage four self-dependent, then stage five is an interdependent stage in which the person is capable of depending on others without losing independence.[59] Now there is empathy with and active concern for all peoples and groups, for the whole human family, and not just for one's own immediate community.

Stage Six: Universalizing Faith. When Fowler speaks about stage six, his language becomes somewhat poetic. This seems to be inevitable, as stage six of faith activity is difficult to name with the concrete language of our everyday speech. He likes to point to examples of it, rare as they are, and Mother Teresa of Calcutta is frequently cited.

Here the self ceases to be the centering reference point, and the ultimate is put there instead. The person has an ongoing experience of immediate participation in the ultimate and makes encounter with the ultimate available to others. The stage six person dwells in the world as a transforming presence. The self of stage six "engages in spending and being spent in order to transform present reality in the direction of a transcendent actuality."[60] Here the particulars of life are cherished as vessels of the universal. Life is both loved and held loosely; it is taken seriously, but not too seriously. For people at stage six the human community is universal in inclusiveness. In theological terms the Kingdom of God is an experienced reality. In spiritual terms stage six is the most complete state of union with God that is possible this side of eternity.

The *National Catechetical Directory* for Catholics of the United States, entitled *Sharing The Light of Faith* and issued by the United States Catholic Conference in March 1979, proposes "maturity of faith" as the goal of all "catechesis."[61] In regard to the social sciences, especially those concerned with human development, it says, "These sciences . . . help us understand how people grow in their capacity for responding in faith to God's grace. They can, therefore, make a significant contribution to catechesis. At the same time, catechists should not be uncritical in their approach to these sciences, in which new discoveries are constantly being made while old theories are frequently modified or even discarded."[62] The point is well made and the caveat appropriate. Although Fowler's "stages" of faith development should not be seen as absolutes, his insights can inform our efforts in Christian religious education (or what the Directory prefers to call catechesis), and I draw upon his insights repeatedly throughout the remainder of this work. He will inform us especially in Chapter Eleven when we reflect on the question of readiness for Christian religious education.

RELIGIOUS EDUCATION TOWARD CHRISTIAN FAITH

The purpose of Christian religious education is to sponsor people toward maturity in Christian faith as a lived reality. We are now in a position to draw together the characteristics of such a faith life and the educational task they pose. What I outline here is not a complete statement of our task, but rather aspects of it. Other dimensions will be added and these expanded upon in light of further reflections. But on the basis of what has been said thus far essential aspects can be named.

1. *Christian faith is a gift of God whose grace touches the inner core of a person and disposes one toward a lived relationship with God in Jesus Christ.* Before we ever speak about our educational task, the "giftedness" of faith must always be remembered. Faith is "God's gift" (Eph. 2:8), and it is "God, who gives the growth" (1 Cor. 3:7). As Rahner explains, "To lead to faith (or rather, to its further, explicit stage) is always to assist understanding of what has already been experienced in the depth of human reality by grace. . . ."[63] The fact that faith is a gift of God does not make our educational efforts unnecessary or superfluous. On the contrary, if faith is to be explicitly Christian, if people are to come to a lived relationship with God in Jesus Christ, then the faith Story of the Christian community must be encountered in lived experience.

The educator's task within the community (the socializing task of the whole community will be dealt with in Chapter Six) is to see to it that the Story is made accessible[64] and people enabled to appropriate it so that it truly becomes their own. Unless someone is "sent" (Rom. 10:15) to share the Good News that Jesus Christ is our Lord and Savior, and to announce the Kingdom as he announced it, a person's potential for explicitly Christian faith and relationship with God in Jesus Christ will not be realized. Our task of enabling people to appropriate the Christian faith tradition also includes the task of disposing them to respond to God's grace. This calls for a sponsoring activity which attempts to remove the human roadblocks so that the grace of God may work God's will.

2. *There is a cognitive dimension to Christian faith, an activity of believing.* All faith includes a knowing and interpreting of human experience, a way of making meaning out of existence, pattern out of chaos. While this interpreting activity is not narrowly "intellectualist," there is a cognitive dimension to it. Going further, when faith as a human universal is given expression by a community of people through a particular religious tradition, then the specificity of that tradition invites members of the community to a knowing of, and an assent to, the stated beliefs of the tradition as a way of making meaning. Christianity, for example, is founded on what Christians understand to be a divine revelation. As Christians have responded to that revelation over the centuries and attempted to live their faith in its light, the meaning they have constructed has come to symbolic expression in statements of belief. Anyone who wishes to express universal disposition for faith through the Christian tradition is expected to give assent to those beliefs. Not all Christian "beliefs" are of equal importance (there is a "hierarchy of truths"), but in general these statements of doctrine call for an activity of believing as *part of* the activity of Christian faith.

The cognitive dimension of Christian faith presents religious educators with the task of instructing new members in the doctrinal expression of our faith tradition. We must also provide opportunities for older members to deepen and expand their understanding of it. Furthermore, because we are rational beings, the instruction needs to be accompanied by an attempt to show the reasonableness of giving assent to such beliefs.[65] (Obviously this takes different forms at different levels of development.) The disposition to believe is, by God's grace, prior to our understanding of what is believed. However, our attempts to understand what is expected in Christian belief are not superfluous. In the divine-human covenant such attempts are one expression of our response to God's invitation to faith in Jesus Christ.

3. *There is an affective dimension to Christian faith, an activity of trusting.* Christian faith is an invitation to a relationship of loyalty to and trust in a faithful God who saves through Jesus Christ by the power of the Spirit. This loyal trusting relationship with God in Christ shapes, as it is also shaped by, the quality of our relationship with other people. As with all human relationships, this aspect of Christian faith points to an affective dimension and calls for an activity of trusting. Educationally, this gives rise to a twofold task.

First, the task is to nurture people in their spiritual development. Christian religious education must foster the spiritual growth of its participants, deepening their relationship with God in Jesus Christ. This requires particular attention to and education for the activity of prayer, both personal and communal. And it requires that our educating attempt to dispose participants to awe, reverence, and wonder at the goodness of a faithful God whose Kingdom is already among us.

Second, our Christian religious educating has the task of promoting a deep and abiding bond of friendship and good will toward the whole human family. I am speaking now of a trust in humankind that endures even in the face of apparent evidence that such trust is unwarranted. The brotherhood and sisterhood of all people must come to be a felt reality at what William Butler Yeats called "the deep heart's core." Christian religious education has the task of promoting such a loyalty and commitment, not only toward "those like us," but toward all God's people.

4. *There is a behavioral dimension to Christian faith, an activity of "doing."* The other dimensions of Christian faith also require an activity, but by "doing" here I am referring to the specific kind of engagement in the world required by Christian faith. Christian faith invites us to engagement in the world, first, in response to the gift, and second, in response to the mandate of God's Kingdom in Jesus Christ. The two responses belong together in the one lifestyle and community, but for the sake of clarity I set them out separately here.

Engagement in response to the gift of the Kingdom. The Kingdom of God is

God's gift to us. Because of the saving action of God in Jesus Christ, Christians believe that the Kingdom is ensured and in a definitive sense has already come. Trusting in a God who saves, and convinced of God's faithfulness to God's promises, we are invited to live even now as a redeemed people. With confidence in God we can afford to live our lives with joy, with hope, with peace, with happiness, with all the best things for which the human heart longs and for which the Kingdom stands. We can enjoy God's creation, we can embrace and live life to the fullness of our human potential for it. The human state is a blessed and redeemed existence.

This dimension of lived Christian faith calls for an educational response whereby the Story is taught always as Good News. Our educating must sponsor people in living life as joyfully and humanly as possible, confident that God's Kingdom both here and hereafter is God's gift to us. Nietzsche once said of Christians, "They would have to sing better songs for me to learn to have faith in their Redeemer: and his disciples would have to look more redeemed!"[66] Our educating must attempt to sponsor people toward living as redeemed people. A Christian religious education that promotes fear, anxiety, self-hatred, or unnecessary guilt is defeating its very purpose.

Engagement in response to the mandate of the Kingdom. God's gift and invitation to the Kingdom brings with it a mandate that we live our lives according to God's intentions for creation. According to Jesus' preaching of the Kingdom, we must engage in the world in response to his radicalized mandate of love. Our response to God's love for us is to reach out in love to God's people. The radical mandate to love God *by* loving other people encompasses within it all of God's intentions for creation. Thus it requires us to live peacefully and to promote peace, justly and to promote justice, equally and to promote equality, and so on. It calls us to a life of loving service, agape, on all levels of human existence—the personal, the interpersonal, and the social/political. This is how, by God's grace in Christ, the Kingdom becomes present already and how we play our part in preparing the material for its completion. The love mandate must never be thought of as if it were an unfair burden imposed by the whim of a capricious God. Love is the source of life. God commands us to love each other so that we may have life, and have it to the full. Thus our response to God's gift and our response to God's mandate of the Kingdom belong together.

This behavioral dimension of Christian faith requiring engagement in the world in response to the mandate of the Kingdom poses what may be the most difficult, but also the most crucial, task of Christian religious education. Our educational efforts must aim at bringing ourselves and our students to lives where there is a unity between what we profess to believe and how we actually engage in the world.

5. *Christian faith is a lifelong developmental process involving the total per-*

son. I referred above to the need for people to grow in their understanding of the "doctrinal content" of the Christian tradition. Here I am speaking of another kind of faith growth, which is, in many ways, more basic than the first. We need to develop in our inner structuring capacity for faith activity.[67] Such "structural" growth is inextricably intertwined with our maturation as human beings. Faith development and human development cannot be separated.

The educational response to this developmental aspect of faith ability requires that the very approach we use in Christian religious education be capable of fostering such development. We certainly cannot settle for "delivery systems" that by their very nature do little more than promote knowledge of the doctrinal content of the tradition and tend to maintain people at stage three of faith development. The *fides quae* (that which we believe) is our concern, but so, too, is the *fides qua* (that by which we believe). Our educational approaches must be capable of promoting both. We must be concerned about the development of the whole person. We may not have the time or opportunity to be involved in developing all the human capacities of our students, but such capacities are our concern, even as our priority remains faith education. In the context of intentional religious education for Christian faith an effort to promote human development in general is not superfluous to our primary purpose.

In summary, lived Christian faith is the immediate purpose of Christian religious education. Christian faith as embodied in human existence calls for at least three activities: believing, trusting, and doing. Through Jesus Christ we are invited by God toward maturity in faith. Christian religious educators are to attempt to lead out toward that end. I use "attempt" deliberately because faith is always God's gift. But the gift does not allow us to settle for poor educational efforts, leaving the rest to God. That would be unfaithful to our side of the covenant. Our efforts can never explain the "results" that ensue from them. It is God who gives the increase. But our "attempts" at Christian faith formation are necessary nonetheless.

We now turn to the consequence for pilgrims in time of living such a life of Christian faith. The consequence is that the Kingdom is made present already, and a contribution is made toward preparing the materials for its final completion in which we will all participate. I speak of this consequence as the process of coming to human freedom.

NOTES

1. Karl Rahner uses the terms *a priori* and *a posteriori* to describe, respectively, the relationship between faith as the gift of God and the human community which acts as the bearer of God's revelation. While faith always begins from inner illumination, "the light of faith," which is God's self-revelation by grace, it is actualized and consciously appropriated only by encountering what Rahner calls the "a posteriori proposition of verbal revelation." The latter is carried

within a historical context by a community of Christian faith (see, for example, *Foundations*, p. 150).

2. That the claims I make here are for *Christian* faith specifically and not for faith as a human universal is an important point to bear in mind. For example, the faith response to many of the great world religions might not necessarily include a lived life of *agape*.

3. Throughout the history of the Christian Church in the West these dimensions have received different degrees of emphasis from the two great traditions. Roman Catholicism has emphasized the intellectualist/belief dimension, while the Protestant Churches have tended to emphasize the fiducial/trusting dimension. In more recent theology, regardless of denomination, faith as doing is being emphasized.

For the following overview I am much indebted to the theology of faith outlined by Avery Dulles (see, especially, *The Survival of Dogma* and his article "The Meaning of Faith"). I will augment Dulles' position with insights from other authors and will constantly bring in what has been outlined already about the Kingdom to help name the existential reality that is Christian faith. This will lead, among other things, to a stronger statement of "faith as doing" than that offered by Dulles. But Dulles, after a most helpful overview of the approaches to Christian faith throughout history (he calls them the intellectualist, the fiducial, and the performative approaches), insists on the three essential elements that I am arguing for here. He writes, "Faith includes three elements: a firm conviction regarding what is supremely important, dedication or commitment to that which one believes in, and trustful reliance on the power and goodness of that to which one stands committed. The three components of faith are thus conviction, commitment, and trust" ("The Meaning of Faith," p. 13). Though the overview here is of Christian faith, I have also been much informed and affirmed by Norman Lamm's work on the Jewish understanding of faith. Lamm describes faith from a Jewish perspective as having three similar elements and calls them "cognitive," "affective," and "functional." He sees all three dimensions as essential to an authentic understanding of faith from the Hebrew Scriptures (see Lamm, *Faith and Doubt*).

4. W.C. Smith, *The Meaning and End of Religion*, p. 181.

5. Tracy, *Blessed Rage for Order*, p. 16 n.13.

6. Many texts can be cited for this position of Augustine. One locus classicus, which also shows the influence of Plato's thought on his position, is *City of God*, Book X, Ch. 2 (see pp. 189–190). For religious educators it may be more interesting to read how Augustine understood faith as illumination in relation to the task of the teacher (see, for example, *The Teacher* [Ch. 11, no. 38, Ch. 12, no. 39], pp. 51–53). He writes of his work as teacher, "Even when I say what is true, and he sees what is true, it is not I who teach him. For he is being taught, not by my words, but by the realities themselves made manifest to him by the enlightening action of God from within" (*The Teacher* [Ch. 12, no. 40], p. 54).

7. In a treatise, "On the Spirit and the Letter," addressed to Marcellinius, Augustine wrote, "We now speak of that faith which we employ when we believe anything . . . for what is believing but agreeing to the truth of what is asserted?" ("On the Spirit," 1 [Ch. 54]:214). "The very will by which we believe in God is . . . reckoned as a gift of God, because it arises out of that freedom of our will which we received at our creation. . . . It surely follows that it is God who works in man the actual willingness to believe. . . . To yield our consent . . . is the function of our will. . . . For the soul cannot receive and possess these gifts . . . except by yielding its own consent. So that whatever it possesses, and whatever it receives, is from God and belongs to God; and yet the act of receiving and having belongs, of course, to the receiver and the possessor" ("On the Spirit," 1 [Ch. 60]:223–224).

8. Augustine, *Lectures or Tractates on the Gospel According to St. John*, 1 (Tractate 29):405.

9. Aquinas, *Summa Theologica*, 2 (Q. 6, Art. 2):1201.

10. Ibid., 2 (Q. 4, Art. 2):1191.

11. Ibid., 2 (Q. 2, Art. 9):1186.

12. Dulles, *Survival*, p. 153.

13. From the point of view of religious educators it is most interesting to note how the famous *Catechism of the Council of Trent* spoke about faith. In fact, what the *Catechism* said about faith had a greater significance for the day-to-day life of the faithful than the Council Decrees. Issued by the Council as an official compendium of Catholic doctrine, it was to be used by priests in preparing their Sunday sermons. It was widely employed and shaped, probably more than any other document, the popular understanding of Roman Catholicism down to our own generation.

About faith the Catechism stated: "This knowledge, however, is nothing else than faith, by which we yield our unhesitating assent to whatever the authority of our Holy Mother the Church teaches us to have been revealed by God; for the faithful cannot doubt those things of which God, who is truth itself, is the author." It adds later: "When God commands us to believe He does not propose to us to search into His divine judgements, or inquire into their reason and cause, but demands an unchangeable faith, by which the mind rests content in the knowledge of eternal truth" (*Cathechism of the Council of Trent*, pp. 11 and 15). Such a defensive statement and the anxiety about "orthodoxy" that underlies it is understandable in the Counter-Reformation and pre-Enlightenment period. But it demands what came to be known as a blind faith and militates against what I will argue for later as a critical faith.

14. *The Church Teaches*, pp. 29–30.
15. Of the equation of faith with belief, he writes, "One factor contributing to this peculiarity, there would seem no question, has been the circumstance of Greek though as a massive influence in Christian history" (W.C. Smith, *The Meaning and End of Religion*, p. 180).
16. W.C. Smith points out that the verbs *pistuein* in Greek and *credere* in Latin, which we translate as "to believe" and understand in a very intellectual sense, originally meant much more than cognitive assent. Originally, both words had strong connotations of trust and commitment. The very etymology of the verb *credere* means "to rest one's heart." Looking at the meaning of the old English word *bileve*, he concludes "that the phrase 'belief in God' originally meant in English a loyal pledging of oneself to God, a decision and commitment to live one's life in His service" (*Belief and History*, p. 42).

   However, in our time the word *belief* does not obviously carry such connotations of trust and commitment. It is wiser, therefore, to push beyond the word *belief* and make more explicit the other dimensions of faith activity.
17. At least some of the present crisis of religious education for Roman Catholics arises from the "modal shift" that has come with Vatican II and its understanding of faith. When faith was defined as belief in officially stated doctrines, then educators made what would appear to be the obvious educational response by writing a catechism, having people memorize it, and convincing them to assent to it. But when our understanding of faith is broadened beyond belief and is understood as an existential reality which encompasses the whole person, how then will we educate for that kind of Christian faith? That, as I see it, is the challenge that now lies before us and to which we have made only the beginnings of a response.
18. My contention that Christian faith activity demands engagement in the world in response to God's Kingdom in Jesus Christ must not be construed as a negation of the contemplative life in the history of the Christian Church. On the contrary, this rich tradition, so well expressed in the great contemplative religious orders of men and women, is always for the sake of the world and never a quest for personal holiness alone. The holiness is sought and the life of contemplative prayer entered, precisely as a form of "active engagement." By their ascetic lives, the contemplative communities become powerhouses of prayer and intercession for the sake of the world and the advancement of God's Kingdom within it.
19. Dulles, "The Meaning of Faith," p. 17.
20. It is not accurate to impute this dichotomy to Aquinas himself. It is true that he situated charity in the will (see *Summa Theologica*, 2 [Q. 24, Art. 1]:1275) and faith in the intellect (see Ibid., 2 [Q. 4, Art. 2]:1191). But far from dividing them, he insisted that in the life of a Christian, faith and charity belong together as inextricably intertwined as is "matter" and "form." He wrote, "Therefore charity is called the form of faith in so far as the act of faith is perfected and formed by charity" (Ibid., 2 [Q. 4, Art. 3]:1192). His interpreters were often not so wise. Aquinas, I believe, would be closer to the position I am advocating here: that faith without charity is not Christian faith at all.
21. Dulles, "The Meaning of Faith." p. 21.
22. Abbott, *Documents*, p. 243.
23. Lamm calls it "affective faith" and says, "Affective faith is personal and emotional, bespeaking a sense of trust, reliance, dependence, and hope. . . . It involves a quest for peace, for tranquility and, above all, for meaning" (*Faith and Doubt*, p. 8).
24. Dillenberger, *Martin Luther: Selections*, p. 24.
25. Ibid.
26. It is not necessary to digress here into the age-old debate that has often divided Christians about the relationship of faith to good works. However, it is interesting to hear Lamm's comment on it

from a Jewish perspective. Judaism, according to Lamm, has never entered into the debate because for them the only question is the relationship between "study and works"; "Faith and works . . . are indissolubly intertwined. . ." (*Faith and Doubt*, p. 9).

27. Dulles, "The Meaning of Faith," pp. 29, 30.
28. Bonhoeffer, *The Cost of Discipleship*, p. 69.
29. Tillich, *Biblical Religion*, p. 53.
30. Sartre's notion of "bad faith" is a complex one, and I am aware of the danger of oversimplification here. However, at the heart of bad faith there is a "lie to oneself," a knowing refusal of the responsible freedom of being what one knows oneself to be (see *Being and Nothingness*, esp. Part 1, Ch. 2, pp. 47–70).
31. Here Christian faith is in continuity with its Jewish roots. Norman Lamm says, "Judaism has always maintained that behavior influences belief, that the cognitive may be fashioned by the functional" (*Faith and Doubt*, p. 20).
32. The Antinomians held that Christians are by grace set free from having to observe any moral law. Proponents (some Gnostic sects, the Anabaptists, etc.) often claimed to be following Paul's doctrine of salvation by faith, but Paul, in fact, made vigorous ethical demands precisely on the basis of faith.
33. Dulles, "The Meaning of Faith," p. 37.
34. For a balanced critique of Fowler's work and a listing of some very valid caveats for religious educators, see McBride, "Reaction to Fowler," pp. 211–218.
35. See Fowler, "Stages in Faith," p. 191.
36. Abbott, *Documents,* p. 219.
37. *The General Catechetical Directory,* par. 30, p. 25.
38. Fowler, "Stages in Faith," p. 173.
39. In the old scholastic terminology Fowler is investigating *fides qua* (that by which we believe) rather than *fides quae* (that which we believe). As he explains it, "We are attending to the 'form' or 'structural characteristics' of faith-knowing, rather than to its 'contents.' We are looking at faith 'as a way of knowing and construing,' rather than as 'that which is known or construed' " ("Toward a Developmental Perspective on Faith," p. 211).

    However, he is far from claiming that *fides quae* and *qua* are not related. On the contrary, calling them the outer and inner structure of faith, he explains that there is "a dynamic, dialectical relationship between the outer and the inner structures of faith" ("Stages in Faith," p. 177).
40. For example, he writes, "One's faith qualifies and gives tone to one's entire way of interpreting, reacting to, and taking initiatives in the world." ("Toward a Developmental Perspective on Faith," p. 208). In seeing faith as an a priori at the core of a person, Fowler is in continuity with the illuminist tradition of Augustine and the Fathers before him.
41. See Fowler, "Faith, Liberation and Human Development," p. 3.
42. Fowler, "Stages in Faith," p. 175. Since there is no word in English to name faith as an activity, Fowler coined the word *faithing*. In more recent writings, however, he avoids using *faithing* and speaks of "faith activity" or "being in faith."
43. Fowler, *Maps,* p. 18.
44. Fowler, "Faith, Liberation and Human Developmnent," p. 6.
45. Fowler, *Maps,* p. 24.
46. Fowler, "Toward a Developmental Perspective on Faith," pp. 207–208.
47. Ibid., p. 211.
48. Fowler, *Maps,* p. 18.
49. In relation to the first part of this chapter, it can well be asked here, What of faith as doing in Fowler's construct? He rarely mentions faith as doing specifically. However, as already seen, he understands faith in both its knowing and relating as an active process. In this sense, for Fowler all faith is a "doing," and he investigates faith as an activity. Secondly, it should be remembered that Fowler is studying the underlying structure of faith as a human universal. The insistence that faith must express itself as an active engagement in the world in response to the Kingdom comes only if we put the term *Christian* (or *Jewish*) before the noun *faith.* Christian faith must be expressed in a specific kind of doing that is, among other things, an active reaching out to others in love, a lived response to the radical mandate of the Kingdom. But that cannot be said of faith as a human universal, and, as such, it need not get central attention in Fowler's work. He does say that "faith as a 'doing' or 'being' includes and flows from faith as a kind of 'know-

ing' " ("Faith, Liberation and Human Development," p. 8). I agree, as long as we insist that the reverse is also true; that faith as doing and being gives rise to faith as a kind of knowing.

50. Fowler, *Maps*, p. 18. He explains elsewhere, "It is a human universal in the sense that human beings universally have to construct a 'world,' and have to give it form and shape by virtue of attachments they form to centering images of value and power" ("Faith and the Structuring of Meaning," p. 2).

51. I am indebted to Sharon Parks of Harvard University, a close colleague and collaborator of Fowler, for this expression of the relationship between religion and faith.

52. Fowler, *Maps*, p. 23–24.

53. In the transition from one stage to another we see an expression of the dialectical process that I will later describe in detail as an essential activity to be promoted by Christian religious education. But Fowler's talk about a painful and protracted process, and my own talk later about a dialectical activity that can give rise to struggle, must always be tempered with the memory that while God came to Jacob as a struggling angel, God came to Elijah in a gentle breeze (see 1 Kings 19:12). Faith development is a dialectical process, but by the grace of God, it *can* be a gentle one.

54. Fowler says, "Each stage of faith has its own particular wholeness, grace and potential integrity" ("Toward a Developmental Perspective," p. 214). I have heard Fowler state in lectures that there have been many saints who apparently did not progress beyond stage three. That may well be true, but they may not be as plentiful as their biographers would have us believe. It is possible that the saints have often been presented to us as docile obedient people (stage three) for ideological reasons, whereas in fact they have more often been stage five or six.

55. A very helpful diagram of these "structural competencies" can be found in *Maps*, pp. 96–99; a glance at the diagram makes it clear that the "structural competencies" Fowler considers part of a person's ability to have faith are so broad that his description of the person's faith development is close to being a description of the development of the total person. The diagram also makes evident how he is informed by other developmental theorists.

56. Fowler, "Toward a Developmental Perspective on Faith," p. 216.

57. Conjunctive faith is now Fowler's preferred title for stage five. Originally he had named it paradoxical/consolidative.

58. This aspect of stage five always reminds me of the reference by Paul in 2 Cor. 4:7 to "this treasure we possess in earthen vessels." A stage five person realizes that our symbols are no more than earthen vessels, but they hold treasures for us of infinite value.

59. For this description of stage three as dependent, stage four as self-dependent, and stage five as interdependent, I am indebted to Sharon Parks (see "Communities as Ministry," pp. 74–75).

60. Fowler, *Maps*, p. 88.

61. See *Sharing the Light of Faith*, especially Ch. 8, pp. 99–123.

62. Ibid., p. 100.

63. *Sacramentum Mundi*, "Faith: I. Way to Faith," by Karl Rahner, 2:311. This statement of Rahner's follows from his description of faith, which is obviously grounded in the illuminist tradition. For example, he writes, "Every human being, even previous to the explicit preaching of the Christian message, is always potentially a believer and already in possession, in the grace that is prior to his freedom, of what he is to believe . . . God's direct self-communication in Christ" (Ibid., 2:310).

64. For this image of "making accessible" to describe religious education activity I am indebted to my colleague Mary C. Boys. Boys writes, "My claim is that 'make accessible' is the verb which ought to function as the primary description of religious education" ("Access to Traditions and Transformation," p. 15).

65. Thomas Aquinas expressed this well when he argued that there is need for "persuasive arguments showing that what is proposed to our faith is not impossible. . . ." (*Summa Theologica*, 2 [Q. 1, Art. 5]:1172).

66. F. Nietzsche, "Thus Spoke Zarathustra," p. 204.

67. This point deserves special attention in planning church adult education programs. It would appear that many of our programs are designed to do no more than deposit new information in people's heads. But such programs are likely to maintain people at stage three of faith development. We must design programs capable of sponsoring people in their inner ability for faith rather than merely giving them the "new theology" that has arisen since they were last in school.

5

For Human Freedom

THE PRIMARY claim made in this chapter is that Christian faith lived in response to the Kingdom of God has the consequence of human freedom.[1] Such Christian faith is grounded in human freedom, and the fruit of it is to live with, in, and for freedom, both here and hereafter.[2] The relationship between Christian faith and human freedom is symbiotic in that, if they exist at all, they exist together, and each one draws from and gives life to the other. For this reason, within the ultimate purpose of the Kingdom of God, Christian religious education has twin immediate purposes, namely, Christian faith and human freedom. We need to have both purposes consciously before us as we make decisions about the nature, context, approach, readiness, and copartners of our religious education. And while we may think of the purposes as dual, they belong together as two parts of the same piece—a life lived in response to the Kingdom of God in Jesus Christ. In our educational activity, and indeed in the living of a Christian life, Christian faith and human freedom are as essential to each other as is an effective cause to its consequence.

In effect, I am here proposing the language of freedom as the most comprehensive way of talking about the corporate consequence and condition of living with and for the values of the Kingdom of God. The description I offer for *freedom* is comprehensive enough to include all the values of the Kingdom (justice, peace, reconciliation, joy, hope, and so on) and at the same time is sufficiently focused both to empower and to critique our efforts in Christian religious education.[3]

CREATED TO IMAGE A FREE CREATOR

The nature of human freedom has been one of the most passionately debated topics throughout the history of philosophy. A variety of understandings of freedom have been proposed, and many debates between the various schools remain unresolved.[4] The ancient Greeks understood freedom not as individual freedom of action nor as freedom of the will, but as freedom of the State and of the citizen within it. In our own day B.F. Skinner claims that because of the conditioned nature of human behavior we are beyond the possibility of either freedom or dignity.[5] Between those extremes, and in the intervening period, a multiplicity of positions have been taken and different dimensions of freedom emphasized.

Even among commentators who attempt to understand freedom from a distinctively Christian perspective there are divergences. Christian philosophers and theologians have traditionally divided on the basis of different understandings of human nature. If one holds that the human condition is totally depraved and fallen, then freedom, if possible at all, can be only by the grace of God, and by the grace of God alone. If, on the other hand, the "fall" did not lead to total depravity for human nature, then human responsibility for freedom is more obvious, and God's grace can work within nature as it struggles toward freedom. While my own position here will lean toward the latter view, my intention is to propose a description of human freedom that is compatible with a broad spectrum of positions and traditions. In a profound sense freedom will always remain a mystery. In fact to capture it within one concise definition would be to limit it. People who suffer from a lack of freedom know it in its absence. People who enjoy some measure of it can have at least a limited understanding of it from their own experience. Still, a working description of freedom is necessary here since I pose it as part of the purpose of our "leading out" in Christian religious education.

Three main themes predominate in the understanding of human freedom throughout the history of philosophy, and all three are essential to a comprehensive understanding of freedom. The first is an emphasis on freedom as the ability to act to satisfy needs and tendencies: a freedom for action and from external constraint or servitude of any kind. The second emphasis is on self-determination without any inner necessity for what is willed: freedom for choosing and from inner compulsion or necessity. The third emphasis is on freedom as the ability to respond to a rational process of decision making. All of these dimensions of human freedom will be included in what follows; the constant perspective for considering them is the Christian and Jewish traditions.

The approach of describing human freedom under the headings of "freedom for" and "freedom from" is very useful, and I follow it here. However, it is necessary first to recall why we have the possibility of freedom in the first place. The ground of our freedom will shape what we are free for and free from.

The starting point for affirming our possibility for freedom is the biblical claim that we are created by a free creator. That God acts as a free creator is foundational to the whole Hebrew and Christian understanding of God.[6] The freedom of God goes out of God and, working unhampered by anything prior, creates out of nothing. In God's creating, creativity and freedom are combined. In this sense, the freedom of God is absolute. And the grounds for God's absolute claim to sovereignty over all people is the fact that God is our creator who brought us into existence and maintains us in it. Following from this, it is also central to the Hebrew and Christian traditions that God made us and fashioned us in God's own image and likeness. If we are a reflection of the free divine act and image that created us, then we must have the possibility of freedom. Otherwise we would not be in God's image and likeness.[7] Thus because of our very existence as the reflection of God we have the possibility of freedom. With this ground for our freedom we are free primarily "for God," and in realizing this freedom we find freedom "for ourselves" and "for others."

We are free primarily for God because it is only by saying yes to the image of whom we are a reflection that we can say yes to our own authentic selves, and only as our own true selves can we be free. In saying yes to the One we reflect, we say yes to our own possibility, and in striving toward the image, we strive toward freedom. Stated negatively, by saying no to the One we reflect, we say no to our own possibility and thus choose unfreedom; one cannot choose evil and be true to the image of God. God objectifies us as reflections of God's self and, therefore, we come to our subjectivity by saying yes to the ground of our being. The fullness of human freedom is realized in perfect union with God. Conversely, to be alienated from God is to be alienated from the ground of one's own being and thus to live in unfreedom.

Because our freedom for is a freedom for God, in a deep sense it is an absolute freedom.[8] It is absolute in that nothing relative, but only God, can fully satisfy it. It is absolute to us as human beings in that nobody can rob us of the *right* to freedom. They may ignore our right. They may consistently deny us the opportunity to exercise it. But as long as we are human beings, the right to freedom can never be erased. Deep within the core of every person there is implanted the longing and the right to be free. We have this right by "copyright" because at that core of ourselves we are most like unto God.

We will see below that our freedom for God and thus for ourselves is realized within history as a freedom for others. In this respect human freedom is a limited freedom to be exercised in a community and for a community. But before I explain freedom for others, there is a more fundamental question that must be answered. The same Bible that tells the story of our being created in the image and likeness of a free creator also tells the story of a "fall." By this fall it appears that humankind chose freedom for itself precisely by saying no to God. As a result, the Bible indicates, although we are created in the image of a free creator, we are everywhere in chains. By what is traditionally called our original sin we have fallen to a state of unfreedom from which we are incapable of self-rescue. And if we look into the reality of our own existential situation (whose horizon is death), we realize that this biblical "revelation" is a verification of what we find in the human condition. Both as individuals and as communities, our condition seems fallen and broken. Given this fallen state, then, have we the possibility of realizing our longing and right for freedom at all? Remembering the three dimensions of human freedom outlined above, have we, in our freedom for God, the capacity to know the good (rational freedom), to freely choose the good (freedom for choice, freedom from inner compulsion), and to do the good (freedom for action, freedom from external constraint or servitude)?

Christians give a common response to these questions. By the grace of God, made available to us through the dying and rising of Jesus Christ, we have the capacity of saying yes to God. Even while Christians disagree about the nature and extent of the divine and human contributions to the quest for freedom, there is agreement that by the liberating work of Christ, sin has been conquered and in God's amazing grace we can be free. In the last part of this chapter I outline the three dimensions of freedom made possible by God in Jesus Christ within history (and the responsibility each dimension places on us). For now we need to continue our sequence of philosophical reflection.

In our freedom for God, how do we exercise our rational freedom, our freedom of choice, and our freedom of action? First, the rational dimension of our freedom for God is rooted in our ability for rational self-reflection. Such rationality expresses the transcendent aspect of being human. Although grounded in existence, the human person can consciously stand over against other things that exist. Through rational reflection the self can transcend what is nonself and reflect upon it. Further, the "I" of the self can stand over the "me" of the self and reflect upon it in self-reflection. The ability for such transcending activity is a reflection in us of divine transcendence. This God-given capacity of the human "spirit," coupled with the actual grace of God working within us, gives us the capacity to know the good with sufficient clarity to be held responsible for what we choose to do. Without this ability for rational discernment between good and evil we could not be held responsible for our actions. Both sin and virtue would be beyond us. Thus by the power of God's grace working within our transcendent nature, we can have rational freedom.

What then of freedom of choice in our freedom for God? Is the need to decide either for or away from God so innate that whichever way we orient ourselves there is no choice involved? This is a complex question. Perhaps more than any other dimension of our freedom for God, it brings us up against the mystery of a free creator who created Self-reflections with the freedom even to reject their own image.[9] In one sense there is an "imperative" to our freedom for God. To say no to God is to choose less than ourselves and thus to choose unfreedom. We realize our freedom for God only by becoming what we are called to become,[10] a people fully alive who reflect God's image and move toward our potential destiny of full divine communion. In this sense, to find our true freedom, we must say yes to God. But where is the choice in such freedom? Can we, with clear knowledge and full consent, say no to God and realize our freedom? The answer seems to be that we can freely and knowingly choose to say no to God, but our refusal begets unfreedom rather than freedom. God respects our choice. But having chosen to say no to God, we must live with the consequences, which are alienation from God and from our own true selves, or, in theological terms, the slavery of sin. In other words, we have freedom of choice even to the point of being able to choose unfreedom.[11]

The biblical story that best illustrates this paradox is the Exodus account. There Moses, by the power of God, led the Israelite people out from the slavery of Egypt toward a Promised Land. The hazards and hardships of the desert, however, soon proved to be too much for them.

> Here in the desert the whole Israelite community grumbled against Moses and Aaron. The Israelites said to them, "Would that we had died at the Lord's hand in the land of Egypt, as we sat by our fleshpots and ate our fill of bread! But you had to lead us into this desert to make the whole community die of famine!" (Exod. 16:2–3)

Gladly would they have turned and gone back to Egypt. But the paradox is that if the Israelites had freely chosen to return to Egypt, they would be choosing unfreedom again. We, too, can willfully and knowingly refuse our potential to become who we are invited to become. We can also, by God's grace, choose to say yes to God and thus move toward actualizing the selves we are invited to become, selves who ever more fully reflect the One in whose image we have our existence.

Coming now to the third essential aspect of freedom, in our freedom for God how do we express our freedom for action? Our freedom for God and thus for ourselves is realized in our freedom for others. Here it is important first to remember that human freedom must find realization within a historical context. It cannot be satisfied with a transcendent freedom alone nor with some ideal form called freedom by philosophers. Nor can it be realized in isolation, but only within a historical community. The point is that the God for whom we are free is a God who did not remain outside of history, but who came within it to act effectively on behalf of God's intentions for creation. God's intentions for all people and creation is what we have been calling the Kingdom of God. Since the

Kingdom is both in and at the end of history, our freedom for God must come to lived expression within our historical context even as it awaits completion by full union with God at the end of our time. Our freedom for God is realized by faithful response to God's Kingdom now. In the law of the Kingdom we love God by loving our neighbor. To be free for God is to be free for others. To say yes to God and to obey God's will requires that we love and serve the people God loves and calls to freedom with us.

When the Pauline and "Catholic" epistles talk of our new-found freedom in Christ, they speak constantly of the obedience of freedom, the law of freedom, and freedom as service. Peter writes, "Live as free men, but do not use your freedom as a cloak for vice. In a word, live as servants of God" (1 Pet. 2:16). And James writes, "Always speak and act as men destined for judgment under the law of freedom" (James 2:12; see also James 1:25). The freedom made possible to us by Jesus Christ brings with it not license, but a "new law." This new law of freedom means that we are now free to love and serve each other. Paul is the one who states this best: "It was for liberty that Christ freed us. So stand firm, and do not take on yourselves the yoke of slavery a second time!" (Gal. 5:1). But he adds later, "My brothers, remember that you have been called to live in freedom—but not a freedom that gives free reign to the flesh. Out of love, place yourselves at one another's service" (Gal. 5:13). In his epistle to the Romans he explains further that our God-given freedom from sin now makes us "slaves of justice" (see Rom. 6:17–22).

Thus the freedom of action in our freedom for God and ourselves made possible by Jesus Christ, is, in fact, a freedom for others. In this sense, it is a "limited" freedom—limited in that we cannot act as we please regardless of the consequences for other people. To borrow Mary Mahowald's language, freedom from a Christian perspective can never be understood as "raw" freedom in the sense of an unbridled "individualistic" freedom. Rather, it is a limited freedom that is actualized and contained within a "communalistic context." [12] Of course, the point, and the paradox, is that only by being limited can it be true freedom and not license. "Unrestricted freedom is a form of slavery. To be 'free' to do what I will in relation to another is to be in bondage to the law of least resistance." [13] To be free for union with God is to be free to enter into communion with other people in a relationship of love and service to each other. This is a far cry from the rugged individualism that is often taken by people in our society to be the epitome of human freedom. [14]

To borrow James Fowler's language, freedom, like faith, is realized in a triadic relationship. The three poles of freedom and the three poles of faith are the same: self, community, and God. Freedom for God is the possibility of authentic freedom for oneself. But freedom for self and for God must find expression in, and is both limited and made possible by, the freedom for and of others. The biblical notion that salvation comes to us as a people means that true freedom can come to us only as and with a people. But even when united as a people, we cannot free ourselves. From a Christian perspective human freedom is not possible, "apart from a liberating transcendence."[15] It is in the possibility of union with God, our ultimate horizon of freedom, that we can have freedom, both individually and socially, here and hereafter.

"Freedom for" from a Christian perspective then is freedom for becoming what we are called to become, which is a freedom for union with God that finds expression in a freedom for communion with and service to other people. The "freedom from" of Christian freedom follows logically. By the saving power of God in Jesus Christ we can now be free from anything that prevents our freedom for. For now we can say that the epitome of freedom from in a Christian perspective is freedom from sin. But what does it mean to be free from sin within our historical context, and what is the historical task posed by such a freedom? That many kinds of slavery abound in our historical reality is obvious. Christians must not allow talk of freedom in Christ to pose easy solutions to the problem of unfreedom in our world. On the contrary, our faith forces us to confront the question: If we are made free for God and from sin by the liberating work of Jesus Christ, why then, in our historical context, are the chains of an old slavery all around us and within us? Further, what are we to do about such slavery? As Marx would have it, a freedom yet to be realized is no freedom at all.

Christians must not be naive about this. To solve the problem by saying that Jesus brought us a spiritual freedom to be realized in an afterlife is only a partial solution, and thus a false one. It overlooks our need for freedom as pilgrims in time and falls into the time-honored but misleading body/soul dichotomy. It also misrepresents the meaning of the saving work of Jesus Christ as being entirely for "another world." We are on a journey toward human freedom through Jesus Christ. That freedom is to begin in our time, and, as with the Kingdom, the fact that it is God's gift does not rob us of our historical responsibility to make it present now.

PILGRIMS TOWARD FREEDOM THROUGH JESUS CHRIST

In each epoch of its history humankind appears to have had some predominant concern. The evidence of our time suggests that our predominant concern is the quest for human freedom. It is in terms of freedom that we most often ask the existential question about the meaning of our existence. Hegel would claim that freedom has been the quest of all history, and that may well be true. However, the longing and struggle for freedom is consciously before our era with an awareness and urgency like never before. It expresses itself in a great variety of struggles and is surely pervasive enough to be called a general movement of humankind in our epoch.

It has been suggested that the primary concern of the ancient world was the quest for immortality.[16] The Christian Church responded to this quest by emphasizing salvation as an otherworldly reality of eternal happiness. Such a response may well have been appropriate for its time and will always be part of our response in every time. The most crucial task facing the Christian community and tradition in this time, however, is to respond to the human quest for freedom.[17] Can our Christian faith empower us in that quest? We can be quite certain that to continue speaking of salvation only in otherworldly and "spiritual" terms will not meet the challenge. In fact, such an understanding of the redemptive work of Christ can lend itself to the legitimation of sinful social structures within history, if only by silence and inaction in the face of them. An otherworldly kind of salvation can and has, to some extent, caused people to tolerate situations of injustice and acquiesce in conditions of bondage. Because of the promise of heaven for the individual soul in another life, the ills and pains of this life could be accepted, even when they were inflicted unjustly. In fact, if borne well and willingly, they were believed to add to the reward awaiting us in heaven.

I am thoroughly convinced that Christianity can be and should be an empowerment to the quest for human freedom. Such a claim, however, must not be taken for granted. We have had our share of serious critics with compelling claims that Christianity cannot be emancipatory, two of the most notable being Marx and Freud. Their criticisms cannot be dismissed lightly. On the contrary, they must be taken with the utmost seriousness by the Christian community, and if we are to make counterclaims we must first respond to the truths in their claims. I deal with them here because religious educators, especially, must be aware of them and must educate in a manner that will prove Marx and Freud wrong.

Marx's often-repeated slogan "Criticism of religion is the foundation of all criticism" is well known, as is his statement, "Religious distress is at the same time the expression of real distress and the protest against real distress. Religion is the sigh of the oppressed creature, the heart of a heartless world, just as it is the spirit of a spiritless situation. It is the opium of the people."[18] A point often overlooked in that frequently quoted statement is that Marx saw religion as an authentic "protest against real distress." At a time when the human state seemed totally hopeless, religion offered heart and hope in the midst of misery. In that sense he detected its possibility for being a subversive element.

The oppressive influence of religion, however, as Marx saw it, was that it not only gave people some spark of hope in a hopeless situation but also caused them to accept their condition as inevitable, irremediable, the will of a God outside of history. As a result, it became an opium which deadened the awareness of people, preventing them from refusing the injustice of their situation. In fact, religion for Marx was no more than an expression of unjust and self-negating social conditions. He saw it as arising from the same source as all other social problems; namely, the alienation of people from the products of their labor and the injustice of a capitalist system in which owners controlled the mode of production and retained the surplus value of other people's labor as their own. Because of false consciousness the workers either were not aware of their alienation from the products of their labor or saw such alienation as inevitable. In their pain they turned to a God outside of history and found some solace in the hope of an "other world" of perfect happiness. The churches preached such a God and such a salvation. The ruling class welcomed this, taking advantage of it to prevent people from seeing the real cause of their pain. Thus religion, in Marx's opinion, became an ideology used by the ruling class to pacify the subjugated class. Marx claimed that human history had now evolved to the point where people were capable of revolutionary praxis to bring about a just society. Consequently, returning the means and goods of production to the workers would destroy religion because it would destroy the unjust social structures which had given rise to the need for it. In fact, in the revolutionary struggle the destruction of false consciousness would have to go hand in hand with the destruction of religion.

Many arguments can be made against Marx's position. To begin with, he was reacting to what contemporary theology considers a false notion of God, namely a God "up there" or "out there" who turns us away from ourselves and the world. Such a notion of God has long since been rejected by Christian theologians as unfaithful to our scriptures and inadequate to the human condition.[19] Moreover, Marx overlooked (as did most theologians of his time) the transforming power of Christianity and its mandate to subvert all that is not of the Kingdom. But before we dismiss Marx's criticism as invalid, we must first face the truth that is in it. In his nineteenth-century context Marx is criticizing a Christianity that saw itself as offering no more than an otherworldly salvation. When Christianity offers no more than that, and by turning people toward an "other world" turns them away from their historical responsibility in this world, his criticism would seem well placed. Today, however, Marx's criticism is being met by Christians who understand Christianity as a call to salvation in both "this" and "other" worldly terms.

If Marx saw religion as oppressive, Freud saw it as repressive. For Freud, God and religion are products of "wish fulfillment" and are based on an "illusion."[20] Threatened by "the superior powers of nature, of Fate," and disillusioned by the limitations especially of their fathers (Freud is often charged, correctly, with sexist attitudes), people follow their "infantile prototype" and turn to an infinite "father" for protection and fulfillment of their needs.[21] Such a father is no more than a creation of our own needs, and while the needs are real, the God they produce is an illusion, in other words, has no basis in reality. Further, the illusion is dangerous because it causes us to repress what is too painful for our consciousness to hold in view and thus perpetuates infantile behavior patterns and prevents us from facing reality as it is. Since the products of our wish fulfillment are interiorized within the psyche, God and religion become the most limiting factors in a person's superego, causing repression and guilt. Freud grants that "devout believers are safeguarded in a high degree against the risk of certain neurotic illnesses: their acceptance of the universal neurosis spares them the task of constructing a personal one." However, he hastens to add, "we may now argue that the time has probably come . . . for replacing the effects of repression by the results of the rational operation of the intellect."[22]

Here again, Freud's analysis could be dismissed by the claim that he was reacting to a false understanding of religion and a false image of God. In fact, what I described in Chapter Four as maturity of faith is the very antithesis of what Freud was condemning. But the truth in Freud's position must also be recognized. If Christians understand salvation only as an otherworldly reality and God as a "big daddy" residing in that other world, then such a view is likely to prevent us from facing historical reality as it is and from taking initiative to transform it toward the Kingdom of God. Or if God is presented as a fearful judge and sin as a private affair between the individual and God, then debilitating personal guilt is likely to be the result.[23]

The criticisms of Marx and Freud should give Christians reason for pause before they glibly claim that "Jesus means freedom."[24] In addition, some of our history would also indicate why we Christians can be doubted as trustworthy companions in the journey toward human freedom, although it would be grossly unfair to say that all of our history indicts us. In their very origin both Judaism and Christianity were critiques of the world of their time, and the prophetic word denouncing oppression and injustice has never been absent from either tradition. Christianity has been a major influence in improving the lot of many oppressed peoples, far greater certainly than many other major world religions.[25] The eradication of discrimination on the basis of sex, race, ethnic background, and so on has made greater strides in areas of Jewish and Christian influence than in areas where other major religions have been dominant. But our history has another side too.

Since the marriage of throne and altar with Constantine, Christians have as often been on the side of oppressive powers (if only by legitimating silence) as we have been critics of them. The historically conditioned nature of our theology, the blinding influence of our social context, and our fear of being personae non grata with the establishment have often distracted us from the critique that is the constant calling of people who claim to live under the Word. When kings reigned, we provided ideological legitimation with theological talk about the divine right of kings. When slavery was part of the economic arrangement of the day, we quoted Genesis (9:18–27) and the curse of Ham, and issued papal documents to bless the arrangement. We have talked about the right to private property in such a manner that Western capitalism appeared to have the sanction of heaven. In a chauvinistic society where women are yet to be treated as equals, we continue to bar them from equal participation in our decision-making processes, and some of us still bar them from our sanctuaries, thus legitimating and helping to perpetuate the sinfulness of sexism. And in the very recent past we witnessed the destruction of six million people, perpetrated at the heart of Christendom, and with no more than feeble or isolated opposition from the Christian community. In fact, in a perverse way, a traditional Christian animosity toward Judaism was encouraged in order to legitimate that terrible Holocaust. It would seem that human freedom, even after the coming of the messianic age in Jesus Christ, is, like the Kingdom he preached, both already and not yet. The not-yetness of human freedom poses a huge historical task for all people, and for Christians precisely because of their faith in Jesus Christ.

There has emerged in the Christian Churches a growing awareness that sin is not only personal and salvation is not simply for later. This is not a new awareness. It has always been there in some form, though not always so obviously preached or lived. However, what has increased markedly in recent times is consciousness of the task an expanded understanding of sin and salvation poses for the Church's whole mission to the world. Deepened insights from the social sciences along with such criticisms from Marxism and psychoanalysis have given rise to a far greater clarity about the social and political implications of being a community of Christian faith in the midst of history. This "social consciousness" finds expression in a broad spectrum of contemporary Christian theology, though theologians as often express community consciousness as they are a cause of it. It finds increasing and more forceful expression in official church statements.[26] There is evidence of it in the developing social consciousness of many Christian organizations and movements. It is seen in places and issues where Christians are actively involved, because of their faith, in struggles for human liberation. It will continue to find greater expression if we press the implications of saying that there is some continuity between our time and the completed Kingdom of God, and that the Kingdom is to be made present already within human history.

SIN AND SALVATION REVISITED

Christians, because of their faith in Jesus Christ and their response to the Kingdom of which he is the effective agent, have an unavoidable obligation to play a concerted part in humankind's quest for freedom. Further, they have a unique contribution to make to that struggle, and their faith can empower them to make it. But if we are to be agents of a freedom that begins within history, then we need an expanded notion of the meaning of sin and of the salvation made possible by the grace of God in Jesus Christ.

Sin as Personal and Social.   The typical notion of sin in popular Christian consciousness understands it as a private and personal matter between an individual and God. As might be expected, repentance of sin is seen typically as an individualized process. To be absolved from it, many Catholics go to Confession (most often in a very private context[27]), and many Protestants settle for believing a little harder in their hearts.

Undoubtedly, there is a personal dimension to human sinfulness.[28] For a particular act to be sinful, it must involve personal choice by somebody. But current Christian consciousness and critical theology are reclaiming what is, in fact, a profoundly biblical notion, namely, that sin is both a personal and a social reality. The consequences of personal sins never remain private. To say no to God is to say no to the Kingdom of God. We sin against God by sinning against God's people and against God's intentions for ourselves and for creation.

The social dimensions of personal sin go far beyond the particular immediate impact of our sinful act on the community. Personal sins and their consequences do not remain isolated from each other. Instead, they accumulate together with all the other "personal" refusals of God's Kingdom. Then the accumulation becomes congealed and institutionalized into social structures and arrangements that are sinful, structures that oppress, exploit, or discriminate (sexism, racism, uncontrolled capitalism, totalitarian socialism, etc.). These structures, although the product of personal sins, take on a life of their own, making the doing of God's will more difficult and militating against the values of the Kingdom. As Robert McAfee Brown explains it, "Not only do we sin against one another individually, we perpetuate those sins corporately through structure whose ongoing existence militates against humanizing possibilities for others."[29]

Furthermore, these sinful social structures tend to maintain us in our private sins. To state this another way, there is a dialectical and mutually supporting relationship between personal and social sin. Personal sin gives rise to social structures that are sinful, and those structures then return to maintain people in or dispose them toward further personal sin. For example, while human greed is a personal sin, the corporate expression of that greed is a consumer society in which people exploit each other for the sake of having more goods to consume. Just to live in such a society is inevitably to be disposed toward further sins of greed. Gregory Baum explains, "Human limitations and personal sins compounded have created social sins and conversely social sins create an environment that promotes personal sins."[30] If we Christians are to consider ourselves, as Paul says, "dead to sin but alive for God in Christ Jesus" (Rom. 6:11), then we are called to live our lives not only without personal sin, but also in opposition to all social arrangements that are sinful.

Salvation as This- and Otherworldly. Salvation as it is popularly understood by Christians and typically preached among us is the possibility of heaven for the individual soul after death.[31] It is both individual and otherworldly. In many ways such a commonly held understanding of salvation would seem to have changed little since Marx's day.

Belief in an afterlife of eternal union with God, or eternal alienation from God, is a consistent and central part of the Christian faith tradition. That belief must always be affirmed. But contemporary critical theology insists that while salvation can only be completed in an "other" world by full union with God, it is to begin in our present historical time. In other words, the salvation made possible by Jesus Christ is both this- and otherworldly.

This expanded notion of salvation goes hand in hand with the expanded notion of sin. We are in need of salvation not only from our personal sins, but also from the sinful social structures produced by and producing our personal sins. We need emancipation from sin both individually and collectively. Since sin is rooted in our present reality, salvation must begin there too. Since the Kingdom has already begun definitively in Jesus Christ, salvation must begin within history, and it must have both a personal and a social dimension to it.[32] Salvation comes to us now as the power, by the grace of God in Jesus Christ, to overcome personal sins and to struggle against all sinful principalities and powers. Rahner explains, "As a reality which is constantly also achieving visible form at the social level, it is quite impossible in principle for salvation not to be concerned with the social realities within which it has to be realized and made manifest in history."[33]

Therefore, if Christians are to live as a redeemed people, we must live in opposition to sin, both personal and social. Such salvation is made possible by the grace of God in Jesus Christ. But as with the gift of the Kingdom (the gift of the Kingdom and the gift of salvation are, in fact, the same gift), our responsibility to respond to that grace remains. By grace salvation is made possible, and that possibility empowers us to struggle with some hope for freedom for ourselves and for all God's people. Far from reducing us to passivity, the gift of salvation places a mandate on us to be involved within history in such a struggle.

JESUS THE LIBERATOR

Traditionally, the meaning of the Christ event for human history has been expressed in the language of salvation and redemption. I am not suggesting that we abandon those terms; they are too old and too rich in possibilities to be discarded. But when Jesus is understood to have freed us from sin that is both personal and social, with a salvation that is both this- and otherworldly, then it is most appropriate also to use the language of freedom to talk about the meaning of Jesus the Christ for us. [34] And given that the traditional language still carries such strongly personal and otherworldly overtones, it may even be advisable to talk more often in the language of freedom (though it, too, can have unfortunate connotations). For our time at least it can better express the intrahistorical and social dimensions of the Kingdom in Jesus Christ and is thus more capable of responding to the needs and concerns of our time. To say, as Käsemann says, "Jesus means freedom" is not to read something into the Gospels at will, but it arises when we bring a contemporary hermeneutic to the reading of scripture and to the theological task of articulating the meaning of salvation/redemption for our time. That this language of freedom is most appropriate can be readily demonstrated if we bring our broadened understanding of sin and salvation to reinterpret the meaning of two central Christological titles, Savior and Redeemer.

In the history of Western Christianity there have been two principal models for understanding the consequences of the Christ event and the meaning of atonement.[35] One, usually called the "classic" model, understands Christ's dying and rising as saving us from the powers of evil. In him the principalities and powers of evil are conquered for us. By defeating evil, Christ saved us for God and for union with God. Thus the most appropriate title for Christ under this model of atonement is Savior.

The second principal model, usually referred to as either the "Latin" or the "satisfaction" model, understands the dying and rising of Jesus Christ as making satisfaction to God's justice for our sins.[36] Here Christ is our Redeemer, and by his redeeming act he buys us back from bondage and pays the price for our sins. In consequence, we are restored to divine sonship or daughtership.

Whichever model is favored—and both have longevity in the tradition—the Christian community throughout its history has believed that Jesus died and was raised up by God to redeem us from our sins, save us from their consequences, and make possible to us a state of union with God. Given the needs of our time, however, and when sin is seen both as a personal and a social reality, when salvation in Jesus Christ is understood as both this- and otherworldly, when the central theme of Jesus' preaching and work, the Kingdom of God, is understood as both already and not yet; then Christ our Savior and Redeemer can also be appropriately called Christ our "Liberator." By God's grace in Jesus Christ we can come to live with "the glorious freedom of the children of God" (Rom. 8:21).

Three Dimensions to Freedom in Jesus Christ.   From Paul's statement to the Galatians that Christ has set us free (Gal. 5:1) down to the present day, Christians have often used the language of freedom to describe the consequence of God's saving work in Jesus Christ. Christ has freed us from our sins is a message that has been preached to every generation of Christians. But I, along with many other contemporary theologians and educators, am proposing an expanded meaning for that language here. Throughout its history, the Church has most often limited freedom in Jesus Christ to a spiritual freedom. The freedom he made possible for us was preached as a liberation from personal sin in preparation for the completed freedom of the soul in an "after" life. But freedom in Jesus Christ is being described here as a freedom for the whole person that begins within the historical social context. In addition, this freedom places on Christ's followers a mandate (even as it gives them the grace to respond to the mandate) to begin, within time, to struggle toward the realization of such freedom. There are, then, at least three dimensions to the freedom made possible by Jesus Christ. They have already been alluded to a number of times, but lest any one be overlooked, it is well to set them out separately here, with the responsibility each one gives us. Christian religious educators must attend to all three of them.

The first and ultimate dimension of human freedom through Jesus Christ may still be rightly called spiritual. It is by the freedom of our "spirit" that we can transcend the mundane and passing to reach out for union with the ultimate Transcendent. We will not be entirely free until we achieve our final destiny of permanent union with God. Only in and with the free Creator, whom we reflect, can the human hunger for freedom be fully satisfied. In this sense, our final freedom is a spiritual freedom. As we move toward the completion of that possibility in eternity, spiritual freedom comes to us within history as the mandate and grace to live as if God is truly our only God, for whom our lives are lived. By entering into a trusting union with this God, before whom there is no other, we can also enter into true communion with all God's people.

The second dimension of freedom in Jesus Christ is personal; it can also be called the interior, psychological aspect of freedom. By the grace of God in Jesus Christ we can turn from slavery to inner compulsion and have an autonomy of will whose horizon is the Kingdom of God. The Kingdom, as Jesus preached it, calls for such a personal conversion. Without this personal conversion that frees and heals the inner self, "spiritual" freedom would seem to be impossible.[37] With this personal freedom comes the mandate and grace to turn from sin in our own hearts, and outward toward God and God's people.

And the third dimension of freedom in Jesus Christ is social/political. Freedom in Christ cannot be only an inner healing or a spiritual possibility. Personal freedom in the depths of one's self and freedom for union with God and communion with others requires freedom within our social and political contexts. Paul van Buren explains, "We are bound together in the structure of God's creation in such a way that there simply cannot be such a thing as individual free-dom. We shall all go free together, or we are all locked into bondage together."[38] To the extent that such social/political freedom exists, it is more likely that there can be personal and spiritual freedom too.

Union with God, communion with others, and inner wholeness are certainly difficult to attain in the midst of sinful social structures. Peter Hodgson goes so far as to ask, "Can there be an inner freedom in the context of an outer bondage and an alien world?"[39] My answer is that personal and spiritual freedom are rendered more difficult by sinful social structures. There have always been peo-ple of courage who have succeeded in rising above the shackles of oppressive so-cial structures and have achieved great personal and spiritual freedom. But it is clearly God's intention (i.e., the Kingdom) that such structures be destroyed. The liberating work of Jesus Christ is God's definitive act in opposition to all such structures, and those who claim to be Jesus' followers must live their lives in opposition to them.[40] Thus the freedom made possible by Jesus Christ is a so-cial and political freedom as well as a spiritual and psychological one. His dying and rising is a means of grace to empower the human struggle within history for an ever-increasing degree of freedom from sin as it is embodied in the economic, political, and cultural arrangements of our world.

CHRISTIAN FAITH AND HUMAN FREEDOM IN RELIGIOUS EDUCATION

I claimed at the beginning of this chapter that Christian faith and human freedom are inextricably, symbiotically related. They draw from and give to each other. They are so closely related that both must be posed as the dual pur-poses of Christian religious education, which has as its metapurpose the King-dom of God in Jesus Christ.

That lived Christian faith is to lead to human freedom (the language used here to describe the corporate consequences of the Kingdom) should now be quite clear. I need to clarify further, however, how Christian faith is also to arise from human freedom.

To begin, the response of a person or a community to God's invitation to lived Christian faith must be a free response. Regardless of one's position on the relationship of grace to nature, if Christian faith is to be meritorious, although it is prompted by the grace of God, it must involve a free response.[41] For God to impose God's saving grace upon us would be to deny the possibility for auton-omy and freedom that is ours as beings created in the divine image and likeness. The most God chooses to do is invite and give grace to respond. The refusal or acceptance of that invitation remains our responsibility, and such responsibility presupposes freedom on our part.

Perhaps the clearest statement in many years concerning the freedom that must underlie all choices of faith was the Second Vatican Council's *Declaration on Religious Freedom*, which was certainly a milestone for Roman Catholicism. It enunciates its basic principle thus: "This Vatican Synod declares that the human person has a right to religious freedom." This right "has its foundation in the very dignity of the human person, as this dignity is known through the revealed Word of God and by reason itself" (Par. 2). In consequence, everyone "has the duty, and therefore the right to seek the truth in matters religious," and "as the truth is discovered, it is by a personal assent that men are to adhere to it" (Par. 3). The Council went on to claim that "man's response to God in faith must be free" as "one of the major tenets of Catholic doctrine" (Par. 9), strong language indeed for a General Council of Catholicism. Finally, the Council saw its position as modeled on the example of Christ, who "refused to impose the truth by force" (Par. 11).[42] Clearly, the response of Christian faith must arise from human freedom.

Christian faith and human freedom belong together, then, as ground and consequence of each other. The two must be consciously posed as the mutual purposes of Christian religious education. When human freedom is posed as integral to our purpose, there are important implications for how we shape our educational praxis. When it is consciously used to inform our day-to-day decision making, it can guide what and how we teach and be a criterion to evaluate our efforts.[43]

In its *Declaration on Religious Freedom* Vatican II made a statement of great relevance to religious education when it declared:

> In spreading religious faith and in introducing religious practices, everyone ought at all times to refrain from any manner of action which might seem to carry a hint of coercion or of a kind of persuasion that would be dishonorable or unworthy. . . .[44]

That statement, and indeed the whole *Declaration*, is not typically interpreted as applying to the Church's educational ministry. However, it may well be religious educators who should take the *Declaration* most seriously. Any form of manipulation or indoctrination is both bad education and blatantly counterproductive to the purposes of Christian education. The educational process we use must itself be capable of promoting human emancipation. Any approach that by its very nature tends to control people or rob them of their word is unfit for our purpose.

To state this more positively, whenever, wherever, and however we educate in the Christian faith tradition, that activity should empower the human quest for freedom in all three of the dimensions outlined. Unless we concern ourselves with all three dimensions of freedom, we are not educating faithfully in the name of Jesus Christ. Our intentions must be to sponsor people toward a lived

Christian faith that is both free and freeing. Human freedom within history will always be an ongoing journey rather than a point of arrival. Our educational praxis must be capable of enabling people along that journey.

In Chapter One I said that the Christian faith tradition can be made available to pilgrims in time in a manner that overpowers and controls them or in a way that empowers and liberates them. Given that human freedom is integral to our purpose, we have the task of making the tradition available in such a manner that people can critically appropriate it to their lives as a source of freedom. In other words, our educational activity must be designed to foster greater degrees of Christian critical consciousness so that our people may respond to the demands of the Kingdom in their own personal, social, and political contexts. The Christian community, and its religious educators, have much ground to cover before our educating for Christian faith is consistently an education for human freedom. But let that be the vision that calls us forward and evaluates our efforts as we go.

NOTES

1. Schubert M. Ogden writes, "Faith is the existence of freedom. By this I mean, quite simply, that the distinctive way of understanding ourselves in the world that is properly described as Christian faith in God is a way of existing and acting in freedom and for it" (*Faith and Freedom*, p. 49). Odgen's whole book is an excellent statement of the mutuality between Christian faith and human freedom.
2. I mentioned previously that a typical and traditional answer given to the question Why be a Christian? was To save my soul, or some variation of that (To get to heaven, etc.). In that old answer there is a truth that must not be lost—the realization that our response to God in Christ, and indeed our educational efforts to promote a response, have eternal consequences. In suggesting the language of freedom as a more compelling and apt way of talking about the consequences of Christ's dying and rising for us, I am certainly not denying the "eternal" consequences of how we now live. On the contrary, as will be evident from this chapter, human freedom can only be fully and finally realized in complete and eternal union with God, hereafter. But it must begin to be realized here, albeit imperfectly.
3. Kasper makes a strong statement of the same point when he writes, "Scripturally, the new being in Christ can be described in a number of ways: life, justice, redemption, peace, forgiveness, and so forth. None of these terms is dispensable. In our present situation, however, the new existence in Christ is most readily comprised in the notion of Christian freedom. Christian freedom is the actualization for us of what Resurrection means in history" (*Jesus the Christ*, p. 156).
4. Peter Hodgson lists as many as six major traditions in the understanding of human freedom, and a number of them have distinct subdivisions (see *New Birth of Freedom*).
5. See Skinner, *Beyond Freedom and Dignity*.
6. Paul van Buren writes, "Both the Christian and the Jewish communities and traditions have maintained that the God of whom they wish to speak is free" (*The Burden of Freedom*, p. 12).
7. My grounding of human freedom in the notion that we are created in the image of God is a choice from a number of possibilities. However, there is a long tradition of understanding the possibility and nature of human freedom because of this *imago Dei* tenet. According to Walter Burghardt, the patristic theologians of the Alexandrian school argued for human freedom on the basis of the Genesis text. For Origen, Gregory of Nyssa, and Cyril of Alexandria the human person is created for freedom because created in the image of God (see Burghardt, "Free Like God," pp. 343–364). The Second Vatican Council in its *Pastoral Constitution on the Church in the Modern World* (par. 17) grounds its understanding of human freedom on the same base.

The *Constitution* states that "authentic freedom is an exceptional sign of the divine image within man" (Abbott, *Documents*, p. 214).

8. Rahner explains that "freedom is ultimately an openness to everything, to everything without exception: openness to absolute truth, to absolute love, and to the absolute infinity of human life in its immediacy to the very reality which we call God" (*Foundations*, p. 402). J. De Finance expresses the same point thus: "Human freedom, participating in God's freedom, perfects itself as freedom only to the extent that it allows itself to be completely enveloped by God" (*New Catholic Encyclopedia*, "Freedom," by J. De Finance, 6:89).

9. Paul van Buren writes insightfully about this point. "There is, I think we must say, a strange mystery about God's freedom" (*The Burden of Freedom*, p. 25). One aspect of this mystery is that apparently God has freely "qualified" God's own freedom and has made it "dependent" by sharing it with us "so that the realization of his freedom awaits the realization of the freedom of the sons and daughters of God" (pp. 9–10). Now God's freedom, by God's free design, waits upon the exercise of our freedom. "It is the mystery of God's freedom that he will not exercise it apart from us. The freedom of God waits upon us. Clearly, the name of that sort of freedom is love" (p. 34).

10. James Cone, writing out of a similar Christian perspective on human freedom, says, "Simply stated, freedom is not doing what I will but becoming what I should" (*Black Theology*, p. 39).

11. Karl Rahner's explanation of freedom of choice in regard to our freedom for God is very similar to the one I am proposing here. A good summary of his position can be found in *Foundations*, pp. 93 ff. Rahner writes, "Although it exists in time and in history, freedom has a single, unique act, namely, the self-actualization of the single subject himself" (p. 95). This self-actualization is possible by saying "yes to God" (p. 100). But there is a choice. "As a being of freedom, therefore, man can deny himself in such a way that he really and truly says no to God himself, and indeed to God himself and not merely to some distorted or childish notion of God" (p. 101). But by saying no to God we say no to ourselves and abort our true possibility of self-realization. "This 'no' is one of freedom's possibilities, but this possibility of freedom is always at the same time something abortive, something which miscarries and fails, something which is self-destructive and self-contradictory. Such a 'no' can give the appearance that the subject really and radically asserts himself only by this 'no.' This appearance can be given because the subject affirms in freedom a categorical goal absolutely, and in doing this he then misses everything else absolutely, instead of giving himself over unconditionally to the ineffable and holy mystery" (p. 102).

12. See Mahowald, "Feminism, Socialism and Christianity," pp. 31–49.

13. Cone, *Black Theology*, p. 41.

14. Freedom for service in a communal context is obviously at odds with what is often called the individual rights tradition of freedom. In the popular consciousness of our society that individual rights position has come to mean the freedom to choose at will between multiple choices and possibilities as long as our choices do not directly violate the rights of other people. In America, at least, this position is usually attributed to the philosophy of John Locke, although Locke would surely disagree with much popular understanding of his position. Locke based human freedom not in God, as I have done here, but in the individual person. He argued strongly for the right to private property to fulfill the need for self-preservation, and within the social contract the state has the duty to uphold that right (see Locke, *Two Treatises on Government*, pp. 129–141). But in practice this has tended to lead to a rugged individualism, with "every man for himself" as its slogan. As a result, Hodgson concludes, "Perhaps the most grievous and persistent failing of American society has been the tendency to neglect the well-being of the social whole to the advantage of private property and capital" (*New Birth of Freedom*, pp. 32–33).

15. Ibid., p. 79. The position I am advocating here is very similar to the position Hodgson takes in *New Birth of Freedom*. After a scholarly overview of the many traditions for understanding human freedom, he claims that from a Christian perspective freedom has what he calls three structures—subjective, intersubjective, and trans-subjective. "The subjective structure of freedom may be defined as autonomy; its intersubjective structure, as community" (p. 116). There is a certain individual autonomy that must not be lost sight of in Christian freedom. The individual as individual has the right to freedom and autonomy, and is not to be simply submerged in the will of the group. And yet autonomy is limited, while it is also made possible and authentic by the freedom of and for the community. As Hodgson puts it, "Subjective and intersubjective freedom are dialectically interrelated" (p. 146). Thus subjective and intersubjective freedom are mutual empowerments and correctives to each other, and both must be maintained in a fruitful

tension with each other. Hodgson talks about the trans-subjective and third dimension of human freedom as "openness to the future" (p. 109), and it is grounded in "a liberating transcendence." As I have argued, openness to the future is openness to the "liberating transcendence" of God, and it is in this third structure of freedom that the other two structures are grounded.

16. Elisabeth Moltmann-Wendel and Jürgen Moltmann, among others, propose this thesis. They write, "Just as the call for salvation from transitoriness to attain immortality could be heard in every corner of the ancient world, today a cry for liberation is shouted by the oppressed, the humiliated, and the offended in this inhuman world" ("Foreword," in Russell, *Human Liberation in a Feminist Perspective*, p. 11).

17. Schillebeeckx writes, "The concrete question with which mankind in history confronts the gospel now is: What do Jesus' message and praxis have to contribute to the overall effort to liberate humanity in the full sense of the term?" (*Jesus*, p. 623). Schubert Ogden similarly claims that the crucial question facing Christian theology over the next fifty years is "Can Christian faith in God be so understood that it positively includes the concern for human liberation in this world?" (*Faith and Freedom*, p. 13).

18. Marx and Engels, *Marx And Engels on Religion*, p. 42. While Marx believed that "criticism of religion is the foundation of all criticism," yet in a sense he assumed that adequate criticism had already been offered. Thus he spent little energy criticizing religion himself. His disparate thoughts about religion are scattered throughout his works. The book cited is an excellent collection of them.

19. There are many notable theological works which counter the notion of God as "up there" or "out there" and pose an alternative of a God who is present to human existence as "the ultimate ground of being," the "holy mystery" at the core of reality who turns us toward that reality. See, for example, Bonhoeffer, *Letters and Papers from Prison*; Tillich, *Systematic Theology*, 2: esp. pp. 5 ff; Robinson, *Honest to God*; Gilkey, *Naming the Whirlwind*, esp. pp. 147–178, 415–470; Rahner, *Foundations*, esp. pp. 44–89.

20. Freud writes, "We call a belief an illusion when a wish-fulfillment is a prominent factor in its motivation, and in doing so we disregard its relation to reality, just as the illusion itself sets no store by verification" (*The Future of an Illusion*, p. 31).

21. See Ibid., p. 16.

22. Ibid., p. 44.

23. Freud was certainly no admirer of religious education. However, his criticisms should serve as a sobering reminder that our task must be taken with great seriousness and care. A poor execution of it can have far-reaching and debilitating consequences. Freud wrote, "Think of the depressing contrast between the radiant intelligence of a healthy child and the feeble intellectual powers of the average adult. Can we be quite certain that it is not precisely religious education which bears a large share of blame for this relative atrophy?" (*Future of an Illusion*, p. 47).

24. I take this phrase from Ernst Käsemann's book of the same title. Käsemann, however, is far from being a naive claimer (see *Jesus Means Freedom*).

25. Walter Kasper claims, "It was Christianity that first recognized the dignity and worth, grounded in freedom, of every man irrespective of race, origin, position and sex. In this perspective it is possible to see the modern era [he is referring specifically to its quest for emancipation and liberation] to some extent as the historical expression of Christianity" (*Jesus the Christ*, p. 42).

26. Beginning with *Rerum Novarum* (1891), the social encyclicals of the Roman Catholic Church have moved carefully but increasingly toward greater social involvement by the Church and Christians in the struggle for justice and human freedom. Recent documents that evidence this increased social consciousness are the Second Vatican Councils, *Pastoral Constitution on the Church in the Modern World* (1965); the encyclicals *Mater Et Magistra* (1961) and *Pacem in Terris* (1963) of Pope John XXIII; *Populorum Progressio* (1967) and *Octogesima Adveniens* (1971) of Pope Paul VI; *Redemptor Hominis* (1979) of Pope John Paul II and many of his speeches during papal visits to Mexico, Poland, Ireland, and the United States (especially his U.N. address). A high point in this increasing consciousness is found in the often-quoted statement by the Second General Assembly of the Synod of Bishops (1971): "Action on behalf of justice and participation in the transformation of the world fully appear to us as a constitutive dimension of the preaching of the Gospel, or, in other words, of the Church's mission for the redemption of the human race and its liberation from every oppressive situation" (Gremillion, *The Gospel of Peace and Justice,* p. 514).

While the statement from the second meeting of CELAM (Conference of Latin American Bishops) at Medellin in 1968 has less official weight than documents issued by the Magisterium for the universal Church, the Medellin documents have had a major influence on the social involvement of the Catholic Church in Latin America, where almost half of the world's Catholics reside (see *The Church in the Present Day Transformation of Latin America in the Light of the Council* for the full text from Medellin). The statement from the third meeting of CELAM at Puebla (Feb. 1979) strengthened the positions taken at Medellin.

The General Assembly of the World Council of Churches meeting in Nairobi (Nov.–Dec. 1975) took "Jesus Christ Frees and Unites" as its theme. The Assembly adopted a strong position favoring an expanded role for the Church in the struggle for human freedom (for the Nairobi documents see Paton, *Breaking Barriers*).

27. The New Rite of Reconciliation (formerly known as Confession) was issued by the Congregation for Divine Worship on Dec. 2, 1973. It was written in response to the mandate of the Second Vatican Council that all the sacraments be revised with regard to the pastoral understanding and administration of them. The New Rite of Reconciliation is an excellent example of the expanded notion of sin I am advancing here. It clearly understands sin as both personal and social and calls for reconciliation to take place ideally in the context of a community celebration (see *Rite of Penance*).

28. I am anxious to insist on the personal dimension of sin. There is a danger, I believe, of emphasizing social sin to the point that all sin is attributed entirely to sinful social structures, and our personal capacity for sin is forgotten.

29. Robert M. Brown, *Theology in a New Key*, p. 74.

30. Baum, *Religion and Alienation*, p. 204. See Baum's work, especially pp. 197–208, for an excellent overview of sin as both social and personal, and his outline of the four levels of social sin. The rediscovery of social sin and the contemporary understanding of it can be seen as a reinterpretation of the traditional Christian notion of original sin. To live in the midst of sinful social structures is to be disposed inevitably toward sinfulness.

31. Kasper writes, "The maxim 'Save your soul' and the description of the pastoral ministry of the Church as 'cure of souls' are therefore at least one sided and can easily lead to flight in face of man's concrete needs, requirements and concerns" (*Jesus the Christ*, p. 207).

32. Baum writes, "The salvation of Jesus Christ has a bipolar, personal-and-social meaning, and any attempt to leave out one pole distorts the original message" (*Religion and Alienation*, p. 211).

33. Rahner, *Theological Investigations* 12:238.

34. Jon Sobrino writes, "Any initial attempt to approach the historical Jesus must be done from the standpoint of the Kingdom of God. . . . This thesis enables us to properly appreciate the activity of Jesus as liberation" (*Christology at the Crossroads*, p. 60). Leonardo Boff has made an excellent statement on Christology in which he takes the historical Jesus as his departing point. Boff's basic claim about Jesus is summarized in the title of his book (see *Jesus Christ Liberator*). But the understanding of Jesus as liberator is no longer confined, if it ever was, to "liberation" theologians. In fact, an amazing consistency has emerged across a very diverse spectrum of theologians in the use of the language of freedom or liberation to describe the meaning of the Christ event for us. Some examples: I have already given a statement from Kasper (see note 3). Schillebeeckx seems to use *salvation* and *liberation* interchangeably; for example, "Liberation or 'salvation,' then, is the conquest of all human, personal and social forms of alienation. . ." (*Jesus*, p. 624). Bernard Häring, perhaps the most respected senior Catholic moral theologian today, has recently published the first volume of a new trilogy on moral theology (his first great trilogy, *The Law of Christ*, was published some twenty-five years ago). The whole trilogy is entitled *Free and Faithful in Christ*. The central themes in his understanding of Christian ethics are freedom and fidelity. In the first volume he explains why. "The law of Christ is . . . essentially a law of perfect liberty" (Häring, *Free and Faithful in Christ*, p. 68).

35. A highly respected and often-cited source for an explanation of "the three main types of the idea of the atonement" is the work of Gustaf Aulén, *Christus Victor*. Aulén, in fact, divides the traditional understandings of the Atonement into two main types, 1) the classic, and 2) the Latin or satisfaction type. He then subdivides the latter into two schools of thought, one with a "subjectivist," and the other with an "objectivist," emphasis. While he claims to tackle the debate between the two main types "purely objectively" (p. 61), he in fact makes a strong argument, drawing from scripture and tradition, on behalf of the classic view, of which he says, "Its central theme is the idea of the Atonement as a Divine conflict and victory; Christ—Christus Victor—fights against and triumphs over the evil powers of the world, the 'tyrants' under which mankind is in bondage and suffering, and in Him God reconciles the world to Himself" (p. 4).

He explains later, "The deliverance of man from the power of death and the devil is at the same time his deliverance from God's judgement" (p. 59). On the other hand, he points to Anselm and his work *Cur Deus Homo* as the *locus classicus* for the Latin or satisfaction understanding of the atonement. In this view Christ, as a human being, makes satisfaction to God's justice for the sins of humanity and, by paying the price for our sins, redeems us from their consequences. In this model, according to Aulén, "the satisfaction must be made by man; and in Christ's atoning work" (p. 87). Aulén subdivides the Latin model into an objectivist school of thought, which emphasizes the saving work of Jesus Christ the human being on our behalf, and a subjectivist school which emphasizes the inner conversion required in the heart of the individual after the model of Christ our exemplar.

36. For the *locus classicus* for this understanding of the Atonement see St. Anselm, "Cur Deus Homo," in *St. Anselm Basic Writings*, pp. 171–288.

37. Gutierrez, who is often wrongly imputed with emphasizing only the social dimensions of freedom in Christ, insists that all freedom must begin with "an interior liberation, in an individual and intimate dimension . . . on a psychological plane . . . in relation to the real world of the human psyche as understood since Freud" (*A Theology of Liberation*, p. 30).

38. van Buren, *The Burden of Freedom*, pp. 42–43.

39. Hodgson, *New Birth of Freedom*, p. 70.

40. Robert M. Brown states this well when he writes, "To believe that Christ has redeemed the situation of every human life means that whenever any human life is threatened, we are called to bring down whatever principalities, powers, forces, or structures are responsible" (*Theology in a New Key*, p. 12).

41. The explanation of Thomas Aquinas may still be the clearest statement of this position. See, for example, Aquinas, *Summa Theologica*, 2 (Q. 2, Art. 9):1186.

42. See Abbott, *Documents*, 678–691.

43. Christian educators must not naively assume that we are the only ones who take human freedom seriously as integral to our purpose. On the contrary, not to pose human freedom as part of our purpose would call for condemnation of what we do as bad education. My own conviction that all education ought to be emancipatory began in my courses with Professor Dwayne Huebner at Teachers College, Columbia University, Fall 1973. Paulo Freire, to whom I am also much indebted, offers perhaps the most compelling argument in our day that all education must be "an exercise in freedom." ("Conscientization," p. 23). But Freire is far from novel in making such a claim. Plato's notion that the philosopher, having seen the light of immortal Truth, must return to the cave and lead others out to that Truth, is an argument in favor of education for freedom. The long liberal arts tradition, going back at least to the middle ages, has the assumption that such enlightenment will bring humanization. The humanistic school of education today, which again has ancient roots in Comenius, Locke, Rousseau, Pestalozzi, and Froebel, has the same goal in mind. Dewey's notion of education as beginning with the interests and potential of the students and causing them to grow toward realizing their possibilities is to understand education as being for freedom. And Whitehead argued consistently that "the dominant note of education at its beginning and at its end is freedom" (Whitehead, *Aims*, p. 31).

The point that underlies education for freedom is the fact that our vocation is to become human. Freedom is essential to being truly human. Therefore, education must respond to that human calling and help to promote it. The whole notion of education discussed in Chapter One is, in fact, an argument for a freeing and liberating educational activity regardless of what community sponsors the educating. When education is understood as a political activity that leads out pilgrims in time toward a future in which their human possibilities are ever being more fully realized, then human freedom must be seen as integral to the purpose of all educational activity.

44. Abbott, *Documents*, p. 682.

THE CONTEXT OF CHRISTIAN RELIGIOUS EDUCATION

Prologue

THE CONTEXT of Christian religious education is the third foundational issue to be addressed. In this Part, I offer reflections on the formative power of the social-cultural context, the community context most desirable for Christian formation, and the influence our educating might have in shaping the social environment.

John Dewey gave many descriptions of education, one of the most insightful being that all education is "the participation of the individual in the social consciousness of the race."[1] Formal education plays only a small part in our participation in and formation by the social consciousness of the race. Far more formative is the influence which arises simply from living within our social context. Clearly, then, we must be aware of how the social context forms the self-identity of ourselves and our students, and of how our educational efforts relate to that process.

We are formed to be who we are through interaction with our social and cultural context. In other words, self-identity is socially mediated and maintained. This claim is now considered a truism among contemporary sociologists, anthropologists, and psychologists. The main area of disagreement concerns the extent to which the social-cultural environment determines the identity of the self and the extent to which the individual self or selves can be creators and transformers of the context and not only the creatures of it.

The understanding previously outlined of Christian faith as a lived reality presupposes that such a faith can only arise, by God's grace, from one's total self. It cannot come from the head alone, nor from the heart alone, nor from one's pattern of action. It emanates from God's activity with the total person and from his or her self-identity. Christian faith is the expression of a Christian self. But if one's self-identity is shaped in large part by one's social and cultural context, then the process of coming to Christian self-identity, and thus lived Christian faith, requires a Christian social context. In other words, to come to be and remain Christian requires a process of socialization in the midst of a Christian faith community.

This insight for us long predates the research of the social scientists. In fact, the communal social context of Christian faith becoming is an expression of one of the fundamental principles of the Christian and Jewish traditions. It is as a people and within a people that we are saved. It is as a people that we have our convenant with God. Only in relationship can we become human, and only as members of a people can we become who God calls us to be. The research of the social scientists clarifies how this social process of human formation proceeds, and educators with the task of promoting lived Christian faith must be informed by their insights. In fact, one of the most favored approaches among religious education theorists today is the "socialization approach." I survey some of these theorists here and affirm their basic position. However, I am also convinced that intentional education cannot be merely an intensified form of socialization.

I was age twenty-two and attending an international student convention when I first became keenly aware of both the empowerment and the limitation of socialization on my life. At the convention I met and eventually became friends with a university student from Moscow. I was an enthusiastic young Catholic seminarian preparing for ordination, and he was a very dedicated member of the Communist Youth movement in his country. At first we spoke only polemical language, and each tried to show the other the error of his ways. Eventually we moved beyond our rhetoric and realized that we had some very similar concerns and commitments. As we said goodby, he, somewhat sadly, said, "If only you had grown up in my home in Moscow, you would have become a fine comrade in the movement." Taken aback at first, I eventually replied, "And if you had grown up in my family and village, you might well be a young seminarian now preparing for ordination." With that we both realized and admitted how our social context had formed us and wondered how much choice there had been in who we had become.

A Christian faith community is necessary for becoming Christian but, in addition, our religious education must promote a critical reflective activity in the midst of our socializing if our faith is truly to be our own and for the sake of the ongoing reform and faithfulness of the whole community.

6

On Becoming Christian Together

THE SOCIAL PROCESS OF HUMAN BECOMING

Like all specialized fields of study, investigation of socialization has given rise to its own particular terminology. Sometimes the words can hide the human process they are intended to describe. In an effort to avoid this, I shall first set out the meaning I intend for some of the key terms used below.

One confusing term is the word *socialization* itself. Psychologists, anthropologists, and sociologists investigate what this term represents from their own particular perspectives.[2] The psychologist concentrates on individual psychic consciousness as it emerges in interaction with a social context. The sociologist studies the phenomenon from the perspective of contemporary social structures and asks how people come to the self-understanding by which they fulfill their roles within society. The anthropologist, who may prefer the term *enculturation*, investigates the process from the perspective of the transmission of culture from one generation to the next by means of a commonly held symbol system. However, all of these scientists understand socialization as the process by which people come to be who they are by interaction with other people in their social environment.[3]

Self and *identity* are also key words in the language of socialization. Here I use the term *self* to include three related aspects of a person, namely, one's self-image, one's world view, and one's value system. *Identity*, on the other hand, is the experience of continuity and sameness we have of ourselves.[4] The two concepts are so closely related that here I prefer to speak of them together as *self-*

identity, meaning the continuous and stable awareness we have of our self-image, world view, and value system.

Two other closely related terms are *culture* and *society*. I understand *culture* as the patterned way of life produced by a people through which its members have guidelines for valuing, believing, and acting. Culture is embodied and expressed in a system of symbols, of which the most basic and pervasive form is language. By appropriating those symbols, people come to know the world and engage in it with the patterned behavior of their particular culture. *Society*, on the other hand, is the institutionalized order and organized arrangements people give to their way of being together. It expresses, as it also promotes, the patterned life of their culture. Although the two realities can be distinguished, cultural patterns and social structures cannot exist apart from each other. Thus I often use the term *social/cultural environment* to mean the whole ethos of a stable group of people. *Socialization*, then, is the process of being inducted into that ethos, which in turn produces our self-identity.

Socialization is a lifelong process because the human estate is always lived out in solidarity with other humans. But clearly the amount of influence people have upon us varies as we grow from childhood into adulthood. As our self-identity becomes more established, we become more discerning about the influence of other people on our lives. As a result, theorists find it helpful to distinguish between primary and secondary socialization. *Primary* socialization, centered in childhood, is the early formative process by which children form their first self-concept, value system, and world view by interiorizing the implied or demonstrated expectations, value systems, and world view of their primary adults. For a description of *secondary* socialization I rely on Berger and Luckman, who describe it as "any subsequent process that inducts an already socialized individual into new sectors of the objective world of his society."[5] As might be expected, primary socialization is more permanent and decisive than the secondary socialization of later life.[6]

How does the process of socialization actually take place? Various explanations have been offered to describe this complex human phenomenon. The one I follow here outlines three movements in the process: externalization, objectification, and internalization. These movements are separated only for the sake of analysis; in reality they are simultaneous and inextricably interrelated.[7]

EXTERNALIZATION

As human beings, we cannot live as self-contained units within the space our bodies occupy. We have an inner necessity to move outside ourselves and enter into relationship. As we externalize ourselves, our needs, desires, capacities, and possibilities, we enter with other people into a collectivity. Together we develop structures, artifacts, and arrangements to support our being together and to care for each other. We reach common agreements, expectations, and patterns for making meaning. We devise ways of expressing and maintaining those arrangements and agreements. Out of our corporate externalizations, cultures develop and societies emerge. If we were able to "keep to ourselves" and refuse to externalize, there would be no culture or society. But such a way of being here is impossible for us if we want to live humanly. Humans can be human only in relationship with other humans.

OBJECTIFICATION

Once we have externalized ourselves, the social structures and cultural patterns which we have created take on a "facticity" of their own. In a sense, they begin to exist without our volition, sui generis,[8] in their own right. The social world that arose from our externalizing activity and that of our predecessors becomes reified into its own objective reality, with a life of its own. We cannot wish it away and expect it to obey. It is very difficult to change it even a little, and our efforts must always begin with what is already there.

Since the collectivities we form are based precisely on expectations and agreements for the well-being of the group, these expectations and agreements must be met by the group's members. In this sense, every social reality establishes certain limits within which the members are expected to live.[9] Limits are not necessarily debilitating restrictions. They can be, and at times are, but as we saw in Chapter Five, even freedom can be found only within certain "limits." In this sense, our social/cultural environment enables us to live humanly precisely because it provides a collective horizon within whose boundaries we can find human solidarity.

In the interest of stability society erects elaborate systems of self-maintenance. These serve to keep people within, or to bring recalcitrant ones back within, its boundaries. Max Weber argued that physical force, specifically "legitimate violence," is the primary source of all social restraint and the one in which other systems of regulation are based.[10] The use of violence, or the threat of it, gets translated into legal and political systems. After violence as a means of social maintenance, Berger lists economic pressure and, to a lesser extent, "the mechanisms of persuasion, ridicule, gossip and opprobrium."[11]

If society is to maintain and regulate itself, then some individual or group must have authority to administer it in the name of the common good. Weber argued that authority in a society springs from one of three sources, which he called "traditional," "legal," and "charismatic." Traditional authority is grounded in the rules and customs of a time-honored and commonly held tradition. It reflects the mores of a people that have been sanctified by time and are powerful enough to dispose people to conform to them. Legal authority does not replace traditional authority, which is always present among every people. But when traditional authority is challenged, there emerge legal ordinances ideally based on rationality and made by people appointed to legislate. The authority of the legislators, Weber explains, is "by virtue of the belief in the validity of legal statute and functional 'competence' based on rationally created rules."[12] Charismatic authority, based on an "extraordinary and personal gift," is exercised by a great demagogue or prophet whose authority is grounded in the strength of personal charisma.

However, if the form and structure of our social world is to be maintained, it cannot survive for long on force or blind submission to authority. Its limits and regulations need to appear both reasonable and warranted to us. There is need, therefore, for "systems of legitimation"[13] and "plausibility structures"[14] that make present arrangements seem both legitimate and justifiable. Societies devise systems of legitimation and plausibility structures by creating ideologies that are appropriate to their needs. Simply stated, an *ideology* is a comprehensive world view that makes meaning out of the world as it is and thus legitimates and makes plausible a given social/cultural environment.[15] Ideologies find expression in and are maintained by "symbolic universes." By appropriating the commonly held and used symbols, of which language is the most basic, people come to appropriate the ideology of their group.[16]

INTERNALIZATION

Having externalized ourselves into culture and society, and culture and society having taken on a life of their own, the empowerments and limitations of that world are now taken back into our consciousness as our own. The possibilities and parameters that our social/cultural context appears to offer become our own perception of our possibilities and parameters. In other words, the objectified culture and society created by us and our predecessors become internalized as the basis of our own self-identity.[17]

George Herbert Mead laid the foundation for our understanding of this third movement with his notions of "role theory" and the "generalized other." According to his role theory, within society certain patterns or typifications of behavior become established and expected of its members. The "done thing" takes on mandatory status, and people are expected to "role play" to that mandate. The self emerges from interaction with these social expectations. There are two stages in the process. At first, one's self is constituted by the attitudes and expectations of individual others on a one-to-one basis.[18] But these significant others coalesce in our consciousness and come to constitute one "generalized other." Thus in the second stage, Mead explains, the "self is constituted not only by an organization of these particular individual attitudes, but also by an organization of the social attitude of the generalized other or the social group as a whole to which he belongs."[19]

The expectations of our generalized other do not remain outside of us. They are internalized as we identify with our significant others (and identify with them we must if they are significant for us). This means that the self is a reflected entity. C. H. Cooley's notion of the "looking-glass self"[20] is still a helpful image here. When we look out into society, we see reflected there certain attitudes toward us and expectations of us that we then take back within ourselves as our own attitudes toward and expectations of ourselves. In other words, the self-image, value system, and world view we come to is a reflection of the self-identity we see mirrored back to us from society. Thus the possibilities and parameters society poses for us from without *tend to become* the possibilities and parameters we allow ourselves from within.

I emphasize "tend to become" because we are not *determined* by the socialization process, and here we come to a crucial factor in understanding the three movements outlined. If our self-identity was totally determined by the socialization process, then change would be well-nigh impossible, and significant differences would be unlikely, at least among people who achieve self-identity within the same social/cultural environment. But change takes place. People are different. These two obvious pieces of empirical data point to the fact that the self is shaped but not determined by society and culture. Instead, the interaction between the self and society is dialectical, the person holding out, at least to some extent, for his or her individual identity.

THE SELF/SOCIETY DIALECTIC

There is, then, a dialectical relationship between a person and the social context. *Dialectical* is a much-used word, often with varying meanings. My understanding and use of it is in the Hegelian tradition. In that sense there are three moments to a dialectical relationship. First, there is a moment of affirming, of giving assent, of accepting. Next, there is a moment of refusal, of rejection, of denial. And last, there is a moment of moving beyond which incorporates and subsumes the first two moments into a higher synthesis. Thus to name the relationship between a person and the social environment as dialectical means that the person accepts and affirms some of the social influence and refuses and rejects some, and from this comes a movement beyond those two moments, for both the person and the social reality. The dialectical relationship means that the social/cultural context does not totally determine an individual's self-identity; in fact, the individual can give an altered shape to his or her social reality.[21] It is now beyond dispute among theorists of socialization that there is a dialectical relationship between the individual and the social world.[22] What the theorists disagree on is the extent and quality of the dialectic. Those who admit little possibility for individuals to refuse the determining power of society are often associated with the tradition of social science identified with Emile Durkheim. Durkheim, they claim, saw society as such an objectified reality, sui generis, that people inevitably act out their expected roles within it. The "collective consciousness" has a "coercive" power over "individual consciousness," and thus people become who society shapes them to be.[23]

Theorists who give more weight to the subjective side of the dialectic have traditionally been aligned with a Weberian school of thought. Max Weber's notion of charisma emphasizes that it is possible, at least for prophetic people, to break through the world that is socially mediated, refuse it, and pose an alternative.[24] The charisma of the prophet can summon other people to more critical self-knowledge, can release new energy and inspire people to take action in recreating their society, rather than maintaining it as it is and themselves as their social/cultural context would dictate. But Weber understood such prophetic activity to have definite limits. It is usually short lived and tends to become absorbed and "routinized" until it becomes an integral part of the status quo (albeit a slightly altered one). Given his position that the social sciences are value free, descriptive rather than prescriptive, Weber never took the step of advocating the promotion of such "prophecy."

The dialectic between people and their environment can vary depending on the individual's age, status, ego strength, and so on. My position is that the dialectic which takes place inevitably is typically quite minimal, but *it can be promoted.* I contend further that for the sake of individual autonomy and the ongoing reconstruction of society, both society and its members need the dialectic to be intentionally promoted. This requires, among other things, a process of critical education. In taking this position I am moving away from the social scientists already cited toward the position of the critical social theorists. I will deal with critical social theory in some detail in Part IV when I explain the critically reflective moment in shared praxis. For now, suffice it to say that the critical social theorists emphasize that the dialectic between a person and the social/cultural environment needs to be intentionally and actively promoted if people are to be transformers of their social world, and not merely the creatures of it. I take up this point again in the final section of this chapter, where I will argue that the dialectic taking place inevitably in a Christian faith community is not sufficient in either quantity or quality to transform reality in the direction of the Kingdom of God. Such a dialectic needs to be intentionally promoted, and in a Christian community, religious education has a vital part to play in promoting it.

To summarize the "social process of human becoming," it is clear that the self-identity we achieve is the result of interaction with our social/cultural environment. Our self-concept, our value system, the world view by which we act and make meaning are shaped, but not determined, by the process of socialization. There is a dialectical relationship between individuals and their society that promotes both the autonomy of the individuals and the restructuring of society. Thus the relationship between them is one of creative tension rather than opposition between two protagonists. The human phenomenon is always both social and individual, and neither can exist apart from the other. The dialectical relationship between the individual and his or her social environment typically remains quite minimal, but it can be actively promoted.

THE SOCIAL PROCESS OF CHRISTIAN BECOMING

Even our cursory venture into the literature of socialization is enough to make the point that what one is, what one does, what one remains, and what one becomes are a result, in very large part, of the interaction of the person with the social/cultural environment. Let us now relate this realization to the description of Christian faith outlined in Chapter Four.

When Christian faith is understood as believing, trusting, and doing in response to the Kingdom of God in Jesus Christ, then clearly such a way of being in faith, by the grace of God, emanates from and is an expression of the total person, of his or her self-identity. But if self-identity is shaped by interaction with a collectivity, then to become Christian selves requires that we have socializing interaction with a Christian faith community which is capable of forming us in such faith.[25] It is within a Christian social/cultural environment that people come to appropriate the symbols which carry forward the tradition. It is there that they encounter role models, a world view, and a value system that can be interiorized as their own Christian self-identity.

From the point of view of our quest for the context of Christian religious education, all of our educational efforts will bear little fruit unless they take place within a Christian faith community, and the more faith filled that community is, the more successful will be our educating for lived Christian faith.

CHRISTIAN SOCIALIZATION AND RELIGIOUS EDUCATION

A socialization approach to Christian formation is certainly not new in the Christian Church. The Catechumenate of the early Church was a process of socialization, and a very effective one.[26] While use of the formal Catechumenate declined, for long periods in the Church's history and for the majority of its members Christian formation was left to the influence of the home and surrounding society.[27]

There has reemerged in recent times, however, a school of religious education theory that recommends again and with fresh insights what is usually called a socialization model for doing intentional Christian education. This approach is in continuity with a long tradition but brings the insights, language, and discoveries of modern social science to develop its model. This recent expression of the socialization approach is itself over one hundred years old. In that time other recommended approaches have come and gone, but proponents of the socialization model have been increasing—and they have been growing in their understanding of it. In this section I will survey some of the key ideas of its major proponents. Together they offer a more complete explanation of the role of socialization in Christian formation, and their key insights will enable us to know our educational task more clearly in relation to our community context.

Horace Bushnell (1802–1876).   A man of great foresight and vision, Horace Bushnell is a forerunner of the modern theorists who recommend a socialization approach to Christian formation. His basic notions on Christian nurture were first written in the 1840s, but they have a remarkably contemporary ring. Bushnell had intuitively many of the insights later verified by research in the social sciences.

He devised his philosophy of Christian nurture in reaction to the revivalism of his day and more remotely in reaction against the "conversion" emphasis of traditional Puritanism. In the 1840s revivalism was again sweeping the land: Charles Finney was doing for mid-nineteenth-century America what Jonathan Edwards and George Whitefield had done for eighteenth-century America. Similar to its predecessors, the revivalism of the nineteenth century emphasized the total depravity of the human person and urged people to undergo a radical conversion to faith in Jesus Christ. Revival meetings were orchestrated to bring about such a cataclysmic "conversion experience."

The attitude of the revivalists toward Christian formation was that, because of human depravity, children could not grow up as Christians but could only come to the faith by being "born again." It was on this specific point that Bushnell began his criticisms of the revival movement and of the whole conversion syndrome. From the beginning he offered an opposing thesis: rather than waiting for conversion at a later age, the child is to be nurtured as a Christian from his or her earliest years. As he stated it more concisely later:

> What is the true idea of Christian Education? ... That the child is to grow up a Christian, and never know himself as being otherwise. In other words, the aim, effort, and expectation should be, not as is commonly assumed, that the child is to grow up in sin to be converted after he comes to a mature age; but that he is to open on the world as one that is spiritually renewed, not remembering the time when he went through a technical experience.[28]

Bushnell fired the first shots in 1838 from the North Congregational Church in Hartford, Connecticut, a church he was to pastor throughout his active ministry. His *Discourses on Christian Nurture* were published in 1847 and immediately caused heated debate. He was condemned for his "naturalism," that is, for implying that children can grow to Christian faith by some human process. The *Discourses* proved to be so controversial that the publisher withdrew them from circulation. His best known work—and the one for which he is most remembered—was published in 1861 under the title *Christian Nurture*. It still stands as a masterpiece in the annals of Christian religious education.

Bushnell grounded his argument for Christian nurture in what he called the "organic unity" of society, by which he meant that all the members of a given society have a common source of life that relates them intimately. The life of the adult world, and especially of the parents, flows into the children as life flows from the trunk into the branches of a tree. Because of this organic unity nurture takes place inevitably, and parents especially must see to it that the nurture their children receive is Christian. This places on them the responsibility of living lives that witness to Christian faith. "Have it first in yourselves; then teach it as you live it; teach it by living it; for you can do it in no other manner."[29]

As the home is the primary source of Christian nurture for Bushnell, parents must see to it that the atmosphere there is a thoroughly Christian one since "the children grow into faith, as it were, by a process of natural induction—only it will be intensely supernatural, because their faith is both quickened and grown in the atmosphere of God's own Spirit, always filling the house."[30] Christian nurture must start as early as possible (he even spoke of prenatal nurture) and is to be the bedrock of all later educational efforts.

Such sentiments place Bushnell squarely at the head of the socialization approach to Christian formation. His emphasis on the primary role of parents and the home in Christian formation is a lasting insight to which Christian educators must deliberately attend.

George Albert Coe (1862–1951).   Coe stands out as the greatest theorist of Protestant religious education for the first fifty years of our century. He was much influenced by the Social Gospel movement and by "liberal" theology. The very title of what is usually taken to be his most significant work—*A Social Theory of Religious Education*—clearly places him among the proponents of the socialization model. His statement that "the constant aim of elementary religious education should be to make conversion unnecessary"[31] shows that he is very much in the "nurture tradition" of Bushnell. But the greatest influence on his educational ideas was his friend and colleague John Dewey.[32] Dewey's notion that education is the participation of the individual in the social consciousness of the race and that it is to be grounded in the reconstruction of experience (which in turn is to lead to social reconstruction) are central themes in Coe's understanding of Christian religious education.[33] It was Coe, more than anyone else before or since, who brought the insights of Dewey to bear on the enterprise of church education.

Coe went beyond Bushnell's emphasis on the family and saw the whole social network of reality as the primary educator. He believed that all education should be a process of social interaction. "The central fact of the educative process is a growing Christian experience in and through the pupils' social interactions."[34] Social interaction is at the heart of Christian education not only as the process, but also as the content. "The primary 'content of the curriculum' is to be found in present relations and interactions between persons."[35]

In addressing the purpose of Christian religious education, Coe was the first to pose the crucial question with which we continue to struggle: "Shall the primary purpose of Christian education be to hand on a religion, or to create a new world?"[36] He favored the creation of a new world, which demands "creative" rather than "transmissive" education. Echoing Dewey, creative education places primacy on social reconstruction and employs transmissive processes only to that end. Such social reconstruction must further the "democracy of God" (a term Coe preferred to Kingdom of God) and is demanded because "reconstruction, continuous reconstruction, is of the essence of the divine work in and through the human."[37]

Beyond Bushnell, Coe's key insight serves to push religious educators out into concern for the whole social reality by which we are socialized. If we take the reality of socialization seriously, then our concern is not just the quality of Christian family life, but reform and reconstruction of the whole social ethos because it shapes us even as we are to shape it toward the democracy of God.

Coe and his companions gave rise to a whole movement in Protestant church education which is called both "liberal" and "progressive." He was certainly influenced by both the liberal movement in Protestant theology and the progressive movement in American education. He also lived long enough to see the high and low points of what he had helped to found.[38] With the financial exigencies caused by the crash of 1929, the progressive movement in religious education suffered a severe setback.[39] Its decline was augmented by the diminishing popularity of liberal theology and the rise of neo-orthodoxy.[40] However, Coe's insight concerning the social dimension and responsibility of Christian education was never lost. The line of continuity to its more recent proponents was kept alive, especially in the department of religion and education of Union Theological Seminary, New York. In leaner times (1940) its chairperson, Harrison Elliott, continued to sound the clarion call—"A recognition of the social nature of the self makes evident the importance of a social theory of education. . . ."[41]

C. Ellis Nelson.   When the socialization model seemed to be in its twilight days, at least in the theoretical writings, C. Ellis Nelson (also a chairperson of Union's department of religion and education) brought a fresh impetus to it and a deeper understanding of the role and need for socialization in Christian becoming. Writing some fifty years after Coe's *Social Theory of Religious Education*, Nelson could benefit from the research and insights of the social sciences that had taken place in the interim and could approach the phenomenon of socialization with a fresh perspective and a more critical eye.[42]

Nelson draws more from anthropology than from sociology in his analysis of the socialization process, concentrating on the means by which culture is transmitted in order to analyze the transmission of religious faith. He finds that "culture . . . is communicated through a process of socialization which 1) establishes a perceptive system in relation to a world view, 2) forms a conscience according to a value system, and 3) creates a self-identification out of personal relations within a social group."[43] These three dimensions are at the very heart of what it means to be a Christian and to live the Christian faith. Thus the "main contention" of his book "is that religion at its deepest levels is located within a person's sentiments and is the result of the way he was socialized by the adults who cared for him as a child."[44] Consequently, the "natural agency" for communicating Christian faith is a Christian faith community.

Nelson is careful to distinguish between a community of faith and the local church. The local congregation should be a community of faith, but he wisely refuses to make the two synonymous. Of a faith community he writes, "This communal reality is found in a self-conscious association of believers who are permanent enough in location to have face-to-face relationship with each other in a variety of situations and who are stable enough to function as a corporate group in carrying out their mutually developed plans and activities."[45] Within such a community of faith, "worship incubates faith. . . . fellowship makes faith operational . . . searching makes faith meaningful . . . confronting issues makes faith ethically alive."[46]

As Bushnell called attention to the family and Coe to the broader social ethos, Nelson stresses the formative power of the whole Christian community. For him everything the Church does, its whole way of being in the world and its way of being together, is educational. We educate by who we are as a faith community, and the quality of our corporate life together is our primary curriculum. Even the items that take priority in our annual budgets profoundly educate or miseducate the members of our congregations. But this realization is hardly a source of comfort for Nelson, who is far from naive about the quality of faith life in our churches. "The problem in main-line Protestant churches is that the process of transmitting a tradition is working too well—it is producing in the rising generation what the adults actually believe!"[47] Nelson clearly realizes the need for a critical dialectical activity in the midst of the Church's socializing.

John Westerhoff III.   John Westerhoff continues to recommend the socialization/enculturation approach to religious education and is its leading spokesperson today. There have been shifts and developments evident in his published works, but throughout there is the constant theme that "faith can only be nurtured within a self-conscious intentional community of faith."[48] This truth, in turn, calls for a new direction, a paradigmatic shift, in our practice and thinking about religious education. For Westerhoff the Church is still caught in a "schooling-instructional" paradigm for its ministry of education, and "the schooling-instructional paradigm is bankrupt."[49] We must shift instead to a "community of faith–enculturation paradigm."

In his earlier work Westerhoff proposed a process of "intentional religious socialization"[50] as the most effective approach to religious education. He now prefers the language of "enculturation" because "intentional religious socialization" implies "that someone does something to someone else."[51] If by this shift in language he is arguing the need for more mutual interaction in the socialization process, then I appreciate and agree with his point. I am convinced that the dialectic between the individual and the socializing community must be promoted rather than taken for granted. I am not so sure, however, that a shift to the language of enculturation will accomplish this.

Westerhoff understands education as "an aspect of socialization involving all deliberate, systematic and sustained efforts to transmit or evoke knowledge, attitudes, values, behaviors, or sensibilities."[52] Thus, it would seem, he understands intentional education as one agency among many of socialization in the community.

Because he is now claiming liberation theology rather than liberal Protestant theology as his theological base, Westerhoff gives even more urgency and depth to the role of religious education in what Coe and Dewey called social reconstruction. He emphasizes the role of catechesis (the term he now prefers[53]) to lead people to social action of "engaging in political activity to reform our economic system until justice and equity are achieved." He is acutely conscious of and draws attention to the "hidden curriculum" in much of our educating which has the consequence of maintaining sinful social arrangements. He insists that "the church needs to train its people to think politically, socially, economically, theologically and ethically."[54]

Arising from his knowledge of anthropology and his collaboration with Gwen Kennedy Neville, Westerhoff's most valuable insights include the role of liturgy, ritual, and symbol in Christian formation.[55] He emphasizes especially the formative influence of the "Church at worship" as it ritualizes and celebrates its faith together. "By uniting learning and liturgy, Christian education could be enhanced; more important, our faith could be transmitted to our children."[56]

Berard Marthaler. The theorists referred to so far have all spoken from the Protestant tradition of religious education. There has been a growing awareness of the socialization model within the Catholic tradition as well. Many recent universal and local Catholic Church documents concerning education have promoted the idea that it is the *ecclesia,* the whole faith community, that educates, and that Christian education must be understood within the mission of the total Church. This thinking is evident in the American Bishops Pastoral Letter, *To Teach as Jesus Did;* it underlies the *Rite of Christian Initiation of Adults* which is modeled on the Catechumenate of the early Church. The *General Catechetical Directory* protrays the work of catechesis as a pastoral activity of the total *ecclesia,* stating that renewal of catechesis "can in no way be separated from general pastoral renewal."[57]

Berard Marthaler is the best known Roman Catholic advocate for the socialization approach to religious education today, especially as that approach is understood in the Bushnell, Coe, Nelson, and Westerhoff tradition.[58] Marthaler points out that "every human being, except perhaps the feral child, is consciously or unconsciously a product of socialization."[59] He thus insists that "the community of faith with all its formal and informal structures is the chief catechist."[60] He outlines the different dimensions of socialization emphasized by anthropologists, sociologists, and psychologists. Then drawing upon the insights of all three sciences, he understands "catechesis" or "education in faith" (his preferred language) as having a threefold objective: "1) growth in personal faith; 2) religious affiliation; and 3) the maintenance and transmission of a religious tradition."[61] Thus psychology indicates that socialization is necessary for growth in personal faith, sociology shows how a faith community is necessary for religious affiliation, and anthropology sees socialization as necessary for the maintenance and transmission of a religious tradition.

A Dialectical Approach to the Socialization Approach

I now pose a dialectical critique of the socialization approach to Christian religious education. In other words, I begin by affirming the truth and value that is in it, I then point out its limitations, and finally (in Part IV) attempt to move beyond it while retaining its validity.

Socialization is a given among any collectivity of people: it takes place inevitably. Thus it would be foolish to debate whether or not we should have socialization in our Christian communities. They are very much correct and wise, then, the theorists who go further and argue that we should give intentionality to our socializing (and learn from the social sciences how to do this) so that our communities will be more likely to bring people to lived Christian faith.

The wisdom in their recommendation is all the more evident when we remember the description of Christian faith offered in Chapter Four. Such lived faith can only emanate, by God's grace, from a Christian self-identity. Because we come to self-identity through interaction with our social ethos, Christian self-identity requires that we be socialized by a community of Christian faith. That is where faith begins and is enabled to grow to maturity. The more faith*ful* our communities are, the more likely it is that younger members will come to authentic Christian faith and older ones continue to grow in it.

In Part IV I propose a shared praxis approach to Christian religious education. When the term *shared Christian praxis* is used in its broadest meaning (instead of as a technical name for a specific approach to intentional education), then it is truly a description of the shared faith life of a Christian community. A community of Christian faith is a group of people who share together in a common effort to live Christian praxis; that is, they are intentionally doing God's will in response to the Kingdom in Jesus Christ. Shared praxis as a specific approach to Christian education, like all other approaches, needs to take place in the midst of a broader shared Christian praxis, that is, a community of Christian faith.

There is a severe limitation, however, to the socialization model when the intentional activity of education is understood as no more than another agency of socialization and called only to socialize more effectively. In fact, Christian religious education that settles for being no more than an agency of socialization will be counterproductive to its true purpose. This is so because neither the dialectical relationship which arises inevitably between a Christian community and its surrounding social/cultural environment, nor the inevitable dialectic that exists between the community of faith and its individual members, are sufficient of themselves, in either quantity or quality, to promote maturity of Christian faith lived with human freedom in response to the Kingdom of God. The dialectical relationship between the Christian community and its social context, and between the community and its individual members, must not be left to chance, but should be intentionally promoted. Promoting such dialectics is the activity of raising critical consciousness. As I point out in Part V, this will take different forms at different age levels, but our religious education always has a vital part to play in this task. Far from socializing our students more effectively, our educational task will often require that we call in question and counteract much of the socialization that is already taking place. I have at least three reasons for claiming that such critical consciousness should be intentionally promoted by our religious education. In brief, it is necessary for the transformation of society, for the reformation of the Church, and for the maturation in faith of individual Christians.

First, if the Christian community is to be any more than a reflection of the broader social/cultural environment within which it exists, then a dialectical relationship must be promoted between the two. Otherwise we become part of the "plausibility structure" that legitimates society as it is, rather than a creative influence for its transformation. That the dialectic which takes place inevitably is far from sufficent in either quantity or quality is borne out by the evidence of history.

As pointed out in Chapter Five, Christianity has often been used as a source of legitimation for sinful social arrangement. Peter Berger explains that religion can be either world maintaining or world shaking; historically it has most often been the former.[62] Gregory Baum's work *Religion and Alienation* (a theological reading of some outstanding social theorists) offers a masterful expose of how Christianity can be controlling/alienating/legitimating or liberating/redemptive/critiquing. Baum points out that there is certainly nothing inevitable about it being used to the latter end, and in fact it has been used most often for the former. Of H. Richard Niebuhr's fivefold typology of the responses of Christianity to its social and cultural environment, only the fifth understands Christ as a "transformer of culture."[63] The other four, more prevalent in history than the fifth, all fail in their own way to promote the transformation of the social/cultural world that Niebuhr convincingly presents as the mission of Christ and of Christians. It would seem that if Christianity is to be a redemptive, humanizing, liberating force in the midst of history, a force that constantly points toward the Kingdom by living and promoting its values, then a constant dialectic must be maintained between Christian communities and their surrounding social environment.

In promoting this dialectic, we must remember that it is not a situation of "us" versus "them." We are both us and them. Here I want to emphasize the plurality of social worlds to which all of us belong and thus the great variety of socializing agencies that impinge upon us. In the face of our pluralistic society I find that the proponents of the socialization model are often less than realistic. If we lived in some idyllic situation in which all the socializing factors acting upon us were authentically Christian, then perhaps we could settle for "intentional socialization." But our Christian faith communities are only one part of our total social/cultural environment. We are members of many communities and segments of a pluralistic society. Ethnicity, geographical location, work site, political association, leisure ethos, and so on, as well as our Christian community affiliation, give us membership in a great variety of collectivities. All, together with the overall cultural environment that is common to them (e.g., the media culture), have their socializing influence on our lives. As a result, a great variety of world views and value systems, some of which are very contrary to a Christian self-identity, vie for our acceptance. Thus the socialization to which we are exposed inevitably might well have a decidedly un-Christian influence on us. Consequently, it is imperative that our religious education develop in us a critical capacity for discerning the mixed influences of socialization on our lives.

Perhaps an example from the media culture will highlight this point. It is estimated that by the time our young people reach the age of seventeen, they have viewed an average of fifteen thousand hours of television.[64] As yet we have not even begun to measure the far-reaching influence, for both good and evil, that such a powerful socializing force must have on our young people and on ourselves. Urie Bronfenbrenner claims that television is a more formative influence on children in our modern society than are their parents.[65] But television certainly cannot be trusted to socialize people into a value system and world view that are consistent with the Christian gospels. The advertising alone, and the excessive amount of it on programming for younger children, will go a long way toward producing bona fide members of a materialistic, consumer society. Anyone who would talk about any kind of socialization in our society must deal with this powerful reality of television and with the many other socializing forces in our media culture (books, magazines, newspapers, movies, etc.). Therefore, for the sake of both our own Christian self-identity and the transformation of our social reality, our ability for critical discernment must be heightened. Religious education has a vital part to play in such consciousness raising.

Secondly, a dialectical relationship must be promoted between Christian communities and their individual members for the sake of the ongoing reform of the Church. This second reason can be understood more clearly if we remember that, in an existential sense, the Church is not yet the Church. It is not yet what it is called out to become and will find its completion only in the Kingdom of God. Meanwhile, we have made only feeble beginnings toward becoming the Church, and we must not settle for that.

Chapter Three described the Church as "the community of those who confess Jesus Christ as Lord and Savior, who ratify that by baptism, and who point toward the Kingdom of God as preached by Jesus, by proclaiming in word, celebrating in sacrament and living in deed the Kingdom already and the Kingdom promised." The Church is to be a sacrament, an efficacious sign, of the Kingdom of God in Christ. To fulfill such a sacramental role, it must preach and celebrate the Kingdom (*kerygma*), it must embody the Kingdom within its own structures (*koinonia*), and it must actively engage in the world to make the Kingdom present already and help prepare the materials for its final completion (*diakonia*).

Indeed, there are dimensions and degrees of such a faith community in the Christian Church. On those beginnings we must build. But the Church is also, as Augustine put it so well, a *corpus mixtum* (a mixed body) that has the task of *semper reformanda* (always being reformed). The socialization that takes place inevitably between any community and its individual members is weighted much more toward the formative power of the group than to the transforming power of its members. In fact, the consequence of socialization is overwhelmingly one of maintenance of the status quo rather than of transformation.[66] In other words, a dialectical relationship in which individual members can be a transforming influence on the Church is far from inevitable.

There is a maintaining, conserving, and transmitting of our Christian tradition that is part of the task of Christian religious education. For that, "intentional socialization" is essential. But there is also a creating, liberating, and transforming activity that must take place as we come to appropriate the tradition and become creative members of the community to which it gives rise. Thus if the Church is to progress toward becoming what it is called to become, if it is to be *semper reformanda* rather than in a state of stagnation, then in the midst of our socializing our religious education must constantly promote a critical dialectical activity.

The third reason why a socialization process is not sufficient by itself to achieve our purpose pertains to the maturation in faith of individual Christians. To begin with, because the Church is still a *corpus mixtum*, it is far from inevitable that to socialize people into our present congregations will sponsor them toward Christian faith lived with human freedom in response to the Kingdom of God. Undoubtedly, some of our local communities are more faith filled than others, and our task is to build ever more faithful ones. But to only socialize people into our present communities may produce little more than a version of civil religion with some Christian trappings.

There is a story told that John Dewey once gave a lecture on the nature of utopia but never mentioned anything about its form of schooling or education. When asked how he could make such a glaring omission, Dewey is reported to have replied that utopia is where there are no schools; they will be unnecessary. I do not use the story to argue for schools as such, but to make the point that if our Christian communities already and fully constituted what the Church ought to be, then a socialization approach to religious education would be sufficient. Meanwhile, something more is needed.

That the ordinary dialectic between an individual and his or her Christian community is insufficient by itself to promote maturity of Christian faith would seem to be verified by the developmental research of James Fowler. It is clear from Fowler's work that the transition from any one stage of faith development to a higher stage is a dialectical process. The truth and goodness in any present stage needs to be affirmed and carried forward, but its limitations also must be recognized if a person is to move to a higher stage. If a dialectic/critique, calling into question the faith activity of one's present stage, does not take place, then a person is likely to remain at that stage. Such transition from stage to stage is far from inevitable. Fowler's research indicates that most people get caught in stage three of faith development, that is, a conventional faith that makes meaning according to what "they" say and do. In his research on moral development, Lawrence Kohlberg similarly found that a great majority of our society remain at a conventional level of moral development all their lives. This is a strong indication that the dialectic between an individual and the social environment which takes place inevitably is not sufficient by itself for promoting human development beyond a conventional level. A socialization approach can bring people to a conventional stage (where "they" are still primary), but conventional faith and morality are not yet one's own.

In pointing out the insufficiency of a socialization approach to Christian religious education, it is important to indicate, in fairness, that many of its proponents also recognize its limitation. This is true especially of Nelson[67] and Westerhoff.[68] But none of them has shown how intentional education within the community can be enhanced by socialization but also a corrective to undesirable socializing influences. They tend to perceive education as one aspect of the overall socialization process, rather than as something that promotes a critiquing and dialectical dimension in the midst of that process. They are perceptive in explaining how the whole Christian community educates but are not nearly as clear on how the community can be educated.

CONCLUSION: BOTH SOCIALIZATION AND EDUCATION

Christian religious education needs the context of a Christian faith community, and such a community needs a critical educational activity that is more than another agency of socialization.

Regarding the first part of our conclusion, both the insights of the social sciences and the Church's own lived experience indicate clearly that becoming Christian requires the socializing process of a community capable of forming people in Christian self-identity. We "become Christian together."

Then, regarding the second part of our conclusion above, far from relieving us of our specifically educational responsibility, awareness of the social process of Christian becoming only serves to make our educational task a little clearer. Harrison Elliott issued a wise warning some forty years ago that has often been forgotten: "A recognition of the social nature of the self makes evident the importance of a social theory of education, but it increases rather than decreases the problem of religious education." And he added, "There needs to be some factor in the religious educational process which will lift human life above its present standards and attainments. Otherwise, both education and religion leave individuals as good or as bad as the present level of society."[69] I claim that the "factor" Elliott called for must be an educational activity which, even as it draws life from the socializing power of the faith community, also promotes a dialectical relationship between the community and its surrounding social/cultural environment, and between the community and its individual members. It must raise the critical consciousness of Christians. In this sense it must be an education which enables people to be aware of, to affirm and to be thankful for, how Christian our community is already. But it must also question, critique, and bring to consciousness the not-yetness both in our own community and in the world, and call us forward toward being more faithful Christians in response to the Kingdom.

That education will be more than another agency of socialization is also far from inevitable. In fact, if education is guided only by the interest of socialization, then it typically educates people for acceptance of reality as it is socially mediated rather than for its transformation. Richard Shaull writes:

> Education either functions as an instrument which is used to facilitate the integration of the younger generation into the logic of the present system and bring about conformity to it, or it becomes "the practice of freedom," the means by which men and women deal critically and creatively with reality and discover how to participate in the transformation of their world.[70]

Critical and consciousness-raising education needs intentionality, and if such education is taken for granted it is likely not to take place.

For Christian becoming it is not a question of either socialization *or* education. We need a socialization process *and* a critical education in the midst of it. An educational approach that might be capable of including both will be explained in Part IV.

NOTES

1. Dewey, "Creed," p. 19.
2. John A. Clausen gives a helpful overview of how the different social sciences understand socialization from their own particular perspectives (see "A Historical and Comparative View of Socialization Theory and Research," in Clausen, *Socialization and Society*, pp. 22–45).
3. John Westerhoff offers a very useful description of socialization that draws insights from all three disciplines—sociology, psychology, and anthropology. He describes it as "the lifelong formal and informal ways one generation seeks to sustain and transmit its understanding and way of life; seeks to induct its young into and reinforce for its adults a particular set of values and responsible adult roles; and seeks to help persons develop self-identity through participation in the life of a people with their more or less distinctive ways of thinking, feeling, and acting" (Westerhoff and Neville, *Generation to Generation*, p. 39).
4. Erikson explains that ego identity "provides the ability to experience one's self as something that has continuity and sameness, and to act accordingly" (*Childhood and Society*, p. 42).
5. Berger and Luckmann, *Reality*, p. 130.
6. Brim explains that primary socialization is more effective because of the strong affective dimension that typically accompanies it (see *International Encyclopedia of the Social Sciences*, "Socialization: Adult Socialization," by Orville G. Brim, 14:555–560).
7. Peter Berger, both in his own work and in his collaborative work with Thomas Luckmann, offers a similar outline of the process. For their explanation they draw heavily on George Herbert Mead. Berger offers a helpful and succinct description of the three movements as follows: "Externalization is the ongoing outpouring of human being into the world, both in the physical and the mental activity of men. Objectivation is the attainment by the products of this activity (again both physical and mental) of a reality that confronts its original producers as a facticity external to and other than themselves. Internalization is the reappropriation by men of this same reality, transforming it once again from structures of the objective world into structures of the subjective consciousness" (*Canopy*, p. 4). I frequently disagree with Berger, however, in his unduly deterministic and mechanistic understanding of the process.
8. This idea is in Hegel's *The Phenomenology of Mind*, and it may well predate him. However,

Emile Durkheim is the social scientist who gave it central emphasis in sociology (see Durkheim, *The Rules of Sociological Method,* pp. 1–13).

9. Berger states this far too strongly when he writes, "Society is the walls of our imprisonment in history" (*Invitation,* p. 92). Although his statement is unduly deterministic, however, we must not underrate the truth that is in it.

10. See Weber, *From Max Weber,* pp. 77–78.

11. Berger, *Invitation,* p. 71.

12. Weber, *From Max Weber,* p. 79.

13. A "system of legitimation" is a stable social arrangement that serves to explain and justify social expectations as they presently exist.

14. A "plausibility structure" is the theoretical base a society gives its present arrangements so that they appear appropriate and for the best.

15. Berger explains, "The ideology both justifies what is done by the group . . . and interprets social reality in such a way that the justification is made plausible" (*Invitation,* p. 112).

16. See Berger and Luckmann, *Reality,* p. 94. For Berger and Luckmann mythology, science, theology, and philosophy are the primary symbol systems of universe maintenance and legitimation. They overlook, however, or fail to stress, that symbols can also be used to critique society. I later argue that they ought to be so used, but that such usage requires intentionality.

17. Berger explains, "Internalization . . . implies that the objective facticity of the social world becomes a subjective facticity as well. The individual encounters the institution as data of the objective world outside himself, but they are now data of his own consciousness as well" (*Canopy,* p. 17).

18. Mead describes the first stage as when "the individual's self is constituted simply by an organization of the particular attitudes of other individuals toward himself and toward one another in the specific social acts in which he participates with them" (*Mind, Self and Society,* p. 158).

19. Ibid., p. 158.

20. See Cooley, *Human Nature and the Social Order,* esp. p. 184.

21. Unlike the Marxist understanding, however, which is also in the Hegelian tradition, I do not understand a dialectical relationship to be inevitably antagonistic. For Marx the dialectic is always a process of conflict, pain, and struggle. It can well be so at times, but it can also be a gentle discerning process which, with proper support and sponsorship, can be peaceful and peace bringing.

22. Some notable examples of contemporary theorists who emphasize a dialectic between the self and its social world are Cottrell, Goslin, Inkeles, Danziger and Dreitzel (see Leonard S. Cottrell, "Interpersonal Interaction and the Development of the Self," in Goslin, *Handbook of Socialization Theory and Research,* pp. 543–570; David A. Goslin, "Introduction," in Goslin, *Handbook of Socialization Theory and Research,* pp. 5–12; Alex Inkeles, "Society, Social Structure and Child Socialization," in Clausen, *Socialization and Society,* pp. 74–129; Kurt Danziger, *Readings in Child Socialization,* p. 3; Hans Peter Dreitzel, *Childhood and Socialization,* p. 15.) Berger, too, insists that there is a dialectical relationship between the individual and the social context. In his work with Luckmann they write that socialization is not "a one sided, mechanistic process. It entails a dialectic between identification by others and self-identification, between objectively assigned and subjectively appropriated identity" (*Reality,* p. 121).

   However, Berger's understanding of dialectic is a weak one in which the shaping power of society is emphasized much more than the creative and transforming ability of the individual. This is evident in such statements as, "It is possible to sum up the dialectic formation of identity by saying that the individual becomes that which he is addressed as by others" (*Canopy,* p. 16). I place him on the minimal side of the dialectic continuum. His talk of "man as player" leaves little room for an authentically critical activity for the individual and sees him or her as capable of no more than learning to "play the system" (see *Invitation,* ch. 6).

23. While this is the typical interpretation of Durkheim in the English-speaking world, Theodore Steeman argues convincingly that it is a misrepresentation of Durkheim's position. He interprets Durkheim as being far less deterministic than is usually claimed (see "Durkheim's Professional Ethics," pp. 163–181).

24. See Weber, *The Sociology of Religion,* pp. 45–59.

25. We have arrived at this conclusion on the basis of general socialization literature. It should also be noted, however, that there is a significant body of empirical research literature on the question of religious socialization and its influence on faith formation. A general conclusion of that research is that socializing agencies, especially the influence of the home on primary socializa-

tion (though later environments can also have significant formative influence), are the major influences on the religious attitudes of youth (see, for example, Greeley and Rossi, *The Education of Catholic Americans;* Carrier, *The Sociology of Religious Belonging;* Argyle and Beit-Hallahmi, *The Social Psychology of Religion;* Flynn, *Some Catholic Schools in Action;* Fahy, *Factors Predictive of Religious Outcomes in Australian Catholic Secondary Schools.*).

If we bring a developmental psychology approach to the question of religious formation, we can draw upon Fowler's work to substantiate our claim that Christian faith, like all other human being, becoming, and doing, is rooted in, made possible by, and limited by interaction with our social/cultural context. For Fowler, as for Piaget and Kohlberg, human development comes from the interaction of the person with the social environment. A look at any of the stages of faith development as Fowler outlines them makes it evident that coming to each stage of faith and being maintained in it is a process of interaction with the "faithing" community within which one is being socialized. This is especially obvious for the first three stages of faith development, but it is also true of the later stages whose development is impossible without interaction with communities of faith.

26. The high points of the Catechumenate were approximately from the beginning of the third century to the end of the fifth. A detailed account of its stages can be found in the *Decree of Hippolytus* (see Easton, *The Apostolic Tradition of Hippolytus,* pp. 41–45). The unfolding of the stages over a period that could last up to three years was a gradual socializing of the catechumens into membership in the Christian community. The community was seen as the primary educator.

27. See, for example, Josef Jungmann's account of catechesis in the last Middle Ages ("Religious Education in Late Middle Times," pp. 38–62).

28. Bushnell, *Christian Nurture,* p. 4.

29. Ibid., p. 71.

30. Ibid., pp. 346–347.

31. Coe, *A Social Theory of Religious Education,* p. 181.

32. Dewey and Coe were "neighbors" for many years while Coe taught at Union Theological Seminary in New York (1909–1922), and Dewey taught across the street from Union at Columbia Teacher's College (1904–1930). After Coe retired from Union in 1922, he moved over and taught at Teacher's College until his retirement five years later.

33. The strong influence of Dewey on Coe is obvious, for example, in his description of Christian education: "Christian education . . . is the systematic, critical examination and reconstruction of relations between persons, guided by Jesus' assumption that persons are of infinite worth" (Coe, *What Is Christian Education?,* p. 296).

34. Coe, *A Social Theory of Religious Education,* p. 80.

35. Ibid., p. 102.

36. Coe, *What Is Christian Education?,* p. 29. Coe's question was taken as the theme of the second annual Boston College Symposium on Foundations of Religious Education, April 1978. It is interesting to see how contemporary scholars (Mary C. Boys, Maria Harris, C. Ellis Nelson, Letty M. Russell, and Dwayne Huebner) respond to Coe's question some fifty years later. For the Symposium papers see O'Hare, *Tradition and Transformation in Religious Education.*

37. See, Coe, *What Is Christian Education?,* pp. 33–54.

38. The beginning of the "progressive religious education movement" in mainline Protestant churches is usually dated with the founding of the Religious Education Association in 1903. Both Coe and Dewey were founding members.

39. One of the main thrusts of the progressive movement was to train professional religious educators well versed in modern pedagogy. These were hired by many congregations to direct their education programs. But with the financial crash of 1929 and the decrease in church budgets, the "directors of religious education" (or whatever their title) were often the first to go.

40. One of the earliest and most significant shots fired against the progressive movement and on behalf of a new-orthodox position was H. Shelton Smith's essay "Let Religious Education Reckon with the Barthians" (originally published in *Religious Education* 24 (January, 1934):45–51, now found in Westerhoff, *Who Are We?,* pp. 97–109). Smith gave a more complete critique of the progressive movement in his later work, *Faith and Nurture.*

41. Elliott, *Can Religious Education Be Christian?,* p. 219.

42. It would seem that Nelson was better grounded than his predecessors had been in the social science literature on socialization. It was from in-depth study of that literature that he came to recommend a socialization approach: "From my study of cultural anthropology and sociology, I

discerned that what these social sciences were describing as the socializing process (or acculturation process) was the process by which faith and its meaning was transmitted by a community of believers. . . . Therefore by using the analytical methods of the social scientists who study human communities we could see how this process operated and use it for understanding and improving our communication of the Christian faith" (Nelson, *Where Faith Begins*, pp. 10–11).

43. Ibid., p. 95.
44. Ibid., p. 9. Nelson explains: "My thesis is that faith is communicated by a community of believers and that the meaning of faith is developed by its members out of their history, by their interaction with each other, and in relation to the events that take place in their lives" (Ibid., p. 10).
45. Ibid., p. 98.
46. See Ibid., pp. 102–120.
47. Ibid., p. 202.
48. Westerhoff, *Will Our Children Have Faith?*, p. 52.
49. Ibid., p. 23.
50. Westerhoff and Neville, *Generation*, p. 42.
51. Westerhoff, *Will Our Children Have Faith?*, p. 79.
52. Ibid., p. 17.
53. See, Westerhoff, "A Call to Catechesis," pp. 354–358.
54. Westerhoff, *Will Our Children Have Faith?*, pp. 66, 67.
55. See, especially, Neville and Westerhoff, *Learning Through Liturgy*.
56. Westerhoff, *Will Our Children Have Faith?*, p. 52.
57. *The General Catechetical Directory*, p. 12. Berard Marthaler in his scholarly commentary on the *Directory*, writes, "Though the Directory does not use the term, the educational role it attributes to the ecclesial community is in effect a description of 'socialization.'" (*Catechetics in Context*, p. 65).
58. Gabriel Moran lays great emphasis on the place of the community, the "religious body," in religious education (see, for example, *Religious Body*). However, he avoids the language of socialization, and it would not be accurate to include him as a proponent of the socialization model as described here.

    James Michael Lee is the Catholic theorist of "religious instruction" (Lee's preferred language) who has done most to call attention to the social sciences as the basis for developing religious education (see Lee, *The Shape of Religious Instruction;* and *The Flow of Religious Instruction*). But Lee concentrates on the actual instructional process that takes place within an intentional educational setting rather than on the formative influence of the broader social/cultural context. I later criticize the theorists surveyed thus far for their lack of attention to the specific form or shape that intentional educational activity might take within the socialization approach. That criticism could never be levelled against Lee. Attention to what he calls the "teaching-learning" act is a central concern of his work.
59. Marthaler, "Socialization as a Model for Catechetics," in O'Hare, *Foundations*, p. 66.
60. Ibid., p. 89.
61. Ibid., p. 77.
62. See, Berger, *Canopy*, p. 100.
63. See Niebuhr, *Christ and Culture*.
64. It is also estimated that by age eighteen a person will have seen 350,000 commercials (see Kauchak, "T.V. Ads: What Are Youngsters Buying?," pp. 530–532, esp. p. 531).
65. See Bronfenbrenner, *Two Worlds of Childhood*, pp. 100–118.
66. In taking this position, I am again being informed by the critical social theorists. They argue that the socialization taking place inevitably in any society is more determining than enabling, more maintaining than transforming. Jürgen Habermas argues that "the process of socialization takes place within structures of linguistic intersubjectivity: it determines an organization of behavior tied to norms requiring justification and to interpretive systems that secure identity" (*Legitimation Crisis*, p. 43). But these "interpretive systems that secure identity" have the interest of what Habermas calls "practical" control, in that their intention is to maintain a common tradition (see Habermas, *Interests*, p. 176). Thus socialization, as it typically takes place, has the consequence and the active interest of maintaining and perpetuating present social arrangements.
67. Nelson's grave concern that socialization is producing in the young what the adult members of our congregations actually believe (see note 47) shows clearly that he is aware of the limitations of the socialization approach. He looks to the sermon as the source of a constant, critical element

for the congregation. Of the pulpit he says, "in the long run it is the only way for a prophetic voice to be heard." (*Where Faith Begins,* p. 191). But while we can hope for more prophetic voices from our pulpits, the traditional division of labor between priests and prophets advises us to be realistic in our expectations. Nelson does not outline an intentional educational activity that might also be a "prophetic voice," nor does he indicate the part intentional educational activity might play in helping to build Christian faith communities.

68. Westerhoff constantly warns that the Christian community must not be a mere reflection of the surrounding society. His "continuing haunting question" is whether or not we can turn local churches into communities of faith that can be entrusted with the task of enculturating people into authentic Christian living (see *Generation,* p. 70). But again, although he knows that the community educates, he has not as yet outlined the role that intentional education might play in helping to educate the community toward Christian faith. He has given some broad guidelines for building educational programs, but he continues to see education as an aspect of socialization. What kind of an aspect it is and its relationship to the socializing process are not clear. In fact, he is so sweeping in his rejection of the "schooling-instructional" paradigm that it is difficult to envision the form intentional educational activity might take within his "community of faith-enculturation" paradigm.

69. Elliott, *Can Religious Education Be Christian?,* pp. 219, 225.

70. Richard Shaull, "Foreword," in Freire, *Oppressed,* p. 15.

AN APPROACH TO CHRISTIAN RELIGIOUS EDUCATION: SHARED PRAXIS

Prologue

THE FIRST Christians told a story about the risen Christ that Christian educators would do well to remember. It is recounted by the evangelist Luke (24:13–35).

The story goes that on the first Easter Sunday two of Jesus' followers were making their way to Emmaus, a small village about seven miles from Jerusalem. As they went their way, they discussed "all that had happened" (14) over the previous days, and, as might be expected, it was a "lively exchange" (15). Who should join them but the risen Jesus, who began "to walk along *with* them" (15). For whatever reason, they were "restrained from recognizing him" (16). He entered into their company by inquiring, "What are you discussing as you go your way?" (17). Somewhat distressed and a little impatient at the stranger's ignorance, they wondered where he had been. Surely everyone in Jerusalem knew "the things that went on there these past few days?" (18). Rather than seizing this obvious opportunity to disclose his identity (Who knew better than he what had gone on there?), he inquired "What things?" (19). They told him the story as they knew it and their dwindling hope that "he was the one who would set Israel free" (21). Now, adding confusion to their disappointment, "some women" (22) of the group were spreading the "astonishing news" (22) that "he was alive" (23).

Jesus cajoled them for not looking at these recent events within a broader context, and in response to their story and hope he told them an older Story and a larger Vision. "Beginning, then, with Moses and all the prophets, he interpreted for them every passage of Scripture which referred to him" (27). He pointed out that the Messiah had to "undergo all this so as to enter into his glory" (26). Surely now they would recognize him. They did not, and he continued to resist telling them. But he had obviously aroused their curiosity, for they "pressed him" (29) to stay the night in their company. He agreed.

At table that evening he blessed and broke bread for them and "with that their eyes were opened and they recognized him; whereupon he vanished from their sight" (31). Then the pieces of their puzzle fell in place, and they remembered how their hearts had "burned" inside them as he talked "on the road." But instead of spending time in self-reproach for not seeing sooner, they set out immediately for Jerusalem (a hazardous journey by night) to tell "the Eleven and the rest of the company" (33). They told the story of what had happened "on the road" and "how they had come to know him in the breaking of bread" (35).

This story has been much commented on by biblical exegetes and interpreters. I offer an educator's reflection. I see the risen Christ portrayed here as the educator par excellence. He begins by encountering and entering into dialogue with the two travellers. Rather than telling them what he knows, he first has them tell the story of their recent experience and what their hopes had been. In response he recalls a larger Story of which their story is part, and a broader Vision beyond what theirs had been. We might expect the typical educator to tell them now what "to see," but he continues to wait for them to come to their own knowing. He spends more time in their company. Surely the dialogue on the road carried over into their table conversation. Eventually, in their table fellowship together, they "came to see." Thereupon they set out immediately to bear witness to what they now knew.

Here the risen Christ educates by encountering, entering into dialogue, inviting people to tell their stories and visions, reminding them of a broader Story and Vision. Then still refusing to "tell them" what to see, he waits gently for them to see for themselves. This story is a fitting memory as we begin Part IV, which suggests one possible approach to doing Christian religious education. It has been a significant influence on my thinking, and I have returned to it many times since I first began to devise such an approach.

As all educators who attempt to practice the art well know, there is no easy and sure way of doing education of any kind. Education is a human endeavor in which, to use Bonhoeffer's phrase, there is no "cheap grace." As Whitehead once cautioned, "I merely utter the warning that education is a difficult problem, to be solved by no one simple formula."[1]

There can never be a simple formula, technique, nor "how to do it" for education of any kind. We educators seem to have more than the usual penchant for jumping on new bandwagons that come along promising an easy solution. But easy solutions are sure to disappoint us.

In this Part, I describe a "shared praxis approach" to Christian religious education. I shudder to think that it could be made to sound like another panacea. In my enthusiasm for it, born of some apparent success in my own praxis, I may sometimes make strong claims for its possibilities. But I know its limitations, having experienced them, too, in my own praxis.

Some preliminary remarks about a shared praxis approach may help to avoid misunderstandings later. To begin with, the word *approach* is important. I avoid calling shared praxis a theory or a method because, in a definite sense, I intend it to be both.[2] Attempting to avoid the traditional dichotomy between theory and practice and to capture the twin moments of praxis (reflection and action), I call it an approach—in other words, an informed reflective (theory) manner of doing (method) Christian religious education.

I also favor the term *approach* because it has the possibility of pointing toward and questioning the underlying outlook and disposition that the initiator brings to an enterprise. The educator's underlying attitude is perhaps the most crucial variable in shaping the activity of Christian religious education. Our attitude shapes, in large part, our way of being with students, and ultimately education is a way of being with people. How we perceive such foundational issues as the nature, purpose, and context of Christian religious education will decide the basic outlook we bring to the task. That attitude is decisive in determining whether we are "with" or "over" people in the educational setting; whether we attempt to educate as leading out people to their future possibility of union with God and each other in Christ, or whether we socialize them into a taken-for-granted world, both ecclesial and social.

If Christian religious education is to lead people out in response to the Kingdom of God in Jesus Christ toward lived Christian faith and human freedom, then our most appropriate underlying attitude is to see ourselves as brother or sister pilgrims in time *with* our students. Whether one favors a shared praxis approach or not, this underlying attitude toward ourselves and our students is most appropriate for our enterprise, however it is done.

I offer what I have come to know about a shared praxis approach because it has the possibility of responding to the nature, purpose, and context of Christian religious education as previously described. However, I hasten to add that what I call a shared praxis approach is far from being a new creation *ex nihilo*. On the contrary, it arises, as it should, from my own praxis and from the praxis of many other religious educators. It comes from reflection on what many of us are already doing. In fact, shared praxis is, to some extent, a drawing together of many trends and insights that have been evident in religious education over the past eighty years. There are many shoulders on which to stand even as we attempt to reach beyond them.

To religious educators who are already doing Christian education by shared praxis, or by some variation of it, the statement here should resonate with their own experience and practice. I hope that offering a language to describe what we do and some clarity about it may enable us to be more deliberate, consistent, and effective in our educational praxis. For those who approach Christian religious education very differently, the statement should be sufficiently challenging to cause reflection on and greater clarity about why and how they educate.

The following chapters are not a final word. On the contrary, any praxis approach must, by its very nature, be a constantly self-renewing process where theory is clarified in praxis to empower further praxis. Only by doing it reflectively can we come to know more clearly how to do it. Thus people who are new to this approach will not "know" how to do religious education by shared praxis at the end of these chapters. Praxis can never be "known" from a book. But a book *can* provide some ideas about how to proceed.

Last, it should be clear that I propose shared praxis as a possible approach to religious education in the Christian tradition. Beyond that I make no further claims for it at this time. Shared praxis may well have fruitful possibilities for education in other religious traditions. But there are major world religions whose telos is not overt engagement in the world in response to anything like the Kingdom of God as preached by Jesus Christ. Their purpose might not be served at all by a shared praxis approach in their religious education. (However, I am confident that it is appropriate for religious education in the Jewish tradition.)

Part IV is the largest section of this work (four chapters), and in many ways it is the heart of my own statement about Christian religious education. But it is informed by, as it has also informed, the other five Parts. In summary, Chapter Seven raises the question of epistemology which is at the bedrock of all forms of education; Chapter Eight presents a brief historical overview of the notion of praxis as a way of knowing; Chapter Nine explains in detail the essentials of a shared praxis approach; and Chapter Ten outlines and gives examples of the five pedagogical movements I presently use when doing shared praxis in Christian religious education.

In Search of a "Way of Knowing" for Christian Religious Education

THE EPISTEMOLOGICAL QUESTION

Epistemology is the philosophical discipline which studies the nature and source of knowing and the reliability of claims to knowledge. As human beings, we are capable of coming to some conscious knowledge of ourselves and of our world. But what is the nature and scope of our knowing? What is its basis? Given the ability we have for self-deception, can we depend on our knowing process? These are the basic questions investigated by epistemology.

Epistemology is of pressing interest to educators. All education, by the very nature of the activity, is intended to promote a "knowing" of some kind. It follows, then, that at the bedrock of all education an understanding of the nature and scope of knowledge has been assumed or explicitly chosen.[3] Educators usually pose the epistemological question as, How may knowing be promoted? But the answer to that question is shaped by our understanding of a prior one, What does it mean to know?

Questions about the nature, source, and reliability of knowledge have been debated by Western philosophers since at least pre-Socratic times. Attempts to answer them have given rise to divergent schools of thought. In fact, since epistemology is such a foundational philosophical issue, the differences between the great schools of philosophy can invariably be traced, at least in part, to differences in epistemologies. The lines of debate were laid down at the dawn of Western philosophy and have been repeating themselves with amazing consistency in one form or another ever since. Modern differences between rationalists and empiricists, idealists and realists, positivists and skeptics have a long history.[4]

Over the history of philosophy many different ways of knowing oneself and the world have been proposed, each with its own criteria for judging the reliability of what is known. Thus if educators are consciously to select a way of knowing upon which to base their teaching, a choice must be made among different epistemological positions. Clearly, educators must give primary consideration to adopting a way of knowing that is capable of promoting the purpose for which their particular educational endeavor is intended. Thus to answer the epistemological question for Christian religious education, we must be mindful first of the nature and purpose of our enterprise and the context within which it takes place.

I have described Christian religious education as a political activity with pilgrims in time that deliberately and intentionally attends with them to the activity of God in our present, to the Story of the Christian faith community embodied in that present, and to the future Vision of God's Kingdom, the seeds of which are already among us. It has the task of attending deliberately to and holding in fruitful tension the three dimensions of our existential time—past, present, and future. Our purpose in such educational activity is to lead people out toward a lived response to God's Kingdom in Jesus Christ. That response, which is possible only by the grace of God, is a life of Christian faith. Lived Christian faith is a way of knowing oneself, God, and the world in Christ; a relationship with God, other people, and the world in Christ; and a way of actively engaging in the world with others in response to the values of the Kingdom of God as preached and made possible by Christ. Our educating for such a lived faith should also have the consequence of promoting human freedom—spiritually, psychologically, and socially. It needs to arise from a Christian faith community and return to that community to increase its faithfulness, rather than simply maintaining what is already there. Whatever way of knowing we adopt, it should be capable of promoting an educational activity of such nature and purpose.

In attempting to find such a way of knowing, it is fitting to begin with our scriptures. The Bible offers nothing like an explicit epistemology in the sense of an articulated theory of knowledge. Yet it speaks constantly about "knowing the Lord" and about how such knowing is promoted. Thus we can detect the way of knowing it proposes (in a sense, its implied epistemology) by investigating what it means by knowing the Lord and how it describes that knowing process.

I am not implying that we can simply settle for what appears to be a biblical way of knowing and consider our problem solved. Scripture never provides short-cuts to such truth. Just as we question much of biblical cosmology, so, too, in epistemology we cannot ignore the past two thousand years of human inquiry and reflection. But the way of knowing we choose as a bedrock for Christian religious education must be consistent with and capable of promoting a knowing the Lord as that is understood in Scripture.

THE BIBLICAL WAY OF KNOWING

THE HEBREW SCRIPTURES

The Hebrew verb for "know" is *yada*. In the Septuagint the Greek verb used for *yada* is *ginoskein*. But in Greek philosophy *ginoskein* has a predominant meaning of "intellectual looking at" an object of scrutiny and strongly connotes objectivity. If *ginoskein* is understood this way in the Septuagint, then it is not an accurate translation of *yada*. For the Hebrews *yada* is more by the heart than by the mind, and the knowing arises not by standing back from in order to look at, but by active and intentional engagement in lived experience. It is significant that the Hebrews had no word that corresponds exactly to our words *mind* or *intellect*. Comparing *ginoskein* and *yada*, Rudolf Bultmann states, "the OT usage is much broader than the Greek, and the element of objective verification is less prominent than that of detecting or feeling or learning by experience."[5] Whereas the Greeks strove for objective knowledge wherein the subjective dimensions of knowing are obliterated as much as possible, this was certainly not true for the Hebrews. "On the contrary," writes Bultmann, "the OT both perceives and asserts the significance and claim of the knowing subject. . . . It is in keeping with this that we do not find in Israel any knowledge which objectively investigates and describes reality."[6] As a consequence—and this is significant—"knowledge is not thought of in terms of a possession of information. It is possessed only in its exercise or actualization."[7]

Another indication of the deeply experiential and relational sense the Hebrews had of what it means to know is that the verb *yada*, when given a direct personal object, is sometimes used for lovemaking. The Book of Genesis states that Adam "had knowledge" of Eve (see Gen. 4:1, 25; also Num. 31:18; Judges 21: 12; etc.). It is significant also that the past participle of *yada* is used for a good friend or confidant (see Ps. 31:11 ff.; 55:13 ff; 88:8 ff).

The Hebrew scriptures speak about "knowing the Lord" as an activity in which God takes the initiative, and this initiative is always encountered in lived experience—in events, in relationships, in creation, and so on. The God of the Hebrews is a God in the midst of history rather than removed from it. God's reaching out calls for a response of the total person, an entering into relationship with God in which God's mighty acts are recognized and sovereignty accepted (see Deut. 11:2; Isa. 41:20; Hos. 11:3 ff). Further, knowledge of the Lord demands active *acknowledgment* of the Lord, and that in turn requires obedience to God's will. In fact, God is not *acknowledged* and thus not known unless God's will is done by the person in response to the experience of God.[8] Being possessed by God demands the response of obedience (see Ps. 119:79).

Because this is what it means to "know the Lord," the fool or ignorant one in the Bible is not the person who does not "know about" intellectually, but rather the one who fails to do God's will. Ignorance in the biblical sense is therefore synonymous with guilt. Bultmann explains, "Thus knowledge has an element of acknowledgment. But it also has an element of emotion, or better, of movement of will, so that ignorance means guilt as well as error. . . . To know Him or His name is to confess or to acknowledge Him, to give Him honour and to obey His will."[9] Punishment is meted out for the sinner's foolishness and on the house of everyone "who *knows* not God" (Job 18:21). On the other hand, as the Book of Jeremiah states, "He did what was right and just, and it went well with him. Because he dispensed justice to the weak and the poor, it went well with him. Is this not true knowledge of me? says the Lord" (Jer. 22:15c–16).

In summary then, knowing God in the Hebrew sense arises from lived experience, requiring that the person is possessed by Yahweh, acknowledges in mind and heart God's sovereignty, and lives a response by doing God's will. It is in experience and response that God is truly known.

THE NEW TESTAMENT

In the New Testament two verbs are commonly used for "to know"—*ginoskein* and *eidenai*. Although there are some shades of difference in their meaning, they are usually used interchangeably.[10] Whichever is used, the Hebrew modification of the common Greek meaning of to know continues in the New Testament. Given that much of the New Testament was composed for Gentile readers and was influenced by Hellenistic civilization, it is not surprising that the intellectual quality of knowing does appear.[11] But to "know God" continues to have the same basic meaning in the New Testament as in the Hebrew scriptures. This is evident from the fact that *ginoskein* continues to be used for lovemaking as well as for knowing (see Matt. 1:25; Luke 1:34, "How can this be since I do not know man?").

Bultmann reviews the meaning of knowing the Lord in the Synoptics and argues that its primary meaning is still that of relationship with, acknowledgment of, and submission to the will of God. "The Christian view of knowledge is thus largely determined by the OT. An obedient and grateful acknowledgment of the deeds and demands of God is linked with knowledge of God and what He has done and demands. It is in keeping that this Christian knowledge is not a fixed possession but develops in the life of the Christian as lasting obedience and reflection."[12]

For Paul, too, true knowledge of God and of Christ is a dynamic, experienced relationship that must find its expression in agape—love of neighbor (see I Cor. 8:1 ff). In I Corinthians 13 *gnosis* (knowledge) is placed under agape, because without agape it is worthless. Knowledge is to be grounded in love and lead to right action (see Phil. 1:9 ff.). To "grow in the knowledge of God," one must "lead a life worthy of the Lord and pleasing to him in every way . . . multiply good works of every sort. . ." (Col. 1:10). Thus for Paul "knowing God" is grounded in a loving relationship and leads to loving service for others.

The Fourth Gospel and the Epistles of John display by far the richest understanding in the New Testament of what it means "to know the Lord." McKenzie finds that John "explicates what is elsewhere implicit. . . ."[13] For John to "know the Lord" is to love, to obey, and to believe.

Knowing and Loving.   John is adamant that "the man without love has known nothing of God" (I John 4:8). Such bold statements lead McKenzie to conclude that "in John knowledge and love grow together, so that it is difficult to say whether love is the fruit of knowledge or knowledge is the fruit of love."[14] They are grounded in and mutually enriched by each other and do not exist apart (see I John 4:7–8; 16, 20). The only way truly to know God is through a loving relationship.

It is because of the love between himself and the Father that Jesus can say, "The Father knows me and I know the Father" (John 10:15). The same knowing is to exist between Jesus and his disciples (John 10:14, 27). But this loving/ knowing, and the awareness of it, is to find expression in agape—loving service of one's neighbor. "Whoever loves God must also love his brother" (I John 4:21). Loving actions for the neighbor arise from and express the awareness of being loved by God. "Beloved, if God has loved us so, we must have the same love for one another" (I John 4:11; also John 13:34; 15:12). Thus for John to know God is to be in a relationship of love with God, to be aware of that love, and to respond by loving our neighbor.

Knowing and Obeying.   Clearly, for John God is not truly known unless there is a loving response. Knowledge of God demands concrete action. Bultmann says that in John "it is plain that γινώσκειν does not mean the knowledge of investigation, observation or speculation, nor of mystical vision remote from historical contacts or action; it achieves concrete expression in historical acts."[15] I referred above to this doing as loving action, but here we can call it obedience to God's commandments. "The way we can be sure of our knowledge of him is to keep his commandments" (I John 2:3 and the following verses). Again, in this aspect of knowing the Father, Jesus is our model. It is because of his perfect obedience to the will of the Father that he can claim to know the Father best. "Yes, I know him well, and I keep his word" (John 8:55). And the converse is also true. The disobedient person does not know God. "The man who sins has not seen him or known him" (I John 3:6; also I John 2:3–5).

Obedience to God's commandments is essential if we are to know God, and it is also required if we are to belong to Jesus. "If you live according to my teaching, you are truly my disciples; then you will know the truth, and the truth will set you free" (John 8:31b–32). In many ways the last statement is a summary of all that I have said so far of Christian faith as a doing that is to lead to human freedom. Scripturally, we would seem to be on good ground.

Knowing and Believing. *Pisteuin* is the verb John uses for "to believe" or "to have faith." Raymond Brown comments that "to a certain extent 'knowing' and 'believing' are interchangeable in John."[16] Certainly many of the characteristics John attributes to knowing God are also essential to believing. To begin with, "to believe" or to have faith is, like knowing, an active process, so much so that John always uses a verb form when he refers to it. The noun *pistes* (faith) never occurs in John even though it is used 243 times in the rest of the New Testament.[17] In addition, belief, for John, is most often belief *in* a person, a relationship of trust, an active commitment, particularly to Jesus. The commitment finds expression in loving obedience.

In the biblical sense, then, to know God is a dynamic, experiential, relational activity involving the whole person and finding expression in a lived response of loving obedience to God's will. Without loving action God is not known. Without such action any other kind of knowing is, in the biblical view, no more than foolishness.

There is, however, another dimension to biblical knowing that is most relevant to our search for a way of knowing in Christian religious education. While the biblical source of knowing is what contemporary educators might call experiential, that knowing is also to be informed by the people's understanding of their past history and of the promises God made to them. Educators must not conclude that the biblical process of knowing the Lord is totally a "discovery method" within present experience, as if what had been known by the people before was of no consequence. On the contrary, both the Hebrew scriptures and New Testament make it abundantly clear that there must be a resolute commitment to remembering and retelling the events of God's activity among the people in the past, and (as seen in Chapter Three) to interpreting all present events within the horizon of God's Kingdom.

Few people have placed as much emphasis on remembering, reenacting, and retelling their faith Story as have the Hebrew people. They have been faithful to Moses' admonition, "Take care and be earnestly on your guard not to forget the things which your own eyes have seen, nor let them slip from your memory as long as you live, but teach them to your children and to your children's children" (Deut. 4:9). Their children would come to the knowledge of God in their own lived experience, but their living in that experience was to be informed by what God had done and promised to their people before them.

The New Testament is replete with accounts of Jesus' preaching and teaching as remembered and interpreted in the faith life of the first Christians. They remembered well his final mandate to the Apostles, which Matthew places on the lips of the risen Christ: "Full authority has been given to me both in heaven and on earth; go, therefore, and make disciples of all the nations. Baptize them in the name 'of the Father, and of the Son, and of the Holy Spirit.' Teach them to carry out everything I have commanded you" (Matt. 28:18–20). They were to forget nothing he had made known to them. According to John's account, this is why he promised to send the paraclete, the One who "will instruct you in everything, and remind you of all that I told you" (John 14:26). Beginning with the missionary outreach of the very first Christians, the Church has striven ever since to do what the Acts report Paul to have done—"he preached the reign of God and taught about the Lord Jesus Christ" (Acts 28:31).

In the biblical understanding then, people come to know the Lord in the midst of historical experience, by reflecting on the activity of God there, by entering a relationship with God and God's people, and by their lived response to that relationship. But their knowing is informed by and interpreted through the Story that has arisen from the previous "knowing" of God's people, and is shaped by the hopes they have in God's promise for their future. From a biblical perspective, then, Christian religious education should be grounded in a relational/experiential/reflective way of knowing that is informed by the Story of faith from Christians before us, and by the Vision toward which that Story points.

AN EPISTEMOLOGICAL SHIFT IN CHRISTIAN RELIGIOUS EDUCATION

In general education, the notion of learning by doing is as old as education itself. The truth of the notion, however, has often been forgotten. In Chapter Eight I will trace the history of the shift, especially in Western philosophy, from an active toward a more metaphysical reflective way of knowing, where knowledge is to lead to "doing" rather than to arise from it. In recent times, however, there is ample evidence among leading education theorists of a shift back toward a more active understanding of the knowing process, away from what Dewey called "the spectator theory of knowledge" toward a way of knowing that is active/reflective and arises from lived experience. Such an epistemology is implicit in Comenius, Locke, Rousseau, Pestalozzi, and Froebel. Piaget has described all authentic cognition as such an interactive/reflective process. The most significant advocate for an education grounded in an experiential way of knowing is John Dewey himself.

Dewey refused the false dichotomy that had emerged in education between the "progressives" (emphasizing experiential learning) and the "traditionalists" (emphasizing beginning with the disciplines of knowledge). He insisted that knowledge must be warranted by the inquiry of experimental logic, giving a "technical definition" of education as the "reconstruction or reorganization of experience which adds to the meaning of experience, and which increases ability to direct the course of subsequent experience."[18] Like Comenius and others before him, Dewey argued that "the child's own instincts and powers furnish the material and give the starting point for all education."[19] But more sophisticated and realistic than they, he also saw the need for those interests to be "directed or guided." By a "method of intelligence"[20] the child's experiences are to be so organized as "to enable him to perform those fundamental types of activity which make civilization what it is."[21] For Dewey experience does not inevitably give rise to knowing. But all true education must be based in experience that is "reconstructed" and properly guided.

In Christian religious education the same epistemological shift is evident. Even a counting of heads among contemporary theorists indicates that there has been a significant shift toward a mode of knowing that is relational, experiential, and active. In the Catholic tradition the shift is more recent, but now very much present. A look at many of the curricula presently being used in parish programs makes it clear that an experiential way of knowing is assumed, if not explicitly recommended. Significant turning points toward such a way of knowing for Catholic religious educators were the International Catechetical Week at Katigando (1964) and Alfonso Nebreda's *Kerygma in Crisis* (1965). The "anthropocentric approach"[22] proposed at Katigando and by Nebreda argued for beginning with the life situation and experience of the learners before the kerygma could be proclaimed. This preparatory activity was seen more as a process of "preevangelization" than as an integral part of the catechesis in its own right. But it marked the turning point toward what Catholics usually call "experiential catechesis."

Pierre Babin and Marcel van Caster are the most notable proponents of experiential catechesis. Babin, relying heavily on a psychological base, argues for a "pedagogy of invention" rather than of "transmission," which will promote the active participation and creativity of the learners.[23] Marcel van Caster, from a strong anthropological perspective, argues for a relational/experiential approach that is grounded in a dialogue between God's revelation and human experience.[24]

The way of knowing which underlies the educational theories proposed by Gabriel Moran and James Michael Lee is also relational/experiential/reflective. Moran's notion of revelation resonates quite clearly with an experiential approach to religious education. When he argues that the starting point of revelation is "the personal, relational, social, and practical experience of people today,"[25] then an experiential approach to religious education would seem inevitable. James Michael Lee draws upon the social sciences to devise a theory of "religious instruction." A basic contention in his theory is that learning is in and from experience. Accepting that "experience is revelational,"[26] he argues that the religion class should be made into "a laboratory and a workshop for Christian living where students learn Christian living precisely by engaging in Christian living in the here-and-now learning situation."[27] Consequently, "The task of religious instruction is to provide the experience in which Christian learning can take place and in which the individual can acquire behaviors which we may legitimately call 'Christian.'"[28]

In the Protestant tradition of religious education the socialization model, already discussed in Chapter Six, is grounded in a relational/experiential/reflective way of knowing. For Coe, Elliott, Nelson, and Westerhoff religious education and formation arise from the lived experience and interaction of people in communities of Christian faith. An experiential way of knowing for religious education is also advocated by many other leading Protestant theorists. I will cite some of the more notable examples.

Lewis Sherrill defined Christian education as "the attempt, ordinarily by members of the Christian community, to participate in and to guide the changes which take place in persons in their relationships with God, with the Church, with other persons, with the physical world, and with oneself."[29] The confrontation/encounter of people with God is through relationship and experience. Much influenced by the theology of Paul Tillich, Sherrill argued for a correlative method for doing Christian education, in which the great themes of the Bible are correlated with the common predicaments of human experience.

In Iris Cully's position there is an interesting combination of the dual influences of Barthian neo-orthodoxy in theology and existentialism in philosophy. Because of her Barthian sympathies she emphasizes the kerygma as the core content of the Church's teaching. But because of her existentialism she proposes a methodology that is "life centered." She avoids the term "present experience" because it can cause educators to overlook history[30] and thus the kerygma, but nevertheless grounds her methodology in an experiential way of knowing.

Randolph C. Miller, after Coe the most influential Protestant theorist of this century, poses an empirical epistemological base for both Christian theology and education. For Miller the clue to Christian education is in theology,[31] but a theology that arises from reflection on human experience. Grounding Christian educational activity in human relationship, he thus sees it as a social process. Consequently, like the advocates of the socialization model, he emphasizes the role of home and nurturing congregation.[32] Christian knowing arises from reflection on one's own experience in relationship with the Christian community experience.

D. Campbell Wyckoff has concentrated on devising a sound curriculum theory for Christian education.[33] He has developed a set of principles to guide curriculum building, and his overall construct is undergirded by an experiential way of knowing. He writes, "I believe that the organizing principle of the curriculum should be the Church's experience,"[34] though he is anxious to ensure that an experiential approach does not rule out the content of the faith tradition. "Clearly, I want the curriculum of Christian education to be heavy on the 'subject matter' side. The call of the church needs to be known, discussed, understood, and its implications (past, present, and future) sought."[35] But his methodology for enabling people to encounter that curriculum is "involvement . . . in the life and work of the worshipping and witnessing community in a cycle of orientation, action, and reflection."[36]

Even as these theorists have emphasized an experiential/relational way of knowing, they have also claimed, to varying degrees, that the "content" of the Christian faith tradition should be made present to people within the pedagogical context. None of them confines Christian knowing to what can be discovered in one's own present relationships and experience. The biblical message and tradition of Christianity must also be taught, even as it can only be truly "known," by encountering it within lived experience and by an active/reflective process.

However, even though many of the leading religious education theorists have shifted to an experiential way of knowing, there also have been a good number who place primary emphasis on teaching the content of the biblical message and the Christian tradition. (Their emphasis places them within the "disciplines of learning" school of curriculum theory mentioned in Chapter One). Josef Jungmann and Johannes Hofinger are two notable Catholic examples of this position; H. Shelton Smith and James D. Smart have represented this emphasis in the Protestant tradition.

The kerygmatic movement spearheaded by Jungmann[37] and championed by Hofinger[38] is best known in this country as the salvation history approach. Its central emphasis is on beginning with and teaching the story of salvation. It gives little place to the role of the student's lived experience.[39]

In mainline Protestantism H. Shelton Smith, taking a strong neo-orthodox position, was the first to call the liberal religious educators of the 1940s back to the basic kerygma of the Christian message. In their enthusiasm for an experiential way of knowing, the liberals seemed to him to be overlooking the biblical and doctrinal content of the tradition.[40] Following Smith's lead, James D. Smart also took a strong neo-orthodox theological position as the basis of Christian education, emphasizing transmission of the biblical and doctrinal message.[41]

In summary, there is evidence in both general and religious education of a major shift toward an active/reflective and relational/experiential way of knowing. Religious educators can rightly claim that this is consistent with a biblical understanding of how we come to "know God." However, in Christian religious education there has also been a strong insistence that our educating must faithfully impart and teach the message of Christianity. Again, this position, too, would seem to be on good biblical grounds as long as the underlying way of knowing is more than "transmission."

TOWARD A PRAXIS EPISTEMOLOGY FOR CHRISTIAN RELIGIOUS EDUCATION

The nature, purpose, and context of Christian religious education calls for a way of knowing that can hold past, present, and future in a fruitful tension, that fosters free and freeing lived Christian faith, that promotes a creative relationship with a Christian community and of that community with the world. To this we can now add that the biblical understanding of knowing the Lord points to a way of knowing that is experiential/relational and active/reflective even as lived experience is informed by the biblical message. And many recent religious education theorists have proposed a shift toward such an experiential way of knowing, even as there has also been a corresponding insistence that the biblical and doctrinal message of Christianity be taught faithfully.

The shared praxis approach to Christian religious education proposed in the remainder of Part IV is undergirded by a praxis way of knowing. Given the kind of knowing that Christian education should promote, I claim that a praxis way of knowing is most capable of meeting the task. It is a relational, reflective, and experiential way of knowing in which by critical reflection on lived experience people discover and name their own story and vision and, in a Christian education context, the Story and Vision of the Christian community. It thus combines the knowing which arises from present lived experience with what was known by Christians here before us. Since a praxis way of knowing always has the purpose of promoting further praxis, the knowing which arises from a reflective/experiential encounter with the Christian Story and Vision seems capable, by God's grace, of sponsoring people toward intentionally lived Christian faith.

In proposing such an epistemological base for and approach to Christian religious education, clearly I stand on many shoulders. There are also a number of ways, however, in which I attempt to go beyond the "experiential" religious educators before me. I attempt to deepen the critical dimension of reflection on experience. I more deliberately hold present experience in a dialectical and critical correlation with the Story and Vision. But that is moving too far ahead, and the differences will not be evident until I outline my own position in some detail. That description must begin with the notion of praxis itself. My own understanding of praxis will be stated in detail in Chapter Nine. First, however, I outline in Chapter Eight the philosophical roots that underlie my understanding. These roots and the way I build on them are essential to my rationale. Readers who are not so philosophically inclined may wish to pass quickly over the historical overview. The philosophical roots may be of more interest later, especially after one has attempted to use a shared praxis approach in religious education.

NOTES

1. Whitehead, *Aims*, p. 36.
2. In my earlier published articles I have referred to it as a "theory/method."
3. Paulo Freire writes, "Education . . . always implies . . . a theory of knowledge put in practice and a way of knowing" (*Process*, p. 88).
4. Anything like a detailed account of the long and complex debates about the process of knowing could fill many volumes. Chapter Eight will provide some detail on the evolution of what I am calling a "praxis epistemology" and will draw especially from the thinking of Aristotle, Hegel, Marx, and the critical social theorists. Chapter Eleven will outline some of the relevant insights for education in the "genetic epistemology" of Jean Piaget. Beyond that, I draw no more than the following broad strokes in an ancient debate.

   The opposing sides in the epistemological debate can be labeled as rationalism versus empiricism, and as idealism versus realism, both groupings being variations on the same theme. Is human knowledge "from within" (rationalism) or "from without" (empiricism)? Is knowledge a reflection of what actually exists in reality (realism), or is it determined by the universal and innate ideas of the knowing subject (idealism)? However oversimplified, such would appear to be the essential lines of division for more than two and a half millennia.

   The debate between rationalists and empiricists is already evident in pre-Socratic times, when Heraclitus emphasized the role of the senses in human knowing and Parmenides stressed the primacy of reason. Some hundred years later the issue became central to the philosophy of Plato, in many ways the first great epistemologist. Plato can be called both a rationalist and an idealist. For him the world that can be known by the senses is changeable and a source of mere relative opinion rather than truth. However, above the sensible world there is a transcendent and superior world of concept-objects, which are nonsensible and universal. They comprise the real world of what he called forms or ideas (justice, truth, freedom, etc.). By what is already within a person, a priori, the human soul or mind possesses the ability to have nonsensible contact with the ideal and eternal objects of the nonsensible world. The forms, known by reason, are the source of real immutable truth, distinct from the relative opinion provided by the senses and the sensible world.

   I deal in more detail with Aristotle's tripartite division of the ways of knowing in Chapter Eight. Here, in contrast to Plato, he can be called an empiricist and a realist. He agreed with Plato that knowledge is always of some "universal" in that we know particular things as instances of universals. But he rejected Plato's notion of a separate transcendent world of forms. For Aristotle what is known is an expression of what is real, and nothing is ever in the mind that was not first in the senses. The soul is a set of faculties possessed by the body, and knowledge arises from the activity of those bodily senses. They provide the data that is appropriated and judged by reason.

   If we jump some two thousand years, the same lines of debate are apparent between the seventeenth-century rationalists (Descartes, 1596–1650) and empiricists (Locke, 1632–1704; Berkeley, 1685–1753; Hume, 1711–1776).

   The dialectic between the idealism of Hegel and the realism/materialism of Marx is treated in some detail in Chapter Eight, but it should be noted here as, among other things, an epistemological difference. Hegel is a philosophical idealist/rationalist in the Platonic tradition, while Marx forged his own brand of realism and empiricism with knowing arising from the concrete historical activity of the knowing subject acting upon the world.

The pragmatists of more recent years attempt to combine the rational and empirical dimensions of human knowing, but add a tentativeness to their conclusions and an openness to human knowing by making utility the ultimate criterion of all truth. They, in turn, have been critiqued by the existentialists and phenomenologists for their lack of attention to the subjective condition and situation in time of knowing subjects. The existentialists and phenomenologists attempt to correct this fault by emphasizing the historical subjective consciousness of all "knowers." And so the debate goes on.

5. *Theological Dictionary of the New Testament*, "*ginōskō*," by Rudolf Bultmann, 1:697.
6. Ibid., 1:697.
7. Ibid., 1:698.
8. John McKenzie summarizes this well when he writes, "The knowledge of Yahweh may be summed up in experience and response" (*Dictionary of the Bible*, "Know, Knowledge," p. 486).
9. *Theological Dictionary of the New Testament*, "*ginōskō*," 1:698.
10. See *Theological Dictionary of the New Testament*, "*Oida*," by H. Seesemann, 5:116.
11. See *Theological Dictionary of the New Testament*, "*ginōskō*," 1:701.
12. Ibid., 1:707.
13. McKenzie, *Dictionary of the Bible*, p. 487.
14. Ibid., p. 487.
15. *Theological Dictionary of the New Testament*, "*ginōskō*," 1:711.
16. Raymond Brown, *The Gospel According to John I–XII*, 1:513.
17. See Ibid., 1:512.
18. Dewey, *Democracy*, p. 76.
19. Dewey, "Creed," p. 20.
20. Dewey, *Experience and Education*, esp. pp. 73–88.
21. Dewey, "Creed," p. 26.
22. See Erdozain, "The Evolution of Catechetics," pp. 7–31.
23. See Babin, *Options*.
24. See van Caster and LeDu, *Experiential Catechetics*.
25. Moran, *The Present Revelation*, p. 222.
26. Lee, *The Shape of Religious Instruction*, p. 16.
27. Ibid., p. 19.
28. Ibid., p. 74.
29. See Sherrill, *The Gift of Power*, p. 82.
30. See Cully, *The Dynamics of Christian Education*, p. 119.
31. See Miller, *The Clue to Christian Education*.
32. See Miller, *Christian Nurture and the Church*.
33. See Wyckoff, *Theory and Design of Christian Education Curriculum*.
34. Wyckoff, "Understanding Your Church Curriculum," p. 82.
35. Ibid., p. 83.
36. Ibid., p. 83. Of all the religious education theorists outlined my own position resonates most readily with Wyckoff's. In his search for a curriculum theory he has posed six foundational questions which closely parallel the six foundational issues on which this book is based. Wyckoff assembles his curriculum principles around the purpose, scope, context, process, partners, and timing of Christian education ("Understanding Your Church Curriculum" gives a brief and clear synthesis of his position on these questions). His emphasis on encounter, action, and reflection is clearly an example of a praxis way of knowing. He attempts to give equal emphasis to the past, present, and future and adds "that story-telling may be Christian education's irreducibly basic approach to content" (Ibid., p. 84).
37. See Jungmann, *Handing on the Faith*.
38. See Hofinger, *The Art of Teaching Christian Doctrine*.
39. For an excellent historical overview and critique of the salvation history approach, see Boys, *Biblical Interpretation in Religious Education*.
40. See H. Shelton Smith, *Faith and Nurture*.
41. See Smart, *The Teaching Ministry of the Church*.

8

Some Philosophical Roots
for a Praxis Way of Knowing

A LARGE amount of contemporary philosophical, theological, and educational literature is liberally laced with the word *praxis*. However, the word is used (and misused) in a variety of ways. The problem arises, in part, from the complexity of the notion itself and the absence of a single English word to translate it. To capture its meaning adequately might well require a whole sentence, such as, Praxis is purposeful, intentional, and reflectively chosen ethical action. It is probably wiser for now to leave the word in its original Greek.

The English word *practice* is not an adequate translation of praxis, especially when practice is used with its common meaning, as in "putting theory into practice." In fact, many contemporary writers use praxis as a corrective to such an understanding of practice, and especially to offset the dichotomy between theory and practice so prevalent in our Western mindset. To understand praxis requires a shift in consciousness away from dichotomizing theory and practice, toward seeing them as twin moments of the same activity that are united dialectically. Instead of theory leading to practice, theory becomes or is seen as the reflective moment in praxis, and articulated theory arises from that praxis to yield further praxis.

The praxis way of knowing for Christian religious education that I describe in Chapters Nine and Ten involves a critical reflection within a community context on lived experience. The reflection is informed by one's own past and future and by the Story and Vision of the Christian community. To understand such a way of knowing, however, and to establish its appropriateness for our enterprise, it is necessary first to indicate the historical roots of my understanding of praxis. I do not pretend to present a complete history of the concept; I intend simply to show how my view of it is continuous with a substantial tradition.

Many people falsely assume that praxis is an exclusively Marxist term. It is true that praxis was central to Marx's thought, and he helped bring the idea back into the mainstream of Western philosophy. It has been used in Marxist literature ever since. However, my understanding of it begins with Aristotle. And while it is also shaped by Hegel, Marx, and Habermas, my own statement differs in significant ways from all of them. I trace the historical overview from the interest of a religious educator and will indicate the implications the epistemological shifts have had on our enterprise over its history.

PRAXIS IN ARISTOTLE

Epistemology as a distinct branch of philosophy is not much in evidence before John Locke (1632–1704). Thus when I speak of Aristotle's epistemology, I am describing his implied position and using a term he himself did not use. But although Aristotle and the Greeks concentrated their thinking more on what is to be known than on the theory of the procedures for knowing it, their different philosophical positions are undergirded by a variety of ways of knowing. Aristotle's understanding of the "three ways of knowing" is where we can most profitably turn to trace the meaning of praxis.

Aristotle saw the free person as having three distinctive ways of relating intelligently to life, or, conversely, three human activities from which understanding could arise. These he called *theoria, praxis,* and *poiesis*.[1] The three ways of life they represent are the speculative life, the practical life, and the productive life.[2] The speculative life is the life of contemplation and reflection. The practical is an ethical life lived in a political context. The productive life is the life devoted to making artifacts, or to artistic endeavors.[3]

These three ways of life were, for Aristotle, three different forms that intelligent human activity can take. In that sense they are three different ways for a reflective subject to relate to the objective world, and therefore three different ways of knowing. A *theoria* way of knowing is the quest for truth by a contemplative/reflective/nonengaged process. A *praxis* way of knowing is by reflective engagement in a social situation. *Poiesis* as a way of knowing found embodiment in and arose from a "making." As ways of knowing they differ primarily in their *telos,* their intended outcomes. Theoretical knowledge is an end in itself, practical knowledge is aimed at ordering human social action, and productive knowledge is to lead to the making of artifacts.[4] It will be well to set out each way of knowing in greater detail and then to review Aristotle's understanding of their interrelationships.

The *theoroi* were the contemplative visitors to the Greek games who abandoned themselves to the sacred events by "looking on." This root of *theoria* remains in Aristotle's use of the word, although he did not see it as a passive state of inertia; for him it was an active state involving *energeia*. However, it continued to mean an activity of contemplative knowing wherein the knowing is for its own sake and arises from one's own speculation independent of evidence from reality. In fact, *theoria* provided knowledge of subjects that wholly transcended reality. For Aristotle there are three "conditions" or "states of mind"[5] that give rise to a *theoria* way of knowing, and, conversely, the exercise of *theoria* helps to develop these habits. The first two are *episteme*, the faculty by which we can reason syllogistically to know principles that are necessary and eternal,[6] and *nous* which is "the state of mind that apprehends first principles."[7] But these two are subsumed in "the most finished form of knowledge,"[8] the state of mind he calls *sophia*. *Sophia* includes both *nous* and *episteme* but goes beyond them in that, in Aristotle's words, "wisdom (*sophia*) is scientific *(episteme)* and intuitive knowledge (*nous*) of what is by nature most precious."[9] *Theoria*, the contemplative reflective pursuit of ultimate truth, leads to possession of *sophia*, the highest form of wisdom. In coming to such transcendent wisdom the most complete form of human happiness can be found, and the life of *theoria* is the only one that leads there.

Aristotle uses the term *praxis* with a number of different but closely related meanings. In its broadest possible meaning *praxis* refers to almost any kind of intentional and deliberate outward activity that a free person is likely to perform. In a more restricted sense it describes "rational and purposeful human conduct."[10] Finally, *praxis* in its most technical sense describes ethical conduct in a political context. Not only is this Aristotle's most precise use of the term, he also sees it as the most appropriate form of *praxis*, that is, to live an ethical life within a political context, or conversely, to conduct political life according to responsible ethical principles. Yet in all his uses of the term there is a basic commonality. For Aristotle in any context *praxis* means a purposeful and reflective action by which knowing arises through engagement in a social situation. Thus *praxis* always includes "twin moments"—action (i.e., engagement) and reflection, but not separated from each other; it is action done reflectively, and reflection on what is being done. In consequence, knowing arises not from one's inward speculation, but from intentional engagement with and experience of social reality. It is thus a practical way of knowing, and *praxis* has its purpose in further *praxis*.

Phronesis, according to Aristotle, is the "state of mind" from which *praxis* arises and which, in turn, is developed by *praxis*. *Phronesis* is the habit of practical wisdom or prudence. Aristotle defines it as "a true state, reasoned, and capable of action with regard to things that are good or bad for man."[11] He insists that *phronesis* should be informed by general principles and adds that "it must also take cognizance of particulars, because it is concerned with conduct [*praxis*] and conduct has its sphere in particular circumstances."[12] In other words, the habit of *phronesis* must be exercised in *praxis* so that the action is informed by both general principles and particular circumstances.

It is relevant to my own description of a praxis way of knowing in Chapter Nine to note here that Aristotle insisted on the role of emotion in *praxis*. This is most obvious in his notion of *proairesis*, which can be translated as "deliberate choice." *Praxis*, as a freely chosen ethical activity, must always involve deliberate choice. He explains: "Now the origin of action (*praxis*) . . . is choice, and the origin of choice is appetition and purposive reasoning."[13] He explains further that "there are in the soul three things that control action [*praxis*] and (the attainment of) truth, viz. sensation, intellect and appetition."[14] Thus *praxis* is not dispassionately chosen action (in fact *apatheia*, lack of passion, always hinders *praxis*), but neither is it an unreasoned following of whim or appetite. The choice involved in *praxis* is, in Aristotle's words, "either appetitive intellect or intellectual appetition; and man is a principle of this kind."[15] From this we can conclude that, for Aristotle, *praxis* is an activity of the total person—head, heart, and lifestyle.

In attributing such a holistic meaning to *praxis*, Aristotle is very much in continuity with its ancient Greek usage. In fact, the ancient Greeks sometimes used *praxis* as a euphemism for sexual intercourse.[16] This is of particular interest to us in light of our discussion in Chapter Seven of the Hebrew *yada* and its use for both the activity of knowing and lovemaking. Here already we have an indication that there is a strong resonance between the biblical and the praxis way of knowing.

What then of *poiesis*? For Aristotle *poiesis* is a way of relating to reality in which a concrete artifact or thing is produced. The product embodies a certain kind of knowing, and its production involves a knowing process. This is the knowing expressed in the work of the sculptor, the craftsperson, the tradesperson, and, in its highest expression, the poet. While *praxis* refers to reflective doing, *poiesis* refers to skilled making. As a way of knowing, then, the former is a practical knowing whose purpose is ongoing action, while the latter involves a productive knowing and has its end in what is produced. Lobkowicz says, "The distinction is not easily rendered in English; what comes closest to it is the difference between 'doing' and 'making.' We do sports or business or politics, and we make ships or houses or statues."[17]

The condition of mind that gives rise to *poiesis* is *techne*, craft, skill, or art. It is by a person's *techne* that a *poiesis* way of knowing takes place, and the exercise of *poiesis* sharpens the person's skill or ability for producing. But it would be misleading to imply that there is no intellectual component in *poiesis*. There is a reflective intellectual dimension in it. The difference is that in *praxis* thought is merged with doing, while in *poiesis* thought is merged with making.

For Aristotle, then, the "three lives" are three different ways of relating intelligently to the world and thus are three different ways of apprehending or knowing reality. He argued, however, that intentional education must be grounded in a *praxis* way of knowing. He insisted constantly that education is a part of politics—the epitome of the life of *praxis*—and as such is a practical rather than a theoretical science.[18] The end of education, to Aristotle, is not an abstract knowing, but a certain kind of moral character that will make a good citizen and promote the well-being of the state. Only a praxis way of knowing can promote this. Given the purpose of Christian religious education outlined previously, we already have part of the reason I argue for a praxis way of knowing as the epistemological base for such educating. However, I will also argue that a praxis way of knowing must unite dialectically both "theory" and "practice," our own stories and visions and the Christian community's Story and Vision. It is relevant, therefore, to dwell briefly on how Aristotle understood *theoria*, *praxis*, and *poiesis* to be related.

A common interpretation of Aristotle's position is that he opposed them to each other.[19] The roots of such an interpretation are certainly to be found in Aristotle. But if we take into account his overall understanding of these concepts, opposition may be too strong a term. It is more accurate to say that Aristotle saw *poiesis* and *praxis* as cooperating with each other to make possible the life of *theoria* and the highest form of wisdom, *sophia*. Good *poiesis* is a means to good *praxis*,[20] and the practical life is to make the speculative life possible.[21] By the same token, the life of *praxis* is to be informed by reflection and universal principles.[22]

But Aristotle is also at least partly responsible for what later came to be an assumed dichotomy between theory and praxis. While the lives of *poiesis* and *praxis* are to make the speculative life possible, *theoria* led to the highest form of wisdom, which is its own end, rather than something to inform further *praxis*. For him *theoria* is also the most ideal of the three lives. He argued that "the intellect is in the fullest sense the man. So this life will also be the happiest."[23] This is true because "the activity of God, which is supremely happy, must be a form of contemplation; and therefore among human activities that which is most akin to God's will be the happiest."[24]

This apparent dichotomy of *theoria* and *praxis*, and Aristotle's obvious preference for *theoria*, must be understood in the context of his time. To begin with, Aristotle was reacting against the Sophists of his day, who had reduced knowing to practical or technical efficiency. *Theoria* was useful to them only insofar as it led to practical behavior. Aristotle saw their position as reductionist, as posing a dangerous threat to the great intellectual enterprise upon which he was embarked. Thus he argued strongly against such pragmatism, contending that knowledge is of value even for its own sake. Second, he understood God as totally transcendent and outside of history and thus most Godlike when in contemplation. But that is the God of Greek philosophy. The Hebrew God, by contrast, is a God who acts and intervenes in history. It is fair to ask whether, if Aristotle had had such a Hebrew image of God, he would have posed the contemplative, nonengaged life as the most Godlike. I doubt it.

Poiesis as a way of knowing seems to have fallen into oblivion after Aristotle's death.[25] The primacy he gave to the life of *theoria* was emphasized further, but "theoretical knowing" was given a new meaning, and *praxis* as a valid way of apprehending the world was greatly downgraded.

The Neoplatonists[26] played the largest part in forging this new understanding of both *theoria* and *praxis*. Their contribution was twofold. First, they separated contemplative thought from scientific theorizing. This distinction needed to be made and was necessary to the development of the theoretical sciences. But the "theoretical knowledge" that arose from such scientific theorizing was seen as the primary form of knowledge: one should know such theory first and then apply that to practice. Second, the Neoplatonists greatly de-emphasized the political life of *praxis*. The speculative, theorizing life was posed without qualification as the ideal one. While Aristotle had seen *theoria* and *praxis* as two aspects of the free human life, *praxis* was now to be spurned and avoided for the sake of scientific theorizing.[27] A speculative and theoretical way of knowing now held sway without balance. As a result, the mindset typical of Western philosophy developed, that to know the world or guide action in it, one should begin with a speculative type of intellectual knowing and then apply that, if it had any application, from outside experience to practice. (I will refer to this hereafter as a "from theory to practice" way of knowing.)

CHRISTIAN EDUCATION AND GREEK
INTELLECTUALISM: A CONFLICT

It is reasonable to suppose that Christian educators would have been well disposed to a praxis way of knowing. In their initial contact with Greek philosophy, however, they encountered an unbridled form of Greek intellectualism. Considering the theoretical emphasis the Greeks gave to the process of knowing, an epistemological conflict between Christianity and Hellenistic philosophy seems inevitable. As outlined in Chapter Seven, the Hebrew and New Testament way of knowing God is not a speculative exercise nor a contemplative removal from the world. It calls, instead, for reflective engagement in the world in obedience to God's reign and in response to the experience of God in the midst of history. The Incarnation itself is an act of divine praxis—the Word becoming flesh in time and place. Rather than being a God who is to be reached by re-moving oneself from the human arena, the Incarnate Son is the supreme sign for Christians of a God who acts within history and can be truly known in our ac-tion of loving service. No one can be "in light" while "hating his brother" (I John 2:9). Even should one "with full knowledge comprehend all mysteries . . . but have not love . . . [he or she] is nothing" (I Cor. 13:2). We could thus expect that the young Christian community would give priority to the lived, practical life of Christian virtue as the most authentic way of coming to know the Lord, and would employ such a relational, experiential, and active way of knowing in its educational ministry.

At first catechetical efforts were indeed grounded in such a biblical way of knowing. The *Didache*, a first-century or early second-century document[28] and one of the earliest extant catechetical instructions outside the New Testament canon, makes it clear that the "way of life" that leads to salvation is a life of moral living in the midst of the world.[29] When the Gnostics emerged in clear prominence in the second century, they were condemned by orthodox Christian-ity for, among other reasons, claiming that a special kind of secret knowledge (*gnosis*) would lead to redemption of those who possessed a special spiritual ele-ment. True "followers of the Way" proposed a life of Christian engagement in the world, not possession of certain knowledge, as the road to union with God. The Catechumenate (which had its high points from the beginning of the third to the end of the fifth centuries) placed increased emphasis on doctrinal instruc-tion but continued to be a relational/experiential process of initiation into the Christian community by which the catechumens were prepared for living the Christian life.[30]

But with the rise of the catechetical school of Alexandria a marked shift be-gan in the Christian understanding of the process for knowing the Lord. Under Clement (c. 150–c. 215) and his successor Origen (c. 185–c. 254), this school be-gan to forge a "Christian paideia"[31] that would reconcile Christianity with Greek philosophy and culture. As a result, the clear-cut difference between knowing in the Hebrew/New Testament sense and knowing in the Greek spec-ulative/intellectual sense became far less distinct. For the Alexandrian school the speculative life and way of knowing was primary and to be preferred. Ori-gen, the "creator of the first grand synthesis of speculative theology,"[32] saw the active life as preparing people for a cognitive knowing that was to lead to con-templative and mystical union with God.

The Alexandrians performed a needed service in their day. The speculative and intellectual component of Greek philosophy was necessary for the develop-ment of Christian theology. However, because they were a catechetical school and became a model for other such schools, they had extensive influence on the Church's educational ministry. As a result, a strong rational and theoretical view of knowing emerged in Christian religious education and increased over the centuries. Eventually Christian educators came to assume that the process of knowing most appropriate to their endeavors began with statements of the "content" of the faith tradition (be that in biblical or Greek rationalist language) and conveyed that to people from outside of their lived experience with the intention that they apply it to their lives. Christian educators had departed as far from a biblical way of knowing as the philosophers had from a praxis one.

The causes of such a major epistemological shift in religious education are complex to trace, and I do not pretend to give an adequate explanation here. Obviously, there are many pieces to the puzzle and, among other factors, the Church's understanding of revelation was part of it. However, it appears that "from theory to practice" was the assumed epistemology in Christian education long before it held sway in Christian theology. Of the first Christian theologians Lobkowicz notes, "The statements of the Gospel simply were too explicit to permit them without further ado to embrace the extreme intellectualism of the pagans."[33] I am moving toward the conclusion that the theologians often favored an experiential/reflective way of knowing for their own enterprise, but when recommending a process of Christian education, they assumed that they had already discovered what the people ought to know. As a result, they proposed a very didactic approach that would impart the message of Christianity without paying much attention to the lived experience of the learners. I will cite some notable examples.

The theological method used by Augustine in *The City of God* and in his *Confessions* is a spiritual reflection on his own relationship with God and on the signs of the times in light of the Scriptures and the Church's teaching. His theological purpose is a quest for practical spiritual wisdom, and his method is based on an experiential/relational way of knowing.[34] Such would seem to be very much in the Biblical tradition of *yada*. Like Aristotle, Augustine also speaks of "three lives." He writes, "Or take the three modes of life, the contemplative, the active, the contemplative-active. A man can live the life of faith in any of these three and get to heaven. What is not indifferent is that he love truth and do what charity demands. No man must be so committed to contemplation as, in his contemplation, to give no thought to his neighbor's needs, nor so absorbed in action as to dispense with the contemplation of God."[35] While he intends to give equal importance to all three modes of life, clearly he insists that the Christian life must be a life of praxis, or what he calls contemplative-active.

Augustine's pedagogical insights were far ahead of his time.[36] However, in contradistinction to his theological method, he proposed a didactic narrational process to instruct people in the story of salvation history with no apparent attention to the lived experience of the students as a dimension of knowing. This is especially evident in his best known catechetical work, *De Catechizandis Rudi-*

bus (written about 400), which is based entirely on the "narrative" approach. He advises the deacon Deogratias to teach with love so that "he to whom you speak by hearing may believe, and by believing may hope, and by hoping may love."[37] There the epistemological assumption is obvious—oral instruction leads to believing first and then to Christian living.

De Catechizandis Rudibus was written for *accidentes*, people just entering into the Catechumenate. Its narrational approach and its lack of attention to an experiential way of knowing can be explained by the fact that the *accidentes* were then to enter into the relational experience of the Christian community where another and deeper kind of Christian knowing would take place. Long after the catechumenal process had disappeared, however, *De Catechizandis Rudibus* was still being used as a standard textbook and approach to intentional Christian education. The salvation history approach of Jungmann and Hofinger in our own day is influenced by Augustine's text. As indicated in Chapter Seven, some fifteen hundred years after Augustine recommended it the salvation history approach was still paying little attention to lived experience or to an active/reflective way of knowing.

Although Thomas Aquinas emphasized the role of intellect in the knowing process, his theological method is not based on a theoria way of knowing. From his mentor Aristotle he knew that nothing is ever in the intellect that is not first in the senses, and thus an experiential/reflective way of knowing is at the bedrock of his great theological *Summa*. As noted in Chapter Four, he also argued that faith and charity are related in the life of Christians as closely as matter and form. In this sense we can say that for Aquinas the Christian life is to be a life of Christian praxis, a knowing/believing that is embodied in a Christian lifestyle.

But when it came to religious education Aquinas espoused a pedagogical process that assumed a "from theory to practice" way of knowing. Not only was a biblical way of knowing overlooked, but Greek philosophical language was given primacy over biblical language. He assumed that theologians and the Church *magisterium* had already synthesized into propositional statements what is required for Christian knowing. These propositions were to be taught to the people, who were then to apply them to practice.[38]

With the scholastics after Aquinas the task of Christian theology became more obviously a quest for "rational knowledge about God."[39] With such knowledge having been established by the theologians, religious education, now more than ever seen as the "messenger" of theology, could be reduced to a question-and-answer catechism to be memorized. For Roman Catholics the great post-Reformation catechisms of Canisius and Bellarmine firmly established a catechism book as the primary tool for religious education and memorizing of its precise propositional summaries as the pedagogical process. Thereafter, the epistemological assumption that the knowing process most appropriate to intentional religious education is to move "from theory to practice," from outside of experience into the lives of people, was firmly established for Roman Catholics. It has remained the predominant way of knowing of our intentional religious education until recent times.[40]

At first sight, it would appear that the Reformers proposed an alternative way of knowing to undergird Christian education. They rejected the intellectualism of the Scholastics and emphasized faith as trust in God rather than belief in doctrinal propositions. But, alas, when it came to recommending an educational process, Luther was the great popularizer of the catechism approach. In the preface to his *Small Catechism* (1529) he ordered pastors and preachers to "take these tables and forms, and instruct the people in them word for word."[41] In time Protestant educators moved away from Luther's catechism approach and placed emphasis on knowing the Bible rather than doctrinal summaries. Nevertheless, a biblical way of knowing was rarely employed to teach the biblical message. In a certain sense, the from theory to practice process continued, with the learning and memorizing of Bible stories and passages replacing the memorizing of doctrinal statements.

Over the history of Christianity we appear to have moved farther and farther away from a biblical way of knowing, at least in our *intentional* religious education. (Undoubtedly, the informal education which took place within the Christian community was always a socialization process, and thus a relational/experiential way of knowing.) I do not mean to condemn the Scholastics or Reformers for making such epistemological assumptions for Christian education. They were people of their time, and so they reflect the educational practice of their historical context. From the Neoplatonists onward Western education was generally understood as the imparting of "theoretical" knowledge (i.e., from outside lived experience), which would then be applied to practice.

The notion of an experiential way of knowing for intentional education re-emerged only with Comenius, Locke, and Rousseau, and their ideas had little impact on the Church's formal education. Had Aristotle's notion of a praxis way of knowing been remembered, it might have had a significant influence on Christian education. But praxis as a reliable way of knowing had been lost to Western philosophy.[42]

A shift away from the unduly speculative mode of traditional metaphysics began with Francis Bacon (1561–1626), the English statesman and philosopher of science. Bacon had little time for speculative philosophy and sought to develop a practical philosophy instead. He proposed an empirical mode of knowing as the basic method for scientific inquiry. Instead of standing back from the world to theorize about it, Bacon argued that the way to knowledge is by experimentation and induction from the facts of experience to fundamental principles, which could then issue in beneficial practical results. By the gathering of empirical data from sense experience, judicious interpretation, and further experiments to verify hypotheses, the world and nature could be known for human benefit.

A whole school of British philosophers continued in this empirical strain, most notably John Locke. Locke was impressed by, but ultimately opposed, the rationalism of Descartes (1596–1650). Locke argued that all knowing begins not in the mind, but in sensation. The mind is a "tabula rasa" whose ideas come from sense experience.

Immanuel Kant (1724–1804) tried to bridge the debate between the continental rationalists (Descartes, Spinoza, and Leibnitz) and the British empiricists (Locke, Berkeley, and Hume). He argued that all knowledge is the result of an intellectual act on what is presented to the mind from without. By claiming that all knowledge requires an ingredient derived from reality, Kant undermined further the foundation of traditional metaphysics and its claim to provide knowledge of subjects which totally transcended nature. At the same time, as a person of the Enlightenment, he helped to establish the role of critical reason in the knowing process and called for a "majority of age" where people would "dare to think."

By now the understanding of human knowing as a reflection on experience had been reestablished in Western philosophy. But it was G. W. F. Hegel (1770–1831) who began to use the term praxis again to describe such a way of knowing. Hegel's understanding of praxis, however, differs significantly from Aristotle's. To begin with, from Kant and the Enlightenment Hegel learned the importance of *critical* reason, thus deepening the rational moment of praxis far beyond the notion of reflection in Aristotle. In addition, Hegel's understanding of history as an ongoing and dialectically evolving process led him to understand praxis as historical, taking up what went before and transcending it to shape the future toward the development of human freedom. In that ongoing unfolding of history, theory and praxis are dialectically united rather than dichotimized from each other as Aristotle had left them. It is in this Hegelian tradition that I take up again the story of my own understanding of praxis as a way of knowing.

HEGEL AND THE PRAXIS OF *GEIST*

The relationship between theory and praxis is central to Hegel's whole philosophy. To understand how he understood them and their dialectical relationship, we must first look at the organizing theme of his philosophy, what he called *Geist*.

Hegel's notion of *Geist* is indeed difficult to summarize. In essence, it means the all-powerful and encompassing "Spirit" that is the sum total and guiding force of all creation and possibility. A kind of pantheism underlies the notion, with all things seen as emanations of the great Spirit and related to each other in that Spirit.

Hegel's *Geist* can be described as a combination of the Greek concept of ultimate Reason and the transcendent/imminent God of the Jewish and Christian traditions. The Greeks understood the world to be inherently rational, and all understanding of its rationality is an appropriation of the ultimate Reason that is its source. For the Greeks, however, Reason is not an active principle in process of becoming but is already in the world and can be brought to human consciousness by *theoria*. If we add to this notion the Jewish-Christian concept of a God who is both "Wholly Other" and One who intervenes in history to effect God's will, then *Geist* is an active rational principle that is actualizing itself within history. For Hegel, then, *Geist* is not abstract and transcendent Wisdom, but an infinite, and active Reason that guides the world by Providence. In his own words, "The truth that a Providence, that is to say, a divine Providence, presides over events of the world corresponds to our principles; for divine Providence is wisdom endowed with infinite power which realizes its own aim, that is, the absolute, rational, final purpose of the world."[43] Here the ultimate Reason of Greek philosophy and the active, effective God of Judaism and Christianity have been combined. *Geist* is Reason actualizing itself in the world. In this sense, *Geist* is not only the ultimate state of reality, but also the material and efficient cause of the world, as it is and as it is becoming. History for Hegel is the story of *Geist* realizing itself, ever progressing from freedom as an abstract idea to its concrete embodiment in history.

In explaining the self-realizing activity of it, he argued that *Geist* is in a constant state of self-initiated activity by which it moves forward to ever higher levels of actuality. "The very essence of Spirit is action. It makes itself what it essentially is; it is its own product, its own work."[44] But this activity is a conflictive process in which *Geist* constantly stands over against itself; its subjective self gives rise to an objectivized, opposite self, and the two enter into conflict. "Spirit is at war with itself. It must overcome itself as its own enemy and formidable obstacle. Development, which in nature is a quiet unfolding, is in Spirit a hard, infinite struggle against itself."[45] Through this dialectical struggle *Geist* overcomes itself and moves forward to another level of self-realization.[46]

If *Geist* is moving toward self-actualization by its own inner dynamic, what, then, we may rightfully ask, is the role of human activity? Hegel explained, "The transition of its [i.e., *Geist*'s] potentiality into actuality is mediated through consciousness and will."[47] Human consciousness and will are no more than the mediation or the reflection of *Geist*'s self-actualizing. They are not the cause of its actualization, they merely mirror *Geist*'s activity and reflect its development within human history.[48] On the other hand, the struggle and ongoing dialectic of *Geist* are of great consequence to history. The self-actualization of *Geist* is, according to Hegel, the inexorable and inevitable realization of complete and total freedom, and *Geist* moves history forward toward that end.

Within this great overarching framework of *Geist* how did Hegel understand praxis and unite it with theory? For Hegel all praxis is the praxis of *Geist* as it realizes itself in history. Human knowing is not realized by speculative theorizing apart from the world, but by reflection on and participation in the praxis of *Geist* within history. Theory is not something to be formulated by intellectual speculation and then applied to practice. Rather, theory is human consciousness of the rational ingredient in *Geist*'s praxis as it actualizes itself in the world. This is what Hegel meant by his famous dictum, "Theory rises only at sundown"; in other words, it comes afterward rather than before. Instead of theory leading to practice, theory arises from consciousness of the rational ingredient of *Geist*'s praxis in the world. Richard Bernstein offers a helpful summary of Hegel's position:

> *Theoria*, in its purest form, as philosophy, is nothing but the articulation of the rationality ingredient in *praxis*. There is then an ultimate harmony of theory and practice—*theoria* and *praxis*—not in the sense that philosophy guides action, but rather in the sense that philosophy is the comprehension of what is; it is the comprehension of the *logos* ingredient in *praxis*, i.e., *praxis* as the self-activity of *Geist*. There is an ultimate unity of theory and practice, a unity that becomes intelligible when we understand that *Geist* is at once *praxis*, and in its self-reflective form, *theoria*.[49]

What, then, can we draw from Hegel to understand a praxis way of knowing? To begin with, by pointing out that all knowing is consciousness of life's praxis, he rejected the epistemological assumption that underlies a from theory to practice (as a "one-way street") way of knowing. In this he challenged the primacy of theoria in the knowing process and posed praxis as primary instead. That is where knowing begins. Second, and more important, he rejected the separation of theory and praxis as a false dichotomy. They belong together in a fundamental unity because praxis is the actualizing of *Geist* and theoria is human consciousness of the rational ingredient in *Geist*'s self-actualizing. If an educational activity is to be faithful to this insight of Hegel, then it must hold lived experience and the consciousness that has arisen from lived experience in previous generations (what I called in Chapter One the "disciplines of learning") in a fruitful tension with, and never apart from, each other. This unity of theory and praxis appears in a shared praxis approach to Christian religious education as I attempt to hold the Christian Story/Vision and present Christian praxis in a dialectical unity.

But there is also a profound shortcoming in Hegel's understanding of the human role in historical praxis, and thus in his understanding of praxis as a way of knowing the world. While he understood human knowing to be consciousness of praxis, for Hegel it is *Geist*'s praxis that is brought to consciousness. If human knowing is no more than consciousness of *Geist*'s praxis, then it does not arise from self-initiated active/reflective engagement in the world. It comes instead by phenomenological observation of *Geist*'s activity and self-actualization. But if human knowing is consciousness of *Geist*'s self-consciousness, then the world is still more to be contemplated than acted upon. In other words, for Hegel there is still an unduly contemplative, receptive, and nonactive dimension in human knowing. We can only conclude that even as he espoused historical praxis as the source of knowledge, Hegel remained caught in a Greek theoretical mode of knowing, or what Dewey called the spectator theory of knowledge.

The problem with such philosophical idealism is compounded further by the fact that, for Hegel, the actualizing of *Geist* is taking place inevitably, guided and empowered by Providence. As a result, human initiative and creativity are left with little part to play in the unfolding of history. History moves forward instead by the self-initiated dialectic taking place within *Geist* and according to its own rationality. But such an arrangement robs us of our human responsibility within history. So while there is some resemblance, Hegel's *Geist* is not the God of the Kingdom whose action calls for our action and whose gift calls for our response. Thus, Hegel brought Western epistemology back again to consider a praxis way of knowing united with theory, but his explanation of such a knowing process is still not adequate for our purpose in Christian religious education.

Karl Marx moved us a step closer to a critical human praxis that demands the reflective-intentional action of humankind within history. In dialectic with Hegel's position, Marx put humankind in the place of *Geist* as the self-constituting agent of historical becoming. As a result, he turned Hegel's world upside down but claimed that that was to place the world on its feet, rather than on its head where Hegel had left it. Even though Marx put humankind in the place of *Geist*, however, the inevitability of the dialectical process in Hegel recurred in Marx and posed a problem for which Marx offered at best an ambiguous solution. In addition, Marx claimed that all historical progress depends entirely on human action, and, as we will see, that, too, is its own error.

MARX'S PRAXIS WAY OF KNOWING

When Marx came to Berlin in the fall of 1836 for graduate studies, he immediately came under the influence of Hegel's thinking and the "Hegelians of the Left." He was fascinated by Hegel's grand system. But even in his doctoral dissertation he began to struggle with what he perceived to be a profound problem in Hegel's work, namely, reconciling a still unchanged world with the salvific heights promised by Hegel's self-actualizing *Geist*. Marx claimed that a freedom which is yet to be realized by an idealized evolutionary process is still no freedom at all. In the eleventh of his "Theses on Feuerbach" he made the oft-quoted statement, "The philosophers have only interpreted the world differently, the point is, to change it."[50]

Eventually Marx came to see Hegel's idealism and his idea of absolute *Geist* as no more than an ideology, a false consciousness that accepts and legitimates reality as it appears to be as if that is how it ought to be. Following Feuerbach, Marx rejected *Geist* as a mystification in Hegel's thought. But still fascinated with Hegel's grand synthesis, he inserted humankind in the place of *Geist*, so that the ideational evolutionary process now became a human and historical one. For Marx knowledge is not a reflection of the consciousness of *Geist*, but a reflection of "historical materialism," by which he meant the material conditions of life, and specifically the mode of producing the material means of existence as these find embodiment in society and history. Human consciousness is a reflection of that social historical reality because "it is not the consciousness of men that determines their existence, but their social existence that determines their consciousness."[51] False consciousness is consciousness that merely reflects the superstructure of an unjust society and accepts that superstructure as legitimate.

For Marx the overarching reality is not *Geist* as Hegel claimed but humankind in relationship within history; the moving power in history is not divine providence but humanity's self-constitutive labor. The self-alienating dialectical process that Hegel saw as an expression of *Geist*'s praxis Marx roots instead in the conditions, and especially the economic arrangements, of human society. "For Hegel," wrote Marx, "human nature, man, is equivalent to self-consciousness. All estrangement of human nature is therefore nothing but estrangement of self-consciousness." But there, according to Marx, Hegel was wrong because "man is a corporeal, living, real, sensuous, objective being with natural powers." As a consequence, "he has real, sensuous objects as the object of his being and of his vital expression. . . . He can only express his life in real, sensuous objects."[52] Alienation is not estrangement from self-consciousness. Alienation from self-consciousness is only an expression of the deeper estrangement and alienation of humankind from the products of their labor.

According to Marx, it is in labor that people externalize themselves and, thus objectified, come to be what they are. The inner life is given expression and takes form in the objects people produce. This concept is similar to the first two moments of Hegel's dialectic—the subject (1) becomes objectified (2) in the product of his or her labor. In this separation the object that the worker produces confronts the worker "as something alien, as a power independent of the producer."[53] This is a necessary stage if one is to come to true self-consciousness and "material synthesis" by reappropriating the products of one's labor. However, in a capitalist economy, Marx claimed, this does not happen. Instead, the products of labor are controlled by the owners of the means of production and the workers cannot reappropriate the objects of labor to themselves.[54] In consequence, Marx claimed, a revolutionary praxis is necessary, by which the social and economic structures can be radically changed so that the laborers can share the ownership of the means and ends of their production. Then, Marx promised, there will be a society in which the products of labor no longer have "mastery over" but will be "controlled by" the laborers, and human praxis will be the praxis of historical freedom.

Whether one agrees with Marx's critique of capitalism or not, he helps to advance our understanding of human praxis as a way of knowing, even as his understanding of it had serious deficiencies.

For Marx emancipation and freedom can only be brought about by human praxis within history. Nowhere does he clearly define his meaning of praxis, and yet it is central to his thought. My reading is that for Marx praxis meant the self-initiated and self-creating activity of human beings that is intentionally and reflectively done and transforms social reality in the direction of human emancipation.[55] Thus human praxis, not *Geist*'s praxis, is the agency in history of freedom and emancipation.

Clearly a praxis epistemology is central to Marx's understanding of knowing. Because he saw labor as that which mediates between a subject and an object, labor is not only a way of engaging in the world, it is also a way of knowing the world.[56] We come to know the world by a critical reflective activity that transforms the world. In consequence, knowledge is not knowledge unless it is "done," and it is only in being reconstructed that the world is apprehended or known. For Marx theory is the articulation of the consciousness that arises from such human praxis, and it must return to inform further praxis. Therein lies the dialectical unity. It is in being actualized that theory is transcended, and further theory arises from its own actualization for the sake of further praxis, and so on, in an ongoing process.

What can Christian religious educators learn from Marx about a praxis way of knowing? First, we can draw from him the insight that human knowing is an expression of historical human praxis. In this he has already taken us beyond Hegel. We can learn further that authentic knowing should be a transforming activity (we will hear a similar word from Piaget in Chapter Eleven) and should transform reality toward human freedom and emancipation. He adds weight to the argument that the traditionally accepted dichotomy between theory and practice is a false one, and it is especially important for educators of any kind to know this.[57] We can also take from him the insight that historical human praxis demands initiative and creativity, reflection and intuition, on our part. With intentionality and creativity we can be, in part, producers of our own history, and not merely the products of it.

But Marx's notion of praxis is also insufficient for our purpose. In fact, it has a number of serious errors. I offer first a theological and then a philosophical criticism of his understanding. In doing so I also intend to make clearer some essential aspects of my own understanding of praxis.

By reducing humankind to the products of its own labor, Marx would rob us of all transcendence, and indeed of the God who is source of that transcendence. Here I intend to state more than my obvious disagreement with his atheism. The important point for us as Christian educators is that such a materialistic praxis can never be an adequate way of knowing for Christian religious education. For Marx we and history are the products of "dialectical materialism," the dialectical interaction between ourselves and the concrete objects of reality. Our praxis is limited to that interaction. In consequence, for Marx, we are what we make ourselves, and no more. The human emancipation he hoped for is to be entirely and exclusively the product of human efforts. But Christians could never settle for such a limited notion of praxis. In theological language this is an extreme form of pelagianism, the view that salvation comes by our own human efforts alone. If we were to accept such an understanding of and expectation from human praxis, we would be denying both the reality of sin and the gift of God's grace and Kingdom.

Our historical praxis is not only a material praxis, nor is it entirely our own "doing." Our way of knowing is through an active/reflective relationship with our created world, but also through a lived relationship with God as this is encountered and reflected upon in a Christian community and in the whole community of humankind.

Marx, of course, would dismiss such a theological criticism as based in false consciousness. He saw all such religious "groaning" as no more than an expression of the pain caused by the alienation of people from the products of their labor in an unjust society. There is also, however, a serious philosophical deficiency in his understanding of praxis. To explain this I draw from Jürgen Habermas' criticism of Marx's epistemology.

Marx rightly contended that there are twin moments in human praxis, action and reflection, consciousness and doing. However, he had a limited and impoverished understanding of both the active and reflective moments. Because Marx posed "sensuous human labor" as that which mediates between the subject knowing and the object known, action is reduced to labor as a "tangible productive activity," and the reflective moment in praxis is reduced to "production feedback" (both Habermas' phrases) from that labor. In consequence, explains Habermas, "Marx reduces the process of reflection to the level of instrumental action."[58] But this position limits the scope and breadth of the active moment and the depth and importance of the reflective moment in praxis.

By limiting activity to productive labor, Marxists were left with only a critique of economic praxis and, as Anthony Quinton points out, "the causes of human misery and frustration include, but go far beyond, the existing system of property-relations."[59] By limiting reflection to production feedback (and since production feedback happens inevitably), the importance of self-initiated critical reflection as a moving force in historical praxis is largely obliterated. Habermas writes of Marx on this point: "By reducing the self-positing of the absolute ego to the more tangible productive activity of the species, he eliminates reflection as such as a motive force of history, even though he retains the framework of the philosophy of reflection."[60]

This ambiguity in Marx led to a "reification" of the revolutionary process— the conviction that it would happen in and of itself and by its own inevitable dialectic. Thus the ongoing process of history itself becomes "fetishized," that is, takes on a life of its own, in the Marxist schema.[61] The problem this engendered for later Marxists is stated well by Trent Schroyer:

> Marx has not really shown why emancipatory struggle is necessary and has reduced the problem to economic determinism, that is, forced cooperation of workers in the midst of a mechanizing production process is held by Marx to result in the growth of a socialist consciousness. Later Marxists have therefore always been faced with an unanswerable question: namely, "how is consciousness of domination possible?"[62]

I would add also that Marxists could never adequately explain why such consciousness of domination is necessary, nor why, if it will emerge inevitably to the point of revolution, anyone should intentionally try to promote critical consciousness. Habermas, on the other hand, offers a broadened understanding of both the active and the reflective moments in praxis which transcends the fetishization and limitations of Marx's position. He also offers a new basis for the unity of *theoria* and praxis, namely, the constitutive interest of the knowing subjects.

HABERMAS' DIVISION OF THE THREE WAYS OF KNOWING

Jürgen Habermas is recognized as the leading contemporary representative of the school of critical theory housed at the Frankfurt Institute.[63] Presently stationed at the Max Planck Institute in Starnberg, West Germany, he is recognized as one of the most influential philosophers in modern Germany. While continuing to be identified with critical theory, Habermas is also critical of the Frankfurt School. In his opinion current critical theorists have dissociated themselves from the original intention of the school, namely, to be the self-consciousness of a political struggle for emancipation.[64]

There are many valid criticisms made of Habermas's social theory. I draw upon his thinking here only insofar as he expands in significant ways the notion of praxis as a way of knowing beyond that left by Marx. In his understanding of praxis, too, there are some serious inadequacies, which I will list below; however, he takes us a step closer to a notion of praxis adequate for Christian religious education and strengthens the argument and base for maintaining a dialectical unity between *theoria* and praxis.

For Habermas all knowing has a "knowledge constitutive interest," that is, a basic orientation of the knowing subject that shapes the outcome of what is known. The "interest" we bring to the knowing process is that which unites theory and practice, where knowing subject and world known come together. We know what we want to know in order that we may act.

To explain this notion of interest, Habermas argues that fundamental to the human species are twin dispositions toward reproduction and self-constitution. The disposition toward reproduction gives rise to work. The tendency toward self-constitution gives rise to human interaction and language. But grounded in both and prior to them is a third fundamental disposition, namely the quest for human emancipation, which gives rise to the struggle for freedom. Interests, then, are the orientations that arise from these basic human dispositions. They find expression in the work and interaction of human beings and in their struggle for emancipation. The interests of the knowing subject connect the object of knowledge with the possible use to which the knowledge derived may be put.[65] Thus for Habermas theory and practice are united by the "knowledge constitutive interests" of the knowing subject.

This position leads Habermas to reject the "objectivist illusion" that claims the possibility of disinterested knowledge. In dialectic with popularized Marxism, it also leads him to reestablish the absolute importance of the critical reflection of the knowing subject. The action *and* reflection of the subject are essential to a praxis way of knowing and to engaging in the world for its transformation. However, not all human praxis is capable of being transforming and emancipatory. It depends upon the extent and critical quality of the reflective moment in praxis, and, according to Habermas, in some of the scientific modes for investigating reality the reflective moment is not sufficiently critical to cause emancipation. To understand his position here it is first necessary to outline his threefold division of the sciences that investigate reality. He divides them into the empirical analytical sciences, the historical hermeneutic sciences, and the critical sciences.

Empirical Analytical Sciences.   These are the sciences of knowing that reflect on our productive activity in the world. According to Habermas, the interest of the analytical empirical sciences is aimed at technical usability in work. Their aim is to investigate reality so that its predictability and reliability are discovered for the sake of controlling reality to our own practical ends. The investigation is "purposive-rational action" and is thus a praxis. But the interest which motivates the empirical analytical sciences is one of "technical control";[66] in other words, they investigate reality to know what can be reliably used to control reality. Critical reflection is suspended in that they ask only What is? rather than What might be? and they do not ask Why? at a fundamental level that might uncover the interest that constitutes the science itself. The technical control is rationalized and legitimated instead by production and the products of labor.

Historical Hermeneutic Sciences.   The second group of sciences reflect on the meaning of the interaction of human beings, especially as expressed in language.[67] While the first group of sciences collects data that describe reality so that it can be used more effectively in a technical way, this second group interprets human interaction in its historical, community context. However, in the standard hermeneutical sciences, according to Habermas, the interest is always in maintaining the present communal reality as it is, and in maintaining intersubjective communication within that reality. The praxis is a communicative praxis, but in effect it asks only, Within the confines of this context (or tradition), what does such and such mean? It does not ask, What were the constitutive activities of the species that made it this way? nor Do we want to continue within this meaning-making system? As a result, the interest of the historical hermeneutic sciences is what Habermas calls "practical control."[68]

Put simply, the outcome of the hermeneutical act is determined by the interest the interpreters bring to the act, and according to Habermas, they bring a practical interest in maintaining mutual understanding within a common tradition. If the interpreters are not aware of this interest, then "the understanding of meaning is directed in its very structure toward the attainment of possible consensus among actors in the framework of a self-understanding derived from tradition."[69] Given the "maintaining" interest of these sciences, they are not likely to uncover distorted and repressed communication within the accepted tradition handed down. As a result, the interpretation remains within the confines of that tradition and serves the interest of practical control. In a word, the reflective moment in this praxis is not sufficiently critical to be emancipatory; it interprets only "what is there" in the tradition, rather than uncovering and questioning the genesis that produced reality as it appears to be, or posing an alternative beyond the walls of the given tradition.

According to Habermas, then, these first two groups of sciences and their praxis ways of knowing are not capable by themselves of being emancipatory because they fail to be aware of and to critique their own knowledge-constitutive interests. The knowing they promote fails to critique ideology and will not promote critical consciousness to see things as they are constituted and create them as they might be. There is a third group of sciences, however, which can cause such a critical consciousness. They arise when an emancipatory interest is foremost in the investigation of reality. Whether or not we agree with this assessment of the first two groups of science[70] (and I claim below that Habermas' criticisms are overstated), in this third group we find his expanded notion of a truly critical praxis which can inform us for a praxis approach to Christian religious education.

Critical Sciences.   The critical sciences are those that arise from and reflect upon the human quest for freedom. They include and are informed by elements from the first two groups of sciences, but their interest is emancipation, and their praxis is a truly critical one. Habermas uses psychoanalysis as his central example of such a science, but when sufficiently critical, these sciences can include the "sciences of social action" that attempt a "critique of ideology."[71] The key ingredient of the critical sciences is a critical self-reflection that uncovers the personal and social genesis of one's attitude and unmasks the interest of one's present action, within the context of societal action. As such, they involve both a self-critique and a social critique. Critical self-reflection within one's social-historical context is essential if emancipation, the interest of these sciences, is to be realized. Habermas claims that with the return to the social and personal genesis of present action, repressed dialogue is released, ideology is unmasked, and an emancipation can ensue that enables people to create a present that has some freedom from a controlling past.[72] Habermas does not contend that our knowing can ever be free of "interest." That is impossible. But when the interest is emancipatory, then "the mind can always reflect back upon the interest structure that joins subject and object a priori: this is reserved to self-reflection. If the latter cannot cancel out interest, it can to a certain extent make up for it."[73]

In conceptualizing what a critical science of society might be, Habermas has been greatly influenced by the psychoanalytic work of Sigmund Freud. Habermas understands the relationship between the therapist and patient in psychoanalysis as one that employs critical linguistic analysis in order to correct distorted communication, release repressed dialogue, and uncover unrecognized dependencies and suppressed controls. The self-knowledge that results coincides with the emancipatory interest of the patient and therapist. Using this as a model, Habermas proposes a similar role for the social theorist in relation to society. In effect, this has moved Habermas to attempt to develop a theory of "communicative competence" that can achieve in society what the therapist achieves with the patient. Only by uncovering the interests, ideologies, and assumptions which are at the base of the historical constitutive activity of the human species and

make society what it is can people participate in a critical praxis for emancipation. This requires a level of communication that goes beyond the level of "ordinary discourse."

Habermas is adamant about the need for dialogue in the midst of a critical
praxis. "In the act of solitary self-reflection the subject can deceive itself."[74] But
when it comes to describing a situation of what he calls "communicative competence," he admits that his position is still in embryonic form.[75] Some of his
thinking on communicative competence will reappear in Chapter Nine in my
description of dialogue in a shared praxis approach to Christian religious education. There, however, I am more influenced by Freire's notion of dialogue,
Buber's I/Thou relationship, and my own experience in attempting to create
situations of authentic dialogue.

What, then, can we learn from Habermas about a praxis way of knowing
for religious education? I list below six disagreements I have with his notion of
praxis, and attempt to correct them in the understanding of praxis I propose in
Chapter Nine. However, I will first note some key insights I have learned from
him in my attempts to construct a praxis way of knowing for Christian religious
education.

To begin with, Habermas has corrected some of the reductionism in Marx
and has gone beyond him on two crucial points. First, he expands Marx's understanding of the active moment of praxis far beyond labor that produces tangible objects. He does this by also stressing the activities that give rise to the historical hermeneutic sciences and the critical sciences. For Habermas knowing is
by human praxis, but the active moment in that praxis includes all intentional
human activity, be that instrumental, interpretive, or critical.

Secondly, Habermas reestablishes the importance and primacy of critical
reason on the part of the knowing subject. This was a contribution of the Enlightenment that was largely lost to party Marxists, if not to Marx himself. Habermas is beyond the Enlightenment, however, in his emphasis on the need for
critical reflection that is both a self-critique and a political/social critique. By
proposing a critical, self-reflective, social praxis, he requires critique of the
whole spectrum of interests, symbols, attitudes, assumptions, technologies, and
ideologies that suspend doubt and control people by distorting communication
and repressing dialogue. It is not just the economic system that needs to be criticized, as Marx contended, but the whole symbol system by which the world is
mediated to us. In summary, Habermas goes beyond Marx in his notion of
praxis in that action is much more than labor, reflection is much more than production feedback, and interest is much more than class interest.

Three other aspects of Habermas' thinking have also informed me. First, he
has argued for the unity of theory and praxis as Hegel and Marx did before
him. But his pointing to the knowledge-constitutive interests of the knowing

subjects as the source of that unity is a unique contribution and a key insight for a shared praxis approach to Christian religious education. It will be reflected especially in the fact that shared praxis attempts to bring people to name their own constitutive knowing (that is, the knowing which arises from their own engagement in the world), and to critically reflect on that knowing in order to uncover its source and consequence (their "interests"). In this way people are brought to know and name their own story and vision. That self-constituted knowing is then placed in a dialectical hermeneutic with the Story and Vision of the Christian community, thus attempting to maintain the unity of *theoria* and praxis in the act of Christian knowing.

Second, while I believe Habermas has overstated his claim (see my third point of disagreement below), he offers a convincing argument that when the reflective moment of praxis is truly critical, it can be emancipatory. This is one of my reasons for using a praxis way of knowing to undergird Christian religious education: it would seem more capable of promoting the human freedom that is part of our purpose.

Last, his argument for the need to release repressed dialogue and work toward "communicative competence" will reappear again in the dialogical dimension of the shared praxis approach.

On the other hand, there are at least six aspects of Habermas's position that I reject and attempt to move beyond. First, I do not accept his position that all hermeneutics has the interest and consequence of practical control. Undoubtedly, hermeneutics can have that consequence, and it often has. But I favor Gadamer's position on this issue (see note 70 here and note 24 in Chapter Nine) and argue that when a hermeneutical activity is dialectical and poses an open horizon for tradition, it can break the bounds of practical control and be emancipatory.

Second, and closely related to my first criticism, Habermas takes the Enlightenment position that poses reason as the only authority and rejects tradition out of hand. He seems to claim that truly critical reflection will find nothing in any tradition, nor in one's personal and social genesis, that is worth retaining. As a result, he is critical to the point of negativism. I avoid using "critical reflection" in that negative sense and view the tradition as a source of life and truth. Critical reflection is a dialectical but positively creative activity which recognizes the limitations of our traditions but also affirms and retains their truth as we attempt to create beyond them.

Third, I do not place the same amount of unlimited faith in critical reflection as Habermas appears to. Critical reflection is not inevitably emancipatory; it only has the possibility of being so. Habermas overstates the power of human critical reason alone to change the world. In that he is as much a pelagian as Marx. I insist that critical reason is essential for a transforming human praxis, but the enlightening Spirit and God's grace of discernment is the a priori gift by which it takes place. Then it *may* be emancipatory.

Fourth, I favor the more obvious emphasis given by both Aristotle and Marx that the end of praxis is more praxis. In other words, within religious education the critical reflection on action that is shared in dialogue (shared praxis) must lead back always to lived Christian faith with the consequence of human freedom. Habermas seems to make "communicative competence" in an "ideal speech situation" (see note 75) an end in itself, but that sounds as if the world would continue to be described rather than transformed.

Fifth, Habermas does not place sufficient emphasis on the affective dimension of a praxis way of knowing and so has forgotten the insights of both Aristotle and Marx. As Habermas describes it, a praxis way of knowing sounds unduly rational and, in a narrow sense of the word, cognitive. His notion of interest certainly includes emotion, but his method for uncovering interest sounds intellectualist.

Finally, my understanding of the critically reflective moment of praxis places greater emphasis on the role of imagination than Habermas appears to give it. Critical reflection needs to be a critique of ideology that unmasks the genesis of the present in the constitutive activity and interests of the past, both personal and social. But it must also bring creativity to imagine a new future beyond the present or past. Without creative imagination, critical reflection is again in danger of leading to a debilitating negativism.

PAULO FREIRE AND HIS PRAXIS OF EDUCATION

The philosophical background to my understanding of a praxis way of knowing would not be complete without pointing to the educational work of Paulo Freire.[76] Freire is the most significant exponent of a praxis approach to education today. He argues for such an approach precisely because he believes it is capable of promoting human emancipation. My first attempts to use a praxis approach in religious education began after meeting Freire and reading his foundational work, *Pedagogy of the Oppressed*, in 1972.

Freire is presently a special consultant on education to the World Council of Churches and is stationed in Geneva, Switzerland. His main theatre of action is the emerging African nation of Guinea-Bissau. However, his understanding of education arose from his own praxis in literacy programs conducted first in Brazil and later in Chile. Using a critical consciousness-raising praxis approach, he taught people to read in as little as six weeks.

There are three basic philosophical assumptions upon which Freire's approach to education is grounded. First, *humanization is the basic human vocation*. That calling, however, is constantly prevented from being realized by the many cultural and social forms of oppression that dehumanize people. "But while both humanization and dehumanization are real alternatives, only the first is man's vocation."[77] Second, *people are capable of changing their reality.* We can become creators of our culture and not merely creatures determined by it. We can have critical consciousness of our reality to the point that we act to change it. Third, *education is never neutral.* It always has political consequences. The consequences can be either to control people by integrating them into conformity with existing society or to liberate them to deal critically and creatively with their reality in order to transform it.

I have drawn upon Freire's description of a praxis approach to education many times already and will continue to cite him throughout the remainder of this work. By way of a brief summary here, Freire argues that education is to be an exercise in freedom. To achieve such an end he proposes a "problem-solving" critical reflection on present reality approach, in opposition to what he calls the "banking method"[78] for doing education. Promoting critical consciousness ("conscientization") that disposes people to act and arises from reflection on their historical experience is essential to his praxis approach. Conscientization, for Freire, is a process of decoding reality, "stripping it down so as to get to know the myths that deceive and perpetuate the dominating structure"[79] so that people are disposed to change that reality in the direction of humanization. Such conscientization is possible only by participation in historical, critical praxis. "Functionally, oppression is domesticating. To no longer be prey to its force, one must emerge from it and turn upon it. This can be done only by means of the *praxis*: reflection and action upon the world in order to transform it."[80] The role of the pedagogue is to be "with" rather than "over" people, enabling them to name their world and through dialogue come to act creatively on their historical reality.

Freire's position has aroused considerable controversy. Among other things, he has been expelled from his native Brazil for "subversive activity." I am one among many religious educators who have been challenged by his insights. However, one shortcoming in his writings so far is that nowhere does he explain clearly what he means by praxis. As a result, it is not at all clear how one might attempt to construct an intentional pedagogical activity by a praxis approach in something other than a literacy program. I also criticize him for placing undue emphasis on the present and future, to the almost total neglect of the past. He sounds at times, as Habermas does, as if nothing from the past is to be made available again to people in the present. I attempt to correct this in the shared praxis approach by insisting that the Story of the faith community be constantly remembered. It certainly cannot be imposed upon the present as a final word. Rather, it is to be placed in a dialectic with the present. If the past is forgotten and left unreclaimed, it will determine and control our present. If it is critically appropriated, it can be emancipatory.

The various strands of thought I have traced from Aristotle to Freire will reappear again in Chapters Nine and Ten as I describe a shared praxis approach to Christian religious education. I am committed to an approach that is grounded in a praxis way of knowing because 1) it seems capable of promoting a "knowing" in the biblical sense; 2) since it maintains a unity between "theory" and praxis, it seems more likely to promote a lived Christian faith and thus decrease the hiatus between the faith we claim and how we live; and 3) it seems more capable than a from theory to practice way of knowing of promoting emancipation and human freedom.

Over the past eight years I have been attempting to develop, use, and explain such a praxis approach. I am now ready to share a description of it at its present stage of development.

NOTES

1. This tripartite division can be found in many places in Aristotle's writings. Perhaps the best statement is in *Topics VI* (see Aristotle, *The Works of Aristotle Translated into English*, 1:145–147).
2. Most often Aristotle refers to this third way of life as "productive," but he also sometimes refers to it somewhat disparagingly as the "life of enjoyment" (see, for example, Aristotle, *Ethics: The Ethics of Aristotle*, Book 1, Ch. 5. Hereafter references to *The Nicomachean Ethics* will be to this 1977 edition of Thomson's translation [cited as *Ethics*] unless otherwise noted).
3. This tripartite division of "lifestyle" is not original to Aristotle in Greek philosophy. It goes back at least to Pythagoras (and he probably did not invent the terms either), who divided the people who came to the Olympic games into three categories. The first group were the *theoroi,* people who came to contemplate the games from a distance with a form of spiritual abandonment to the events taking place. The second group were those who came to participate in the events by active competition. The third group were the artisans and craftsmen who came to exchange their artifacts and generally to have a good time (see Burnet, *Early Greek Philosophy*, p. 98).
4. Lobkowicz states the distinction between them well when he writes, "While theoretical knowledge is an end in itself . . . practical knowledge aims at ordering human action and productive knowledge, at producing a material thing" (*Theory and Practice*, p. 127).
5. "Conditions of mind" is Greenwood's translation of *psyche* (see Aristotle, *Nicomachean Ethics*, trans. L.H.G. Greenwood, p. 93). Thomson translates it as "states of mind."
6. See Aristotle, *Ethics*, p. 207.
7. Ibid., p. 211.
8. Ibid., p. 211.
9. Ibid., p. 212.
10. Lobkowicz, *Theory and Practice*, p. 11.
11. Aristotle, *Ethics*, p. 209.
12. Ibid., p. 213.
13. Ibid., p. 205.
14. Ibid., p. 205.
15. Ibid., p. 206.
16. See Liddell and Scott, *A Greek-English Lexicon*, πρᾶξις, p. 1459. An example of praxis being

used for sexual intercourse can be found in Fragment 127 of Pindar's poetry. Pindar was an ancient Greek poet who lived approx. 522–433 BCE (see Pindar, *The Works of Pindar*, Fragment 127:341).

17. Lobkowicz, *Theory and Practice*, p. 9.
18. See Burnet, *Aristotle on Education*, p. 1.
19. Lobkowicz, for example, argues that Aristotle opposed the life of *theoria* to *praxis* and opposed *praxis* to *poiesis* (see *Theory and Practice*, pp. 9, 17).
20. See, *Nicomachean Ethics*, trans. Greenwood, pp. 41–43. Greenwood claims that for Aristotle, "*poiesis* is essentially a means to *praxis*" (Ibid., p. 41).
21. See Burnet, *Aristotle on Education*, p. 9.
22. See Stewart, *Notes on the Nicomachean Ethics of Aristotle*, 2:443–444.
23. Aristotle, *Ethics*, p. 331.
24. Ibid., p. 333.
25. Lobkowicz comments, "As we have seen, Aristotle had divided knowledge into theoretical, practical, and productive. Yet the third member of this division seems to have fallen into oblivion soon after Aristotle's death, the main reason probably being that Aristotle tended to identify productive knowledge with arts and thus had suggested that it was not a genuine type of knowledge in the strong sense of the term" (*Theory and Practice*, p. 81). Lobkowicz's explanation is probably correct. However, I rather think it also happened that *praxis* and *poiesis* were collapsed into meaning what we refer to in English as *practice*. In a sense, that does not do justice to what Aristotle meant by either *praxis* or *poiesis*.
26. Plotinus (205–270) is usually considered the founder of Neoplatonism, although the undue intellectualism I am referring to here was evident in the Platonists before him. Some Neoplatonists rejected Aristotle out of hand, while others considered him as a useful preparation for studying the higher wisdom of Plato. The Neoplatonists were a powerful school of thought until about the seventh century.
27. Lobkowicz summarizes the position of the Neoplatonists on this point thus: "Nothing opposed to contemplation was any longer a perfection in its own right; only contemplative life truly counted and everything else was either its radical absence or a path leading toward it. Virtue and human perfection were now divorced from all sociopolitical context" (*Theory and Practice*, p. 55).
28. For a discussion of the date of its composition see "The Didache," p. 151.
29. See Ibid., pp. 15–19.
30. For a brief but scholarly description of the Catechumenate see *New Catholic Encyclopedia*, "Catechumenate," by J. A. Jungmann, 3:238 ff. An account of the various stages of initiation it involved can be found in the *Decree of Hippolytus* (see B. Easton, *The Apostolic Tradition of Hippolytus*, pp. 41–45).
31. See *New Catholic Encyclopedia*, "Paideia, Christian," by T. P. Halton, 10:862–864.
32. Congar, *A History of Theology*, p. 42.
33. Lobkowicz, *Theory and Practice*, pp. 60–61.
34. In light of this Gutierrez contends that Augustine in fact used a praxis method for doing theology. However, it is more of a spiritual praxis than a historical praxis (see *A Theology of Liberation*, pp. 6 ff).
35. Augustine, *City*, p. 467.
36. Augustine had some very valuable and avant-garde insights on education. He advised teachers to love and gain the trust of their students; to have one central unifying theme in their presentation; to explain the material without wandering; to alter teaching styles in order to maintain student interest; to suit the material to the learning capacity of the students; to provide summaries; and, above all, to give good example. His two most concise statements on education are his *De Catechizandis Rudibus* and his treatise *De Magistro* (see Augustine, "The First Catechetical Instruction," and *The Teacher*).
37. Augustine, "The First Catechetical Instruction," p. 24.
38. The best example of such a summary statement of doctrine for catechesis can be found in Thomas' catechetical sermons delivered to the people of Naples at the end of his life (see Aquinas, *The Catechetical Instructions*).
39. Gutierrez argues that, in general, the task of Christian theology for the first 1,200 years was seen as a quest for "spiritual wisdom." Its method of inquiry was based, in large part, on a praxis way of knowing. After Aquinas, however, the task of theology became a quest for "rational knowledge about God." Then theology became a theoretical science, separated from

Christian spirituality and praxis (see Gutierrez, *A Theology of Liberation*, pp. 5 ff).
40. The first major turning point toward an active and experiential way of knowing in Catholic religious education came with the "Munich method" in the early years of this century. Strongly influenced by the "activity school" of pedagogy and by Herbartianism, it was a striking departure from the catechism approach and at least had the potential for being an active/reflective way of knowing. The exponent of the Munich method best known to American readers was R. G. Bandas (see, for example, his *Catechetical Methods*).
41. Martin Luther, "A Short Catechism for the Use of Ordinary Pastors and Preachers," in Eby, *Early Protestant Educators*, p. 88.
42. Duns Scotus (c. 1265–1308) did ask the question *"quid sit praxis,"* but Lobkowicz makes the interesting note that "no Latin author before Scotus ever used the expression 'praxis' in a philosophical or theological context" (*Theory and Practice*, p. 71).
43. Hegel, *Reason in History*, p. 15.
44. Ibid., p. 51.
45. Ibid., p. 69.
46. The German word Hegel used for the "transcending" moment is *aufheben*, which means both "to cancel" and "to preserve." Thus a view or position is *aufgehoben*, or transcended, by refusing its limitations while retaining its truth, thus moving beyond it to a new level of actualization. The typical popular understanding of Hegel's dialectic as thesis, antithesis, and synthesis does not fairly represent what Hegel intended. It is more accurate to think of the dialectic as a dynamic process in which there are three interrelated moments of affirming, refusing, and moving beyond (see Bernstein, *Praxis and Action*, p. 20).
47. Hegel, *Reason in History*, p. 69.
48. People reflect the dialectic of *Geist* in their quest for self-consciousness, which is also a dialectical struggle. In order that a self-consciousness may realize and know itself, it is essential that another self-consciousness recognize it. Hegel explained, "Self-consciousness exists in itself and for itself, in that, and by the fact that it exists for another self-consciousness; that is to say, it *is* only by being acknowledged or 'recognized'" (*The Phenomenology of Mind*, p. 229). A struggle arises from the fact that we typically attempt to reach self-consciousness by dominating the "other." Hegel used his famous analogy of master/slave to explain this.

The master dominates the slave on the assumption that it is by such domination that one comes to self-consciousness. But the relationship of domination cannot bring the master to an independent self-consciousness because the master is dependent on the slave for self-definition as master. Hegel explains, "Just where the master has effectively achieved lordship, he really finds that something has come about quite different from an independent consciousness. It is not an independent, but rather a dependent consciousness that he has achieved" (Ibid., pp. 236–237). It is the slave who first comes to see his or her value as being in the ability to produce for the master. But in the act of producing objects, the slave comes to recognize his or her mind and will in the objects produced and thus comes to realize that one has a mind and will of one's own. As a result, the slave recognizes a self-value and identity beyond the mere ability to produce for the master. Hegel explained, "In fashioning the thing, self-existence comes to be felt explicitly as its own proper being, and he [the slave] attains the consciousness that he himself exists in its own right and on its own account" (Ibid., p. 239). The slave then comes to realize that the master only consumes and destroys and is dependent on the slave for position as master. That is the beginning of freedom for both slave and master.
49. Bernstein, *Praxis and Action*, p. 34.
50. Marx, "Theses on Feuerbach," p. 199.
51. Marx, *A Contribution to the Critique of Political Economy*, p. 220.
52. Marx, "The Critique of Hegelian Philosophy," pp. 58–60.
53. Marx, *Economic and Philosophic Manuscripts of 1844*, p. 69.
54. Marx's critique of capitalism is both complex and yet disarmingly simple. Our difficulty in understanding it is the technical terms in which it is couched. The best place for his own explanation of the key terms, *value, use value, exchange value, surplus value, universal equivalent,* and *fetishism* is *Capital*, Vol. 1, Part 1, Chapter 1. Section 4 on "The Fetishism of Commodities and the Secret Thereof" is especially helpful.

I offer the following brief sketch of his critique of capitalism. According to Marx, in the capitalist system objects produced for their "use value" (i.e., their qualitative worth to the laborer) are appropriated by the capitalists for their "exchange value" (i.e., their quantitative worth for the sake of exchange by the "owners"), and in the process the objects of labor are "fetishized."

Fetishism occurs when the objects of labor become commodities of exchange and take on what appears to be a life of their own, independent of the labor that produced them. Human labor becomes "abstracted" when commodities produced for their use value are reduced to their exchange value. As a result, what should be a social relationship between laborers becomes a relationship between "things," as if these things have value in themselves. But this is a "mystification," what Marx calls "the mist through which the social character of labor appears to us to be an objective character of the products themselves" (*Capital*, p. 74). As a result, the producer exists for the sake of production instead of vice versa, and the producer appears to have no value. Within such a system, according to Marx, "Our mutual value is for us the value of our mutual objects. That is, we mutually consider man as having no value" (*Economic and Philosophic Manuscripts of 1844*, p. 546).

Going a step further, Marx argued that in a capitalist system where a select group of "owners" have appropriated the means of production to themselves, they also appropriate the objects produced by the labor of the workers. As a result, the workers cannot reappropriate the products of their labor and so remain in a state of alienation and estrangement. It is also a state of exploitation, since human labor has a "surplus value" (i.e., labor produces goods worth more than its wages), and the capitalist never pays laborers the full value of their labor. Instead, in the process of exchange the "surplus value" gets translated into the "universal equivalent" of money, which is in fact no more than the congealed labor of the workers, but is retained by the capitalists as "their own." Marx wrote, "The directing motive, the end and aim of capitalist production, is to extract the greatest possible amount of surplus value, and consequently to exploit labor-power to the greatest possible extent" (*Capital*, p. 331). According to Marx, then, alienation from the products of labor is a necessary moment in the dialectic of labor, but in a capitalist system reappropriation of the objects of labor by the laborer is prevented, and the laborer is held in a state of oppression, alienation, and exploitation.

55. Martin Jay also offers a useful summary of Marx's understanding of praxis and states clearly how Marx saw *theoria* and praxis as united. "Loosely defined, praxis was used to designate a kind of self-creating action, which differed from the externally motivated behavior produced by forces outside man's control. Although originally seen as the opposite of contemplative *theoria* when it was first used in Aristotle's Metaphysics, praxis in the Marxist usage was seen in dialectical relation to theory. In fact, one of the earmarks of praxis as opposed to mere action was its being informed by theoretical considerations. The goal of revolutionary activity was understood as the unifying of theory and praxis which would be in direct contrast to the situation prevailing under capitalism" (*The Dialectical Imagination*, p. 4.)

56. Habermas correctly summarizes Marx on this point when he writes, "The nature that surrounds us constitutes itself as objective nature for us only in being mediated by the subjective nature of man through processes of social labor. That is why labor, or work, is not only a fundamental category of human existence but also an epistemological category" (*Interests*, p. 28).

57. On this point Marx, in large part, stated no more than the obvious. John Hoffman expresses this well when he writes, "No form of human practice is possible without the presence of theory, so that when Marxism calls for the unity of theory and practice, it is simply demanding the conscious recognition of what in fact has always been the case" (*Marxism and the Theory of Praxis*, p. 101).

58. Habermas, *Interests*, p. 44.

59. Quinton, "Critical Theory," p. 51

60. Habermas, *Interests*, p. 44.

61. This is a much-debated question even among Marxists themselves as well as being a frequent criticism of Marx by his opponents. Many commentators claim, in defense of Marx, that the reification of the historical process is the vulgarized understanding found in party Marxism, but not in Marx himself. As I read him, Marx was at best ambiguous on the question, and certainly left himself open to be interpreted as seeing the revolution as coming inevitably. On the one hand, he insisted on the need for critical consciousness in revolutionary praxis. A classic statement reads thus:

We wish to find the new world through criticism of the old. . . . Even though the construction of the future and its completion for all times is not our task, what we have to accomplish at this time is all the more clear; relentless criticism of all existing conditions, relentless in the sense that the criticism is not afraid of its findings and just as little afraid of the conflict with the powers that be. (Lloyd Easton and Guddat, *Writings of the Young Karl Marx*, p. 212).

Such a statement shows that Marx was no crude materialist. True, he argued that philosophy must be transcended and that "you cannot transcend philosophy without actualizing it"

(Ibid., p. 256). He looked to the proletariat as the agents of such actualizing activity, but in their struggle they must always be informed by critical philosophy. "As philosophy finds its material weapons in the proletariat, the proletariat finds its intellectual weapons in philosophy" (Ibid., p. 263). Thus, it would seem, he insisted on the need for critical consciousness in the midst of historical praxis.

On the other hand, Marx also saw such critical consciousness as arising inevitably from the contradictions inherent in the capitalist system. For example, in the "Preface" to the first German edition of *Capital* he wrote, "Intrinsically, it is not a question of the higher or lower degrees of development of the social antagonisms that result from the natural laws of capitalist production. It is a question of these laws themselves, of these tendencies working with iron necessity toward inevitable results" (*Capital*, p. 8). These tendencies that work with "iron necessity toward inevitable results" are within a capitalist system, which, for Marx, would develop to such a point of obvious contradiction that the proletariat "necessarily will abolish private property" (Marx, quoted in Lobkowicz, *Theory and Practice*, p. 420). But then we are left with the problem (which later Marxists tended to amplify rather than solve) that if it is happening inevitably, does that not obliterate the role of human initiative and critical consciousness? Or to pose the question from an educational perspective, if critical consciousness will arise inevitably from the transparent contradictions of society, then why should anyone try to do a critical consciousness-raising form of education?

62. Schroyer, *The Critique of Domination*, p. 32.
63. The Frankfurt Institute for Social Research is an amazing group of thinkers who for more than sixty years have been a powerhouse of theoretical innovation and unrestrained social research. They are a very diverse group of scholars, but the overall position of the general corpus of their work has come to be called "critical theory," following the essay in 1936 by their then director Max Horkheimer, "Traditional and Critical Theory." Their numbers have included such major thinkers as Horkheimer, Theodore Adorno, Eric Fromm, Herbert Marcuse, Friedrich Pollock, Karl Wittfogel, and Alfred Schmidt, as well as Habermas. The common characteristic of their work is critique and a relentless attempt to take seriously Marx's slogan, "We wish to find the new world through criticism of the old." But they also realize that such critique will have to be carried on outside the ideological confines of party Marxism.

They are a reaction to the fetishized and reified concept of the revolutionary process of party Marxism that was unable to explain the reluctance of the proletariat to fulfill its historical role. They turned to human reason and critical reflection again as essential ingredients to the ongoing human quest for emancipation. Here they are in the tradition of Kant and the Enlightenment. (Kant said, "Sapere aude! 'Have courage to use your own reason!'—that is the motto of the enlightenment" [Kant, "What Is Enlightenment," p. 3].) They are also in the Hegelian tradition of judging reality before the "tribunal of reason," but they reject the Hegelian notion of Reason as a transcendent ideal. As a result, they reunite the object of knowledge with the constitutive activity of the knowing subject within a historical process. Thus they call for critical human reason to offset the "objectivist illusion" of both the capitalist and the Marxist systems.

There are many scholarly works on the Frankfurt school of critical theory available in English, including many of the original works of its leading members. For scholarly analysis of the overall contribution of the school see Wellmer, *The Critical Theory of Society*; Jay, *The Dialectical Imagination*; Schroyer, *The Critique of Domination*. For a collection of key essays tracing the historical evolution of the Frankfurt school, see Connerton, *Critical Sociology*. For brief but scholarly summaries see Schillebeeckx, *The Understanding of Faith*, Ch. 6; and Quinton, "Critical Theory," pp. 43–53.

64. For a commentary on this and on Habermas' shortcomings in responding to his own critique see Schillebeeckx, *The Understanding of Faith*, pp. 105 ff.
65. Habermas explains, "Of course, the expression 'interest' is intended to indicate the unity of the life context in which cognition is embedded: expressions capable of truth have reference to a reality which is objectified (i.e., simultaneously disclosed and constituted) as such in two different contexts of action and experience. The underlying 'interest' establishes the unity between this constitutive context in which knowledge is rooted and the structure of the possible application which this knowledge can have" (Habermas, *Theory and Practice*, p. 9).
66. Habermas explains, that in these sciences:

we can say that facts and the relations between them are apprehended descriptively. But this way of talking must not conceal that as such the facts relevant to the empirical sciences are first constituted through an a priori organization of our experience in the behavioral system of instrumental action.

Taken together, these two factors, that is the logical structure of admissable systems of propositions and the type of conditions for corroboration suggest that theories of the empirical sciences disclose reality subject to the constitutive interest in the possible securing and expansion, through information, of feedback-monitored action. This is the cognitive interest in technical control over objectified processes. (*Interests*, p. 308–309)

67. Habermas describes hermeneutics as "the scientific form of the interpretive activities of everyday life" (Ibid., p. 175).

68. Habermas writes, "We call the knowledge-constitutive interest of the cultural sciences 'practical.' It is distinguished from the technical cognitive interest in that it aims not at the comprehension of an objectified reality but at the maintenance of the intersubjectivity of mutual understanding within whose horizon reality can first appear as something." (Ibid., p. 176). (Note: Habermas frequently refers to the historical hermeneutic sciences as "the cultural sciences." He uses the terms interchangeably.)

69. Ibid., p. 310.

70. Habermas' analysis of the hermeneutical sciences especially has been challenged rightly and most obviously by Hans-Georg Gadamer. The debate between Habermas and Gadamer evolved, in large part, around Habermas' critique of the hermeneutical sciences. (In English see, for example, Gadamer, "On the Scope and Function of Hermeneutical Reflection"; and Habermas, "Summation and Response".) In Chapter Nine I make clear how and why I disagree with Habermas in his undue criticism of the hermeneutical sciences, and I side with Gadamer in the debate. I argue that a dialectical hermeneutics which is authentically critical is capable of more than mere maintenance. In fact, it can be emancipatory.

71. Habermas, *Interests*, p. 310.

72. Habermas explains: "A state defined by both cognitive performances and fixed attitudes can be overcome only if its genesis is analytically remembered. A past state, if cut off and merely repressed, would retain its power over the present" (Ibid., pp. 18–19).

73. Ibid., pp. 313–314.

74. Habermas, *Theory and Practice*, p. 28.

75. The best source in English for his thoughts on "communicative competence" are his two articles, "On Systematically Distorted Communication" and "Toward a Theory of Communicative Competence." He contends that it is only by sharing self-critical reflection "with communicative competence" that ideologies can be known, and unmasked, the truth be known, and emancipation promoted. He says "communicative competence means the mastery of an ideal speech situation" ("Toward a Theory," p. 367). An ideal speech situation is one in which there is complete mutuality and intersubjectivity between the participants. He writes in his article "Summation and Response," "With a view to the distinction between a true and a false consensus we name a speaking-situation ideal where the communication is not only not hindered by external, contingent influences, but also not hindered by forces which result from the structure of the communication itself." (p. 131). And he explains further, "The condition that the structure of the communication itself does not produce any forces is fulfilled when completely symmetrical relations exist between the participants in the discussion, i.e. when none of the participants is favored" (Ibid.). However, "A speech situation determined by pure intersubjectivity is an idealization" ("Toward a Theory," p. 372). And yet it is only as we move toward such an ideal that we can approach truth and freedom (and Habermas' constant assumption is that the truth will set us free). In his idealization Habermas is appealing to the highest sentiments in people, and his position is grounded in a faith that all people, at their best, wish to know the truth. To dismiss as an unrealistic ideal the possibility of such communicative competence would seem to be a lack of faith in the human quest for knowledge. In principle, the possibility of "communicative competence" is a latent assumption in any situation of serious discourse. Habermas explains, "Nevertheless it belongs to the structure of possible conversation that we contrafactually operate as if the imputaton of an ideal speaking-situation were not simply fictitious, but real" ("Summation and Response," p. 132).

76. There is much being written by and about Paulo Freire. I suggest that one start with his own foundational writings: *Pedagogy of the Oppressed*; *Cultural Action for Freedom*; *Education for Critical Consciousness*; and his most recent work, *Pedagogy in Process*. For an insightful critique of Freire's work see Elias, *Conscientization and Deschooling*. For a more positive treatment see Collins, *Paulo Freire*. For reflections on the relevance of Freire to religious education see Clasby, "Education as a Tool for Humanization and the Work of Paulo Freire," pp. 48–59;

van Caster, "A Catechesis for Liberation," pp. 281–303; and Warford, "Between the Plumbing and the Saving," pp. 60–76.

77. Freire, *Oppressed*, p. 28.
78. The "banking method" is characterized by Freire as the approach of depositing information in passive receptacles (see *Oppressed*, pp. 57ff).
79. Freire, "Conscientization," p. 27.
80. Freire, *Oppressed*, p. 36.

Shared Christian Praxis

THE COMPONENTS OF A SHARED PRAXIS APPROACH

Christian religious education by shared praxis can be described as *a group of Christians sharing in dialogue their critical reflection on present action in light of the Christian Story and its Vision toward the end of lived Christian faith.*

setting

To begin with, shared praxis takes place in a situation of group dialogue. Shared in the dialogue is an articulation of critical reflection upon one's present active engagement in the world as a Christian. That present engagement is in fact the embodiment of one's own story and vision, and critical reflection upon it takes place in light of the Christian communities' Story and the response which that Story invites. This requires that the Story and its Vision be made available in the pedagogical context. The telos or end of it all is further Christian praxis that is faithful to the Story and creative of its Vision. Thus I understand there to be five main components in Christian education by shared praxis, each requiring some detailed explanation. These are: 1) present action, 2) critical reflection, 3) dialogue, 4) the Story, and 5) the Vision that arises from the Story.

PRESENT ACTION

Present action here means much more than the overt productive activity of the present moment.[1] It means our whole human engagement in the world, our every doing that has any intentionality or deliberateness to it. Present action is whatever way we give expression to ourselves. It includes what we are doing physically, emotionally, intellectually, and spiritually as we live on personal, interpersonal, and social levels. In a sense, it encompasses any kind of human activity beyond the inevitable metabolic activity of our bodies.

It is this comprehensive reality of present action that is the object of critical reflection. Since the action arises from the self, the *primary* object of reflection is the self who reflects. All reflection is primarily self-reflection because when we reflect upon our activity, we are in fact reflecting upon the self that is expressed in such activity. It is only by reflection on its own objectification in action that a subject can come to appropriate himself or herself.[2] Reflection on the self is also primary in the sense that in a praxis way of knowing one begins with one's own constitutive knowing, with how one makes meaning out of one's own present action. To begin with what "they say" would be to fall back into a *theoria* epistemology. However (as seen in Chapter Six), the self is socially mediated. Thus while critical reflection is *primarily* on the self, it is *ultimately* on the social context by which the self comes to its self-identity. The whole sociocultural context, with its norms, laws, expectations, ideologies, structures, and traditions, constitutes the present action for the participants' critical reflection.

I intend the word *present* here to have the meaning I gave it in Chapter One: the present of things present, the present of things past, and the present of things future. In other words, it is the historical self and society that are reflected upon, since our present action is the consequence of our past and the shaper of our future. By reflecting on present action, we can uncover the "pasts" that have brought us to such action, and raise to consciousness the "futures" in that action by becoming aware of its likely or intended consequences. This is why critical reflection on our present action is a way of coming to know and name what I will call our own stories and visions.

CRITICAL REFLECTION

Critical reflection is an activity in which one calls upon 1) critical reason to evaluate the present, 2) critical memory to uncover the past in the present, and 3) creative imagination to envision the future in the present.

Critical Reason to Evaluate the Present. At its first level of reflection critical reason attempts to perceive what is "obvious" about the present. Very often the obvious is so much part of our given world that it is "taken" for granted and either no longer noticed or seen as inevitable. Critical reflection, then, is first an attempt to notice the obvious, to critically apprehend it rather than passively accept it as "just the way things are." This is why Freire, the most notable proponent of a praxis approach to education, often refers to himself as "a vagabond of the obvious."[3]

But while critical reason begins by noticing the obvious in the present, at a deeper level of reflection it must delve below the obvious. By a critical evaluative analysis we can attempt to discover the interest in present action, critique the ideology that maintains it, and recognize the assumptions upon which it is based. This requires returning to the genesis of present action, and so we come to the role of memory.

Critical Memory to Uncover the Past in the Present.   With the activity of memory critical reflection becomes a reflection upon one's reflection, a process of remembering the source of one's thinking. If critical reason is to discover the interest of present action, critique the ideology that maintains it, and recognize the assumptions upon which it is based, then the personal and social genesis of our action needs to be brought to consciousness. This is done by remembering.

The remembering cannot be a facile calling to mind. Simply to recall will do no more than maintain the influence of the past upon the present in a reified manner. Rather, *critical* memory is needed to break open the hardened shell of the past in the present, so as to prevent it from determining the present.

A critically remembered past can be a basis from which to choose the present and its future. A "forgotten" past, on the other hand, holds unconscious sway over the present and thus limits our freedom in shaping the future.[4] Remembering is not only a looking backward to the personal and social biographies of individual and community. It also requires a looking outward, a re-*membering* of our present action with the source of that action in its present social context. It is becoming aware of the world of which we are *members* and how that membership shapes our present action.

By critical memory, then, together with reason, we can discover the personal and social genesis of our present action. In reflecting upon the source of our activity, we come to know our own story and to name our own constitutive knowing, that is, the knowing which arises from our engagement in the world. Without this our own stories are forgotten, and the world is named for us. But critical reflection is incomplete if it rests only on reason and memory. The purpose of naming our present and knowing our story is that we may have some freedom to imagine and choose our future.

Creative Imagination to Envision the Future in the Present. Critical reflection is incomplete without imagination. Imagination is needed as we look at both the present and the past, but its predominant focus is the future. The reason we attend to the present and the past is that we may intend the future. But intending the future requires imagination; otherwise the future will be little more than repetition of the past.

The imagination I am describing here cannot be idle wonderment about the future. Rather, it must be a creative and shaping activity that gives intentionality to the future as it arises out of the present and the past. Imagination involves a refusal to duplicate what is given or to take the shape of the future as inevitable. It looks from the present to the future to envision the consequences of present action and returns from the future to shape the present in the direction of what might be preferred consequences.

In critical reflection on present action (praxis) the exercise of creative imagination is an expression of hope. Hope is what makes the real seem less real than it is, and the imagined more real than it is already. Only humankind has this ability for hope, because we alone can dream, envision, fantasize. If our educating is to promote this essential dimension of being human, then it must encourage imagination.

When education is understood as an activity of "leading out," the role of imagination seems even more obvious. The future thrust, essential to all education, demands imagination. But so much of our educational efforts stifle the imagination of the participants, telling them what to think and how to think it. So often what is authentic imaginative activity is dismissed as idle day dreaming or as naive idealism. We tell our students to "grow up," and by that we often mean "join our world and settle for it." But Jesus did not tell us to grow up. He told us, instead, that unless we become like little children, we cannot enter the Kingdom of God (see Mark 10:15). Little children are still capable of discovery, fantasy, and openness to what is not yet. The invitation of Jesus to become as children is, among other things, an invitation to imagination, creativity, and freedom. For education to lead out to that possibility requires imagination on the part of both students and teachers.

Critical reflection, then, requires the exercise of reason, memory, and imagination. I hasten to add that such are the predominant but not exclusive concerns of each dimension. All three are necessary for attending to the past, the present, and the future. While the focus of attention for our memories is the past, we also need to call on our reason and imagination if it is to be a critical memory that reclaims the past in a new way. In bringing reason to the present, we also need our memories to understand the genesis of the present and our imagination if we are not to settle simply for what we find there. And as we use imagination to envision the future, the images we use come out of our memory and are evaluated by our reason. In other words, a distinction among the functions of reason, memory, and imagination is valid, but a separation is false.

There are two other points about critical reflection that need clarification before we move on. The first pertains to the word *reflection* and the second to the word *critical*. Each word has the possibility of being misinterpreted.

Critical *reflection* engages both the rational and the affective capacities of the human person. In saying this, I am faithful to Aristotle's understanding of praxis as appetitive as well as cognitive. I first became convinced of the affective dimension of critical reflection in my own experience with groups of people in a shared praxis situation. I have found that in such groups emotions often run high. The language of critical reflection tends to mask this dimension and gives the impression of an intellectualistic and strictly cognitive activity. However, I must insist that in the praxis critical reflection is an affair of both the heart and the head.

Two factors explain why the rational and affective are inevitably fused in a praxis way of knowing. First, when we critically reflect on present action, it is primarily our own selves that we come to know, and we cannot know ourselves dispassionately. Head and heart are fused inevitably in self-knowledge. Second, the affective dimension enters into critical reflection because of the components of memory and imagination. Perhaps critical reason alone can be dispassionate (though I doubt it), but when linked with memory and imagination it certainly cannot be so. One cannot remember one's own story dispassionately, nor choose a future action without appetite to move the will. The acts of hoping and choosing not only include, but demand, desire. So when critical reflection is self-critical of one's own lived participation in the world for the sake of choosing further action, then the rational and passional are copartners in the process.[5]

My second clarification pertains to the word *critical*. Critical here is not intended to mean negative criticism that finds only what is wrong in our present action and in the story and vision embodied there. I intend critical, instead, in the sense I have previously described as a dialectical critique. A dialectical critique affirms what is good and true in present action, recognizes its limitations, and attempts to move beyond it. Thus a critical reflection, far from being an exercise in debilitating negativism, is a positive creative activity. This is where imagination plays a vital role. Imagination is essential for the creative and transforming moment of moving beyond. Without it we end up, as Habermas appears to do, with only negative criticism.

It must also be emphasized that in critical reflection the source of discernment, as always, is not solely our own reason, memory, and imagination. It is only by the Spirit's grace of discernment working within our own human efforts that we can come to know reality in light of God's activity and contribute to its transformation according to God's will.

Dialogue

In a shared praxis approach to Christian religious education the participants' critical reflections on their present action as Christians are shared in dialogue within the pedagogical setting. Dialogue is necessary for building Christian community within the group. As the general context of Christian education needs to be a community of Christian faith (Chapter Six), so the immediate context (i.e., the learning environment) of the intentional pedagogical activity itself needs to be a Christian community. To the extent that a Christian community can be created within the educational context, that context is likely to be effective in sponsoring its members toward lived Christian faith. Sharing in dialogue certainly contributes to building such a community. Only in the dialogue of what Buber calls an I/You relationship[6] is it possible for us to form human community, and Christian community requires no less.

Dialogue is especially necessary in a religious education context using a shared praxis approach because the dialogue of participants is an essential part of the catechesis. In fact, the whole content and process of a shared praxis approach is to be dialogical. To be dialogical does not mean that the participants are to talk back and forth "at" each other constantly; such a situation might not be dialogical at all. Paradoxical as it may seem, dialogue begins with one's self. At bedrock it is a conversation with our own biographies, with our own stories and visions. Of course, to be truly known by us, our self-dialogue must be externalized and shared with others, and they, too, must be heard if we are to know more clearly our own stories and visions. Thus dialogue is a subject-to-subject encounter (I/You), in which two or more people share and hear their reflective stories and visions. By such human dialogue the world can be named and common consciousness created for its transformation. "In the beginning is the word," but it must be a word of dialogue to be a beginning and not a conclusion.

Two essential activities are constitutive of dialogue, telling and listening. So often when people say they are ready to dialogue, they mean that they are ready to talk. But dialogue involves listening as much as telling. It must, however, be a listening that attempts to hear with the heart what the other person is attempting to communicate. Much more than the mere words or gestures of the other must be "heard." Our task in dialogue is to hear the whole world and person those expressions bespeak. Only in this way can either of us be affected by the exchange. Douglas Steere, who learned how to listen in his Quaker tradition of "corporate silent waiting on God," says, "How falsely a listener may construe what we say if he takes only our words."[7] When dialogue involves authentic expressing/listening activity, then the consequences are both disclosure and discovery for the people involved. By listening to others disclose themselves to me, I can help them discover themselves. And in disclosing myself to others, I can discover myself. If the dialogue is an expressing/hearing of our reflective stories and visions, then there is in it for everyone the possibility of discovering much more than we set out to disclose.

To say that the whole content/process of a shared praxis approach is dialogical does not mean that the educator cannot make present the Christian Story and its Vision by a variety of pedagogical techniques, including lecture. As I make clear below, and expand upon when describing the third movement of a shared praxis approach in Chapter Ten, the Christian community Story and its Vision must be made present within the pedagogical context, and this is the responsibility primarily of the teacher. But dialogue requires that the Story and Vision be made available in a *disclosure* rather than a *closure* manner. This means that it cannot be imposed upon the participants monologically, but must be made available in a way that invites dialogue with the tradition from their own lived experience.[8]

The dialogue I am describing and proposing here as the modus operandi of a shared praxis approach to Christian religious education is qualitatively different from discussion. This is one of the earliest lessons I learned while working with "The Crossroads,"[9] one of the first groups with which I used a shared praxis approach. We became keenly aware that telling one's story and vision and attempting to name one's world elicit a sense of reverence on the part of the listeners. I found it impossible, as did the regular members of the group, to respond to another's story with discussion-style rebuttals like "Don't you think that . . ." or "I disagree," even when their stories were quite different from my own. This was brought home rather forcefully to the group one evening when a garrulous newcomer jumped in from the beginning and began to make such comments. He was quickly but gently told by one of the participants, "That is not what we are about here." I thought, How true! and realized then how different dialogue is from discussion. Freire explains the difference forcefully:

> And since dialogue is the encounter in which the united reflection and action of the dialoguers are addressed to the world which is to be transformed and humanized, this dialogue cannot be reduced to the act of one person's "depositing" ideas in another, nor can it become a simple exchange of ideas to be "consumed" by the discussants. Nor yet is it a hostile, polemical argument between men who are committed neither to the naming of the world, nor to the search for truth, but rather to the imposition of their own truth.[10]

Freire gives an insightful and moving summary of the requirements for such dialogue (which he also learned about in his own educational praxis). To begin with, "Dialogue cannot exist . . . in the absence of a profound love for the world and for men." Second, dialogue requires humility because "the naming of the world, through which men constantly re-create the world, cannot be an act of arrogance." Third, it requires "an intense faith in man, faith in his power to make and remake, to create and re-create. . . ." It is not a naive faith, however, that ignores failure, but one that refuses to accept failure or human refusal as the final verdict. This love, humility, and faith must lead to a relationship of "mutual trust between the dialoguers." Such trust is more a result of dialogue than a prerequisite. "Whereas faith in man is an a priori requirement for dialogue, trust is established by dialogue." Fourth, dialogue requires hope, a hope that is aware of our incompleteness but is determined not to settle for silence or escape from reality. It is an active hope, but not an impatient one that gives up or continues only if there are results. Freire warns, "As the encounter of men seeking to be more fully human, dialogue cannot be carried on in a climate of hopelessness." And last, as we might expect, authentic dialogue presupposes "critical thinking."[11]

Thoughts such as these cause Freire to be dismissed at times as a naive romanticist and utopian. And, indeed, a reasonable reaction would be to ask where such a community of dialogue can be found. It certainly cannot be found anywhere ready-made, nor is it ever likely to be realized perfectly. But in religious education by shared praxis it is the ideal that ever calls us forward. In my use of shared praxis with diverse groups and in very different contexts I have been amazed at the level of trust and dialogue that can build up quite rapidly. Instead of waiting for an atmosphere of perfect trust, openness, and dialogue before beginning, I have often begun with a group of strangers to each other and, in the praxis, have witnessed what Reuel Howe calls "the miracle of dialogue."[12]

The last point to be made is that the dialogue is not only among the participants but also between the participants and God. Here again I am reporting what I and others have experienced in the praxis as much as prescribing what ought to take place. Very often, while listening to a participant tell his or her story, I and other participants have found our inner dialogue merging into dialogue with God. On many occasions shared praxis groups have reached a point of shared prayer together (sometimes taking a liturgical form) as the most fitting response to what was being heard.

The participants in shared praxis, then, share in dialogue their critical reflections on their present action. There is nothing uniquely Christian about such a process that would entitle it to be called Christian religious education. However, when our reflective activity is in response to the Christian Story and Vision, then our praxis is specifically Christian. When the Story and its Vision are retold and our own stories and visions critiqued in their light, then our educating can be called Christian. The fact is that there is an overall genesis or Story that explains where we as a Christian people have come from and an all-encompassing Vision that calls us forward. In an educational context using a shared Christian praxis approach the participants reflect upon and share the stories and visions embodied in their present action, and those stories and visions are critiqued in light of the faith tradition of Christianity (Story) and the promise of and response invited by that tradition (Vision).

THE STORY

Scripture and *tradition* could be used to convey what I intend by the metaphor *Story*. But those terms are so overladen with the memory of past polemics (scripture *or* tradition) and divisive feuds among Christians that I am reluctant to use them here. I use the word *Story,* but if taken only in its literal meaning, Story is misleading. It may be advisable, then, to begin by saying what I do *not* mean by it.[13]

By Story I do not mean simple narrative. Narratives are indeed part of our Story, but our Story is much more than our narratives. For this reason, and to distinguish it from our individual stories, I capitalize the word. By Christian Story I mean *the whole faith tradition of our people however that is expressed or embodied.* As our people have made their pilgrimage through history, God has been active in their lives (as God is active in the lives of all peoples). They, in turn, have attempted to respond to God's actions and invitations. From this convenanted relationship there have emerged particular roles and expected lifestyles, written scriptures, interpretations, pious practices, sacraments, symbols, rituals, feast days, communal structures, artifacts, "holy" places, and so on. All of these embody, express, or re-create some part of the history of that covenant. The term *Story* is intended as a metaphor for all such expressions of our faith tradition as they are all part of our Christian Story. From that Story, by God's grace, we draw our life of Christian faith, and by making it accessible again, we experience God's saving deeds on our behalf.

As indicated in Chapter Seven, remembering and representing the Story is an essential part of the Jewish and Christian process of knowing God. The life of Jewish and Christian faith is to be lived within the context of a community that embodies and remembers the Story. When in worship and sacrifice we bring ourselves before Yahweh, we are to remind both ourselves and God of God's saving deeds (see Deut. 26:5-11). The Eucharist is the recalling and remembering of God's saving intervention in Jesus Christ. We experience salvation for our time by remembering and reencountering the Story of God's saving deeds. When we remind God and ourselves of the Story, it is as if even God cannot but be moved by the memory, and for us it becomes a saving "event" once more. There is little more that a Christian community can do than authentically re*present* its Story. As H. Richard Niebuhr explained, the Church has an "inability" to state what its meaning is "otherwise than by telling the story of its life."[14]

We must be careful, too, lest it ever be assumed that we are referring to "just another story," as if someone made it up. Bernhard Anderson issues a valid caution that in the shift from talking about scripture as history to calling it story, scripture scholars must not lose sight of the fact that "the God of the Bible is the God who acts historically, in real events and concrete circumstances. . . ." Anderson warns, "The notion that the Bible is *only* story, or that revelation . . . is only a mental event, sounds suspiciously like a new kind of docetism." Our Story is grounded in historical events and has its highpoint, for Christians, in "God's historical presence in the life, death, and resurrection of Jesus Christ."[15] The historical Jesus is the Story incarnate.

True, the written testimonies we have of Jesus were written by post-resurrection communities of faith, but the Christ of faith can never be separated from the Jesus of history. Jesus is the Christ, and the Christ is Jesus of Nazareth.[16] Now the crucified and risen Jesus Christ stands as God's unbreakable promise that God is always with us, continuing to make God's will known, inviting and empowering us to respond by living the realized Kingdom already and forging ahead toward its final completion.

God is still active in our history, and we are constantly called upon to respond and participate in that activity. But if we are to have aught by which to recognize God's will and work, then the Story of our faith community must be made accessible over and over again. God is active in our lives, but God was also active in the lives of our parents and grandparents and so on, back over the history of our people. If we are to know God and find salvation in our present, then we must remember the Story of that faith community.

THE VISION

I intend the metaphor *Vision* to be a comprehensive representation of the lived response which the Christian Story invites and of the promise God makes in that Story. As explained in Chapter Three, God's intention and promise for creation is the Kingdom. By Vision, then, I mean the Kingdom of God, God's Vision for creation. From us it invites a lived response that is faithful to the reign of God. As we respond, we help to make the Kingdom present already. Meanwhile, God's promise of the completed Kingdom comes to us as a sure hope. Thus the call and hope through which we are to live our lives is the Vision of God's Kingdom.

It is important to emphasize that the Story and Vision are not separate realities, but two aspects of the same reality. The Story is the Story of the Kingdom; the Vision is the Vision of the Kingdom. The Vision is our response to and God's promise in the Story, and the Story is the unfolding of the Vision. I believe there are pedagogical advantages in setting them out separately (as will be more evident when I outline the five movements of a shared praxis approach), but we must avoid making a dichotomy of them.

The Christian Story and its Vision find expression, though not perfectly, in a community of Christian faith. They can be encountered there in the reflectively lived and shared faith of the whole community. But within the community, and in a context of intentional religious education, the educator has the responsibility of ensuring that the Story is encountered and its Vision proposed. In the community encounter between our own stories and the Story, between our own visions and the Vision, we can come to "know God" in an experiential/reflective manner. It will be a praxis way of knowing that arises from our own praxis, from the praxis of our community of pilgrims in time, and from the praxis of God in history.

Having said that the critical reflection on present action is to be done in light of the Christian Story and its Vision, we must now go a step further if we are to avoid posing the version of the Story and Vision that we know as hardened ideology, as a final *theoria* imposed upon our praxis from outside of lived experience. That would be to fall back into the old "from theory to practice" epistemology. The reasons against that and for holding *theoria* and praxis in a dialectical unity instead of a dichotomy have already been outlined in Chapter Eight. But there are also pressing historical and theological reasons for not accepting any version of the Story and Vision as hardened ideology to be simply applied to the "present."

To begin with, the Story is not yet completed, and it will not be so until the final coming of God's Kingdom. Meanwhile, as God's plan unfolds, we continue to find ourselves in new historical situations. God's activity in each age calls for its own response, which will always be somewhat the same as, but also unique from, the response possible or expected in previous eras. If our pilgrimage is to unfold the Vision rather than merely repeat the past, then the present cannot passively inherit and repeat the Story. We must appropriate the Story critically within the present experience, reclaim it, add to it with our own creative word, and in that sense "change" it. (Theologically this points to the need for development in our understanding of the tradition.[17])

Second, the Story is itself to be critically reflected upon, rather than passively accepted by the present, because the version of the Story that any group of Christians own and share can have elements of distortion. The distortions arise unwittingly and sometimes with the noblest of intentions, but the fact is that God's revelation has always come to us in the context of history. Each historical context, with its particular social/cultural ethos and ideologies, influences our interpretation and can give rise to distortions and certainly to "incompleteness." Avery Dulles insightfully remarks, "The Church may be seen as a variety of traditions, coming down from Christ and the apostles, undergoing constant development and adaptation. In the course of this development the traditions are sometimes enriched, sometimes impoverished, sometimes contaminated, sometimes purified."[18] An example of such distortion today is when the patriarchal world view of biblical times is used to exclude women from full participation in Christian community life and ministry. If such distortion is to be avoided as much as possible, then present critical consciousness must be active in reclaiming the Story of our faith tradition.

Last, there is no single agreed-upon expression of the Christian Story. There are many versions, all combining to make up the common Story of Christianity, but no one subtradition exhausts the richness of the whole tradition. Thus no one version can be imposed on a group of students as the only or final expression. Again, this may be avoided if people in the present and out of their lived experience are encouraged to bring their own creative word to reclaim the Story.

For similar reasons the present praxis of Christians cannot be rendered silent in the light of the Vision that arises from the Story. The Vision indeed is a critique of our present praxis and a measure of our faithfulness. But ours is also an open future, and its shape is being influenced by present praxis. The Vision can only be truly known as it is realized, and the understanding we now have of it must be adjusted as we move toward it. Thus our present praxis cannot be reduced to insignificance or silence in the face of our Vision.

All of this points to the need for critical scripture scholarship and theology to inform us as we attempt to critically appropriate the tradition. (The relationship between theology and religious education will be dealt with in detail at the end of Chapter Ten.) But even when the version of the Story and its Vision made accessible in a pedagogical context is informed by the best of scholarship, that version still cannot be passively accepted by the participants as the final word to critique their practice. That would also be to fall back into the old from theory to practice epistemological mode.

The objection could be raised here that it is misleading of me to make theory synonymous with Story. I agree that our Story is far more than theory, and with the presence of Biblical language and imagery in it it is less likely to be reduced to *theoria* than when couched in the language of Greek philosophy. But in the pedagogical context if our version of the Story's meaning is proclaimed from outside of lived experience instead of being critically appropriated and encountered in the midst of present praxis, then we are still caught, for all practical purposes, in a from theory to practice way of knowing. To maintain the unity I argued for earlier between theory and praxis, the Story/Vision and present praxis must be held intentionally in a dialectical unity with each other. This points to the hermeneutical principle that underlies a shared praxis approach to Christian religious education. I call it "present dialectical hermeneutics."

PRESENT DIALECTICAL HERMENEUTICS

I will first explain how I intend each of the three words that make up this idea and then describe the process they give rise to in a situation of shared praxis.

Hermeneutics.   Richard E. Palmer points out that the enterprise of hermeneutics has been understood in at least six different ways, but in general the enterprise has been understood by all of them as a "science of interpretation."[19] Etymologically, the word comes from the Greek *hermeneuein*, which means "to make clear" and "to interpret." Thus it connotes both the search for meaning in a "text" or tradition and the activity of explaining to others what one has found.[20] Christian religious education obviously requires a hermeneutical activity[21] because its task, in part, is to guide people in their attempts to discern God's will for them in their lives and to provide a space within which their discernment can be shared.[22]

Present.   My understanding and technical use of the term *present* has already been outlined in detail (Chapter One). In this hermeneutical context I mean by present the time of our existence in which the consequences of the past and the possibilities of our future reside. Thus to do a hermeneutic of the present requires that we look at the present and from the present to both the past and the future within it. Even as we critically reflect on our present and on our own stories and visions within it, we must also look to the faith Story of the people before us, and to the Vision which arises from that Story. However, for the reasons already given, the Story and Vision must be critically appropriated into our own understanding, and thus we need a dialectic in the midst of our present hermeneutics.

Dialectical.   In the context of present hermeneutics a dialectical relationship has three united but discernably different moments, and they are not easily named. The most helpful terms for the three moments may be *affirming*, *refusing*, and *moving beyond*. In a dialectical hermeneutic of any "text" there is an activity of discerning its truth and what is to be affirmed in it, an activity of discerning the limitations in our understanding of it that are to be refused, and an attempt to move beyond it, carrying forward the truth that was there while adding to it in the new understanding.[23] It is important to emphasize again that a dialectical relationship is positive and creative, rather than negative and destructive. The first affirming moment in the relationship is already a positive one, and the third moment of moving beyond becomes a creative and radical yes rather than a debilitating no. Thus a hermeneutical dialectic between present praxis and the Christian Story and Vision recognizes the limitations in both our own praxis and in the Story and Vision as we know them, but it also recognizes the truth that is in them both and carries that forward to a new point of understanding and way of living the tradition.

The present dialectical hermeneutics used in a shared praxis context of Christian education can be set out as a four-part process. The first two parts pertain to the dialectic between present praxis and the Story, the second two pertain to the dialectic between present praxis and the Vision.

In the dialectical hermeneutic between our present and the Christian Story the Story is a source of critique for the present (Part 1, Story to present). In this it affirms some of our present praxis, makes us aware of shortcomings in our present praxis, and calls us to live the tradition more faithfully.

But the direction of the dialectic is not only from the Story to present praxis; it is also from present praxis to the Story as the present brings its own consciousness, insights, and needs to the appropriation of the Story (Part 2, present praxis to Story). In this part there are dimensions of our Story that are reclaimed as of value and lasting truth. But no one interpretation of our Story is ever its complete and final meaning. We can always return to it to find truths that were not recognized before because "the breadth and length and height and depth" (Eph. 3:18) of it can never be totally known by us. In this sense, every version of the Story is limited. In addition there are aspects of our Story we must refuse to inherit (to cite two obvious examples, dimensions of our tradition that have discriminated against women and legitimated slavery). Thus, we always have the task of affirming the truth in our Story but also forging beyond our present understanding of it and way of living it. In other words, it is not merely a matter of asking What does the Story say to our present praxis? This question must also be posed: What does present praxis do to and ask of the Story?

Similarly, in the dialectic of interpretation to be maintained between present praxis and the Vision, the Vision functions as a measure of our present praxis (Part 3, Vision to present). By this we can discern what to affirm in our present historical praxis. The Kingdom is already among us whenever and wherever God's will is done. Its presence already and the sure promise of its completion come to our present as consolation and affirmation. But given the reality of sin in ourselves and in our world, there are ways in which the Kingdom is not yet. Thus the Vision of the Kingdom enables us to discern the limitations in our present praxis that are not of the Kingdom, and calls us to a Christian praxis that will be more creative of the Kingdom and more faithful to God's invitation.

The last part of the process (Part 4, present praxis to Vision), although not as evident, is equally important.[24] For while the Kingdom is a measure of and promise to our present, that Vision is also an open future being shaped in part by present praxis, and our knowing of it is possible only as we shape it. Thus our present understanding of it can never be accepted as a blueprint for its final form. In a Christian educational context this fourth part of present dialectical hermeneutics calls for intentional decision making that is appropriate to the reign of God.

At this stage of my statement the reader may understandably be wondering how all these parts and pieces fit together, if in fact they do, and how they may be done in a concrete pedagogical setting that uses a shared praxis approach to Christian religious education. I will outline in Chapter Ten how I presently bring them together and how I have used them in a variety of pedagogical settings. When those examples are given, the statement I am attempting here may take on greater clarity.

GUIDELINES FOR DECISION MAKING IN A GROUP USING SHARED PRAXIS

In an educational group using a shared praxis approach the participants attempt to appropriate the faith tradition critically in their own praxis and are invited to choose further Christian praxis in response to their shared dialogue and reflection. But as they appropriate the faith tradition, there is surely need for criteria to evaluate their appropriation and response. Without guidelines for discerning what is to be affirmed, refused, and moved beyond in the Story, there is danger that something essential and of "lasting" truth in the Story may be rejected. History teaches the lesson that while developments in our understanding and living of the Story take place, corruptions also occur. There is need, obviously, for limits to what may be refused in the past Story, limits beyond which what is appropriated ceases to be the Christian Story and places one outside the tradition. Thus a shared praxis group needs some guidelines (or what Newman called "marks of authenticity"[25]) to guide their discernment and decision making.

A shared praxis group must constantly approach its task of discernment with prayer for the presence of the Holy Spirit. The risen Christ who promised to be with us always and God's gift of the Spirit are divine assurance to any group of Christians that they can know God's will and that errors, if chosen, will eventually be corrected.

But the ambiguity of life and its meaning can never be banished by simply appealing to the Holy Spirit. Within our human condition and covenant with God our own efforts at discernment, guided by God's grace, are always essential, and for them we need guidelines. I suggest the following three: *consequences, continuity,* and *community/Church.* None is sufficient unto itself. All three are needed in constant interrelation and mutual balancing.

CONSEQUENCES

The first and constant question before a shared praxis group as it makes its decisions and choices about further Christian praxis is: Do the likely consequences of my (our) decision contribute to making the Kingdom present now and to preparing the material for its final completion? In other words, is the envisioned response creative of the freedom, peace, justice, and wholeness that are essential to God's Kingdom? If the praxis chosen does not seem likely to have such consequences (and only time will tell with certainty), then it is erroneous. Thus the type and quality of Christian praxis likely to arise from shared praxis is itself a guideline for the group's choosing of a faith response. Nor can this "mark of authenticity" be dismissed as begging the question. It is often recommended by the gospels—"You can tell a tree by its fruit" (Matt. 7:20).

CONTINUITY

The decisions made by people in a shared praxis group must be in continuity with the Story of the Christian community before them.[26] They cannot take positions in contradiction to what is essential to the Story (and that can only be discerned by the whole community/Church). There will be practices from the

Christian Story that a shared praxis group will decide not to continue, and beliefs, especially those on the lower echelon of the "hierarchy of truths,"[27] that they will refuse or radically reformulate. But the truth of the tradition must be affirmed, and new "truths" must be in continuity with it. Otherwise the decision made is erroneous. To give an obvious example, no group, having reflected on its experiences, could decide that the basic mandate of the gospels is no longer binding and that certain peoples or races may be hated. That would be in total discontinuity with the previous tradition and with the primordial revelation on which Christianity rests.

COMMUNITY/CHURCH

I describe the third guideline in this twofold manner because, although they are intimately related, two groupings of people provide a guideline for decision making. By *community* here I mean the immediate shared praxis group itself, and by *Church* I mean the larger Christian community to which the small group belongs.

Community. In an actual shared praxis group, as participants struggle to discern God's will for them, the discernment of that community itself, guided by the Holy Spirit, becomes a guideline for decision making. After many experiences with shared praxis groups I have come to know that the corporate quest for discernment has a reliability greater than the discernment of any individual alone—and indeed greater than the sum total of the individuals. However, no small community of Christians can be a reliable guide of truth in isolation from the rest of the Christian community to which the small group belongs. To claim as much would contradict the catholicity of Christianity.

Church. The Christian community as Church has the right to teach. Such would seem to be the constant tradition from the earliest days of the Church down to our present. Therefore, the small community constituted by a shared praxis group must be informed by and measure its decisions against the belief and practice of the whole Church. In its *Declaration on Religious Freedom* (Par. 14) Vatican II stated that "the Church is, by the will of Christ, the teacher of the truth."[28] The teaching of the whole Church must always be heard by the smaller communities that constitute it.

This raises the question, however, of what is meant by *Church* in this teaching context. If Church is understood only as what Dulles calls the institutional model,[29] then teaching would appear to belong exclusively to the official hierarchy of the Church (and who the "hierarchy" is varies among denominations), with little role for the "sense of the faithful" and the research of the theologians. If, however, one understands Church according to a more community-like model, which would certainly seem to be the recommended ecclesiology that emerges from Vatican II, then to say that "the Church teaches" is to say that the whole Church teaches and learns together. The *ecclesia docens* is also the *ecclesia dis-*

cens.[30] Thus while protecting the notion of a teaching Church, we must deny the extreme conservative understanding that one small group (the hierarchy) teaches and the faithful only "learn," while the theologians prove that the official teaching already given is correct (what Dulles calls "regressive theology").

Assuming that the whole Church teaches and learns together, then, graced by the presence of the Holy Spirit, there are three sources of such teaching and learning (or what Raymond Brown calls "organs of teaching and belief"[31]) within the Christian Church. These are the teaching of the official magisterium,[32] the research of the theologians and scripture scholars, and the discernment of the people[33] (what has been traditionally called the *sensus fidelium*, or the sense of the faithful).

The three together can be imagined as a tripod, joined in the ongoing reach to know and discern the meaning of God's revelation and our fitting response. To begin with, all three need to be in dialogue with communities other than the Christian one. When Christians talk only to each other about the meaning of God for our lives, we assume that we are the only people to whom God has ever revealed the divine self, that we are the only people among whom God is active. Such an elitist and imperialist attitude contradicts our own Christian conviction about the universal love of God for all people and God's activity within all history.

Then, all three agencies are to interrelate with each other in mutual dialogue, support, insight, correction, and affirmation. The official magisterium (and within the denominations this may be papacy or primate, general assembly or synod, and so on) performs the function of articulating a consensus position, but all three sources interrelate in service to the truth the whole Church seeks and teaches.

The faith life of the people must be informed by the reflection, research, and systematic investigation of the theological and biblical community. But the reflection of the scholars should be grounded in and arise from the lived faith of the Christian community. The Christian praxis of the people is informed by the consensus of belief and practice taught by the official magisterium. But the official magisterium must also listen to and be informed by the sense of the faithful.[34] The official magisterium cannot claim to have a short cut to the truth; it must be informed by the research and scholarship of the theological community.[35] But the theologians need the official magisterium to articulate a consensus position that is in keeping with what has come down from the apostles. Otherwise, theology is a maze of conflicting opinions and different schools of thought and by itself a confusing ground for decisions of faith.[36]

Clearly, none of these three "sources" of teaching and learning in the Church can stand in isolation from the others. All three must work together in service to the "faith handed down." Yves Congar has a threefold arrangement that is somewhat similar to the one I have outlined. He writes, "One must put

truth, the apostolic faith which has been handed down, confessed, preached and
celebrated, at the top. And under it, at its service, we must place the magisterium of apostolic ministry and the research and teaching of theologians, together
with the belief of the faithful."[37]

In summary, it must always be remembered that only by the help of the
Holy Spirit can the truth be known (see John 16:13). When a group assembles
to do Christian religious education by a shared praxis approach, it should come
together in the prayerful presence of the Paraclete. But the participants also
need guidelines to direct them as they fulfill the human side of their responsibility to discern the meaning of God's activity in history and their appropriate response. I have contended that if they 1) maintain continuity with and faithfulness to the Story of the Christian people, 2) choose a response that is
appropriate to the Vision of God's Kingdom, and 3) are informed by the teaching and learning of the whole Church as well as by their own group discernment, then, with the help of the befriending Spirit, they are most likely to discern God's intentions for them and what their response should be. There can
never be absolute certainty or final form to any understanding or praxis of the
truth.[38] We will know God's truth only as we do it, and from doing it learn to do
it more truthfully. When such is our knowing, then the truth will set us free
(John 8:32).

In the words the Fourth Gospel places on the lips of Jesus, the constant calling of all Christians is "to know you, the only true God, and him whom you
have sent, Jesus Christ" (John 17:3). It is the purpose of Christian religious
education to promote our attempts at such knowing. In this chapter I have posed
a shared praxis approach as one way of organizing intentional educational activity toward that end. It is a reflective/active knowing that arises from the present, is informed by the past, and is to shape our future. I have explained the
main components of such an approach and the marks of authenticity that can
guide the decision making of such a group. Now this question must be faced:
How can such an approach be used in different concrete educational settings? I
can do no more here than describe how I have been doing it. In fact, the reflections offered in this chapter have arisen from my own praxis.

The process for using a shared praxis approach has gradually evolved into
five distinguishable pedagogical movements. Chapter Ten outlines and gives examples of them.

NOTES

1. To reflect only on "overt productive activity" would limit reflection to the "production feedback" of Marx and reduce us to the knowing which Habermas attributed to the empirical analytical sciences. Thus we see immediately here the importance of expanding our notion of human action far beyond what Marx described.
2. See Ricoeur, *Freud and Philosophy*, pp. 43–45.

3. Cited by Warford, *The Necessary Illusion*, p. 64.
4. There is a theological echo in this from our Hebrew roots. The quest for salvation requires remembering and recalling, "lest we forget" and be brought to slavery again.
5. The position I am taking here is supported by the research of Jean Piaget on cognitive development. Though the concentration of Piaget's research is on the cognitive dimension of human behavior, he insists that the cognitive and affective are "two indissociable aspects of every action" (*Studies*, p. 33). The genetic epistemology of Piaget has been expanded by Robert Kegan in his research on ego development. Kegan, informed by both his own research and that of Piaget, contends that in the self knowing activity of the ego, "there is nothing about cognition that is non-affective (and there is nothing about affect that is noncognitive)" ("Ego and Truth: Personality and the Piaget Paradigm," p. 100). The fact that the conclusions of these men are based on empirical research lends credence to my claim that self-critical reflection on one's present action is a way of knowing the world that is both rational and "passional." Since the "knowing" arises from the "doing," it is also "actional."
6. Buber's whole notion of relationship, summed up in his famous phrase "Man becomes an I through a You," is very much what I intend by a dialogical relationship (see Buber, *I and Thou*, p. 80).
7. Steere, *On Listening to Another*, p. 188.
8. Reuel Howe, perhaps the most noted proponent of dialogue in Christian education for our time, notes insightfully: "A sermon or a lecture may be dialogical even though there is only one speaker, but the dialogical lecturer is one who is able to draw his students into an implicit dialogue with him in such a way that the meanings they bring to the occasion are activated by the meanings he brings to them" ("The Dialogical Foundations for Christian Education," p. 88).
9. I have described "The Crossroads" elsewhere. See Groome, "The Crossroads: A Story of Christian Education by Shared Praxis."
10. Freire, *Oppressed*, p. 77. Freire also offers a powerful definition of and argument for dialogue in education when he writes, "Dialogue is the encounter between men, mediated by the world, in order to name the world. . . . If it is in speaking their word that men, by naming the world, transform it, dialogue imposes itself as the way by which men achieve significance as men. Dialogue is thus an existential necessity" (Ibid., pp. 76–77).
11. Ibid., pp. 77–81.
12. See Reuel Howe, *The Miracle of Dialogue*.
13. David Tracy, in *Blessed Rage for Order*, uses the term *Christian fact* to convey, I believe, what I am trying to capture by *Story*. But Christian fact sounds too final and complete. Tracy certainly intends the Christian fact to be critically appropriated, but I prefer the term Story because it connotes something that is more open ended. Good stories can be told and retold and improved with the telling. In an empirically minded culture we tend too much simply to accept "the facts."
14. Niebuhr, *The Meaning of Revelation*, p. 35.
15. Anderson, *The Living Word of the Bible*, pp. 48–61.
16. The importance of not separating the "Christ of faith" from the "Jesus of history" is a central theme in the Christology from below outlined in Chapter Four. For a powerful statement of this position see Sobrino, *Christology at the Crossroads*, especially Chapter Nine.
17. The claim made here about the incompleteness of the Story and our right and responsibility to develop it is a religious education expression of the issue which theologians discuss as the "development of doctrine." If doctrines cannot be developed and reinterpreted, then my whole argument for critical reflection upon the Story (and doctrines are at least part of our Story) is denied. I offer the following brief reflection on what is a rather complex theological problem.

The Christian community over history has articulated its understanding of God's revelation and its meaning for their lives in statements of belief. In time, because of their longevity and prominence in the tradition, because of the consensus and weight of official teaching from general councils of the Church, some of those beliefs have come to be accepted as "doctrines" of the faith, that is, statements of belief that require assent from members of the community. In Roman Catholicism, with one of the strongest traditions for such doctrinal statements, they are often called dogmas (which seems even more final and unquestionable than doctrines). Karl Rahner defines a dogma as "a proposition which is the object of *fides divina et Catholica*, in other words, one which the Church officially propounds as revealed by God, in such a way that its denial is condemned by the Church as heresy and anathematized" (*Sacramentum Mundi*, 2: "Dogma," No. 1 "Theological Meaning of Dogma," p. 96).

At first sight, all possibility of critiquing and expanding such formulations would appear to be ruled out, but that has not been the case. The "empirical evidence" of history makes it clear that dogmas have in fact developed over the years. As Candido Pozo writes, "The historical fact of development is undeniable, however it is to be explained, since certain dogmas cannot be found as truths of faith before a given moment in history . . ." (*Sacramentum Mundi*, 2: "Dogma" No. 2 "Development of Dogma," p. 100). The fact is that revelation comes to us within historical, social/cultural settings, and our understanding and articulation of it will always be conditioned by those historical contexts. This leads to what Avery Dulles calls "the historical relativity of all doctrinal statements" (*Survival*, p. 178). Dulles explains that the "truth of revelation" always comes to us in "timebound formulations" (Ibid., p. 181) because the literary forms, world view, and philosophical presuppositions of a particular age shape the formulation of doctrine in that age. When that ethos has changed, the formulations will need to change to be appropriate for a later age. In addition, every era has its own "social pathology and ideology," and these, too, have shaped the formulation of doctrines in their time (see Ibid., pp. 182–186). The consciousness of our time must strive to detect and refuse such pathologies and ideologies and attempt to formulate doctrinal statements that are free of such distortions. Dulles concludes, "The divine truth is not taught by the Church in divine form, but in a human form, and thus it is always difficult to draw the line between what is a matter of Christian faith and what is to be set aside as a human perversion" (Ibid., p. 188).

Awareness of the need for such development has been present in mainline Protestantism perhaps since the Reformation itself. But Roman Catholicism, with its strong magisterial tradition of teaching "official doctrine," has been more reluctant to recognize the need for and reality of doctrinal development. In light of such traditional reluctance the statement of Vatican II in Par. 8 of the *Constitution on Divine Revelation* is itself a significant development. (And in the Council's deliberations was a much debated statement. See Schoof, *A Survey of Catholic Theology*, p. 251.) The Council states, "This tradition which comes from the apostles *develops* in the Church with the help of the Holy Spirit. For there is a growth in the understanding of the realities and the words which have been handed down" (emphasis added). In the same paragraph the Council admits that the Church, rather than possessing the fullness of truth, is only on its way toward that truth. "For, as the centuries succeed one another, the Church constantly moves forward toward the fullness of divine truth until the words of God reach their complete fulfillment in her" (Abbott, *Documents*, p. 116).

In conclusion, then, the fact that the Christian Church formulates its beliefs into doctrinal statements does not in any sense mean that the Story is completed or that the version of it we now know cannot be critiqued. On the contrary, a critical appropriation of the Story is entirely in order and necessary if the tradition is to continue as life giving.

18. Dulles, *The Resilient Church*, p. 146.
19. Palmer, *Hermeneutics*, p. 33.
20. Paul Ricoeur explains that within the hermeneutical act itself there is a dialectic between the explanation one gives and the explainer's own understanding (see *Interpretation Theory*).
21. For an excellent article on the hermeneutical aspect of all education see Palermo, "Pedagogy as a Critical Hermeneutic."
22. I deliberately say that hermeneutics is only part of the task of Christian religious education because to pose it as the total task is to attend only to *discernment* of God's will and thus does not take sufficient account of the affective and behavioral dimensions of Christian education. Coming to know God's will must be accompanied by a formation in disposition to do that will. Thus the total task could never be fulfilled by an activity of hermeneutics, but it certainly is a part of the task. Hubert Halbfas may well be correct when he says, "The basic principles of teaching should be sought in hermeneutics" (*Theory of Catechetics*, p. 81).
23. Hans-Georg Gadamer explains that hermeneutics is "no mere repetition of the text that has been handed down, but is a new creation of understanding" (*Truth and Method*, p. 430). My own attempts at forging a dialectical understanding of hermeneutics came before my reading of Gadamer (I was more influenced by Walter Wink's *The Bible in Human Transformation*), but I have found his position to be both confirming and clarifying. Richard E. Palmer insightfully summarizes Gadamer's notion of dialectical hermeneutics as " 'historically operative consciousness' dialectically interacting with tradition as transmitted through the text" (*Hermeneutics*, p. 42). Bernard Lonergan also contends that the ongoing development of doctrine in the Christian tradition is a constant dialectical process. In his work *The Way to Nicaea* (which is a translation of the first part of the first volume of *De Deo Trino*) Lonergan gives a masterful exposé of the

dialectic at work in the development of the Nicene doctrine from the Early Church to the First Council of Nicaea (325).

24. The third and fourth parts of present dialectical hermeneutics are vital if we are to avoid being subject to Habermas' critique of the traditional hermeneutical sciences. As outlined in Chapter Eight, Habermas criticizes the traditional hermeneutical sciences as having the interest of "practical control" and claims that they maintain people within the confines of tradition. I agree with him that if the interests of the knowing subjects are not critiqued as well as the constitutive genesis of the tradition, and if the hermeneutical activity looks only at the present and the past, then indeed "the understanding of meaning is directed" in its very structure toward the attainment of possible consensus among actors in the framework of a self understanding derived from tradition" (Habermas, *Interests*, p. 310). But to attain consensus about self-understanding within the framework of tradition does not necessarily have the result of imprisonment within the walls of past tradition. Habermas incorrectly makes such an assertion when he claims that "hermeneutics bangs helplessly, so to speak, from within against the walls of tradition" (Habermas' words quoted by Gadamer, "On the Scope and Function of Hermeneutical Reflection," p. 87). Such "helplessness" is not necessarily the case, and here I draw upon and favor Gadamer's position in his famous debate with Habermas.

Gadamer takes a more realistic approach to the giveness of tradition. We live inevitably in, and come to make meaning from, tradition. Tradition is to people as water is to fish. By our language alone we live in tradition because language is the "reservoir of tradition and the medium in and through which we exist and perceive our world" (Gadamer, "Hermeneutical Reflection," p. 86). But by a dialectical hermeneutic, Gadamer claims, we can expand our horizons beyond the limits of tradition, while also bringing with us the truths of that tradition. In the present dialectical hermeneutics I have posed, one's horizon is expanded and the confinement within past tradition is refused in parts three and four of the process. These call not merely for preserving consensus within the limits of a past tradition, but for a newness and creativity toward an open future. Although the creative activity must be in continuity with the past tradition, we are not locked within it as prisoners held bound. Thus in the intentional posing and critiquing of a new horizon—the Vision of the Kingdom of God—Habermas' criticism of the historical-hermeneutical sciences is avoided.

25. John Henry Newman's work on the development of doctrine has greatly informed my own search for criteria to guide the decision making of a shared praxis group. While a shared praxis group is concerned with more than "doctrinal" decision making, yet orthopraxis must always be informed by orthodoxy, and Newman's classic statement *An Essay on the Development of Christian Doctrine* (first published 1845) has proved to be most helpful.

Having established from the evidence of Church history that doctrines can and do develop, Newman attempted to set out "certain characteristics" by which "faithful developments" could be discerned from "corruptions." He arrived at "seven Notes of varying cogency, independence and applicability, to discriminate healthy developments of an idea from its state of corruption and decay" (*An Essay on the Development of Christian Doctrine*, p. 169). Newman's seven "notes" were: 1) "Preservation of Type," by which he meant "the parts and proportions of the developed form, however altered, correspond to those which belong to its rudiments" (Ibid., p. 171); 2) "Continuity of Principles," by which he meant that a true development must be in accordance with the basic principles of the original teaching (Ibid., pp. 178–180); 3) "Power of Assimilation," by which he meant that a true development must have a "unitive power" of incorporation, rather than fragmenting the previous body of teaching (Ibid., pp. 186–188); 4) "Logical Sequence" for a doctrine is a true development "in proportion as it seems to be the logical issue of its original teaching" (Ibid., p. 195); 5) "Anticipation of Its Future," by which he meant that there must have been intimations and an anticipation of the development in the original teaching (Ibid., pp. 196–199); 6) "Conservative Action upon Its Past," by which he meant (stating it negatively) that ideas which "contradict and reverse the course of doctrine which has been developed before them, and out of which they spring, are certainly corrupt . . ." (Ibid., p. 199); 7) "Chronic Vigor," by which he meant the test of time; i.e., that a true development will stand the test of time (Ibid., pp. 205–206).

The crucial point to Newman's position is that any doctrine must have "unity and identity . . . through all stages of its development from first to last" (Ibid., p. 206). Here we have his overarching principle for the development of doctrines, namely "dynamic identity." By this he meant that while dogmas must necessarily develop (i.e., be dynamic), they must also retain their identity and continuity with what has gone before. He uses his "seven notes" as ways of discerning whether this is the case or not for particular questions. All of them will reappear, though in altered form, in the three guidelines I offer for discernment in a shared praxis group.

26. Theologians who write on the development of doctrine use different language to state it, but all seem to be in agreement on this criterion of "continuity." Rahner insists that developments must take place "in vital contact" with the original sources of revelation (see *Theological Investigations*, 1:56). In a later work he explains, "The new [truth] justifies itself always and only through its origin from the old . . ." (Ibid., 5:25). Pozo explains that any new interpretation "must remain demonstrably of a piece with it (i.e., the 'original deposit')." (*Sacramentum Mundi*, 2: "Dogma," p. 101). The notion of continuity can be seen in Newman's overarching principle of "identity" but is especially evident in his first, "Preservation of Type," second, "Continuity of Principles," and sixth, "Conserving of Its Past" notes of a true development.

27. This phrase is taken from Vatican II's *Decree on Ecumenism*. Par. 11 states that "in Catholic teaching there exists an order or 'hierarchy' of truths, since they vary in their relationship to the foundation of the Christian faith" (Abbott, *Documents*, p. 354). Rahner points out that it is difficult to decide what dogmas are essential and what are not (see *Sacramentum Mundi*, 2: "Dogma," p. 96). Thus I cannot take on the enormous theological question here of what should be placed on the upper levels of the "hierarchy of truths," although I am comfortable with the historical practice of placing the Apostles and Nicene Creeds there.

28. Abbott, *Documents*, pp. 694–695.

29. For an insightful description of the institutional model of the Church see Dulles, *Models of the Church*, Ch. 2. Dulles explains that when the Church is viewed solely under the institutional model, then "from the point of view of its teaching function, it resembles a school in which the masters, as sacred teachers, hand down the doctrine of Christ. Because the bishops are considered to possess a special 'charism of truth' . . . it is held that the faithful are in conscience bound to believe what the bishops declare. The Church is therefore a unique type of school—one in which the teachers have the power to impose their doctrine with juridical and spiritual sanctions. Thus teaching is juridicized and institutionalized" (Ibid., p. 34–35).

30. Raymond Brown puts this well when he writes: "At one time or another and in some way, everyone in the Church is part of the *ecclesia docens* . . . and, at one time or another and in some way, everyone in the church is also part of the *ecclesia discens*, including Pope and bishops. Again the words of our Master are almost a reproach: 'You have only one Teacher—all the rest of you are brothers and sisters' (Matt. 23:8)" "Bishops and Theologians: 'Dispute' Surrounded by Fiction," p. 675).

31. Ibid., p. 675.

32. I am using the term *official magisterium* here to refer to the official teaching voice in any denomination of Christianity. For Roman Catholics this obviously means the Pope in communion with the bishops of the world. The general assemblies of the World Council of Churches have come to have a similar place in the faith life of many Protestant Christians. It is important to note, however, especially for establishing the "teaching rights" of the theologians, that *magisterium* has not always been understood in this way. Yves Congar points out that "until the 1820s and 30s magisterium simply means the function or activity of any teacher (magister)—any authority in a given domain" ("The Magisterium and Theologians," p. 17). Congar then draws attention to Aquinas' distinction between two magisteria—" 'the magisterium of the pastoral or episcopal chair' and the 'magisterium of the teaching chair.' The first enjoyed an excellence of power, the second a publicly recognized personal competence" (Ibid., p. 16). The second magisterium certainly included the theologians. This leads Dulles to conclude: "In a certain sense, then, we may speak of two magisteria—that of the pastors and that of the theologians" ("What Is Magisterium?," p. 86).

33. The discernment that emerges from the lived faith life of the people who belong neither to the theologians nor the hierarchy has often been forgotten as a source of teaching. But by their baptism "the faithful" have the Holy Spirit to guide them. Jesus promised the Paraclete to anyone who loves him and keeps his commandments (John 14:15–16). To deny the value and validity of their discernment is to claim that the Holy Spirit inspires only the hierarchy and the theologians. Vatican II, however, in the *Dogmatic Constitution on the Church*, par. 12, declared: "The body of the faithful as a whole, annointed as they are by the Holy One (cf. John 2:20, 27), cannot err in matters of belief." (Abbott, *Documents*, p. 29). Consistent with this position, Dulles writes about "the interior guidance of the Holy Spirit, who implants in the hearts of the faithful an instinctive sense of what is, and what is not, a valid expression of revealed truth" (*The Resilient Church*, p. 50).

34. "Magisterium must not be isolated from the living reality of the Church" (Congar, "The Magisterium and Theologians," p. 20).
35. Raymond Brown explains, "I recognize fully that the office of Pope and bishop is a charism that involves divine help; but, as far as I know, in good Catholic theology grace is thought to cooperate with nature. To use properly the teaching role that is theirs by the charism of their office bishops must take the step of learning about what they are teaching—that is not only common sense; it is the age-old understanding of the church" ("Bishops and Theologians," p. 676).
36. Dulles explains the need for this two way relationship between the magisterium and the scholars thus: "Neither of these two magisteria, however, is self-sufficient. Rather, they are complementary and mutually corrective. Were it not for the theologians, bishops might settle issues by the sole criterion of administrative convenience, without regard to scholarship and theory. In their zeal for uniformity, they might attempt to impose assent by sheer decree, overlooking the values of Christian freedom and maturity. The theologians, on the other hand, would suffer the opposite temptation. They would want unlimited freedom for discussion without regard to the demands of fidelity to Christian revelation. For the unity of the Church as a community of faith and witness, and for its perseverance in its assigned task, the pastoral magisterium is indispensable" ("What Is Magisterium?," p. 86). Adding to this from a religious educator's perspective, creativity and controversy are necessary for the ongoing scholarly enterprise of the theologians and scripture scholars. However, the latest opinions or theses should not be taught to children as if they are the accepted belief of the whole Church. Teachers must exercise a lot of discretion on this point, especially with younger students.
37. Congar, "The Magisterium and Theologians," p. 20.
38. Throughout this whole section of guidelines I have cited Vatican II and many Catholic authors, and obviously have been in dialogue with my own Catholic background. I have avoided discussion of papal infallibility, however, although it might be of particular interest to Catholic readers, and for two reasons. First, given the size and confused state of the question, to deal with it adequately here would take us too far afield. Secondly, it is not necessary to deal with it because the position taken here is not in conflict with the Catholic position on infallibility, when the notion is properly understood. Dulles explains that "infallibility does not demand that a given formulation of the truth be always and everywhere imposed, but only that it be not directly contradicted. It means that when the Church, through its highest teaching organs, defines a truth pertaining to revelation, divine providence, working through a multiplicty of channels, will preserve the Church from error. But it may well be necessary, as the generations pass, to reinterpret the defined dogma in accordance with the presuppositions, thought categories, concerns, and vocabulary of a later age" (*The Resilient Church*, pp. 53–54). It is clear from that statement that nothing I have said is in conflict with the Catholic notion of infallibility. Later, Dulles, situating his position in a historical context, puts the issue of infallibility within a much more reasonable perspective than it popularly enjoys. He writes, "The moderates at Vatican I managed to get many restrictions written into the text and into the explanations given to it on the council floor. As a result, the celebrated definition of papal infallibility really commits one to very little" (Ibid., p. 127).

10

Shared Praxis in Praxis

THE FIVE MOVEMENTS

Given the five components of the approach outlined in Chapter Nine, in a context of Christian religious education using shared praxis one should expect to find an opportunity for the participants to name some dimension of their present Christian action, to reflect critically to whatever extent they are capable (the question of readiness is dealt with in Chapter Eleven) on what they have named, and to share their reflections in dialogue. Since the critical reflection on present action is to be informed by the Christian faith tradition, then the Story and its Vision as they pertain to the issue or topic being dealt with must be made accessible to the group. Finally, in keeping with "present dialectical hermeneutics" and the dialectical unity between *theoria* and praxis, there should be an opportunity for participants to personally appropriate the Story and its Vision to their own lives and choose what may be a fitting lived response.

Over the past years I have used a shared praxis approach with adults and high school and grade school students (in both school and parish contexts), in weekend retreats, seminars, symposia, conventions, community renewal and teacher training programs, and so on. Gradually, from both apparent successes and failures, five recognizable pedagogical movements[1] have emerged. These are the five movements I generally follow now (possible variations will be dealt with later). I will outline them briefly before moving into a more detailed description of each one.

Each shared praxis exercise has a particular focus of attention.

1. The participants are invited to name their own activity concerning the topic for attention (present action).

2. They are invited to reflect on why they do what they do, and what the likely or intended consequences of their actions are (critical reflection).
3. The educator makes present to the group the Christian community Story concerning the topic at hand and the faith response it invites (Story and its Vision).
4. The participants are invited to appropriate the Story to their lives in a dialectic with their own stories (dialectic between Story and stories).
5. There is an opportunity to choose a personal faith response for the future (dialectic between Vision and visions).

There is nothing sacred about the number five, and other educators may find it helpful to adjust, combine, or increase the movements. I hope that we can improve upon them as our praxis continues. The movements can be put into operation by a variety of teaching methods, and many different pedagogical techniques can be used within each movement.

In the following accounts I first describe each movement, then give some samples[2] from my own praxis, and finally make some general reflections upon the process. For the sake of clarity I draw generally from the same instances throughout the five movements.

Each shared praxis unit must have a particular focus, that is, some dimension or experience of Christian faith to which the group will attend. The educator is usually the one who establishes the focus of attention in the group. This can be done in a myriad of ways. In one sense, the focusing exercise becomes a common experience for the participants. Sometimes this may require an overt activity by the group. However, I have also begun with a scripture reading, a film, a photograph or painting, a poem, a story, an example of the issue, a case study, a role-playing exercise, a simple statement of the focus, and so on.

First Movement: Naming Present Action

The first movement is an invitation to the participants to name their present action in response to the particular focus of the unit. We must remember here the broad meaning for *present action* that I proposed in Chapter Nine. I described it as "every doing that has any intentionality or deliberateness to it . . . whatever way we give expression to ourselves. It includes what we are doing physically, emotionally, intellectually, and spiritually as we live on personal, interpersonal, and social levels." Thus, depending on the focus of attention, the opening movement could invite an expression of the participants' reactions, feelings, sentiments, overt activity, valuing, meaning making, understanding, beliefs, relationships, and the like. The important task is to elicit a personal statement on present action rather than a statement of *theoria* based on what "they say." For example, in units on the Eucharist I have formed the opening question as "What do you do with the Eucharist in your life?" or "What does the Eucharist mean in your life?" "What is your own basic reaction to Eucharist?" or some other variation of such questions, instead of asking "What is the Eucharist?" (the latter question being more likely to elicit a *theoria* response). In other words, the goal is to elicit an expression (it could be in words, art, mime, etc.) of one's own "knowing" (doing) as that arises from the person's own engagement in the world. With some issues this will also require a naming of the present action that the participants experience in their social context and community, but it must be their own perspective on that particular social praxis.

In forming the opening question, I often find the old distinction between systematic and moral theology to be helpful. When the group is attending to a particular belief, I usually begin with a question like "What is your own understanding of [the belief]?" If an ethical issue or some Christian practice is being dealt with, I begin by inquiring how they presently respond to that issue in their lives. The actual forming of the opening question will depend greatly on the characteristics of the particular group, but the form is crucial if a statement of praxis rather than *theoria* is to be elicited. Some samples from my own praxis may clarify what I intend here.

In a weekend seminar for eighteen faculty members and administrators from a university concerned about its role in educating for social justice, the opening question was: "What can you name at your university that promotes or prevents education for social justice?" In a graduate course for religious educators when the topic was the purpose of Christian religious education, I opened by asking, "As you look at your own work in parishes, schools, or wherever, what for you is the purpose of Christian religious education?" In a group of Church education leaders who were focusing on the Emmaus story of Luke 24, having read the passage slowly, my opening question was, "What is the primary message *you* hear from this passage?" In a workshop preparing people to be evaluators of a Catholic school network and intended to focus especially on the Christian environment of the schools, the opening question was, "How do you feel about being evaluated?" With a group of eleventh-grade students dealing with loneliness, I focused the topic by showing a short movie on loneliness and then invited them to reflect on and share the feelings the movie had stirred in them (thus causing them to name their "present action" in regard to loneliness). In a unit on Eucharist with ninth-grade students the opening question was "What do you do with the Eucharist in your life?"

Some examples from a fourth-grade class indicate what the first movement might look like for students at that age level. In a unit on prayer (other than prayers in Church, which we had covered in previous units) I began by asking a series of questions such as, "What prayers do you say? How do you say them? What do you say when you talk to God? When do you pray? Tell me about the time that you prayed really hard." In another fourth-grade unit on Reconciliation, focusing in particular on the Penitential Rite at the beginning of the Roman Mass, I began by asking the students to draw a picture of a fight they had had recently. Then I had each of them tell the group about the fight. I asked what had caused the fight, whether they were "really mad with the other person," and how that felt. In another unit on the Offertory of the Mass, I began by asking the fourth-graders about gift giving and receiving. I asked questions such as, "Do you ever give a gift to anyone? Do you ever receive a gift? Can you tell me about a time that you gave a gift to someone? Tell me about a time that you received a gift from someone."[3]

This movement is where the shift from a *theoria* to a praxis way of knowing begins. After the focusing activity the opening question must be put in such a way as to elicit a naming of the participants' praxis rather than their *theoria*. This can be especially difficult with topics of a systematic theological and more abstract nature, for instance, the Blessed Trinity. But even there the opening question can inquire about the participants' understanding of it and way of making meaning out of it, and the implications this belief has for their living of Christian faith. When I prepare for a shared praxis unit, a great deal of my time is spent in formulating the opening question.

It is important to pose the opening question in a gentle, nonthreatening manner. I have learned the hard way that if a praxis-type question is asked without prior explanation, adults can hear it as a challenge to justify their existence, especially if they are unaccustomed to the process. With all age levels I attempt to eliminate the feeling of being investigated by explaining that they are not being cross-examined in an evaluative manner, but rather are invited to come to self-awareness of their own knowing and name it for themselves. It has also helped, especially with participants who are strangers to each other, to begin with some "ice-breaking" and community-building exercises to establish at least a minimal level of trust in the group. After a group has been through the process a number of times, the opening question is rarely heard as a challenge.

Before the participants share their statements, it is important to make clear that each one should feel free to remain silent. I often invite a large group of adults to move into smaller groups of four but to feel free not to join a group or to join a group and not speak. When the group is small enough to be kept together for the sharing (the setting and time frame will often decide this), I have learned by mistake not to "go around the circle." This can force people to speak when they do not wish or are not ready to do so. It is the educator's role in this first movement to facilitate participants in articulating as clear a statement as possible. This sometimes means inviting a person to say more or explain further. It is also the educator's task to keep the group focused on the question posed. The opening movement is not the time for "explaining why," telling anecdotes, and so on, and the educator should gently bring the group back to the question at hand as necessary.

The different ways that people can be brought to express their naming of present action are myriad, and many are more imaginative than the ones I have described here. I often find it helpful to have groups of adults write a brief statement in response to the topic. A more imaginative example is one from a weekend retreat with college-age people focusing on the Church, where the leaders opened by giving the participants playdough and having them fashion their "impression" of the Church and then explain their representations.[4]

SECOND MOVEMENT: THE PARTICIPANTS' STORIES AND VISIONS

The second movement is the beginning of critical reflection proper. It takes different forms for different age levels, but for all participants it is a reflection on "why we do what we do and what our hopes are in doing it" as related to the topic for attention. In this sense the movement is the participants' becoming aware of their own stories and visions as they are expressed in present action. This second movement is first looking discerningly at present action to see the "obvious" about it, but it is also an attempt to go below the obvious, to become aware of its source, the genesis of present action. In this the movement attempts to help participants come to a consciousness of the social conditioning, norms, assumptions, and the like that are embodied in their present action. This can be achieved by using critical memory to probe into the biography of the self and by trying to uncover the social influences that bring us to do what we do—in other words, one's own story. As critical reflection the movement also entails the use of imagination, a "looking forward" that attempts to ascertain the likely consequences of one's action and to determine what one would want the consequences to be (i.e., one's own vision). A discrepancy between the likely and the desired consequences often arises; however, in the dissonance lies the possibility for change, development, and growth. The movement often releases dialogue that was previously repressed, which is part of its purpose.

I usually introduce this movement by posing some questions that invite the participants to explain to themselves what brought them to give the expression they gave in the first movement. I then follow with questions about the likely consequences and the desired consequences of their present action. Here again, the questions are not meant to challenge the participants to defend what they do. Instead, they are an invitation to reflect upon one's reflection (children, of course, are capable of no more than a very rudimentary form of such reflection)[5] and to articulate for oneself and the group why one takes that present action and what the intended consequences of that action are. Some samples from my own praxis may clarify the activity of the second movement.

In the weekend with the university group I introduced the second movement by posing three questions, which we addressed separately: "Why is what we do or fail to do to promote social justice at the university happening? How likely is it that our students will graduate with a commitment to social justice? What would we want to do to promote education for social justice at the university?" The third part I introduced as "blue-sky time" and encouraged some dreaming. The second movement questions are not always set out as separately as this, and responses often overlap. Some people concentrate on their stories and others on their visions.

With graduate students reflecting on the purpose of Christian religious education (a unit I have done many times) I have asked questions like, "What brought you to have that purpose?" (their story) and then, "How does that purpose shape your religious educating?" (their vision). In the group of Church educators reflecting on the Emmaus story I asked two questions, and we dealt with them separately: "What memories does this passage raise up for you?" and then, "What hopes does it give you?" With the people preparing to be evaluators I asked, "What has brought you to feel that way about being evaluated?" and then, "How could those memories influence you when you become an evaluator?"

In the unit on Eucharist with ninth-graders I began by having them remember their First Communions and then invited them to describe how the role of the Eucharist in their life had changed since then. I finished the second movement by asking, "What do you want the Eucharist to become in your life?"

With the fourth-graders I have attempted to encourage reflection according to their capacity, promoting Why? questions in the hope that when they are developmentally capable, they will be more likely to do what could be properly called critical reflection. In the unit on prayer I set the scene by asking them to imagine that I was a little man from outer space. (Most of them had recently seen the movie *Star Wars*.) "I land in my space ship beside you on the way home from school and say, 'Please do not run away. I have a question. I was on this planet one night last week, and I looked through a bedroom window and saw a little boy kneeling beside his bed. He was talking to someone, but there was nobody in the room with him. What was he doing?'" The fourth-graders entered into the spirit of the scene and explained elaborately that the little boy was praying. "Praying," I asked, "what is that?" Now they had to explain to me what praying was, and it was fascinating to hear their explanations. I pushed them further by asking, "Why do you pray?" Invariably the answers were along the lines of "to get things from God." I did not settle for this answer because to do so would have been to affirm them in what Fowler would call the "reciprocity" of stage two faith. I affirmed for them that prayers of petition are important, but asked if there were any other kinds of prayer we could say or any other reasons for praying. In this I was inviting them to undertake critical reflection of a sort, affirming but pushing beyond present attitudes. After further dialogue they agreed that we could also pray simply to tell God that we love God, without asking for anything. In fact, they concluded, the only reason we pray is that God loves us. One girl said reflectively, "Praying wouldn't make any sense if God didn't love us." I then asked them what happens when they pray, how it makes them feel, and how they think God feels about it (their visions). At the end of this dialogue one of them gave the perfect transition to the third movement (community Story and Vision) when she said, "Okay, let's pretend that we are people from outer space and we meet you on the way home from school and ask you the same question. What would you say?" The transitions do not always come so easily.

In the unit on Reconciliation (and specifically on the Penitential Rite of the Catholic Mass) movement two focused on the questions "Why do we fight?" and "What are the consequences of fighting?" A general answer seemed to be that we fight because we want "to get our own way." I asked, "Why do we want things our own way?" and "Is it possible to always get what we want?" I inquired into the feelings they have when they are angry, how it affects them and others when they fight, and if it is possible to "make up" after a fight. I also asked how they think God feels about fighting and if God would want us to make up. They agreed that God does not like us to fight. I inquired if God forgives us when we do, and not all of them were sure about that. One girl said that God would forgive us only if we promised "not to be mad" at the person with whom we had had the fight.

In the unit on the Offertory of the Mass I asked such questions as, "Why do we give gifts? How do you feel when you get a gift? How do you feel when you give a gift? How do you think it makes the other person feel? To whom can you give gifts? What gifts has God given us? Is there any gift we can give back to God? Is God pleased when we offer gifts?"

This second movement can also take many forms and be effected in many ways. The movement looks and sounds quite different with participants of different age levels and in various contexts, but there is a basic similarity no matter who participates or what the focus may be. The primary task is always to enable participants (the educator included) to reflect critically on their present action, their reasons for it, and the consequences of it. Any pedagogical strategy or teaching model which can promote such reflection and dialogue is appropriate for this second movement.

Children take to this movement quite readily, and they often appear to enjoy it. For adults, on the other hand, it seems to be the most difficult and painful movement of the whole process. I am often reminded of Dewey's warning that education grounded in experience "involves reconstruction which may be painful."[6] For this reason, again, it is important not to put pressure on people to speak. We should not assume, however, that the silent ones are not participating in the dialogue. My own experience has been that when I am truly listening, I find myself entering into dialogue within myself with each person who speaks.

Although I described critical reflection as a combination of reason, memory, and imagination, the examples above make clear that not all three dimensions are equally attended to in every unit. The emphasis varies from one topic to another and with different groups. When I work consistently with the same group over a number of units, I often attend to different dimensions for variety, one time concentrating on reason, at another on memory, or again on imagination.

THIRD MOVEMENT: THE CHRISTIAN COMMUNITY STORY AND VISION

The third movement is an opportunity for the group to encounter the Christian community Story concerning the topic of attention and the Vision or response that the Story invites in light of the Kingdom of God. As indicated before, I use Story and Vision as metaphors to represent the faith tradition of the Christian community and the lived response and promise toward which this tradition invites us.

Normally the Story and its Vision are made available to the group by the educator, though I have frequently been with groups of adults where this was done by a well-prepared group member or by an outside resource person. It is crucial that the Story and Vision made accessible to the group be an accurate representation of the faith understanding of the broader Christian community in whose name the educating is being carried on. This requires that the presenter be well informed (as should be true with any approach) by contemporary scholarship and Church teaching. This does not mean that every Christian religious educator should be a professional theologian or scripture scholar, but he or she must have reliable resource material from which to draw. The Story/Vision presented at even the earliest grade levels must be a version that will not have to be contradicted later, but rather can be added to. Bad theology is harmful to the faith life of people at any age.

This is the most obviously catechetical movement in the process. It is the "echoing," the handing down, of what has come to us over our past pilgrimage. Presenting the Story and proposing its Vision can be done in many different ways using a variety of teaching techniques;[7] I have personally used a number of different styles of lecturing, audio-visuals, and research assignments. It is vitally important that the Story be made available in a dialogical rather than in a monological manner. This does not mean that the presenter and the group constantly talk back and forth to each other. Rather, it requires that the Story/Vision be made present in a disclosure rather than a closure way, that is, a way that invites people, bringing their own stories and visions, to reflect upon, grapple with, question, and personally encounter what is being presented. One key condition is that the presenter must never make his or her version of the community Story/Vision sound like the fullness and final statement of the "truth." If the presentation is absolutized and made to sound as if "this is exactly what you must believe or do . . . and as I say so," then a personal appropriation by the participants, in dialogue with their own lived experience, is unlikely. The tradition can give life, but dogmatism is barren and arrests the journey toward maturity of faith.

One wonders if the fact that the great majority of people remain at stage three of faith development is not due, at least in part, to a religious education that taught too much, too soon, too finally, and from outside lived experience. If our expression of the Story/Vision is to be part of an "education toward adulthood"[8] and toward maturity in Christian faith, then they must be presented in a disclosure rather than a closure manner. They must be made accessible in a way that invites people to reflect, to personally appropriate, to see the why and the wherefore of the tradition—in a sense, to rediscover it for themselves. This is also essential to prepare for the fourth movement, where the present dialectical hermeneutics described in Chapter Nine begin. A rule of thumb I have found useful in my own presentations and that helps to promote a dialogical disclosure-type presentation is to end with a statement such as, "And that is my understanding of the tradition on this topic. What do you think?" Such an admission gains respect for my position while inviting the participants to appropriate it to themselves and to their own knowing, out of their own Christian praxis.

When I describe this third movement as a making present of the Christian community Story and its Vision, this should not be understood as two separate presentations, the first of the Story and the second of the Vision. Two foci are sometimes called for within the same presentation, but most often I find that as I present the Story I also present its Vision, the response it invites and promise it offers. A more detailed account of samples from my own praxis may make the workings of this movement clearer.

During the weekend with the university people considering their university's role in educating for social justice, the third movement was handled by three resource people. The first person gave a summary, as she had heard it, of the corporate Story and Vision of the group as it had emerged from the previous two movements. The second two "input" people, who were from outside the group, worked full time in social justice ministry. Drawing heavily from scripture, current theological writings, and papal documents, they gave presentations on their understanding and rationale for social justice and outlined what they envisioned as the possible contribution of the university in meeting that challenge.

With religious educators attending to the purpose of Christian religious education, I gave a summary of the purpose as outlined in Chapters Three, Four, and Five of this work. In the unit on the Emmaus story the third movement was an exegesis of the passage which drew from a number of scripture commentaries and proposed it as a model of Christian education (somewhat as outlined in the Prologue of Part IV).

In another adult group dealing with the role of women in the Church I talked about the low status of women in the pre-Christian world, the oppressive attitude of the Fathers toward women (looking especially at Tertullian, Jerome, and Augustine), and the poor treatment of women in Church legislation and practice down to our own day. Then, bringing some present consciousness to the reading of scripture, I contrasted this story with the open and liberating attitude of Jesus toward women. Many of his words and actions directly contravened the laws and sexist mores of his cultural context. I shared some insights from current feminist theology and spoke about the Vision of the Kingdom in which there is no longer to be discrimination of any kind, where Jew and Greek, slave and free person, male and female will all be one in Christ Jesus our Lord (Gal. 3:28).

With the ninth-graders on the Eucharist I emphasized the responsibility which Eucharist places on us (receiving requires giving) and then screened a film titled *Eucharist,* which very powerfully develops this theme.

In the unit on prayer with the fourth-graders I used a narrative format. I explained how Jesus had told us to pray and pray often. Using scripture stories, I explained how Jesus had given us an example of saying to God what was most on our mind, be it joy and praise or pain and petition; how he had prayed at different times and in various places and had even taught us a special prayer to say. We said the Lord's prayer together. I told them about prayers that are not just prayers of petition and about prayers of petition that are not just for members of our own family or group. I concluded by explaining that Christians are called to be a praying people and that God will always hear our prayers, though not always as we think they should be heard.

In the unit on Reconciliation I used a short film, *The Dropout,* a children's version of the parable of the Prodigal Son. I explained how God is always willing to forgive us when we say we are sorry for what we have done wrong. Then, using the scripture passage about leaving our gift at the altar and being reconciled with our brothers and sisters before offering it (Matt. 5:23-24), I explained the meaning, purpose, and structure of the Penitential Rite at the beginning of Mass and how this prepares us as a community to celebrate the Eucharist in a spirit of love and forgiveness. I explained further that we could always be confident of God's mercy if we say that we are sorry, but we must also be willing to forgive those who hurt us.

Again, in this third movement a great variety of teaching modes and methods of presentation can be used. It may be done in a ten-minute presentation or take a number of weeks or even months. The primary purpose is to enable the group to encounter the broader community Story and Vision that arises from the Christian faith tradition. Fourth-graders, for example, should not have to invent the idea of a loving and forgiving God who offers us mercy and wants us to forgive each other. That is a part of the revelational heritage of our faith community which they deserve to inherit. However, if they are to personally appropriate this idea for their lives, then they need, first, to have it made present in the context of their lived experience and, second, to be enabled to take it to themselves and accept responsibility for their response to it. The second point is the agenda for the next two movements.

The fourth and fifth movements combined are a bringing together of what was done in the first two movements with what was made accessible in the third movement. They place *theoria* and praxis in a dialectical unity with each other. The stories and visions are placed in dialogue and dialectic with the Story/Vision to invite appropriation of the tradition to lived experience and decision making for further praxis. In my own praxis, especially with younger children, the two movements often overlap. However, with adults especially it is often important to keep them separate in the praxis, and I will present them separately here.

FOURTH MOVEMENT: DIALECTICAL HERMENEUTIC BETWEEN THE STORY AND PARTICIPANTS' STORIES

The fourth movement is a critique of the Story in light of the stories and a critique of the participants' present stories in light of the past Story. Though I would rarely pose the question in such metaphorical language, the fourth movement asks, in essence, What does the community's Story mean for (affirm, call in question, invite beyond) our stories, and how do our stories respond to (affirm, recognize limits of, push beyond) the community Story?

Let me repeat again here that I am speaking of critique in the dialectical sense, and not of criticism in the narrowly negative sense. Thus there will be affirmation as well as negation, and very often there will be much more of the former than of the latter. There are times when the Story comes to us as a source of affirmation, encouragement, healing, and hallowing. But knowing that we—in our personal, interpersonal, and social/political lives—are never completely faithful to our faith commitments, there are also times when the Story confronts us, calls us in question, and calls us forward. God's self-revealing and reaching out into the world should always be recognized as both consolation and confrontation, encouragement and correction, affirmation and invitation. Conversely, as our stories respond to the community Story, there are whole dimensions of the larger Story with which our own lived experience resonates (since it arises from the lived experience of the Christians who went before us). Thus we can readily affirm it. On the other hand, there may be dimensions of the larger Story or at least the presentation of it as encountered in movement three in which we recognize limitations.

That there are limitations in our understanding of the Story seems inevitable since we can never exhaust its meaning and truth for our lives. The ground of our Story is a God of ultimate mystery and thus no version or understanding we have of God's activity among our people (our Story) can ever be the last word. Rather than passively accepting or simply repeating the version made accessible, we need to recognize the limitations in our present understanding and attempt to move beyond them.[9] This is far from being an exercise in negative criticism. On the contrary, the dialectic is a liberating and creative process that uses the tradition itself to empower us to move forward. Some examples of how I have done the fourth movement, and then a more precise description of the fifth movement, may clarify what I am saying here.

In the weekend on social justice with the university people, I opened the fourth movement by asking for general reactions to the input of the morning (third movement). How had the input shed light on their situation at the university, what did they see as feasible or not feasible, and what would they add to what was said that morning? In the unit with people preparing to be evaluators of Christian schools the third movement (presented by a well-prepared member of the group) was a very moving presentation on stewardship, well grounded in scripture and rich in imagery. For the fourth movement I invited the participants to choose and share the image that had spoken most powerfully to them and to explain why. (This puts the two stories in dialogue with each other.) With the group focused on the Emmaus story after my presentation I asked the participants, "What insight did my presentation renew for you, and what would you add to or clarify in my statement?" In units with graduate students on the purpose of Christian religious education I typically ask them to write down three points they particularly agree with in my presentation, and three points they want to question, add to, or rephrase. I then have them share their notes with the whole group, or in groups of four if the whole group is too large.

In a unit on "freedom of conscience in a teaching Church," one woman made a very moving statement that is a good example of what can happen at this fourth movement. She said, "In my own life the Church as teacher lost a lot of its credibility after the encyclical on birth control. For some time I just turned it off when it tried to offer me moral directives. Yet I have realized from this evening that I need the consensus and support of a Christian faith community in my ethical decision making. I do not want to decide everything for myself as a private, isolated Christian." Here, I felt, neither the individual story nor the community Story was having the only word, but the two were in a creative dialogue with each other.

After screening the film with the ninth-graders on Eucharist I asked, "If you lie in bed tonight and think about that film, what image or scene will jump out at you first and why?"

In the unit on Reconciliation and the Penitential Rite of the Mass with the fourth-graders, I asked what they thought of the Rite and if it was a good idea to have it at the beginning of Mass (the Story and their lived experience in dialogue). Most of them seemed to think that it was a good idea. We spent some time talking about how it could help us prepare to celebrate Mass with feelings of peace and love. In that class there was also an interesting example of a small story talking back to the big Story. One boy had difficulty pronouncing the words *Penitential Rite*. Then it occurred to me that, for fourth-graders, I had used very poor language. What does that big word *penitential* mean to children? And is it *write* or *right* or *rite?* They did not know. So I asked them to think of a better name for it. After some discussion, one girl volunteered, "It's the time for forgiveness." We settled for that name, the time for forgiveness, and that was how it was referred to for the remainder of the semester. They had come to name it for themselves far better than I had named it for them.

I draw attention also to the difference between asking them what *they* think and feel about the time for forgiveness during Mass and playing the traditional role of teacher by asking them to tell me what the Penitential Rite is. The latter procedure, though typically followed by teachers after their presentation to a class, is not likely to achieve the purpose of the fourth movement. The expectation that usually underlies such a question is that the students will feed back to the teacher the "right answers," that is, the answers the teacher has given them. This is not to imply that the fourth movement is reduced to an exercise in personal opinions or feelings. On the contrary, the participants are indeed expected to know their community Story. In this case I wanted the fourth-graders to know clearly what the Penitential Rite was, and when it was obvious that that was not clear, I repeated my explanation of it. But even more important, I wanted them to come to see what the Penitential Rite might mean for their lives.

At the fourth movement in the unit on Prayer I asked the participants what they now thought about prayer and about how Jesus had prayed. They seemed to agree that we should talk to God not only to ask for things, but also to express love and gratitude. This led to a discussion about whether or not we really can talk to God in our own words, at any time or place, or about anything. This seemed strange to them, and many were reluctant to accept the idea. Two people said that prayers we make up ourselves are not "real prayers." Real prayers, they insisted, are the Our Father, Hail Mary, and other set prayer formulas that they had learned. In response I pointed out that Jesus did not often use a set formula and that I very often talk to God in my own words. Here is an example of the discussion that followed: When I asked one little boy, "Billy, what is the most important thing in your life right now?" he said, "My dog." I did not expect that answer, but this was a dog he had received just a few days previously. I inquired if he could talk to God about his dog. He laughed ("What a stupid question") and said, "No." "Why not?" I asked. He said, "Cause he's not sick." We talked about that with the group, and they agreed that Billy could talk to God about his dog even though the dog was not sick. I asked Billy if he could thank God for his dog and do it in his own words. After a good deal of thought, Billy agreed that he could. I then asked, "Will you?" (fifth movement overlapping), and with some enthusiasm he said that he would.

The vital task to be promoted by the educator in the fourth movement is two-fold: that lived faith experience be informed by the Christian faith tradition and that the appropriating of the tradition be informed by, and be in the context of, lived faith experience. Only thus can a praxis way of knowing be promoted. There is also a sense in which the fourth movement is an opportunity for the participants to see the "why" of the Christian Story or, as Piaget would say, "to reinvent it." As the second movement is an opportunity to reflect on their individual knowing, the fourth movement is an opportunity to reflect on the community knowing, to appropriate it, to name their "new" knowing of it with a sense of discovery. It attempts to promote a moment of "aha" when the participants come to know the Story as their own, in the context of their lives.

At first, people who are new to the process, be they young or old, tend to feed back the answers they presume the teacher expects. This tendency decreases as they continue to use the process. The way in which the fourth movement questions are posed is crucial for moving them beyond such a "right-answers" mentality (e.g., not saying, "Now tell me what prayer is," but rather, "How do you understand prayer? What could it mean for your life?" etc.).

FIFTH MOVEMENT: DIALECTICAL HERMENEUTIC BETWEEN THE VISION AND PARTICIPANTS' VISIONS

The intention for the fifth movement is to critique the visions embodied in our present action in the light of the Vision of God's Kingdom and to decide on future action that will be an appropriate response to that Vision. Stated in its technical language, the fifth movement is asking, "How is our present action creative or noncreative of the Vision, and how will we (I) act in the future?" Stated more simply, the movement is an opportunity for the individual and the group to choose a faith response, a Christian praxis, in light of all that has gone before.

In the dialectic that is intended here there is a recognition of the signs of the Kingdom already among us, but there is also a perception of its not-yetness and a decision of how to respond to both in our lives. To people who are new to the process especially (and given our penchant for abstractions), it is difficult at first to make praxis decisions about our future action. This became obvious in my first experience using shared praxis with adults. All of us tended to make statements like, "People need to realize that . . ." or, "The Church should. . . ." But such are likely to be *theoria* statements, at best, and decisions for other people rather than for ourselves. To help us come to our own new knowing, we found it helpful to preface our remarks with statements like "I will do . . ." or "For me this means. . . ."

Remembering again our comprehensive description of action, the decision for future action here can be a decision for overt activity, or it can be an articulation of a new awareness, understanding, sentiment, feeling, hope, and so on. It could also be a decision for further reflection and attempts at clarification. Many times during this movement participants have said something like, "I have never thought of it this way before, and I need to think a lot more about it." Such a statement is actually a decision for future action.

The examples of what has happened during this fifth movement are almost as varied as the number of people who have participated multiplied by the number of times I have used a shared praxis approach. In the unit on social justice this final movement was spent in outlining concrete strategy for the next step. Many ideas were shared about what might be done, the suggestions were noted, and a committee was formed to write a proposal. The proposal was later circulated to the other members of the group for comments, and then a final statement was prepared for submission to the university administration.

In the Emmaus story unit we began the fifth movement by asking ourselves, "How will these reflections influence how we educate in the future?" In units on the purpose of Christian religious education, my graduate students are invited to write a reflection paper on "What for me is the purpose of Christian religious education?" The fifth movement with the evaluators began with a half hour of silence during which the participants were invited to reflect upon and write down five sensitivities or awarenesses they would want to bring to their task as evaluators. These were later shared with the whole group.

With the ninth-graders on Eucharist we ended by responding to the question, "How will I give 'Eucharist' to people?" Some offered concrete suggestions, while one said, "I will have to think a lot more about that." In other units on Eucharist we have ended by celebrating a liturgy together, and on one occasion a group of high school boys decided to organize a fast for world hunger.

With the fourth-graders in the unit on Prayer I simply asked questions like, "Will you pray? What will you say? When will you pray?" They talked about praying in the morning and at bedtime, before and after meals, saying prayers of petition and also prayers of praise and thanksgiving. One little girl was missing from class that day because she was in the hospital. The class decided that they would pray for her. I suggested that we each write out a prayer and I would take them to her in the hospital. I had the children read their prayers aloud before I collected them, and one boy said that he would say his again that night.

In the unit on Reconciliation we talked about how we might enter into the "time of forgiveness" at Mass the next Sunday. I asked if there was anyone whom they could forgive or "make up" with. Everyone had someone to whom they needed to say "sorry," and I invited them to do that when they had an opportunity. It so happened that two of the boys had had a fight before class that day, and this was reported to the group. The class suggested that they shake hands with each other, and they did. In the unit on the Offertory we spent some time talking about what we might try to remember at the Offertory of the Mass next time we participated. It was just before Christmas time, so there were many decisions concerning Christmas gifts.

The fifth movement is essential if our religious education is to lead to further Christian praxis. As we discussed in Chapter Four, Christian faith is a whole way of being in the world, a lived response rather than a theory about, and our religious education should invite people to decision. Many contemporary curriculum materials, especially at the grade school level, cover the first four movements of shared praxis in one way or another (though the dialectical element is often absent). But unfortunately the fifth movement is frequently left out. An opportunity for choosing needs to be built in as a consistent part of the process, rather than simply being taken for granted.

Even as I pose the fifth movement as an opportunity for choosing a faith response, it is important to remember the guidelines for decision-making outlined in Chapter Nine. This movement is certainly not a free-for-all in which people are invited to choose arbitrarily as they please. On the contrary, the guidelines of continuity, consequences, and community/Church must guide the decision-making. It is also relevant to recall the description of the Kingdom as both invitation and mandate, and the description of Christian freedom as very different from rugged individualism and the antithesis of license. An example may clarify what I mean here: in a unit on justice, the educator could never pose the fourth and fifth movement questions in the forms of "Will you or won't you be just?" as if the Christian Story and Vision offer an option on the question. Justice is a mandate of the Kingdom. The participants may indeed choose to overlook injustice in their lives, but the educator can never pretend that is a valid response to the Kingdom. The educator can, however, invite students to discern what justice means, why they are called to it, and how they will live justly in their own lives.

But even when the guidelines for decision-making and the mandate of the Kingdom are kept in mind, there still remains an obvious risk in inviting our students to such decision-making and personal appropriation. All of us have hopes for what our students will choose, and we should never be without purpose and intentionality. We have the right to give witness to what our hopes are, and our students have a need to hear them. But I am often asked, "What if the participants make choices contrary to what we hope they will choose?" This is a risk we must take. Indeed, we have a responsibility to provide an environment of openness in which they will have that option. Otherwise, we are likely to fall back into domination, rather than education. The model here is Jesus himself. When the rich young man came to him inquiring, "What must I do to share in everlasting life?" he received the invitation to "sell all you have and give to the poor. . . . Then come and follow me." The rich young man refused the invitation. Jesus, while saddened by that refusal, respected the young man's choice (Luke 18:18–25). In John 6, after the discourse on the bread of life, "many of his disciples broke away and would not remain in his company any longer" (John 6:66). Far from refusing their choice and trying to cajole or threaten them into accepting his position, Jesus turned to the Twelve and asked, "Do you want to leave me too?" (John 6:67). Throughout the Bible the call of Yahweh and the call to discipleship always carry with them the right of refusal. That is the risk God takes in giving us free will. Our risk as Christian religious educators can be no less.

We must never presume that because our students do not choose the response we had envisioned for them that they are inevitably being unfaithful to the Story and Vision. *Our* intentions for them are not necessarily God's intentions. In fact, our students may choose other than as we had hoped, but in that go beyond our limited vision as teacher to a more faithful Christian response. One mark of a great educator is the ability to lead students out, not just to his or her own position but beyond that to new places where even the educator has never been. On many occasions in shared praxis groups I have been brought to decisions I never set out to make. Such moments remind us again that the educator should be the "leading learner" and that, especially in the journey of faith, we are all brother and sister pilgrims together.

SOME GENERAL REFLECTIONS ON USING SHARED PRAXIS

VARIATIONS AND SEQUENCE OF MOVEMENTS

As is evident in the different examples from my own praxis, many techniques and strategies can be used to put each of the movements into effect. Shared praxis is not so much a particular method as a general approach within which various pedagogical methods can be used. In general, however, it calls for some basic group skills. I have learned most of what I know in the praxis. When an educator is clear about exactly what the task of each movement is, creativity and imagination must be called up to effect that task.

The sequence used to outline the movements here is the general pattern I have been using in my own praxis. Naming present Christian action and reflecting upon it, then making present the Christian faith tradition as it relates to the focus of attention, followed by an opportunity for the participants to appropriate that to their lives and make decisions for a Christian response, seems a logical sequence that arises from the whole rationale of shared praxis previously outlined.

But I have frequently followed another sequence and arranged the movements in a variety of combinations, with different movements receiving different emphasis from one unit to another. For example, in theology courses with undergraduates I usually begin with a series of lectures to introduce and focus the curriculum of the course, thus, in a sense, beginning with a statement from the Story/Vision. I frequently overlap the first movement and the first part of the second movement, asking the What? and Why? questions together. I have often kept the role of imagination until the fourth movement (imagination is always part of the dialectic), asking, "What can you do with this?" which usually leads to overlapping with the fifth movement. On a number of occasions I have begun units with an exercise in imagination, and on other occasions with an exercise in memory.

The main point is that the movements should flow together in an orchestrated whole, rather than follow a lock-step sequencing. One teacher who has been using a shared praxis approach with high school students for a number of years commented in a recent letter, "Shared praxis is really an attitude and style of teaching, which the teacher must develop and grow into from using it. Then the movements flow from that in a variety of combinations." I agree.

The opening focusing activity is very often a common action together. I have found this particularly necessary with topics where there had been little prior experience. For example, when I began to go through the Mass with the fourth-graders, I found that a number rarely attended Mass and could not even begin to recognize what I was talking about in class. This led me to cancel my "planned curriculum" for the next month, and we spent four weeks preparing, rehearsing, and finally celebrating a Eucharist together. After that we had a common action upon which to reflect.

This brings to mind a criticism of my earlier descriptions of a shared praxis approach—that it has not been sufficiently "praxeological."[10] That criticism may well be true of much of my own praxis up to this point. But with the broadened definition of praxis offered in Chapter Nine there is a real sense in which the first two movements are themselves a praxis. The very opening question immediately invites cognitive action by the participants. When possible, however, it is appropriate to begin with a common experience rather than with a naming of what has been experienced. On some occasions, when I had worked with the same group over a number of units and we came to a decision for common action, we then began the next unit by reflecting on the action together.

However, I do not see a common, overt action by the group to be a sine qua non for using the approach. There is a certain commonality to all human action, and even more particularly to Christian praxis, so that it can at least be named and reflected upon together.[11] Here we are reminded again of the need for a Christian faith community as the context for Christian religious education. When the context is such, there is a constant shared Christian praxis (broadly defined) in the community that can then be named and reflected upon in a shared praxis approach to intentional education.

TIMING AND SHARED PRAXIS

A question I am frequently asked is: "How long does it take to work through a unit using a shared praxis approach?" Since a shared praxis approach is as much an attitude that the educator brings to the educational enterprise as it is the five movements I have outlined, it can be present in any Christian educational context, however we attempt to give it form. There have been ten-minute interchanges with students in which I was consciously attempting to use a shared praxis approach, inviting people to name and reflect on their own experience, offering some "input" out of the Christian faith tradition as I know it, and then inviting them to appropriate that in light of their own experience and come to some decision about it.

In a classroom context the shortest period I have used to cover a complete unit is forty minutes. Obviously, the depth and extent of both the reflection and the dialogue are limited by such a time frame. On the other hand, I have also planned a whole semester's curriculum around the five movements at both the high school and undergraduate levels. Such a time frame provides ample opportunity for reflection, dialogue, research, and lecturing.

In a high school program that met for one hour once a week I structured units to last for a six-week period, giving two evenings to the Christian community Story and its Vision. On many occasions I have conducted weekend retreats and symposia, structuring them around the five movements. Such a setting and time span often appear ideal in that they bring about a certain cohesion in the group while allowing sufficient time to give attention to all five movements. The Crossroads group referred to earlier covered each unit in one evening lasting a minimum of four hours. My weekly fourth-grade class lasts one hour, and we usually complete a unit in that time. Thus the general conclusion I have reached from my own praxis is that the five movements of shared praxis are sufficiently flexible to be organized effectively in many time frames.

THE ENVIRONMENT OF SHARED PRAXIS

Years ago John Dewey noted insightfully, "We never educate directly, but indirectly by means of the environment."[12] That is eminently true in a shared praxis situation. Later research has consistently indicated that Dewey's insight is beyond question. The educational environment in a shared praxis situation is vital to the quality of education that takes place. There are two related dimensions to what I mean here by environment: the emotional and the physical.

Emotional Environment.   The whole atmosphere of the gathering needs to be one of welcome, warmth, and openness. Here I am speaking of the ancient Christian virtue of hospitality. Paul's admonition to the Romans, "Be generous in offering hospitality" (Rom. 12:13) and Peter's exhortation, "Be mutually hospitable without complaining" (1 Pet. 4:9) describe the modus operandi of a shared praxis group. The participants need to feel welcome, at home, and at ease. They need to believe that their contributions will be valued and taken seriously. In such a hospitable environment people are likely to feel free in expressing themselves, speaking their own words rather than saying what they think the group wants to hear. It is in the willingness to listen that the hospitality of a shared praxis group is tested.

Closely related to the need for a hospitable environment is the need for an atmosphere of trust. Trust and hospitality build on each other, and a group cannot have one without the other. The very nature of the shared praxis approach requires trust among the participants if authentic dialogue is to take place, if critical reflection is to happen, if the Story and the stories are to be heard, and if the risk taking of decision making is to have sufficient support.

Françoise Darcy-Bérubé has pointed to the need for trust as one of the "practical problems involved in introducing educators to a shared-praxis approach in religious education."[13] The problem cannot be perfectly solved since realistically there can never be total trust by everyone in a group on every occasion. But, in fact, every situation of discourse presupposes trust among its participants. We cannot wait until we are sure there is a high trust level before we can take the risk of entering into discourse. That would bespeak mistrust and would paralyze us into inactivity. On many occasions there has seemed to be only minimal trust at the beginning of a shared praxis unit, but as the process proceeded through the dialogue and struggle of each person, I have seen the trust level build with amazing rapidity. This would seem to be consistent with Freire's experience, from which he concludes that "trust is established by dialogue."[14] By being a model of dialogue, trust, and hospitality, the educator has a crucial role in creating such an environment in the group.

Physical Environment.   Over fifteen hundred years ago St. Augustine insisted in *De Catechizandis Rudibus* that the learning environment in religious education should be physically "comfortable" for the participants. Unfortunately, we have often forgotten his insight. The ideal physical context for a shared praxis process is what I call a "soft" environment, as distinct from a hard one, for instance, a covered floor rather than a bare one, or comfortable chairs (not armchairs; they discourage participation) instead of desks. In creating such an environment, we must pay attention to the lighting, seating, color scheme, floor covering, and furnishings. Again, the ideal will rarely be realized, but a little imagination and a few supplies can add warmth and hospitality to even the "hardest" of environments. Imagine the difference it would make if our intentional educational settings could be made into a "home" for the participants, where even the physical environment gave a sense of warmth, openness, and hospitality.

The size of the group is also part of the physical environment. I found in the praxis that twelve seems to be the ideal number for a group. If at all possible, the participants should be able to have eye contact with each other, and thus circular formation is required. However, I work constantly with groups far larger than twelve. In such situations it becomes difficult to keep the whole group together for all of the movements and to allow ample time for everyone who wishes to share reflections. Yet it is imperative that all members of a group have an opportunity to speak their word to someone. Meeting this need will challenge the creativity of the leader. I usually subdivide large groups of adults into groups of four to share their reflections and, depending on time and numbers, take feedback from the small groups into the whole group after at least one of the five movements.

RELATIONSHIP OF THEOLOGY TO CHRISTIAN RELIGIOUS EDUCATION

Christian theology, in the strictest and most technical sense of the term, is the discipline that articulates an understanding of the meaning of God in our lives based on an in-depth and systematic investigation of both the Christian faith tradition and the lived experience of people. The teaching magisterium of the Church, scripture scholars, and theologians all participate in that enterprise after their own fashion. Theologians have the special skills and training for research that give them competence to interpret, explain, and develop the meaning of our faith tradition as it interrelates with the human situation at any given time in history. Scripture scholars have competence to investigate in a scholarly manner the texts and contexts of the written statements of the way the founding members of our faith tradition understood the "primordial revelation" of God to our people. The official teaching magisterium is more obvious in some Christian denominations than others and varies in form among them. But in all mainline Christian churches there is some agency or source that is looked upon as the guardian of the "faith handed down"—the assembly, council, confession, meeting, papacy, patriarch, primate, synod, and so on. Informed by the theologians, scripture scholars and (as pointed out in Chapter Nine) the *sensus fidelium*, the magisterium articulates an understanding of the faith tradition that is then a guide for the whole Church. These three sources—magisterium, scholars, and the "sense of the faithful"—cooperate in mutual dialogue, support, and correction in a Church where all God's people are part of the *ecclesia docens* as well as the *ecclesia discens*.

As noted previously, however, at an early stage of the Church's history the relationship of theology to Christian education came to be based on a from theory to practice epistemological assumption. In consequence, the reflections and teachings of the scholars and magisterium were looked on as the truth to be delivered to the people, and Christian education was a key part of the delivery system. This led to what James Michael Lee so aptly describes as a "messenger boy" role for Christian religious education.[15] But such a relationship is based on a false understanding of both theology and education. It sees theology as an intellectualized theoretical endeavor isolated from Christian praxis and views education as a delivery system that banks information in passive receptacles. Quite obviously, a shared praxis approach rejects such a relationship and insists on one of mutuality instead.

From the perspective of a shared praxis approach the relationship between theology and Christian religious education must be a two-way street, one that holds *theoria* and praxis in a dialectical unity.

To begin with, education in the Christian faith tradition and on behalf of (i.e., "from within") a Christian community should be informed by the best current understanding Christians have of their tradition.[16] Christian religious education that is theologically uninformed is an aberration most likely to defeat its intended purpose. That a shared praxis approach needs to be well informed by reliable Christian theology is most evident at the third movement. To make present the Christian community Story and its Vision and to do so reliably requires that the "presenters" know their scripture and theology. Otherwise, distortion of the Story and its Vision seems inevitable. This certainly does not mean that educators must be expert theologians or scripture scholars. But they and their resources should be informed by the experts and by the official teaching of the Church. Teacher training programs for Christian religious educators need to be as concerned with theological formation as with educational development.

On the other hand, while Christian religious education must be informed by reliable theological scholarship, the scholars must also be informed by the lived faith of a Christian community. As the scholars attend to the sources of the tradition, they must also be informed by the present historical experience of the faith community reflected upon in light of that tradition. In this sense, theology should arise from and be informed by precisely the kind of reflection on present Christian action that goes on in a shared praxis group. In fact, when a group of people reflect critically on present historical experience in light of the Christian Story/Vision, they are "doing" theology. This is not to negate the role of the "specialists" in the various theological disciplines. Their expertise in the sources and history of the tradition, their ability to systematize and articulate reflections from the faith of the people lived in response to the tradition, is essential. But we must refuse to hand the theological enterprise over to the exclusive domain of the specialists. Theology is to arise from Christian praxis as much as it is to inform further Christian praxis. It should arise from the faith of a community reflected on in light of the Story/Vision and not from a group of scholars isolated from the community to reflect on the community's behalf. The latter kind of "theology" (and we have it in abundance) contributes little to the ongoing faith life of the Christian community.

Thus, while shared praxis needs to be informed by the expertise of the scholars, the scholars need to be informed by the shared praxis of the people. Only in this way can the Christian community reunite *theoria* and praxis in a dialectical unity in which *theoria* both informs praxis and arises from praxis. Only in this way can theology and Christian religious education cooperate as mutual partners in promoting lived Christian faith in the world.

The importance of the mutuality I am arguing for here can be highlighted further by a historical perspective on the present social arrangement in the Church between theology and religious education. It appears that in the early Church the ministry of the *didaskaloi* (and it was an official ministry—see Acts 13:1; 1 Cor. 12:28–29; Eph. 4:11) was both to know "sound doctrine" (2 Tim. 4:3) and to teach it. In this sense the *didaskaloi* were both theologians and educators.

But over the years an unfortunate division of labor arose between the ministry of knowing sound doctrine and the ministry of Christian education. This division has even led to antagonism, with charges and countercharges on both sides. Theologians often accuse Christian educators (and with some good cause) of not being theologically informed. But educators can, with equal cause, direct a similar criticism to many theologians and accuse them of abandoning their responsibility to be educators. The gap between theology at a scholarly level and the theology that is typically preached or taught at a pastoral level is a growing problem in the Church. Theologians must take some responsibility for that unfortunate pastoral situation. They have certainly augmented the problem by neglecting their pastoral responsibility to be educators. There continues to be a false assumption among theologians that the person who "knows theology" will automatically be able to teach it. As a result, in graduate programs that prepare professional theologians there is typically no attention paid to or preparation for the educational responsibility that comes with being a professional theologian. More unfortunate still is the current dearth of good religious education courses in our seminaries.[17] Very often parish programs break down or are hindered by ordained ministers who may know their theology but have no knowledge of or sensitivity to education. From the perspective of lived Christian faith theology is as useless without good education as Christian education is dangerous without informed theology.

In the division of labor between Christian theology and education, a hierarchical relationship evolved. Theology gained "big brother" status, whereas education became the "little sister." (The sexist connotations of my terms are intended.) The social structures, both professional and academic, that formed tended to maintain this subservient relationship. Christian religious education was seen as not a serious enterprise for the theologically advanced (invariably men) and was relegated to those who were less capable (assumed to be women). These unequal social structures reflect a false consciousness and must be changed. We must come to view theology and Christian religious education as equal partners in the vocation of the Christian community to live the faith it claims to believe and to form people in it. Without a relationship of mutual collaboration both enterprises are greatly impoverished. Richard P. McBrien puts this well when he writes, "Good theology is essential to good religious education. And good educational theory and practice are essential to the learning and communication of good theology. Consequently, there is no other acceptable relationship between religious education and theology except a relationship of mutual respect and collaboration."[18]

LITURGY AND A SHARED PRAXIS APPROACH

As I understand them, Christian liturgy and education both have their own primary purpose, and for each this purpose should remain primary. Liturgy is to enable people to ritualize and express together in worship their relationship with God. Christian religious education is to sponsor people in Christian faith and human freedom. To use either liturgy or education merely to serve the other is a travesty of the purpose of the one made subservient. Thus it is contrary to the very purpose of liturgy to turn it into simply an educational tool. Nor can our educational programs be geared primarily to preparing people to celebrate the sacraments, as frequently appears to be the case in many Catholic parish programs. But while the liturgical and educational activities of the Christian community have their own distinct purposes, there is a profound mutuality between them. In the praxis of community life the two can never be separated. In a sense, they have their own primary purpose but have each other as a secondary purpose. Let me explain.

Liturgy ritualizes and celebrates as worship the lived faith relationship of the people with God and the covenant of God with the people. But liturgy is not merely to express that faith relationship; it is also to deepen and promote it. Liturgy arises from lived Christian faith and should return to increase the living of Christian faith. Liturgy can never be an end in itself. Sacraments and the Word are for the sake of the world and are to promote a lived faith response of engagement in the world. When liturgy causes this to happen, as it ought to, then, de facto, it is educational. It is sponsoring people toward lived Christian faith and hopefully toward human freedom.

Chapter Six outlined the relationship between Christian religious education and socialization in a community of Christian faith. People are enculturated into a community by appropriating the community's symbols. Therefore, the liturgical symbols of the Christian community, given their centrality and importance, are a primary source of enculturation and socialization. These symbols, Word and sacrament, and how they are celebrated, used, and understood in the community have a powerful formative influence on its members, both new and old. In that sense, liturgy has an educational influence beyond its primary purpose of calling and enabling the community to celebrate its relationship with God. Consequently, the liturgical symbols cannot be used only to bring comfort and consolation to people. They must also confront, invite, and cause growth. For example, when the Eucharist is used only to make us feel better or to express thanks for God's blessings to us, and does not cause us to reach out in care and concern for others, then it has the consequence of domestication and is miseducational.

Looking at this relationship from the other side, Christian religious education has liturgy as its secondary purpose in that the faith life which education enables people to live is what we celebrate in liturgy. Even more particularly, as indicated by many previous examples, a shared praxis group will often have as its focus of attention an aspect of the liturgical life of the Church. In that way it will prepare people to participate in the liturgical and sacramental life of the Christian community. I have also been struck by the number of times a shared praxis unit has ended in some form of ritual or liturgical celebration. Indeed, there are times when, in contemplating our own lives and the Story of God's activity in them, the first and most fitting response is awe, wonder, reverence, and worship. Those sentiments should often be ritualized and when possible celebrated in a liturgical format. But the ritualizing of what emerges from a shared praxis group can never be seen as an end in itself. If a shared praxis approach brings people to no more than ritual or liturgy, and if the liturgy has no ongoing influence for leading lives of faith in response to the Kingdom, then it has brought people to "religion," instead of to Christian discipleship.

Thus to collapse liturgy and education into each other betrays the purpose of each. But to presume that they are separated is to miss the profound mutuality that exists between them in the life of a Christian community.

NOTES

1. The fact that I now call the five activities *movements* is a development beyond my earlier published articles, where I called them *steps*. *Steps* can be a misleading term and may give rise to an inflexible mentality where the activities are seen to be rigidly separate and necessarily sequen-

tial. *Movement*, on the other hand, is intended with something of its musical overtones. The movements flow together, overlap, are repeated, and blend into an orchestrated activity with its own wholeness and aesthetic.

2. I purposely use the word *sample* here in preference to *example*, lest the impression be given that I am posing what I have done as model examples. Indeed, there is ample room for critique of my handling of any of the movements. Creative educators will hopefully devise much more imaginative ways of putting the five movements into operation.

3. With my fourth-grade C.C.D. class I use the Benziger "The Word Is Life" series. I have found it to have much in common with a shared praxis approach. In fact, many of the standard grade school Christian education series are easily adaptable to shared praxis. I especially recommend the "Shared Approaches" developed by Joint Education Development and published by United Church Press, Philadelphia.

4. For a description of this retreat see Kennedy, "Young Adults Confront a Bishop."

5. I am well aware that critical reflection in anything like its fullness is not possible for children. But they are capable of concrete reflection, of asking Why? at least from the stage of what Piaget calls concrete operations. In Chapter Eleven I claim that unless some rudimentary form of reflection is encouraged from the beginning, anything like the fullness of critical reflection will be unlikely in adulthood.

6. Dewey, *Art as Experience*, p. 41.

7. Many of the models of teaching that Marsha Weil and Bruce Joyce have worked out can be used at different movements. However, the advance organizer model and the concept attainment model are particularly suited to this third movement (see Weil and Joyce, *Information Processing Models of Teaching*).

8. I take this phrase from the title of Gabriel Moran's most recent book, *Education Toward Adulthood*. Moran has done more than any religious educator to promote the idea that all religious education should be adult centered, in the sense not of excluding children, but of promoting lifelong learning toward adulthood.

9. What I intend here is very close to what I understand David Tracy to mean by "critical correlation." Tracy sees that there are "two main 'sources' of fundamental theological reflection" (*Blessed Rage for Order*, p. 64), namely, "the Christian fact" and common human experience and language. Both sources must be themselves critiqued and then critically correlated with each other.

10. See, Françoise Darcy-Bérubé, "The Challenge Ahead of Us," in O'Hare, *Foundations*, pp. 126–127.

11. The problem of beginning an educational unit with a common praxis experienced by all of the participants together has plagued progressive educators since Dewey. In an intentional educational setting how does one provide common experiences that then can be "reconstructed" (to use Dewey's term) by the group for the purpose of learning and directing of future experience? The original Dewey devotees ended up with an inordinate number of "field trips," and even from an organizational point of view this can pose enormous problems. Audio-visuals can be helpful in that they provide a vicarious way of experiencing an "action" in common. I am confident that more imaginative educators than I can devise an even more "praxeological" way of beginning the process.

12. Dewey, *Democracy*, p. 19.

13. Darcy-Bérubé, "The Challenge Ahead of Us," In O'Hare, *Foundations*, pp. 128–129.

14. Freire, *Oppressed*, p. 80.

15. See Lee, *The Shape of Religious Instruction*, Ch. 8.

16. This is another reason I favor the term *Christian religious education* beyond the term *religious education*. *Christian religious education* makes it clear that the educating taking place is to be informed by and faithful to the theological self-understanding of Christians. Religious education might be a more general enterprise that investigates the human quest for the transcendent; it need not necessarily be informed by the Christian tradition at all or by its theology. But if we call our enterprise Christian religious education, then the essence of that enterprise requires that our efforts be informed by Christian theology.

17. See Radtke, "The State of Catechetics in U.S. Catholic Seminaries."

18. McBrien, *Basic Questions for Christian Educators*, pp. 30–31.

READINESS FOR CHRISTIAN RELIGIOUS EDUCATION BY SHARED PRAXIS

Prologue

CONTRARY TO popular belief among educators, it is an ancient, not a modern, insight that education should be suited to the psychological readiness of students to participate in it. Augustine frequently stressed the importance of suiting instruction to the age level of pupils,[1] and the idea has been emphasized by many of the great education theorists throughout history. What *is* new to our time is the amount of advanced research being done on various aspects of human development. Among the leading developmentalists, and of special interest to educators, are Piaget (cognitive development), Kohlberg (moral development), Fowler (faith development), Loevinger (ego development), and Selman (development of empathy). Their research is ongoing, and their findings must be seen as helpful indicators rather than final and complete descriptions. Although I tend to approach "data" collected by the research of social scientists with a healthy skepticism, there seems to be sufficient and reliable evidence to discern an accurate composite picture of the developmental process of human growth. The issue of readiness in education now takes on added urgency, and there are new possibilities for answering old questions. What is an appropriate educational response to students at the various stages of growth? What educational process is capable of affirming people in the "truth" of their particular stage, while summoning them beyond the limits of that stage to a new level of human maturation? These are questions that arise anew for educators in light of contemporary developmental research.

We have only begun to struggle with such questions. In religious education Ronald Goldman and others[2] have laid some valuable groundwork, but much remains to be done. Educators must be cautious as they begin to draw from the insights of developmental research. What is offered as descriptive cannot be taken as prescriptive, just as what "is" should never be taken automatically as what "ought to be." Nor should education now become the "messenger boy" of the developmental psychologists. We must bring our own issues, questions, insights, and language, as well as a modicum of skepticism, to the "data" being offered. Otherwise our enterprise will become a mode of operationalized social science, and our efforts will be reduced to techniques.[3] On the other hand, to ignore the findings of developmental psychologists seems foolhardy.

In the overall design of this book Part Five deals with another foundational issue for Christian religious education, the question of readiness. However, I do no more here than point to the tip of the iceberg.[4] My treatment is limited in that I consider readiness only for a shared praxis approach to Christian religious education and reflect on that only from a Piagetian perspective. Within this limited perspective, however, I hope to shed light on what is undoubtedly a broader issue. In addition, I consider my treatment to have value precisely because it draws upon Piaget to evaluate a specific approach to religious education, rather than to evaluate the "content" of a curriculum. The latter use of developmental research seems to be most typical in education, and I do not deny its value. For example, in religious education, Piaget's research has shown us that attempts to teach abstract concepts like the Trinity to small children is, among other things, a waste of time; small children are not capable of the kind of formal thinking that such a concept requires. But Piaget has deeper and more significant possibilities for us beyond evaluating content. His exploration of the activity of knowing itself, including the nature of that process at its various developing stages, can help us to evaluate and devise our educational process.

I intend in a future work to juxtapose the stages of faith development as Fowler outlines them with a shared praxis approach and indicate what might be an appropriate educational response to each of the six stages. While I refer to Fowler's work, I choose to attend specifically to Piaget here for three reasons. First, Piaget's work is prior and foundational for most of the other researchers on the stages of human development. Although concerted criticisms can be and have been made of his work (and I add my own below), there has been sufficient additional research, both longitudinal and cross-cultural, to indicate that his basic thesis and descriptions are reliable. Second, Piaget's work is essentially an investigation of epistemology from a developmental perspective. His primary interest is how and when we come to different structures of cognition. Since a shared praxis approach to Christian religious education calls for, among other things, a shift from a *theoria* to a praxis way of knowing, it seems most fitting to evaluate this proposal from a Piagetian understanding of genetic epistemology. That certainly will not exhaust the question of readiness in Christian religious education, but it will indicate whether or not shared praxis is on sound epistemological ground from a developmental perspective. Finally, I believe Piaget's work can legitimate and further clarify what I have already said. While I approach the question of epistemology out of a very different literature, it can be readily enriched by a Piagetian perspective. I see an obvious resonance between Piaget's understanding of knowing as arising from intelligent action upon the world and a praxis knowing that is active/reflective engagement in the world. At their core they are attempts to say something very similar, albeit with different emphases and different language.

On the question of readiness for a shared praxis approach to Christian religious education, I make one key claim in this section pertaining to critical reflection. Anything like the fullness of critical reflection as I have described it is rare, even among adults. Critical reflection is an ever-deepening and expanding capacity in which we grow, rather than a static faculty that we either have or don't have. From about the age of twelve on (the beginning of formal operational cognition, in Piaget's terms) a person can begin to reflect critically in a qualitatively improved way. But developmentally a person is capable of active reflective knowing before that stage. From an educational perspective that reflective dimension of knowing must be promoted and encouraged at the earlier stages of cognitive development if the person is to have the likelihood of full critical reflection later on. As the tree is in the seed, the possibility for critical reflection in a more complete form (critiquing ideologies, unmasking assumptions, etc.) must grow out of the earlier stages of active/reflective cognition. Thus what I will continue to call critical reflection needs to be encouraged from the beginnings of intentional education. If children are not encouraged to ask and reflect on the Why? of reality, and dream about what might be, it is likely that they will continue to appropriate and settle for reality uncritically in adulthood. Perhaps a personal story will help to clarify my point.

Some time ago I was privileged to be with a mother and her son of eight and a half years as he said his night prayers. He prayed earnestly for himself, for his family, for his relatives, and for some of his friends. But he did not pray for his best friend at school, whom he often referred to as Johnny the Tinker. (In Ireland, where the incident took place, tinkers are gypsies who are treated by many people as social outcasts.) The boy's mother inquired, "Are you not going to pray for Johnny?" The boy replied, "But Mammie, Johnny is a tinker." The mother said, "But God loves tinkers, too, in a very special way." The boy thought about that for a long time and then, with enthusiasm, said "And God, please bless Johnny the Tinker." Later I learned that "Johnny the Tinker" had become a permanent intention in the boy's night prayers. The mother explained, "Now I am trying to get him to call Johnny by his correct name rather than 'Johnny the Tinker.'"

What went on in the boy's head and heart during that exchange with his mother is a matter of conjecture. But as I reflected on the incident, I remembered Fowler's stage two of faith development, in which children are concerned only for "people like us." In essence, the mother had invited her son to expand his boundaries of social awareness. While affirming him in his prayers for his family and relatives, she gently challenged her son's exclusion of Johnny and invited him to move beyond his present social perspective. In that sense there was a certain dialectic that took place between mother and son, and she seems to have caused her son to engage in some critical reflection appropriate to his stage of development. That critical reflection is certainly not yet capable of analyzing the social, cultural, and economic structures that cause Johnny to be treated as a "tinker" by his society. But if that little boy is not invited to question his assumptions and expand his bounds of social awareness to include his friend Johnny at night prayers, it is unlikely that he will *ever* be capable of critiquing and acting to change his society. Children of that age are not capable of critiquing social structures that promote injustice and discrimination, but excluding, lying, cheating, stealing, and so on are often part of their lives. They must be enabled to reflect critically on such activities, coming to see the reasons for and the consequences of them (rather than simply being told not to do them) if they are to recognize and oppose social inequalities as adults.

From my experience of using a shared praxis approach across a wide age span I have noticed that even among older adults there are degrees, or I should say stages, of critical reflection. My observation is little more than an intuition at this time, but it seems to be confirmed by developmental research on other dimensions of human growth. As Fowler and Kohlberg have argued for six stages of faith and of moral development, respectively, it is my hypothesis that there are six corresponding stages in the ability of a person to engage in critical reflection. If this hypothesis is sound, then, consonant with the findings of all the developmentalists, growth in the early stages of critical reflection needs to be promoted and encouraged in order for a person to come to a mature critical consciousness in adulthood.

It seems appropriate, then, to ground the very earliest efforts at formal Christian education in an approach that causes children to reflect on their lives as critically as they can in order to promote authentic Christian engagement in the world. My claim is that a shared praxis approach, properly suited to particular age levels, is capable of promoting such a Christian education, and that it can begin in the first years of formal Christian education (from about age seven onward). To explain that position and expand it further, I now draw on the work of Jean Piaget.

Shared Praxis
from a Piagetian Perspective

Died Sept '81

JEAN PIAGET was born 1896 in Neuchâtel, Switzerland.[5] At present he is still active in research, teaching, and writing at the Institute of Educational Science in Geneva, the University of Geneva, and Geneva's Center for the Study of Genetic Epistemology, which he founded. He has published or edited over one hundred books and innumerable articles.[6] The volume of his published works alone gives an indication of the breadth of his lifelong enterprise. With a brilliant, highly disciplined mind and the ability to organize and interpret research, he has made a lasting contribution to our understanding of the human process of knowing.

Piaget is a philosopher, a biologist, a logician, and a psychologist, but he is most accurately described as a genetic epistemologist. Epistemology, the study of the process and nature of human knowing, has been his overriding concern throughout his long career. His earliest intuition was that the epistemological question could best be answered by a study of how people actually develop in their capacity for cognition. He hypothesized that to understand knowledge and the process of knowing, one must first understand how the ability to know develops from the earliest days in a person's life. Sensing that human intelligence parallels and is grounded in biological maturation and adaptation to the environment, he set out to link biology and epistemology and looked to developmental psychology for the necessary link. Given these intuitions, he embarked on what he intended to be a brief study of the underlying structure and pattern of human thinking and reasoning. That study has lasted his lifetime.

It is the inherent structures and processes of knowing manifested in behavior, and how these develop with the person's biological maturation and social interaction, that Piaget has studied. By researching the development in behavior patterns, he has been able to discern the stages of mental growth and the underlying structures of those stages. It appears that he has verified his earliest hypothesis and has constructed his envisioned "biological theory of knowledge."[7]

THE ACTIVITY OF KNOWING AND ITS DEVELOPMENT

For Piaget "knowledge is essentially active"[8] and "is derived from action"[9] upon the world. To be more precise, knowledge arises from the action and interaction between the subject knowing and the object known. The action of the knowing subject can be perceptual, intuitive, or motoric (that is, a feeling/action response). When thought emerges, it is the mental, interiorized abstraction of one's action upon the world.[10]

There are two different but complementary dimensions to the activity of cognition: a figurative aspect and an operative aspect. The figurative, which is the more passive, consists in making a copy, an imitation, of things as they presently appear to the senses. "The figurative aspect is an imitation of states taken as momentary and static."[11] The operative, on the other hand, is the more dynamic aspect. It results in a transformation of reality as it is perceived. In other words, it is the aspect of cognition by which we perceive reality from our own active perspective, and in this sense reality is changed (either physically or perceptually) and assimilated according to our action upon it.[12] True cognition always requires the transforming activity of the knower; the objective world is not known if it is merely copied in a passive manner. This is why Piaget argues that "to know is to assimilate reality into systems of transformation."[13]

But a person does not come to interact with the world as a blank, malleable entity, a tabula rasa. All of us bring our own particular abilities and dispositions to organize, interact with, and make sense out of the objective world. At each stage of our development we have a particular mental system or schema for organizing thought and behavior to adapt to the environment. This capacity or disposition is what Piaget calls one's "psychological structure." The structure is grounded in our innate tendency to organize reality into a coherent system, and it systematizes reality into a manageable enterprise. It is our innate psychological structure that gives rise to the general form of our behavior, and for Piaget knowledge is the behavioral manifestation of the inner structure which the person brings to interact with reality.

As one's psychological structure gives rise to and shapes the interaction between the person and reality, there are two complementary aspects to the interaction: assimilation and accommodation. Assimilation is the process by which reality is modified as its data are incorporated into the present psychological structure of the subject. Thus the child comes to know reality in his or her own way. Accommodation is the activity by which the person's structure itself is modified and changed in response to the stimulus from the incoming data. In other words, the knowing is not just on the child's own terms; those "terms" are altered by the data from reality. Unlike the strict behaviorists, Piaget is arguing here for a two-way dialectical process. By assimilation a person's structure incorporates and changes reality; by accommodation a person's structure is modified in response to reality. As Piaget explains, "The filtering or modification of the input is called assimilation; the modification of internal schemas to fit reality is called accommodation."[14] These twin activities of the innate organizing structure are what enable a person to "adapt" to the environment: "The balancing of the processes of assimilation and accommodation may be called 'adaptation.'"[15] From the interaction of the two a person adapts to the environment and thus maintains equilibrium.

Equilibrium is the tendency of the person to maintain a steady state by balancing assimilation and accommodation. As a person responds to external intrusions, he or she attempts to compensate for them, so that a balance is maintained. Piaget explains that the activity of equilibration has three characteristics. "First, equilibrium is notable for its stability." Thus it signifies a steady state. "Secondly, every system is subject to external intrusion which tends to modify it." In other words, even in the midst of stability change takes place in the person. "Finally . . . equilibrium, thus defined, is not something passive but, on the contrary, something essentially active; the greater the equilibrium, the more activity is required."[16] True stability does not mean immobility, and equilibrium cannot lead to passivity—a resting on our oars, as it were. If equilibrium is to be maintained, it requires a constant self-regulating activity.

There is an important point to be noted here for the sake of our later discussion of educational implications. In the interaction between a person and the environment the assimilation and accommodation that go on in the quest for equilibrium are always dialectical. David Elkind, one of the most competent interpreters of Piaget's thought, insists that this dialectical dimension to cognition is a key aspect of Piaget's whole system. Elkind explains that, for Piaget, "the principle of equilibrium which regulates the interaction of maturational and environmental influences is essentially dialectical in nature." This is true because "at each level of development there are two poles of activity: changes in the structure of the organism in response to environmental intrusion (accommodation), and changes in the intruding stimuli due to the existing structure (assimilation)."[17]

The constant and dialectical activity of seeking equilibrium is what gives rise to the ongoing development of a person's ability to know the world. With the ongoing interaction of a person with the world the quest for equilibrium and balance between internal and external factors causes the cognitive structures to develop so that the person becomes more capable of knowing the world at higher levels of cognition. Piaget outlines three factors or influences upon a person, the equilibration of which gives rise to cognitive development. First, it is evident, even from the very title he gives his work—"genetic epistemology"—that biological, physical maturation is one of the factors in a person's cognitive development. While developing biologically, a person also develops in the capacity to act upon and thus know the world. In the introduction to a work that he describes as "a synthesis, a summing up, of our work in child psychology" (the "our" refers to collaborator Bärbel Inhelder), Piaget states that "mental growth is inseparable from physical growth."[18] In addition, a person's cognitive development is caused by action upon and interaction with the outside environment. Piaget describes this second factor as "the role of exercise and of acquired experience in the actions performed upon objects."[19] The third factor is the interaction of the person with the social context and with what is socially transmitted in that interaction. Piaget describes the third factor as "social interaction and transmission."[20] As a person attempts to hold these three factors in a steady state of equilibrium, the interaction of the three and the constant quest for equilibration bring about cognitive development.

Before we look at the stages of cognitive development as Piaget outlines them, it will be well to raise a question that is often put to Piaget, namely, what of the other dimensions of human growth and development? A classic criticism of Piaget is that he is too narrowly "cognitive." This criticism of Piaget is not one that I share. In fact, the implication in the criticism—that he talks of all development as cognitive development—is not true. To begin with, Piaget believes that cognition is always the result of one's behavior and that it, in turn, directs future behavior. In this, to use the language I favored earlier, he insists on both a rational and an active dimension to human cognition. But in addition, he insists, especially in his later works, that the intellectual and the affective dimensions are "two indissociable aspects of every action."[21] In fact, "the two aspects, affective and cognitive, are at the same time inseparable and irreducible." One cannot exist without the other, nor can either one be subsumed by the other. He explains further, "There is no behavior pattern, however intellectual, which does not involve affective factors as motives; but reciprocally, there can be no affective states without the intervention of perceptions or comprehensions which constitute their cognitive structures."[22] All intellectual activity must be motivated by affect, and all affect, if it is to be comprehended, presupposes a cognitive structure for that comprehension. Because no one person can investigate everything, Piaget chose to focus his research on the specifically cognitive development of the human person. But because of his holistic understanding of the human person and of the human "knowing" process, Piaget concludes that his research and findings on the stages of cognitive development have also shed light on all the other aspects of human development, although he himself may not always spell out the full implications of this conclusion.[23]

The Stages of Cognitive Development

According to Piaget, the cognitive development of a person passes through certain distinguishable but overlapping stages that begin with the first moments of life and usually reach completion by about age fifteen. By a "stage" he means the integrated set of mental operations and generally stable psychological structures that characterize each phase of cognitive development. He has outlined four such stages: the sensorimotor stage (birth to two), the preoperational stage (two to seven), the concrete operational stage (seven to eleven or twelve), and the formal operational stage (eleven or twelve and above). It should be noted that the chronology is approximate; it can vary from person to person and from one social context to another.

Each stage is characterized by an overall psychological structure in terms of which the main behavior patterns can be explained. The stages are hierarchical in that the upper stages are more developed than the lower ones. Further, the order of the stages is constant or invariant, which means that every individual must go through the stages in the same order and no one can bypass a lower stage to reach a higher one. The stages are sequential in the sense that one stage builds upon the previous one. As Piaget explains, "Each of these extends the preceding period, reconstructs it on a new level, and later surpasses it to an ever greater degree."[24] Thus each stage carries forward the competencies of the previous stage but recognizes its limits and moves beyond them. In this Piaget is pointing to the dialectical nature of human growth and development. Because it is dialectical, there is an ongoing unity to the whole process. "In conclusion, let us point out the unity of the processes which, from the construction of the practical universe by infantile sensorimotor intelligence, lead to the reconstruction of the world by the hypothetico-deductive thinking of the adolescent, via the knowledge of the concrete world derived from the system of operations of middle childhood."[25]

Piaget understands each stage, even the earliest one, as having its own particular form of intelligence. He often uses the word *intelligence* to refer to an advanced form of reflective thinking, but he also uses it in a more general sense to refer to the ability of a person to interact with the environment at any stage. In this general sense intelligence is present at all levels of cognitive development, and thus Piaget can talk about even the earliest stage as having a form of "logic." At first it is a logic of behavior. Later a logic of thinking is added.[26]

Sensorimotor Stage. In the sensorimotor stage (birth to two) the form of knowledge is derived from specific sensory input and from one's motoric actions upon the world. While Piaget outlines six progressively more developed levels within this first stage, the common feature is that the child makes feeling/action responses to both the human and the physical environment. Beginning with the first days of life, every action (sucking, turning the head, moving legs or arms, etc.) is an instinctual response to a need or an external stimulus. Thus the child learns to deal with the world "intelligently" by a sensorimotor coordination of actions. As Piaget explains it, "Constructions are made with the sole support of perceptions and movements and thus by means of a sensorimotor coordination of actions, without the intervention of representation or thought." Representation, or thought, is absent because the person is as yet incapable of a symbolic function; in other words, "he does not have representations by which he can evoke persons or objects in their absence."[27] Rather, by reflex action to inner need and outside stimulus, a child learns to deal with reality with a certain kind of "practical intelligence."

The psychological structure here is more accurately understood as an "action schema," a generalized and repeated organization of behavior. It begins with the spontaneous reflexes and movements of the first days of life and progresses to acquired habits. In this progress the child profits from the experience of acting upon objects. Experience modifies the action schema.

Preoperational Stage.   When a child begins to develop the ability to speak and use words to represent things or people, this leads to a new stage of cognitive development. The preoperational stage is the time of transition from preconception to intuition (two to four years) and from intuition on into the ability for concrete reasoning that begins at about age seven. Piaget sometimes calls this the "symbolic stage," which hints at its fundamental characteristic. The child now becomes capable of representing reality by means of symbols or signifiers and representing "objects or events that are not at the moment perceptible by evoking them through the agency of symbols or differentiated signs."[28] The symbols can be "language, mental image, symbolic gesture, and so on."[29] However, the function of symbol here is only representative, and thus reasoned mental operations proper are not possible. Instead of a reasoned knowing of the world, the child knows the world by either preconceptual thought (two to four years) or intuitive thought (four to seven years).

Preconceptual thought is transductive; that is, instead of reasoning from the general to the particular as in deductive thought, or from the particular to the general as in inductive reasoning, the child moves from one particular to another without connection. The preconceptual child can use words, can know the concrete objects those words represent, but cannot build up statements to form a concept. The intuitive child, on the other hand, can have concepts, but they are based on perceptions rather than on reason. As a result, the child "constantly makes assertions without trying to support them with facts."[30] If asked why something is so, the child is likely to reply, "Because it is."

Children in the sensorimotor stage are in a complete state of egocentrism because they cannot differentiate between the self and the environment. Children at the preoperational stage can differentiate themselves from the environment because they can "decenter actionally" (know behaviorally that the objective world is separate from the self), but they cannot "decenter representatively" to comprehend that there are mental universes outside of the self. Piaget describes this egocentrism as "a lack of differentiation between his own point of view and that of others."[31] Cognition at this stage is characterized by a self-centered type of thinking and illogical (by later standards) intuitions based on perception.

Concrete Operational Stage.   The concrete operational stage (seven to eleven or twelve) occurs when a person moves beyond the previous intuitive stage and becomes capable of mental operations, that is, processes of reasoning. While it is a quantum leap beyond the preoperational stage, this mental capacity is still limited to concrete operations. Piaget explains that concrete operations "relate directly to objects and not yet to verbally stated hypotheses."[32] In other words, a person can perform mental operations as long as the thinking is about concrete objects, situations, or their representations. "In sum," explains Piaget, "concrete thought remains essentially attached to empirical reality."[33]

The source of this new capacity for mental operations is the emerging ability to internalize action into processes of thought rather than into isolated symbols. As a result, the concrete operational child is now capable of a step-by-step form of logical reasoning, and of seeing the rational relation between cause and effect. Essentially, this means that a child at the concrete operational stage is capable of reflection as long as the thought processes are directed at concrete objects, situations, or their representations. Since this will have important implications for us later, it is important to be clear on what Piaget means when he uses the term *reflection*. He writes, "Reflection is nothing other than internal deliberation, that is to say, a discussion which is conducted with oneself just as it might be conducted with real interlocutors or opponents."[34] At the concrete operational stage the child becomes capable of such "internal deliberations." It is still a rudimentary form of reflection, but reflection nonetheless.

There are some other characteristics of this stage that deserve specific attention because they are relevant to my claim that a form of shared praxis can be used for Christian religious education from this stage onward.

Reversibility/Conservation: Reversibility for Piaget is the main criterion of concrete operational thinking.[35] This means that the child is now capable of reversing the thinking process, can now move forward or backward and see the parts that explain the whole, or the whole constituted by the parts (for instance, can see that 2 plus 2 equals 4 and 4 minus 2 equals 2). Closely related to this capacity for reversibility is a new ability for "conservation." This means that a child can realize that certain attributes of an object are constant even though the object may change its appearance. The preoperational child cannot understand that the amount of water remains the same when it is in a tall thin glass as when it is in a short fat glass, even though the child may do the actual pouring. But the concrete operational child is capable of such conservation, and as a result can see objective relations and can reason with deductive logic. With the emergence of these new abilities the concrete operational child is capable of seeing the cause and basis for aspects of concrete reality. Consequently, a form of critical reasoning can begin.

b. Memory: A baby is capable of what Piaget calls the "memory of recognition," that is, the ability to recognize an object previously encountered. For example, the baby at the breast can recognize the mother's nipple from previous experience. With the beginning of language at the preoperational stage the child becomes capable of the "memory of evocation," the ability to evoke an object in its absence by means of an image or memory. With the coming of concrete operational thinking the child is capable of a qualitatively different and improved capacity to remember. Piaget laments that "too little research has been done on the memory of the child."[36] Nevertheless, the new abilities for conservation and reversibility presuppose a quantum leap in the child's ability to remember. The child can remember what the whole looked like before it was changed (conservation) and can remember in the whole the parts that comprise it (reversibility).

c. Projection/Anticipation: A child at the stage of concrete operational thinking is capable of a whole new level of projection and anticipation of consequences. As long as it is a concrete situation the child is addressing, he or she can look ahead, anticipate the results, and make forecasts about the outcome. "Compared to preoperational or intuitive thought, concrete operational thought is characterized by an extension of the actual in the direction of the potential."[37] This capacity to look ahead and anticipate outcomes, coupled with the expanded ability to both conserve and look backward, is obviously relevant to a shared praxis approach to Christian religious education.

d. Cooperation: At this stage the child has a new capacity for decentering from the self. Egocentricity decreases because of the child's ability to begin to enter into the mind of another person and to know that there are mental worlds different from one's own. Now the child can experience real feelings of reciprocity and, as a result, possesses a whole new capacity for cooperation and collaboration with others.[38] This ability is relevant to our interest because a shared praxis approach presupposes an ability to consciously participate in a group. It is interesting to note that Fowler's research on faith development highlights this emerging capacity for community even further. At seven or eight years and the beginning of stage two of faith development the child comes consciously to join and participate actively in a faith community (beyond the immediate family) and has the new-found ability to learn "the lore, the language and the legends" of the group.

Dialogue: Piaget carefully observed the language patterns of preoperational children at play and concluded that "they speak as though they were talking to themselves." He called this "collective monologue."[39] At the concrete operational stage, however, because of the decrease of egocentricity the child is now capable of at least the beginnings of authentic dialogue. Piaget writes, "True discussions are now possible in that the children show comprehension with respect to the other's point of view and a search for justification or proof with respect to their own statements."[40]

Moral Reasoning: According to Piaget, the preoperational child is at a stage of "moral realism." This means that "obligations and values are determined by the law or the order itself, independent of intentions and relationships."[41] Thus a child who breaks two cups by accident is considered more culpable than a child who breaks one cup on purpose; the intention is not taken into consideration. The concrete operational child, on the other hand, is capable of making moral decisions on a basis of mutual respect and reciprocity rather than by the heteronomy (obedience to a law imposed from without) and moral realism of the preoperational child. "The mutual respect that gradually becomes differentiated from unilateral respect leads to a new organization of moral values. Its principal characteristic is that it imputes relative autonomy to the moral conscience of individuals."[42] While the autonomy is only relative, it is a significant step toward taking responsibility for one's actions. Now justice, both distributive and retributive, can take priority over obedience.

Formal Operational Thinking.   The stage of formal operations begins at about age eleven or twelve and, according to Piaget's research, is completed by about age fifteen. With the advent of formal operational thinking, a person becomes capable of reasoning about hypotheses that are removed from concrete and present observation. In simple terms, a person can now reason about abstract issues and concepts and is freed from servitude to concrete realities. In Piaget's terms, "As of eleven to twelve years, formal thinking becomes possible, i.e., the logical operations begin to be transposed from the plane of concrete manipulation to the ideational plane. . . ."[43] Because of this new capacity the person is capable of reasoning from theoretical hypotheses, which Piaget describes as "propositions from which it is possible to draw logical conclusions without it being necessary to make decisions about their truth or falsity before examining the result of their implications."[44] This is what Piaget calls "hypothetico-deductive" thinking, which even he admits is a "barbarous" term.[45] With this ability the adolescent is capable of and in fact enjoys constructing conceptual systems and theories and struggling with problems that are stated abstractly. Now the person can think about thinking, be conscious of consciousness, or represent a representation of a possible action.

At first, the formal operational stage has its own form of egocentricity: "Adolescent egocentricity is manifested by belief in the omnipotence of reflection, as though the world should submit itself to idealistic schemes rather than to systems of reality." However, in the transition through the years from twelve to fifteen and into the complete expression of formal thinking, the metaphysical thinking of the adolescent becomes, as Piaget puts it, more "realistic": "The metaphysical egocentricity of the adolescent is gradually lessened as a reconciliation between formal thought and reality is effected. Equilibrium is attained when the adolescent understands that the proper function of reflection is not to contradict but to predict and interpret experience."[46]

The formal operational stage marks the last stage covered by Piaget's research. He has often been criticized for not pushing beyond this age. Surely cognitive development does not cease, nor is it at its fullness, at age fifteen. But no one person can study everything, and Piaget has done what he set out to do—to outline the stages and the source of the child's growing capacity to know the world.

PIAGET AND EDUCATION

This final section deals specifically with a shared praxis approach to Christian religious education from the perspective of Piaget's genetic epistemology. First, however, I wish to draw attention briefly to key implications of Piaget's theory for education of any kind.

Throughout his long career Piaget has been actively concerned with the implications of his work for education.[47] The purpose of education I have been proposing throughout this work is very much in keeping with its purpose as Piaget understands it:

> The principal goal of education is to create men who are capable of doing new things, not simply of repeating what other generations have done—men who are creative, inventive and discoverers. The second goal of education is to form minds which can be critical, can verify, and not accept everything they are offered. The great danger is of slogans, collective opinions, ready-made trends of thought.[48]

There is one obvious educational implication that is most often cited by educators informed by Piaget's findings today: the content level of a curriculum must be such that the students will have the necessary cognitive structures to assimilate it. To cite an obvious example, teaching abstract concepts to children who are capable of no more than concrete operations is largely a waste of time. But, as I claimed in the Prologue, using Piaget only to critique the cognitive level of content in a curriculum misses out on his more significant contribution to our enterprise. Increasingly, educators who take him seriously are contending that his most profound contribution to education lies in his explanation of the process of knowing and how that takes place (and thus how educators might promote it).[49]

Two closely related dimensions to Piaget's understanding of the nature and process of knowing are of particular relevance for educators of any kind. The first is that authentic cognition is an active, creative process in which the knower behaviorally interacts with what is to be known, rather than passively making a copy of it. All true knowing must arise from the constitutive activity of the knowing subject. While he uses different language to say it, Piaget is as opposed to "banking education" as is Paulo Freire. For Piaget the teacher's job is never to transmit facts and concepts to passive recipients, but rather to direct the learning process so that students act on both a physical and a mental level to arrive at facts and concepts as their own. Piaget wisely warns against an unduly "liberal" attitude, in which students are given over entirely to unguided experimentation and "discovery." But he argues consistently for "the use of active methods" that are intentionally planned by the teacher and in which the teacher "compels reflection" (strong language indeed). His condemnation is not as strong as Freire's, but he claims that the simple transmission of knowledge to passive recipients is "archaic."[50] Education must promote an "active discovery of reality," rather than "providing the young with ready-made wills to will with and ready-made truths to know with."[51]

Second, the activity of knowing to be promoted by intentional education is dialectical. There needs to be a dialectical relationship between assimilation and accommodation, and again between figurative and operative knowing. There must be a dialectic between the figurative knowing that makes a copy of reality and the operative knowing that transforms reality. This transformation of reality happens as the child actively assimilates reality, but here, too, there is a dialectic: the child's cognitive structure must also accommodate to the new reality and thus be transformed by it. "The problem of intelligence, and with it the central problem of the pedagogy of teaching, has thus emerged as linked with the fundamental epistemological problem of the nature of knowledge: does the latter constitute a copy of reality or, on the contrary, an assimilation of reality into a structure of transformation?"[52] Piaget very obviously favors the latter understanding of knowledge. Thus education must promote an active, dialectical, and creative process in which knowing is a constitutive activity of the knowing subject.

My criticism of Piaget is that his understanding of such an educational process is insufficiently critical of the social reality. I have been using critical reflection throughout this work to mean a dialectical and creative dimension in the act of knowing. Piaget certainly argues for such a relationship between the knower and the subject to be known. But I have also used critical reflection to mean a calling into question, and, as critique in a dialectical sense, this includes refusing some of the limits posed by what is socially transmitted. The transformation of social reality for Piaget sounds like a transformation more of how we perceive social reality than of that reality itself. This is especially apparent in his discussion of "adaptation." He tilts the scales unduly toward the knower's adapting to what is socially given rather than acting to change it. For example, when he describes adolescents at the formal operational stage as becoming "realistic," it sounds too much like becoming "fitted into" social reality as presently constituted. When he goes beyond description to become prescriptive for education, he proposes that education be brought "into line with the needs of society"[53] and that it must "adapt the individual to the surrounding social environment."[54] Thus I find him insufficiently critical of the social reality and, at heart, a social conservative.

PIAGET'S THEORY AND A SHARED PRAXIS APPROACH

We are now ready to look specifically at a shared praxis approach to Christian religious education from a Piagetian perspective. To begin with, it should be immediately obvious that a praxis way of knowing as I have outlined it resonates with Piaget's understanding of the nature and process of knowing. By his contention that "knowledge is essentially active"[55] and "to know an object is to act upon it and to transform it . . . ,"[56] he is making the case for a praxis epistemology (though he avoids that language). At the very least, we can say that a praxis way of knowing is on very sound ground from a Piagetian perspective.

Second, shared praxis as a general approach to Christian religious education (leaving aside the "readiness" question for now) also seems appropriate to Piaget's genetic epistemology. Nowhere does Piaget spell out in detail an educational process that would be consonant with genetic epistemology, but his emphasis on reflective action in the process of knowing, his emphasis on social interaction and experience, and his dialectical understanding of the relationship between subject knowing and object known call for an educational process that would surely be very similar to the basic workings of a shared praxis approach. Shared praxis is grounded in the constitutive activity of the knowers, promotes critical reflection on present lived experience, is undergirded by a dialectical hermeneutic, and promotes social interaction in the learning situation. As such, it would seem a most appropriate educational response to Piaget's understanding of cognition.

On the question of the age at which participants are ready for a shared praxis approach, I contend that a form of shared praxis can be used as an approach to Christian religious education from the age of seven or eight onward (i.e., the beginning of concrete operational thinking). I contend further (becoming prescriptive now) that a shared praxis approach ought to begin there for students to be more likely to come at a later age to a personal, creative, and mature Christian faith. The reasons for such claims have already been given, at least implicitly. To make them explicit, I will review the various dimensions of a shared praxis approach to Christian religious education in light of Piaget's description of the concrete operational stage of cognitive development. I begin with the aspect of a shared praxis approach that is most often challenged as being unsuited for young children of this age group (seven to eleven or twelve), namely, "critical reflection." Critical reflection requires the use of *reason, memory,* and *imagination.* Thus the question really is Is the child at the stage of concrete operations capable of such activity?

According to Piaget, the child at this stage is capable of *reasoning* as long as the object of thinking is a concrete issue, object, situation, or representation that is observable in the child's lived experience. Further, the child at this stage is capable of a level of *memory* qualitatively higher than the level of memory possible at the preoperational stage (due to the new ability for conservation and reversibility). In other words, the child is now capable of consciously recalling and reflecting upon previous experience. And there can be little doubt about the child's capacity for *imagination*, the third aspect of critical reflection. Piaget's research indicates that the child at this stage is capable of foreseeing the consequences of an action before it is taken and can manage some level of choosing. He explains, "Instead of the impulsive behavior of the small child, accompanied by unquestioned beliefs and intellectual egocentricity, the child of seven or eight thinks before acting and thus begins to conquer the difficult process of reflection."[57]

It could be contended that while a child at the stage of concrete operation is capable of reason, memory, and imagination at a significant level, he or she is still not capable of critical reflection (especially if emphasis is placed on the word *critical*). There is an obvious sense in which this claim is true. Anything like the fullness of critical reflection (critique of ideologies, uncovering of assumptions, etc.) requires the ability to reflect upon one's reflection, and that is not possible before the stage of formal operations. But Piaget's findings also indicate that the ability for any kind of reflection develops through sequential stages, and the genesis of the advanced stage must be laid in the previous stages. When he claims that "in terms of their functions, formal operations do not differ from concrete operations except that they are applied to hypotheses or propositions,"[58] he makes the point that the concrete operational child is capable of the same function of reflection as the formal operational child so long as the object of reflection is concrete. This means that I cannot ask my fourth-graders to reflect on the presence of hatred and animosity among humankind or on the call to universal love for all humanity, but I can ask them "Why do you fight with your sister?" or "How did you feel when you beat up your little brother?" I cannot ask them to theologize about the Blessed Trinity, but I can ask them to reflect on the implications for their lives of having Jesus as their brother. Educationally that is more appropriate than merely telling them what I believe the implications to be and expecting them to tell me back what I have already told them. It seems to me that when Piaget calls on teachers to "compel reflection" in students at this concrete operational stage, he is calling for such critical reflection, "critical" in that they attempt to comprehend the reasons for and consequences of present action. If education fails to promote such reflection at the stage of concrete operations, it is far less likely that critical reflection in anything like its fullness will be exercised later.

We must also remember that Piaget's descriptions should not be taken automatically as prescriptions. Because he found that abstract thinking does not typically take place before the stage of formal operations, this does not mean we should not encourage students at an early stage to begin to do it. On the contrary, since our purpose is always to lead people beyond present limitations, education should take place at the outer limits of the student's ability. Thus a form of critical reflection on concrete issues and examples should begin with the inception of concrete operational thinking. In the later years (ten to eleven), students should be invited to reflect upon their reflections and thus move toward a deeper critical reflection.[59]

The "action" dimension of a shared praxis approach, in which knowing occurs through reflection on action that leads to further action, is very much consonant with Piaget's epistemology. According to Piaget's findings, a child's way of knowing is de facto by an active/interactive/reflective process. In other words to promote authentic cognition we do not have a choice about whether or not to use an active reflective knowing process. Such a process is essential and our only choice concerns how we might structure our educational activity to intentionally promote an active reflective way of knowing.

Quite clearly, at the concrete operational stage the activity must include specific concrete experiences. One criticism I have of my own work with children at this stage is that often the activities have not been concrete enough, although it is certainly possible to have concrete activities for seven-year-olds in an intentional setting of Christian religious education.[60] In suggesting this criticism of my own work, I must be careful not to imply too narrow an understanding of *activity*. Piaget warns that "an active school is not necessarily a school of manual labor." He goes on to explain that for this concrete operational stage the activity can be a "reflective" activity that enables students to make "a personal rediscovery of the truths to be acquired."[61]

A third aspect of a shared praxis approach is that it is to take place in a community of dialogue. Children at a concrete operational stage are capable of entering into such a process. To begin with, Piaget contends that, from the concrete operational stage onward, children are capable of "effective collaboration" and cooperation in a group. An educational process that encourages and provides an opportunity for the development of this capacity would seem well suited to the purposes of Christian religious education. Piaget contends that dialogue can begin in an incipient form at the stage of concrete operations because there is a decrease of social egocentricity, an increase in feelings of reciprocity, and a greater ability to enter into the perspective of another person. As a result, "true discussions are now possible. . . ."[62] Ginsburg and Opper, two of the finest interpreters of Piaget, offer the following comment: "The implication of Piaget's view is that social interaction should play a significant part in the classroom. Children should talk with one another."[63] Rather than encouraging this growing capacity for community and dialogue, we typically structure our learning environments (both emotionally and physically) to prevent children from talking to each other.

The last dimension of a shared praxis approach to be evaluated from a Piagetian perspective is the making present of the Story and its Vision. I have found no writings by Piaget on what we might traditionally call the content of education. However, James Fowler, in his description of the stages of faith development, has talked about the period from seven to twelve as the time when children are most enthusiastic about learning "the lore, the language, and the legends" of their faith community. This age, then, seems to be a most fitting time to present the Story and Vision of the Christian community to children. Some cautions are in order, however.[64]

The Story and its Vision need to be made present within the lived experience of the children if it is to be a "concrete" encounter for them. This can be done by making present the Story and its Vision in response to the named and reflected-upon experience of the participants (i.e., the first two movements of shared praxis). The presentations should also emphasize that there will always be more to discover about the Story and its Vision; to make the version of them presented sound too final at this stage can arrest the pilgrimage toward maturity of Christian faith.

I have had a compelling insight on this point from working with college students over the past five years in undergraduate theology courses. I have often invited them to write "faith biographies" as one option for fulfilling part of the course requirements. A common theme in many of the papers is some version of the question Why were we taught so much "religion" as little kids that was made to sound like the final truth and which we had to believe without question? There has often been a good measure of anger expressed at, as one student put it, "being kept in the dark so long." Many have all but given up on the possibility of being questioning and thinking members of the Christian faith community. We have not only taught young children too much, too soon; we have also made the teachings sound too final. If, at the stage of concrete operations, the Story and its Vision are made accessible in an open-ended and dialogical manner and in the context of children's lives, if they are encouraged to reflect critically about both their own praxis and the Christian tradition, then they should be less likely to claim, as college seniors, that they were kept in the dark too long.

In conclusion, Piaget's work must not be taken as a rigid system that is beyond question. Nevertheless, his discoveries are being corroborated by other investigators, and his work offers an adequate description of the processes and stages of cognitive development. While that description cannot be taken by educators as prescriptive, it can inform us. Perhaps one reason children are late in coming to formal operational thinking, or to formal operational thinking that is critical, is because in our educational efforts we do not invite them to think enough, or to think critically. In a society where education is still treated largely as transmission of knowledge critical consciousness will be rare at any age level. And if a Christian faith community uses a transmissive approach in its intentional education, then maturity of faith at any age will be equally unlikely. I do not mean to imply that shared praxis is the only appropriate way of doing Christian religious education from the concrete operational stage onward. But if we choose something else in its place, it cannot be a "copying" (Piaget) or a "banking" (Freire) form of education. To do that on the grounds that the children are not ready for anything else is to delay, if not to prevent, them from ever being ready for anything else.

NOTES

1. "But as we are now treating of instructing candidates, I can testify to you from my own experience that I am differently stirred according as he whom I see before me waiting for instruction is cultivated or a dullard . . . of this or that age or sex" (Augustine, "The First Catechetical Instruction," p. 50).
2. See Goldman, *Religious Thinking from Childhood to Adolescence*, and *Readiness for Religion*.
3. John Hellesnes warns correctly against this danger: "Educational practice, as the practical application of empirical-analytical science, is technique" ("Education and the Concept of Critique," p. 43). When this is allowed to happen, according to Hellesnes, the consequence is authoritarianism and control.
4. Iris V. Cully offers an insightful summary of the developmental process from the interest of a Christian educator in *Christian Child Development*. She draws upon a wide range of developmental psychologists and adds her own insights, gleaned from many years of experience in church education.
5. For my summary of Piaget, a difficult task given the volume of his writings, I have relied heavily on original works that constitute his summary statements, rather than on writings that go into the intricate details of his experiments. My selection was also influenced by the educational interest I brought to his work. His 1969 work *The Psychology of the Child* (hereafter cited as *Child*), which he wrote with his able collaborator Bärbel Inhelder, is especially helpful. He

prefaces it by saying, "In this volume we have tried to present, as briefly and as clearly as possible, a synthesis or summing up of our work in child psychology" (p. 1). I have also drawn heavily from his *Genetic Epistemology* (referred to hereafter as *Genetic*). His *Six Psychological Studies* is an excellent collection of essays that span twenty-five years of Piaget's work, and together they provide a helpful summary (referred to hereafter as *Studies*). I have drawn on his work with Inhelder (see Inhelder and Piaget, *The Growth of Logical Thinking*). Given that our interest here is so strongly educational, I found Piaget's own statements on the matter most helpful, especially *Science of Education and the Psychology of the Child* (hereafter referred to as *Science*) and his short but helpful collection of addresses, *To Understand Is to Invent: The Future of Education* (hereafter referred to as *Invent*).

For commentaries I have been influenced especially by Ginsberg and Opper, *Piaget's Theory of Intellectual Development*, a well-regarded introduction to Piaget's work. I have also used Furth's writings, especially *Piaget and Knowledge* and *Piaget for Teachers*.

6. See Elkind, "The Children Man," p. 7.
7. Jean Piaget, "Autobiography," in Furth, *Piaget and Knowledge*, p. 253.
8. Piaget, *Genetic*, p. 15.
9. Piaget, *Child*, p. 155.
10. On this point John F. Emling writes, "The essential fact establishing Piaget's revolutionizing concept of intelligence is that knowledge is derived from action" ("To Invent Is to Understand," p. 559).
11. Piaget, *Genetic*, p. 14.
12. See Furth, *Piaget for Teachers*, pp. 47–48; and Ginsberg and Opper, *Intellectual Development*, pp. 152–153.
13. Piaget, *Genetic*, p. 15.
14. Piaget, *Child*, p. 6.
15. Piaget, *Studies*, p. 8.
16. Ibid., p. 151.
17. Ibid., p. xii.
18. Piaget, *Child*, p. vii.
19. Ibid., p. 155.
20. Ibid., p. 156.
21. Piaget, *Studies*, p. 33.
22. Piaget, *Child*, p. 158.
23. He hints at some implications when he writes, "The affective and social development of the child follows the same general process [as the cognitive], since the affective, social, and cognitive aspects of behavior are in fact inseparable" (Ibid., p. 114).
24. Ibid., p. 152.
25. Piaget, *Studies*, p. 69.
26. See Piaget, *Studies*, p. ix ff.
27. Piaget, *Child*, pp. 3, 4.
28. Piaget, *Science*, p. 31.
29. Piaget, *Child*, p. 51.
30. Piaget, *Studies*, p. 29.
31. Ibid., p. 29.
32. Piaget, *Child*, p. 100.
33. Inhelder and Piaget, *The Growth of Logical Thinking*, p. 250.
34. Piaget, *Studies*, p. 40.
35. See Furth, *Piaget for Teachers*, p. 42.
36. Piaget, *Child*, p. 80.
37. Inhelder and Piaget, *The Growth of Logical Thinking*, p. 248.
38. See Piaget, *Studies*, p. 55.
39. Ibid., pp. 20–21.
40. Ibid., p. 39.
41. Piaget, *Child*, p. 125.
42. Piaget, *Studies*, p. 57.
43. Ibid., p. 62.
44. Piaget, *Science*, p. 33.
45. Piaget, *Studies*, p. 62.
46. Ibid., p. 64.

47. Two of his most famous essays on education have been drawn together in a work already cited many times, *Science of Education and the Psychology of the Child*. The more recent essays collected in *To Understand Is to Invent: The Future of Education* were written for the UNESCO International Commission on the Development of Education, 1971.
48. Piaget, quoted in Ginsberg and Opper, *Intellectual Development*, p. 231.
49. C. Kamii and R. DeVries have done significant work on the implications of Piaget for preschool education. The logic that underlies their position is that Piaget's greatest contribution to education is his explanation of the nature of knowing rather than his description of the stages. They contend that the active nature of knowing as described by Piaget requires that educational environments be designed to promote the students' own constitutive knowing activity (see *Physical Knowledge in Preschool Education: Implications of Piaget's Theory*). Deanna Kuhn writes, "Regardless of the position one takes with respect to the controversial issue of developmental stages as an aim of education, the theory [i.e. Piaget's] may nevertheless contribute to education by providing insights regarding the *processes* of learning and cognitive development" ("Application of Piaget's Theory to Education," p. 347). Dwayne Huebner states a similar position in even stronger terms: "The significance which most educators attach to the work of Piaget, namely that he describes the cognitive functioning of the individual during different stages of growth, is . . . a masking of Piaget's more important contribution" ("Toward a Political Economy of Curriculum and Human Development," p. 95).
50. Piaget, *Invent*, pp. 15, 16, 17.
51. Piaget, *Science*, p. 26. He makes a similar point in *Invent* (p. 20), when he writes, "To understand is to discover, or reconstruct by rediscovery, and such conditions must be complied with if in the future individuals are to be formed who are capable of production and creativity and not simply repetition."
52. Piaget, *Science*, p. 28.
53. Piaget, *Invent*, p. 12.
54. Piaget, *Science*, p. 151.
55. Piaget, *Genetic*, p. 15.
56. Piaget, *Science*, p. 29.
57. Piaget, *Studies*, p. 40.
58. Ibid., p. 63.
59. My contention here has been affirmed by my reading of L.S. Vygotsky. Vygotsky, also a developmentalist, died too early (1934) to be much influenced by Piaget's work, though they were both aware and appreciative of each other. Vygotsky lays more obvious emphasis on the dialectical and critical aspect of knowing than does Piaget. Perhaps he is more favorably disposed to such sentiments because of his Marxist background. Vygotsky also insists that "the only 'good learning' is that which is in advance of development" (*Mind in Society*, p. 89).

    The conclusions which Furth reaches from his use of Piagetian insights in the education of children at a concrete operational stage also affirm what I am claiming here. Furth, by Piaget's own admission, is an able interpreter of Piaget's work (see Piaget, "Forward," in Furth, *Piaget and Knowledge*, p. viii). He has been attempting to construct and pilot an approach to education that is faithful to Piaget's insights. Furth argues that education should promote critical thinking in children from the concrete operational stage onward. In his splendid little volume *Piaget for Teachers* he argues that education should enable the child to know not only what is obvious in the social environment, but also what is "hidden" there (see, especially, pp. 128–144). Furth insists that "we should make every conceivable effort to provide an education that will help them exercise their developing operative intelligence on the burning questions of today's social and political life, in order to prepare them for the questions of tomorrow" (Ibid., p. 133).
60. For example, a teacher friend of mine began her First Communion program this past year by spending the first weeks teaching the children how to bake bread. Having had much fun with that adventure, they next organized and had a meal together, which all the children helped to prepare. She began the unit on Baptism with a trip to a local swimming pool, where they drank, splashed, swam in, and washed with, water. These are certainly concrete activities with which to begin, and the children seemed to have little difficulty reflecting on their experiences as they attempted to understand the meaning of the corresponding sacramental events. I would also point out again that many of the grade school religion curricula available have excellent ideas for how to begin a lesson with a concrete activity or experience.
61. Piaget, *Science*, pp. 68, 72.

62. Piaget, *Studies*, p. 39.
63. Ginsberg and Opper, *Intellectual Development*, p. 228.
64. Ronald Goldman, drawing on Piaget's research, has warned that the Bible must be used sparingly and carefully with children before the age of about eleven because understanding the Bible requires formal operational thinking (see Goldman's works already cited). His call for caution is well founded, but his extreme position that would all but exclude Bible stories is convincingly contested by Leroy T. Howe (see Howe, "Religious Understanding from a Piagetian Perspective," pp. 569–581).

THE COPARTNERS IN CHRISTIAN RELIGIOUS EDUCATION

Prologue

THIS FINAL Part takes up a sixth foundational issue for Christian religious educators, namely, Who are the copartners in the enterprise? Who are our students? and How do we perceive our own self-identity in the event of Christian religious education? Throughout this work I have called for critical consciousness on the part of Christian religious educators in understanding the nature, purpose, and context of our educational endeavor. I have proposed what an intentional approach might be and reflected on the readiness of participants for that approach. In calling attention now to the identity of ourselves and our students in the act itself, I am inviting consciousness about the anthropological assumptions that underlie our educating. That there is a self-understanding of our own role and a concept of our students implicit in all our educational work is beyond doubt, but, once again, our implicit position must be brought to consciousness.

By placing the copartners question last, I do not wish to imply that it is least important. On the contrary, it may well be the most fundamental issue of them all. Nor has an anthropology been absent in what has gone before. In fact, a very definite understanding of the human person has been operative throughout. The image of us as pilgrims in time who can consciously appropriate the past time and intentionally shape the future possibilities in our present time implies an understanding of ourselves as historical agents who are capable of history-making activity. In contending that the purpose of Christian religious education is lived Christian faith and human freedom, I am arguing that people are sufficiently capable of self-transcendence to choose such responsible and free engagement in the world. Likewise, in proposing that Christian religious education be done in a community context of dialogue where people are invited to critical consciousness of their participation in the world, for the sake of choosing further Christian praxis, I am claiming that people are capable of such self-constitutive activity in their own historical becoming.

The purpose of this section, however, is more modest than an attempt to delineate a philosophical anthropology of the person. Instead, I take the anthropology on which the previous five parts are based and propose an image we might have of our students and a concept of our own self-identity as we come together in the ministry of Christian religious education. This proposal is as much a Vision as it is a Story, an ideal that ever calls us forward to a life of constant conversion (constant and critically conscious choosing) as educators. To "lead people out" requires that we ourselves be ever moving inward to move outward and that we be turned toward becoming in the likeness of whose Image we are forming and being formed.

Our Students, Our Selves

OUR STUDENTS: SUBJECTS WHO MAKE HISTORY

Our students are brother/sister pilgrims in time with us. All of them have their own unique history (story) and destiny (vision). In presuming to be educators with them, we are taking on a sacred trust, a trust that is betrayed when we deny who they have been or decide who they should be. The concept of our students I am proposing can be expressed in two summary statements.

1. *Our students are subjects, not objects.* They have an "inalienable" right to be treated with dignity and respect because they possess their own individuality and have the capacity to respond to their own calling. There are many philosophical arguments that could be offered to substantiate this claim, but for Christian religious education legitimation can be found most readily in the Christian faith tradition itself.

Our students are to be treated as subjects, not from any particular magnanimity of ours or merit of theirs, but because all people are created in the image and likeness of God. Our students, and we pilgrims with them, have the calling and therefore the right to grow in the likeness of our Creator. The journey of each person back to God is a sacred one, and each, in its own way, is unique. To treat our students as anything less than subjects does violence to that process. Thus they are not objects to be acted upon and molded as we decide, but subjects with whom we enter into a relationship of mutuality and equality. Christian religious education is to be a subject-to-subject relationship of copartners.

As subjects, our students have the right to speak their own word and to name their own reality. As teachers, we have a right to speak our own word, but also an obligation to hear theirs. We can share our stories and visions with them and make present the Story and Vision of the Christian community in whose name we educate. But we must also bring them to know their own story and vision and to critically appropriate the "knowing" of other people of faith in their pilgrimage to God.

Such talk about the dignity and rights of individuals is often dismissed as naive, as unrealistic romanticism, or, in theological terms, as forgetting the reality of sin in ourselves and our world. But to treat our students as less than subjects is an expression of our sinfulness, rather than a corrective for theirs. While all of us are capable of evil, we are, by the grace of God, more inclined to the good. By being treated with respect and dignity, our students are more likely to act in a manner worthy of such treatment (remember Chapter Six and Cooley's "looking glass self"). If our educational praxis treats them as less than subjects, they are less likely to move toward their possibility of intersubjective communion with others and union with God in Jesus Christ.

2. *Our students (like ourselves) are called to be and are capable of being makers of history.* The human being need not be a pawn caught in the inevitable wheel of fate. We are shaped by history, but we can also shape history. We can make choices and act upon the world to influence its future. Within the context of Christian faith formation this means that our students can reach a Christian consciousness that causes them to engage in the world to make present the Kingdom already and prepare the material for its final completion. This is a mutual and equal responsibility of educators and students alike.

We cannot build the Kingdom by ourselves. It is always God's gift. But we are called upon to keep our side of the covenant, and this means being people who act freely to shape history toward the ongoing/coming of the Kingdom. God's free activity will bring about the completed Kingdom. But while the fruits of our human efforts will need to be refurbished there, they will remain. Rahner writes,

> Christianity is not an indoctrination into certain conditions or facts or realities which are always the same, but is the proclamation of a history of salvation, of God's salvific and revelatory activity on men and with men. And because God's activity is directed to man as a free subject, Christianity at the same time is also the proclamation of a history of salvation and its opposite, of revelation and the interpretation of it which man himself makes. Consequently, this single history of revelation and salvation is borne by God's freedom and man's freedom together and forms a unity.[1]

The point I am making here could have far-reaching implications for how we do Christian religious education. If we could come to see our students not as people to be made into "good Catholics" or "good Baptists" or the like, in a narrow sense, but rather as people who are called upon to engage in the world for the making present of the Kingdom of God and the shaping of the present in the

direction of the completed Kingdom, then imagine what the transforming consequences might be for ourselves, our church, our society, and our world.

Treating our students as subjects and makers of history could well require a
major shift in consciousness for most of us educators. For one thing, it is likely
that, as students, we ourselves have been treated in a way that is the antithesis of
what I am describing here. Since the tendency is to imitate our models, to teach
as we were taught, we need to look critically at our own educational biographies
and at the models that most shape our practice. I can remember a number of
teachers who treated me as a subject with personal responsibility, but I can also
remember their opposites. It is the first group that must be my models as I now
attempt to be an educator who is occupied largely with preparing other Christian religious educators. It is difficult to live up to my own ideals. As I point
ahead to my students, I also point ahead of myself.

The social structures within which education typically takes place can add
to the difficulty of treating students as subjects. We inherit those structures, and
sometimes, if we want to work within them, we must take on the role of being
"lived contradictions." But we must never acquiesce in, nor add to, the contradiction. Rather, we must take on the task of reconstructing our educational environments so that intersubjectivity is promoted rather than prevented.

Christian religious education is for and by the whole Church. It is to be
"toward adulthood" in that its aim is maturity of Christian faith. But it typically begins in childhood, and to have intersubjectivity with children is an even
greater challenge. If we look critically at our society, we must surely notice that
children are often treated as objects. While the struggles for economic, cultural,
sexual, and racial freedom are of profound concern to us, as educators we must
also be concerned with the liberation of children.[2] The literature on the history
of childhood demonstrates that many of our social ills are to be found in the op-
pressiveness with which children have typically been treated throughout history.[3] The apparently increasing phenomenon of child abuse indicates that our
own era is equally capable of treating children in a pathological manner.[4] Much
of our legal code regarding children goes back to a ninth-century legal assumption that children have no rights and are the property of their parents. Christian
religious educators should be in the forefront of efforts to fashion legislation that
will give increased protection to the children in our society. We also have the
task of educating our society to a new recognition of children as persons. To do
this, we must begin with our own educational praxis.

OUR SELVES: THE MINISTRY OF THE
CHRISTIAN RELIGIOUS EDUCATOR

In Chapter One I contended that there is a specificity to the task of the educators in a Christian community. It has become very difficult, however, to say

precisely what that task is. There was a time when the nature of our role in the community seemed obvious and was taken for granted: we were to teach children their catechism answers or their Bible stories and memory verses (depending on our denomination). For pedagogical, theological, and social reasons that self-image is no longer adequate for us, if it ever was. Yet relinquishing that self-image has left us with nothing as clear-cut in its place. We have had our own identity crisis about who we are in the community and what it is we are expected to be about. Forging an alternative image for ourselves as educators should involve the reclaiming of a tradition that has been largely lost: namely, that what we do is a bona fide Christian ministry.

It seems beyond question that the early Church recognized the teachers, the *didaskaloi*, as ministers among a variety of ministries (see 1 Cor. 12:28; Eph. 4:11; etc.). We must come again to see our role as a valid and authentic Christian ministry which cooperates with other ministries for the good of the whole Body. We are not appendages or mere helpers to the priestly and episcopal ministries when they are too busy.

On the other hand, teaching is not our prerogative alone; other ministers also have an educational responsibility.[5] In fact, as I have argued, the whole Church educates by its very way of being in the world. In that sense, all Christians, by their baptism, have an educational responsibility. So there must be a further specificity to how Christian educators fulfill their ministry of teaching. My attempt at stating that specificity is this: *the Christian religious educator is to represent Jesus Christ in service to the community by an "incarnational" ministry of the Word.*

To begin with, each form of ministry in the early Church had the task of representing Jesus, the risen Christ, in service of some kind to the faith community and, ultimately, to the world. Ministers represented Christ in service because "it is he who gave apostles, prophets, evangelists, pastors and teachers in roles of service for the faithful to build up the Body of Christ" (Eph. 4:11–12). Thus the ministry of teacher is a form of service rendered in the name of Jesus Christ.

Second, it is clear from the early Church that the ministry of the teacher was to be a ministry of the Word. In that sense it had a commonality with other ministers of the Word, the evangelists and prophets. But (and here we are coming to the specific task) the ministry of the teachers was to attend deliberately to the process by which people came to incarnate the Word in their everyday existence. Theirs was the task of formation, of sponsoring people to embody the Word in their everyday lives. The task of the evangelist, for example, was more one of "announcing" the basic message, the kerygma (e.g., Acts, 2:22–36; 3:12–26; 10:34–43). This kerygma invited a decision for faith in Jesus Christ and repentance. Having announced it, the evangelists could move on to announce it elsewhere. But the teachers were the ones who settled down to impart the *di-dache* (the teaching), who stayed on to promote the slow process of human growth, understanding, and formation necessary for embodying the Word in lifestyle and celebrating it in a Christian community. This certainly seems to have been their role in the Catechumenate from about the end of the second century onward. *The Decree of Hippolytus* (about 215) makes it clear that the teacher and the Catechumens entered into a long-lasting and intensive relationship by which the neophytes were gradually formed in Christian living. I believe that this "incarnating" ministry of the Word is still our specific task. Our ministry of the Word is not so much to preach or announce (though there is obviously a handing down of the message, a catechesis), as it is to form people in living the Christian message. And since it is an incarnational ministry, bringing people to participate in the sacramental life of the Christian community is an aspect of this ministry of the Word. In life the Word is to be lived, and in sacrament the Word as lived is to be celebrated.

We must remember that if we are to fulfill this incarnating dimension of our ministry, we must apply it first to ourselves. This may sound like a truism, but it bears repeating. If we are to teach the Word as effective models for the formation of others in living it, then we ourselves are to embody the Word in our way of being with people. Edward Powers, referring to the task of the Christian educator, says, "If it took God an incarnation to embody his message, we will not do it with less."[6] Because of the "modelling principle," our representing Jesus Christ as teachers must be grounded in our own attempts to live the Christian faith.

This notion of representation is a subtle concept. If its subtlety is not comprehended, it can put us back into an old "power over" mentality. To claim that we are representing Jesus Christ can border on presumption; unless we are clear about what is involved, we can fool ourselves and attempt to fool others.

In her book *Christ the Representative* Dorothee Sölle makes a very important distinction between "representation" and "substitution." She points out that to substitute for someone is to replace the person totally, nullifying the rights and responsibilities of that person. The person substituted for is *replaced* rather than represented. To represent people, on the other hand, is to act temporarily for them when they cannot act for themselves. In representing them, we are acting on their behalf, not on our own. The represented ones retain at least part of the responsibility and still retain their initiative and identity. Sölle uses this distinction and the concept of representation to express the relationship between Christ and Christians. In Christ's role of mediator between ourselves and God we cannot be cancelled or replaced by Christ. But we can be represented. As Sölle says, "The individual man is irreplaceable yet representable."[7] Through Christ's representation we are reinstated into a covenanted relationship with God, but our human responsibility for, and contribution to, that relationship is essential. This is why Christ's representation requires our assent. "Christ depends on our yea or nay, on our assent, otherwise He would merely be a replacement."[8] We give this assent by living a life of Christian faith.

For Christian religious educators the importance of this distinction between substitution and representation becomes evident when we turn the relationship around, as Sölle does,[9] and realize that we are now Christ's representatives to each other. This is true for all Christians, but Christian educators have the specific task of representing Christ in the context of intentional Christian education. When we fulfill that ministry, it is imperative to remember that our task is not to replace Christ and substitute ourselves for him. In God's grand design we have been taken into partnership. But the risen Christ must be allowed to act on his own behalf. I am I, and Christ is Christ.[10] We can represent each other, but not substitute for one another. If we forget this distinction, then as educators we are likely to give the impression that to accept Christ one must accept exactly and only the Christ and the version of his message that we model and teach. This promotes personal empire building, rather than Kingdom building. It leads people to ourselves, rather than to Jesus Christ.

Most people have a tendency to want other people to be like them, and I am often tempted to think that we educators have more than our share of that disposition. But our ministry of Christian religious education is to bring people to know God in Jesus Christ, not to create replicas of ourselves. To forget this is to do violence to the individuality and freedom of those we educate, and indeed to the Christ for whom we would presume to substitute. Our representing of Christ is to sponsor people to live representatively for Christ themselves, in their own ways. In fact, it is important for educators to remember that the people with whom we work are themselves Christ's representatives to us and Christ's representatives to each other. In this sense, all the participants in an event of Christian religious education participate in an act of ministry. The teacher is distinguished as the leader in creating the context, and, as we will see below, has certain specific responsibilities within it. But in that context the participants minister to each other, teacher to students, students to teacher, and students to students. Only as this partnership is realized can a relationship of true intersubjectivity be maintained.

We must also guard against presumption in our claim to be representatives of Christ. We need to remind ourselves constantly that, given our human shortcomings, we are never any more than poor representatives—a mere shadow of the real thing. Only by the grace of God and the power of the Holy Spirit can we approach being faithful to our responsibility. The Fourth Gospel especially makes it clear that without the help of the Paraclete we cannot represent Christ.

The Gospel of John speaks about the obligation of Christians to witness to

Christ. I read *witnessing* to mean what I intend here by representation. Just as Christ was God's witness to the world, so we now become Christ's witnesses to each other. "As you have sent me into the world, so I have sent them into the world" (John 17:18). Raymond Brown points out, in his exegesis of John's Gospel, that it is only by the power of the Paraclete that a Christian can have the presence of Jesus and thus be capable of representing him. "It is our contention that John presents the Paraclete as the Holy Spirit in a special role, namely, as the personal presence of Jesus in the Christian while Jesus is with the Father."[11] Commenting on the role of the Paraclete portrayed by the Fourth Gospel, Ernst Käsemann writes, "In John, the Spirit is nothing else but the continual possibility and reality of the new encounter with Jesus in the post-Easter situation as the one who is revealing his Word to his own and through them to the world."[12] It is impossible for us, then, to truly represent Jesus Christ without the presence of the Holy Spirit to empower our efforts, a presence that should be constantly and prayerfully invoked. In a context using a shared praxis approach, for example, the attempt to critically reflect on present action to come to further praxis is always dependent on the grace of the Spirit, even as the Spirit works within our human efforts. Here we are reminded again that while we have a part to play in the covenant, Christian faith is ultimately the gift of God.

Thus the specificity of our identity as Christian religious educators is clear when our role is seen as a ministry of the Word and even more particularly as a service of sponsoring people in their ongoing formation to live the Word. I believe we can pinpoint our identity in the Christian community even further by looking at the particular responsibilities this ministry places on us in an actual context of intentional education. As I see it, our responsibility within the historical context can be outlined as requiring three related activities: 1) to make present the Story; 2) to propose the Vision; and 3) to choose life.

To Make Present the Story

No people can be "a people" without a shared past. The Christian faith community is heir to a tradition of divine revelation and lived response to that revelation. We are founded on a specific historical intervention by God in his son Jesus Christ, an event that was preceded by God's interventions in the life of Israel, of which we are also heirs. God has continued to intervene in our history, and our people have struggled to live in response to God's interventions and invitations. We are a pilgrim covenanted people, moving through history toward the fulfillment of God's Kingdom. Like all pilgrims, we must know and remember whence we have come if we are to share a common present and shape our future together. New members of the covenant have a special need to hear the Story of the community, and present members need to be constantly reclaiming it. If we forget our Story, then we become a wandering, aimless people with no way of knowing the meaning of God's activity in our present or the response expected of us in our time.

Ideally, the Story should be embodied in the whole Christian community, and to some extent it is. By living in that community, a person can be disposed to inherit the Story and come to relive it in his or her own life. But our communities are far from embodying the Christian Story with complete faithfulness. If our Christian communities were completely faithful, we would not need intentional Christian education; it would be sufficient to raise children in our midst. But because we often forget our Story, or are unfaithful to it, we need people in our Christian communities who see to it that the Story is intentionally remembered and people disposed to relive it with faithfulness. This is not the responsibility of the educators alone, but we share in the task in a special way.

Huebner, writing about education in general, says, "Without education the community could not maintain its pilgrimage beyond a single generation. It would die out along the way and foreclose the rest of the journey."[13] Because our educating is carried out on behalf of the Christian community, we are accountable for how faithfully we remember the Story and how well we dispose people to relive and reclaim it in their lives.

Reliving and reclaiming the Story cannot be seen as a curtailment upon our present in which the present is asked simply to repeat the past. The Story is to be critically appropriated by the present to empower us for the ongoing journey. Nevertheless, it is important to recognize that this remembering and making present of the Story is a *conservative* activity in the best sense of that term. It is a refusal to lose the past and its life-giving possibilities for us. It conserves and preserves our tradition. Without that both our present and our future are impoverished, but from it we can draw new life and hope.

In a sense, this conserving function of the Christian religious educator is a priestly activity. Apart from the responsibility to offer sacrifice the priest in the ancient world and among the Hebrew people was the "custodian of sacred tradition."[14] The priests were the conserving force in the community.[15] In that Christian religious educators serve a conserving function in the Christian community, there is a priestliness to our ministry.

To Propose the Vision

Our Christian Story invites a response and makes a promise. Thus out of the Story we conserve, a Vision emerges that we must make present already by living lives of Christian faith even as it offers the sure hope of God's completed Kingdom. It is by proposing this Vision which arises from our Story that our pilgrim progress is ensured and stagnation avoided. While we affirm and conserve what has been, we must also recognize and respond to what is "not yet." To accept our past as final or our present as complete is a refusal of our Christian vocation to be pilgrims.

If remembering the Story is a conserving activity, proposing the Vision is the liberating dimension of our ministry as Christian religious educators. We must reside in the midst of that dialectic—between conservation and liberation—and attempt to maintain dual loyalties to what has been and to what is not yet. As Jesus said, "Every scribe who is learned in the reign of God is like the head of a household who can bring from his storeroom both the new and the old" (Matt. 13:52). By performing this aspect of our task—that is, by refusing to allow people to settle for what we have or who we are in the present—we are in fact performing something akin to a prophetic function in the community.

The old Hebrew prophets were men and women who refused to accept the "given" world and way of life as being inevitably in accordance with the will of God. The Jeremiahs, the Ezekiels, and the Amoses caused people to critically question their lives to discern the real meaning of God's will for the people. In the biblical tradition God constantly used prophets to call people to such critical discernment. "From the day that your fathers left the land of Egypt even to this day, I have sent you untiringly all my servants the prophets" (Jer. 7:25). Bruce Vawter writes of the prophets and the literature they gave rise to: "The social message was admittedly a major emphasis, but its explanation is to be found in the function of the Israelite prophet—serving as a conscience for his people in precisely those matters where conscience was needed." [16]

In the New Testament Jesus is addressed as "Teacher" forty-eight times and his work referred to as "teaching" some fifty times (a reminder to us that *teacher* is a noble title). But he is very much a prophetic teacher. In fact, writes McKenzie, "he resembles the prophet more than any other Hebrew religious figure." [17] In the same incident when Mark describes Jesus' activity as teaching, Jesus refers to himself as prophet (Mark 6:1–6).

Whenever Christian teachers bring the Word to bear on lived experience to interpret it and invite a Christian response, they are performing a prophetic activity. Whenever we cause people to critically reflect on their lives in light of the Story, and propose a Vision that calls people beyond their taken-for-granted world, we are being prophetic. Precisely because true education does not fit people into reality but causes them to deal with it critically and creatively, Freire calls such education "prophetic." [18] Without this prophetic element in our Christian religious education we are more likely to be involved in domestication than in education.

A Christian educator might well protest, "But I do not have the courage and strength it takes to be a prophet." Such a response is reasonable and indicates an understanding of what is involved in being prophetic. Great prophets always need great courage, and they often pay the price for their risk taking. Prophecy has always been a hazardous occupation—witness Jesus. In his lament over Jerusalem, Jesus says, "Oh Jerusalem, Jerusalem, you slay the prophets and stone those who are sent to you!" (Luke 13:34). Vawter insists that the prophet had to be a person "who was personally involved in the word, who lived for it and was prepared to die for it."[19] Hesitation about being prophetic would thus seem in order. In fact, if you ever meet an overly willing prophet, doubt him or her. Christ the prophet was also Christ the suffering servant. Prophecy in our time requires no less courage. But if we cannot be great prophets, we can at least try to be small prophets. As best we can, we need to cause people and ourselves to question our social world and act to create it in the direction of the Kingdom.

I believe reclaiming this prophetic dimension of our ministry as Christian religious educators has rich possibilities for our praxis. But like prophets themselves, such a reclamation could be dangerous, and there are at least three cautions that I want to voice. First, we should never think that our prophetic activity involves only criticism and questioning in a negative sense. As Abraham Heschel explains, "Almost every prophet brings consolation, promise, and the hope of reconciliation along with censure and castigation."[20] As I have stressed throughout this book, critical reflection is a creative and positive activity whose moment of questioning and refusing is only for the sake of recreating and moving beyond. I also repeat that the Story and its Vision is always a "two-edged sword," which in the midst of its mandate brings affirmation, in the midst of its criticism brings consolation. There is a world of difference between prophets and "complainers."

My second caution is that we must be careful not to reclaim the prophetic dimension of our ministry to legitimate us in what could be an elitist and oppressive way of being "over" those we educate. Such a danger exists in the popular image of the prophet (and of the educator) as someone who has "the word" to give everyone else. In addition, there seems to be a basic tendency in all of us to assume that we know what is best for others and a willingness to tell them so. Such notions are a misunderstanding of the prophetic dimension of our ministry. Our prophecy must be a being with, rather than a being over, others. Here I repeat again that Jesus the Prophet was also the suffering Servant. He came among us, was with us as one of us, "not to be served by others, but to serve, to give his own life as a ransom for the many" (Matt. 20:28). Christian educators especially must heed the words of Paul:

> Your attitude must be that of Christ. Though he was in the form of God, he did not deem equality with God something to be grasped at. Rather, he emptied himself and took the form of a slave, being born in the likeness of men. (Phil. 2:5–7)

This same kind of *kenosis* (self-emptying) is required of us educators, whereby we empty ourselves of the need to "lord it over" our students and instead enter into solidarity and partnership with them. We must be willing to share our prophetic word with them but open, in turn, to hear their prophetic word to us. In this self-emptying to be with, there is a dialectical relationship between the prophet and the community.[21] The prophetic word and witness are being ever refined and transcended because of the prophetic response of the community itself, to which the prophet must be willing to listen. And there is a dialectical relationship between the prophet and the prophetic word that he or she speaks. We are constantly being called forward by our own word. In the educational context this means that when we educators cease being learners, we also disqualify ourselves as educators.

Last, we cannot assume that educators "have a corner" on prophecy in the Christian community. As the prophetic aspect is only one dimension of our ministry, so, too, we fulfill no more than one aspect of the prophetic ministry needed by the community. But the faith life of the community will be impoverished if educators do not fulfill our part of the prophetic task.

Again, if Christian religious educators only cause people to look back and look forward, we could very well miss out on the present and the life that is now God's gift to us. It is here in our present historical context that we are to celebrate and respond to God's invitation to life. Christ came that we might have life and have it to the full (John 10:10), that his joy might be ours and our joy might be complete (John 15:11). Thus there is a third activity that needs to be a dimension of the Christian educator's ministry: enabling people to choose life, to embrace it, and to live their present with full humanity and joy.

To Choose Life

In a profound sense, both the Jewish and the Christian traditions are radical affirmations of the goodness of life. They are life-affirming rather than life-denying. This is evident from the opening pages of the Bible onward. In the creation myth in Genesis, God is portrayed as seeing creation as "good" and human life as "very good." This affirmation is repeated for Christians in the Incarnation. That the divine expressed itself uniquely in human form in the person of Jesus Christ, that the Word was made flesh, is an affirmation of the blessedness and potential of our human existence. Life is to be affirmed, chosen, and lived to its fullest.

The Gospels are Good News for our time and for all time. They are the joyful news that death has been conquered and that we may have life; that the Kingdom has already come and is sure to come in all its fullness. Because of this, in the midst of our looking back and looking forward, we can choose life in our present; we can live it fully and with joy.

We can afford to choose and live our present with joy because the coming of the Kingdom does not depend entirely on us. If we begin to think that bringing about the Kingdom is our task alone, then the anxiety of that burden will distract us from our present and the life it offers; we would need to occupy ourselves totally with what is not yet. But the Kingdom is always God's generous gift to which we respond, rather than something we deserve or earn by ourselves. Rubem Alves, writing about the Exodus of the Israelites and their journey toward the Promised Land, says that the Israelites "could rest because the politics of liberation was not carried on by the power of man alone, but rather by the passion and activity of God. Therefore, it was not only possible to rest in the present without losing the future but rather necessary to rest in the present in order not to lose the future."[22]

The same is true of us in our time. There is a profound sense in which the Kingdom is already among us. In this we have the consequences of our past (especially the dying and rising of Jesus the Christ) and the seeds of our future. But if we concentrate only on our seedlings, we will miss out on the blossoms that are fruits of past generations, to whom our time was future. Thus Christian religious educators can afford to choose life, to live their present humanly and with joy, and they have the task of sponsoring other people to so live in Jesus Christ.

And again, enabling people to choose and celebrate life requires the same incarnational activity on our part that making present the Word always requires. In a special way it requires solidarity with the poor, the oppressed, the marginal, and all those who must struggle against life-denying social structures in order to stay alive. But our solidarity cannot be only with those who are economically and socially poor. We live in a time when the impoverished of our world are actively struggling for the right to life while, ironically, the affluent have increasing difficulty in finding reasons to live. Christian religious educators must be "with" both groups. The challenge of bringing the Good News to the poor is no greater than the task of bringing Christ's authentic message to the so-called wealthy, who are often so poor in the possessions of the Kingdom. As long as some have too much of the earth's goods and others have too little, no one can have true life.

To summarize, we must relate to the people we educate as subjects who are capable of being engaged in history to shape it in the direction of the Kingdom. As we attempt, in the ministry of Christian religious education, to represent Christ in service to the community, it is a ministry of the Word and of incarnating that Word. The substance of our teaching act consists of a threefold responsibility: to make present the Story, to propose its Vision, and to choose life in the present. Being aware to some extent of my own bias, I will avoid claiming that education is the most important ministry in the Christian community. But I do claim that it is second to none.

NOTES

1. Rahner, *Foundations*, p. 138.
2. As educators we need to pay close attention to the children's rights literature. See especially, Gottlieb, *Children's Liberation*; B. and R. Gross, *The Children's Rights Movement*; and for the educational implications of the children's rights movement see *Harvard Educational Review* 43:4 and 44:1.
3. See, especially, deMause, *The History of Childhood*. See also *The History of Childhood Quarterly*.
4. It is now estimated that more than one million children annually are seriously abused or neglected in the United States alone (see Helfer and Kempe, *Child Abuse and Neglect*).
5. Bernard Cooke implies that there are educational dimensions in all forms of Christian ministry; see his *Ministry to Word and Sacraments: History and Theology*, pp. 33 ff, 405 ff.
6. Powers, "On Keeping One's Balance," p. 58.
7. Sölle, *Christ the Representative*, p. 50.
8. Ibid., p. 123.
9. See Sölle, *Political Theology*, p. 107.
10. If the Church as an institution could realize this distinction between representation and substitution, we might have fewer of the problems that arise from making the Church synonymous with Christ without any qualification whatever.
11. Raymond Brown, *The Gospel According to John XIII–XXI*, 2:1139.
12. Käsemann, *The Testament of Jesus*, pp. 45–46.
13. Huebner, "Toward a Remaking of Curricular Language," p. 41.
14. *The Interpreters Dictionary of the Bible*, "Priests and Levites," by R. Abba, 3:879. See also McKenzie, *Dictionary of the Bible*, "Priest," pp. 689–692, esp. p. 691.
15. It is interesting to note that throughout their history priests as a group have generally been looked upon and have served as "conservers of tradition." I do not say this in a pejorative way. It is an essential service in any community that is to maintain itself. But it becomes a problem when all other ministries are subsumed into or subordinated to the priestly ministry. In that event reform and renewal is less likely to occur, and the prophetic element is often stifled. People who look exclusively to priests for reform in the Church are likely to be disappointed. Being reformers is not their tradition.
16. *The Jerome Biblical Commentary*, "Introduction to Prophetic Literature," by Bruce Vawter, 1:233.
17. McKenzie, *Dictionary of the Bible*, "Prophet, Prophecy," p. 699.
18. The educator as prophet is a common theme throughout Freire's work. For a strong statement see, for example, Freire, "Forword," in Goulet, *A New Moral Order*.
19. *The Jerome Biblical Commentary*, "Introduction to Prophetic Literature," by B. Vawter, 1:237.
20. Heschel, *The Prophets*, 1:12.
21. Freire recognizes that in the activity of consciousness raising, or what I call here prophetic activity, it is sometimes necessary for the leader to take a position contrary to that of both the oppressors and the oppressed (to use Freire's language) if a genuine alternative is to be forged. Freire explains, "Due to certain historical conditions, the movement by the revolutionary leaders to the people is either horizontal—so that leaders and people form one body in contradiction to the oppressor—or it is triangular, with the revolutionary leaders occupying the vertex of the triangle in contradiction to the oppressors and to the oppressed as well. As we have seen, the latter situation is forced on the leaders when the people have not yet achieved a critical perception of oppressive reality" (*Oppressed*, pp. 164–165).
22. Alves, *A Theology of Human Hope*, p. 156.

Postscript: Until Break of Day

"I will live in the Past, the Present, and the Future!" Scrooge repeated, as he scrambled out of bed. "The Spirits of all Three shall strive within me. Oh Jacob Marley! Heaven, and the Christmas Time be praised for this! I say it on my knees, old Jacob, on my knees!"

CHARLES DICKENS, *A Christmas Carol*

THE TASK of the Christian religious educator, much like the task Dickens posed for old Scrooge, is to live in the past, the present, and the future; to be with pilgrims in time. In this work I have dwelt on six foundational issues that must be addressed in every time. They are not our only questions, and the responses offered here are certainly not posed as final. On the contrary, I invite other Christian religious educators to enter into dialogue and dialectic with my statement. We must continue to wrestle with these issues for our time even as we build upon what we have inherited, and hope to leave something worth inheriting after us. I am convinced that to faithfully fulfill our mandate as educators in the Christian community, all would-be educators must ask and answer these questions for themselves: What is the nature, purpose, and context of our task? How do we approach doing it, giving attention to the readiness of the participants? Who are the copartners in the enterprise? These questions can never be answered once and for all; they must be answered over and over again. This calls us as educators to an ongoing conversion, or, in the language I have used, to critical consciousness about the what, why, where, how, when, and who of our educating. As Scrooge remembered Jacob Marley, we must remember another Jacob and the story of Jacob's wrestling (Gen. 32:23–33).

Jacob was on his way to meet his brother Esau whom he had cheated out of his birthright. He came to the ford of the Jabbok and rested for the night. But in the course of the night he arose, took his family, servants, and possessions across the stream, and then "Jacob was left there alone" (25a). In the darkness and solitude, "some man wrestled with him" (25b). It was a long and fierce struggle that lasted "until the breaking of the dawn" (25c). Jacob was broken but not vanquished in the encounter. "When the man saw that he could not prevail over him, he struck Jacob's hip at its socket, so that the hip socket was wrenched as they wrestled" (26). Jacob wrung a blessing from his assailant, whom eventually he identified as God (31). He was given a new name, Israel, "because you have contended with divine and human beings and have prevailed" (29b). Jacob asked to know the wrestler's name, but the wrestler refused. If Jacob knew the name, he would also know the nature and would have bound the wrestler to himself. As the sun rose, Jacob went away to meet his brother with a new name and a blessing for his people, but carrying in his body the mark of his conversion: "Jacob limped" (32a).

Is this simply a story about a man, Jacob, who confronted God standing erect and with eyes open? Or was Jacob wrestling with his past and with his future, the wrongs he had done against his brother and the thought of meeting him the next day? Or have we presented here prophetically the entire history of Israel and their relationship with God? Or is the story paradigmatic of the whole human quest to know God, the wrestling it requires and the limits of our knowing.

Perhaps it is all of these and more. At the end of this work I cannot help but think of it as a story for religious educators that captures the struggle to which we are called and helps keep in perspective all of our attempts to sponsor people toward personally owned and authentic faith.

Elie Wiesel describes the passage as "a confused and confusing episode in which the protagonists bear more than one name; in which words have more than one meaning and every question brings forth another" (*Messengers of God*, p. 22). Undoubtedly, the names and words used throughout this book have more than one meaning, and the six foundational questions bring forth others. But as the name Israel came to mean struggle and endurance, we must continue to wrestle with the task of being educators who lead out toward the Kingdom of God, "until break of day." That is our Story and Vision.

Bibliography

Abbott, Walter M., ed. *The Documents of Vatican II.* Translated by Joseph Gallagher. New York: America Press, 1966.

Alves, Rubem A. *A Theology of Human Hope.* St. Meinard, Ind.: Abbey Press, 1969.

Anderson, Bernhard W. *The Living Word of the Bible.* Philadelphia: Westminster Press, 1979.

Anselm, Saint. *St. Anselm: Basic Writings.* Translated by S. N. Deane. The Open Court Library of Philosophy, No. P54. LaSalle, Ill.: Open Court, 1962.

Aquinas, Saint Thomas. *The Catechetical Instructions of St. Thomas Aquinas.* Translated by Joseph B. Collins. New York: Joseph F. Wagner, 1947.

Aquinas, Saint Thomas. *Summa Theologica.* 3 vols. Translated by Fathers of the English Dominican Province. New York: Benziger Bros., 1947.

Argyle, Michael, and Beit-Hallahmi, Benjamin. *The Social Psychology of Religion.* London: Routledge and Kegan Paul, 1975.

Aristotle. *The Basic Works of Aristotle.* Edited, with an Introduction, by Richard McKeon. New York: Random House, 1941.

Aristotle. *Ethics: The Ethics of Aristotle.* Translated by J. A. K. Thomson. New York: Penguin Books, 1977.

Aristotle. *Nichomachean Ethics.* Book Six. Translated by L. H. G. Greenwood. Philosophy of Plato and Aristotle. New York: Arno Press, 1973.

Aristotle. *The Works of Aristotle Translated into English.* Edited by W. D. Ross. Oxford: Clarendon Press, 1949–1956.

Assmann, Hugo. *Theology for a Nomad Church.* Maryknoll, N.Y.: Orbis Books, 1975.

Augustine, Saint. *City of God.* Edited by Vernon J. Bourke. Translated by Gerald G. Walsh et al. Garden City, N.Y.: Doubleday, Image Books, 1958.

Augustine, Saint. *The Confessions of Saint Augustine.* Translated by John K. Ryan. Garden City, N.Y.: Doubleday, Image Books, 1960.

Augustine, Saint. "The First Catechetical Instruction." Translated by Joseph P. Christopher. In *Ancient Christian Writers,* Vol. 2. Westminster, Md.: Newman Press, 1962.

Augustine, Saint. *Lectures or Tractates on the Gospel According to St. John*. 2 vols. Translated by John Gibb. The Works of Aurelius Augustine, Vol. X. Edited by Marcus Dods. Edinburgh: T. and T. Clark, 1873.

Augustine, Saint. "On the Spirit and the Letter." In *The Anti Pelagian Works of Saint Augustine*. 3 vols. Translated by Peter Holmes. The Works of Aurelius Augustine, Vol. IV. Edited by Marcus Dods. Edinburgh: T. and T. Clark, 1872.

Augustine, Saint. *The Teacher*. Translated by Robert P. Russell. Washington, D.C.: Catholic University of America Press, 1968.

Aulén, Gustaf. *Christus Victor*. Translated by A. G. Herbert. New York: Macmillan, 1967.

Aulén, Gustaf. *Jesus in Contemporary Historical Research*. Translated by Ingalill H. Hjelm. Philadelphia: Fortress Press, 1976.

Babin, Pierre. *Options*. New York: Herder and Herder, 1967.

Bandas, Rudôlph G. *Catechetical Methods*. New York: J. F. Wagner, 1929.

Baum, Gregory. *Religion and Alienation*. New York: Paulist Press, 1975.

Beckett, Samuel. *Waiting for Godot*. New York: Grove Press, 1954.

Bellack, Arno. "History of Curriculum Thought and Practice." *Review of Educational Research* 39:3 (June 1969):283–290.

Berger, Peter L. *Invitation to Sociology: A Humanistic Perspective*. Garden City, N.Y.: Doubleday, 1963.

Berger, Peter L. *The Sacred Canopy*. Garden City, N.Y.: Doubleday, Anchor Books, 1969.

Berger, Peter, and Luckmann, Thomas. *The Social Construction of Reality*. Garden City, N.Y.: Doubleday, 1966.

Bernstein, Richard J. *Praxis and Action*. Philadelphia: University of Pennsylvania Press, 1971.

Boff, Leonardo. *Jesus Christ Liberator: A Critical Christology for Our Time*. Translated by Patrick Hughes. Maryknoll, N.Y.: Orbis Books, 1978.

Bonhoeffer, Dietrich. *The Cost of Discipleship*. New York: Macmillan, 1969.

Bonhoeffer, Dietrich. *Letters and Papers from Prison*. Edited by Eberhard Bethge. New York: Macmillan, 1971.

Bonino, José Míguez. *Christians and Marxists*. Grand Rapids, Mich.: William B. Eerdmans, 1976.

Boys, Mary C. "Access to Traditions and Transformation." In *Tradition and Transformation in Religious Education*. Edited by Padraic O'Hare. Birmingham, Ala.: Religious Education Press, 1979.

Boys, Mary C. *Biblical Interpretation in Religious Education*. Birmingham, Ala.: Religious Education Press, 1980.

Bronfenbrenner, Urie. *Two Worlds of Childhood: U.S. and U.S.S.R.* New York: Russel Sage Foundation, 1970.

Brown, Raymond. "Bishops and Theologians: 'Dispute' Surrounded by Fiction." *Origins* 7:43 (April 13, 1978):673–682.

Brown, Raymond. *The Gospel According to John*. 2 vols. The Anchor Bible Series, Vol. 29. Garden City, N.Y.: Doubleday, 1966.

Brown, Robert McAfee. *Theology in a New Key*. Philadelphia: Westminster Press, 1978.

Buber, Martin. *I and Thou*. Translated by Walter Kaufmann. New York: Charles Scribner's Sons, 1970.

Buren, Paul M. van. *The Burden of Freedom*. New York: Seabury Press, 1976.

Burghardt, Walter J. "Free Like God: Recapturing an Ancient Anthropology." *Theology Digest* 26:4 (Winter 1978):343-364.

Burnet, John. *Aristotle on Education*. Cambridge: Cambridge University Press, 1936.

Burnet, John. *Early Greek Philosophy*. 4th ed. London: Adam and Charles Black, 1952.

Bushnell, Horace. *Christian Nurture*. New Haven, Conn.: Yale University Press, 1967.

Carrier, Herve. *The Sociology of Religious Belonging*. Translated by Arthur J. Aurrieri. New York: Herder and Herder, 1965.

Caster, Marcel van. "A Catechesis for Liberation." *Lumen Vitae* 27:2 (June 1972):281-303.

Caster, Marcel van, and Le Du, Jean. *Experiential Catechetics*. New York: Newman Press, 1969.

Catechism of the Council of Trent for Parish Priests. Edited by John McHugh and Charles Callen. New York: Wagner, 1923.

Chadwick, Owen. *From Bossuet to Newman: The Idea of Doctrinal Development*. Cambridge: Cambridge University Press, 1957.

The Church in the Present-Day Transformation of Latin America in the Light of the Council. Washington, D.C.: U.S.C.C., 1970.

The Church Teaches: Documents of the Church in English Translation. Translated and Compiled by John F. Clarkson et al. Rockford, Ill.: Tan Books, 1973.

Clasby, Miriam. "Education as a Tool for Humanization and the Work of Paulo Freire." *Living Light* 8:1 (Spring 1971):48-59.

Clausen, J. A., ed. *Socialization and Society*. Boston: Little Brown, 1968.

Coe, George Albert. *A Social Theory of Religious Education*. New York: Arno Press and the New York Times, 1969.

Coe, George Albert. *What Is Christian Education?* New York: Charles Scribner's Sons, 1929.

Coleman, John A. "Vision and Praxis in American Theology." *Theological Studies* 37:1 (March 1976):3-40.

Collins, Denis. *Paulo Freire*. New York: Paulist Press, 1978.

Comenius, J. A. *The Great Didactic*. Edited and translated by M. W. Keatinge. New York: Russell and Russell, 1967.

Cone, James. *Black Theology and Black Power*. New York: Seabury Press, 1969.

Congar, Yves M. *A History of Theology*. Edited and translated by Hunter Guthrie. Garden City, N.Y.: Doubleday, 1968.

Congar, Yves. "The Magisterium and Theologians—A Short History." *Theology Digest* 25:1 (Spring 1971):15-20.

Connerton, Paul, ed. *Critical Sociology*. New York: Penguin Books, 1976.

Cooke, Bernard. *Ministry to Word and Sacraments: History and Theology*. Philadelphia: Fortress Press, 1976.

Cooley, C. H. *Human Nature and the Social Order*. Glencoe, Ill.: The Free Press, 1956.

Cremin, Lawrence. *Traditions of American Education*. New York: Basic Books, 1977.

Crossan, John Dominic. *The Dark Interval: Towards a Theology of Story*. Niles, Ill.: Argus Communications, 1975.

Cully, Iris V. *Christian Child Development*. New York: Harper & Row, 1979.

Cully, Iris V. *The Dynamics of Christian Education*. Philadelphia: Westminster Press, 1958.

Cyril, Saint, Archbishop of Jerusalem. *The Catechetical Lectures.* Translated by E. H. Gifford. A Select Library of Nicene and Post-Nicene Fathers of the Christian Church, Vol. VII. New York: The Christian Literature Company, 1894.

Danziger, Kurt. *Readings in Child Socialization.* London: Pergamon Press, 1970.

Davis, Charles. "Theology and Praxis." *Cross Currents* 23:2 (Summer 1973):154–168.

Deloria, Vine. *God Is Red.* New York: Grosset and Dunlap, 1973.

Dewey, John. *Art as Experience.* New York: Capricorn Books, 1934.

Dewey, John. *Democracy and Education.* New York: Macmillan, 1916.

Dewey, John. *Dewey on Education.* Compiled by Martin S. Dworkin. Classics in Education, No. 3. New York: Teachers College Press, 1971.

Dewey, John. *Experience and Education.* New York: Collier Books, 1938.

Dewey, John. "My Pedagogic Creed." In *Dewey on Education.* Compiled by Martin S. Dworkin. Classics in Education No. 3. New York: Teachers College Press, 1971.

Dictionary of Biblical Theology. Edited by Xavier Léon-Dufour. New York: Seabury Press, 1977.

The Didache. Translated by James A. Kleist. In *Ancient Christian Writers,* Vol. 6. Westminster, Md.: Newman Press, 1948.

Dillenberger, John, ed. *Martin Luther: Selections from His Writings.* Garden City, N.Y.: Doubleday, Anchor Books, 1961.

Dreitzel, Hans Peter, ed. *Childhood and Socialization.* New York: Macmillan, 1973.

Dulles, Avery. "The Meaning of Faith Considered in Relationship to Justice." In *The Faith That Does Justice.* Edited by John C. Haughey. New York: Paulist Press, 1977.

Dulles, Avery. *Models of the Church.* Garden City, N.Y.: Doubleday, 1974.

Dulles, Avery. *The Resilient Church.* Garden City, N.Y.: Doubleday, 1977.

Dulles, Avery. *The Survival of Dogma.* Garden City, N.Y.: Doubleday, Image Books, 1971.

Dulles, Avery. "What Is Magisterium?" *Origens* 6:6 (July 1, 1976):81–87.

Durkheim, Emile. *The Rules of Sociological Method.* New York: The Free Press, 1964.

Easton, Burton Scott, ed. *The Apostolic Tradition of Hippolytus.* Cambridge: The University Press, 1934.

Easton, Lloyd D., and Guddat, Kurt, eds. and trans. *Writings of the Young Karl Marx on Philosophy and Society.* Garden City, N.Y.: Doubleday, 1967.

Eby, Frederick. *Early Protestant Educators.* New York: McGraw-Hill, 1931.

Elias, John. *Conscientization and Deschooling.* Philadelphia: Westminster Press, 1976.

Elkind, David. "The Children Man." *New York Times Book Review.* May 14, 1978, p. 7.

Elliott, Harrison S. *Can Religious Education Be Christian?* New York: Macmillan, 1953.

Emling, John F. "To Invent Is to Understand: Creative Aspects and Perspectives of Jean Piaget's New Discipline." *Religious Education* 73:5 (Sept.–Oct. 1978):551–568.

The Encyclopedia of Philosophy. 8 vols. Edited by Paul Edwards. New York: Macmillan and The Free Press, 1967.

Erdozain, Luis. "The Evolution of Catechetics." *Lumen Vitae* 25 (March 1970):7–31.

Erikson, Erik H. *Childhood and Society.* New York: W. W. Norton, 1963.

Fahy, Patrick. *Factors Predictive of Religious Outcomes in Australian Catholic Secondary Schools.* Ph.D. dissertation, Boston College, January 1980.

Flynn, Marcellin. *Some Catholic Schools in Action.* Sydney, Australia: Catholic Education Office, 1975.

Fowler, James W. "Faith and the Structuring of Meaning." Unpublished, longer version of a presentation to the American Psychological Association Convention, San Francisco, August 26, 1977.

Fowler, James W. "Faith Development Theory and the Aims of Religious Socialization." In *Emerging Issues in Religious Education.* Edited by Gloria Durka and Joanmarie Smith. New York: Paulist Press, 1976.

Fowler, James W. "Faith, Liberation and Human Development." *The Foundation* (Atlanta: Gammon Theological Seminary) 79 (Spring 1974).

Fowler, James W. "Stages in Faith: The Structural-Developmental Approach." In *Values and Moral Development.* Edited by Thomas C. Hennessy. New York: Paulist Press, 1976.

Fowler, James W. "Toward a Developmental Perspective on Faith." *Religious Education* 69:2 (March–April 1974):207–219.

Fowler, James, and Keen, Sam. *Life Maps: Conversations on the Journey of Faith.* Edited by Jerome Berryman. Waco, Tex.: Word Books, 1978.

Francke, Augustus Hermann. *Memoirs of Augustus Hermann Franke.* Philadelphia: American Sunday School Union, 1831.

Freire, Paulo. "Conscientization." *Cross Currents* 24:1 (Spring 1974):23–31.

Freire, Paulo. *Cultural Action for Freedom.* Cambridge, Mass.: Harvard Educational Review, 1970.

Freire, Paulo. *Education for Critical Consciousness.* New York: Seabury Press, 1973.

Freire, Paulo. *Pedagogy in Process.* New York: Seabury Press, 1978.

Freire, Paulo. *Pedagogy of the Oppressed.* New York: Seabury Press, 1970.

Freud, Sigmund. *The Future of an Illusion.* New York: W. W. Norton, 1961.

Froebel, F. W. *The Education of Man.* Translated by W. F. Hailmann. New York: D. Appleton, 1912.

Fuller, Reginald H. "The Double Commandment of Love." In *Essays on the Love Commandment.* Edited by Luise Schottroff et al. Translated by Reginald H. Fuller and Ilse Fuller. Philadelphia: Fortress Press, 1978.

Furth, Hans G. *Piaget and Knowledge.* Englewood Cliffs, N.J.: Prentice-Hall, 1969.

Furth, Hans G. *Piaget for Teachers.* Englewood Cliffs, N.J.: Prentice-Hall, 1970.

Gadamer, Hans-Georg. "On the Scope and Function of Hermeneutical Reflection." *Continuum* 8:1–2 (Spring–Summer 1970):77–95.

Gadamer, Hans-Georg. *Truth and Method.* New York: Seabury Press, 1975.

The General Catechetical Directory. Washington, D.C.: U.S.C.C., 1971.

Gilkey, Langdon. *Naming the Whirlwind: The Renewal of God-Language.* Indianapolis: Bobbs-Merrill, 1969.

Ginsberg, Herbert, and Opper, Sylvia. *Piaget's Theory of Intellectual Development.* Englewood Cliffs, N.J.: Prentice-Hall, 1969.

Goldman, Ronald. *Readiness for Religion.* New York: Seabury Press, 1965.

Goldman, Ronald. *Religious Thinking from Childhood to Adolescence.* New York: Seabury Press, 1965.

Goslin, David A., ed. *Handbook of Socialization Theory and Research.* Chicago: Rand McNally, 1969.

Gottlieb, David, ed. *Children's Liberation.* Englewood Cliffs, N.J.: Prentice-Hall, 1973.

Goulet, Denis. *A New Moral Order*. Maryknoll, N.Y.: Orbis Books, 1974.

Greeley, Andrew M., McCready, William C., and McCourt, Kathleen. *Catholic Schools in a Declining Church*. Kansas City: Sheed & Ward, 1976.

Greeley, Andrew M., and Rossi, Peter H. *The Education of Catholic Americans*. Chicago: Aldine, 1966.

Gremillion, Joseph. *The Gospel of Peace and Justice: Catholic Social Teaching Since Pope John*. Maryknoll, N.Y.: Orbis Books, 1976.

Groome, T. H. "The Crossroads: A Story of Christian Education by Shared Praxis." *Lumen Vitae* 32:1 (March 1977):45–70.

Gross, Beatrice, and Gross, Ronald, eds. *The Children's Rights Movement*. Garden City; N.Y.: Doubleday, Anchor Books, 1977.

Gutierrez, Gustavo. *A Theology of Liberation*. Maryknoll, N.Y.: Orbis Books, 1973.

Habermas, Jürgen. *Knowledge and Human Interests*. Boston: Beacon Press, 1971.

Habermas, Jürgen. *Legitimation Crisis*. Boston: Beacon Press, 1975.

Habermas, Jürgen. "On Systematically Distorted Communication." *Inquiry* 13 (1970):205–218.

Habermas, Jürgen. "Summation and Response." *Continuum* 8:1 & 2 (Spring–Summer 1970):123–133.

Habermas, Jürgen. *Theory and Practice*. Boston: Beacon Press, 1973.

Habermas, Jürgen. "Towards a Theory of Communicative Competence." *Inquiry* 13 (1970):360–375.

Halbfas, Hubert. *Theory of Catechetics*. New York: Herder and Herder, 1971.

Häring, Bernard. *Free and Faithful in Christ: Moral Theology for Clergy and Laity*. New York: Seabury Press, 1978.

Häring, Bernard. *The Law of Christ*. Translated by Edwin G. Kaiser. Cork, Ireland: The Mercier Press, 1963.

Harkness, Georgia. *Understanding the Kingdom of God*. Nashville, Tenn.: Abingdon Press, 1974.

Harvard Educational Review 43:4 (Nov. 1973) and 44:1 (Feb. 1974).

Hegel, G. W. F. *The Phenomenology of Mind*. 2nd ed. Translated by J. B. Baillie. London: George Allen and Unwin, 1949.

Hegel, G. W. F. *Reason in History: A General Introduction to the Philosophy of History*. Translated by Robert S. Hartman. New York: Liberal Arts Press, 1953.

Heidegger, Martin. *Being and Time*. Translated by John Macquarrie and Edward Robinson. New York: Harper & Row, 1962.

Heidegger, Martin. *On the Way to Language*. New York: Harper & Row, 1971.

Helfer, R. E., and Kempe, C. H., eds. *Child Abuse and Neglect: The Family and Community*. Cambridge, Mass.: Ballinger, 1976.

Hellesnes, Jon. "Education and the Concept of Critique." *Continuum* 8:1 & 2 (Spring–Summer 1970):40–51.

Herbart, J. F. *The Science of Education*. Translated by H. Felkin and E. Felkin. Boston: Heath, 1896.

Heschel, Abraham J. *The Prophets*. 2 vols. New York: Harper & Row, 1962.

Hodgson, Peter C. *New Birth of Freedom*. Philadelphia: Fortress Press, 1976.

Hoffman, John. *Marxism and the Theory of Praxis*. New York: International Publishers, 1976.

Hofinger, Johannes. *The Art of Teaching Christian Doctrine: The Good News and Its Proclamation*. Notre Dame, Ind.: University of Notre Dame Press, 1957.

Howe, Leroy T. "Religious Understanding from a Piagetian Perspective." *Religious Education* 73:5 (Sept.–Oct. 1978):569–581.

Howe, Reuel L. "The Dialogical Foundations for Christian Education." In *An Introduction to Christian Education*. Edited by Marvin J. Taylor. Nashville: Abingdon Press, 1966.

Howe, Reuel L. *The Miracle of Dialogue*. New York: Seabury Press, 1963.

Huebner, Dwayne. "Curriculum as Concern for Man's Temporality." In *Heightened Consciousness, Cultural Revolution, and Curriculum Theory*. Edited by William Pinar. Berkeley, Calif.: McCutchen, 1974.

Huebner, Dwayne. "Toward a Political Economy of Curriculum and Human Development." In *Curriculum Theory*. Edited by Alex Molnar and John A. Zahorik. Washington, D.C.: A.S.C.D., 1977.

Huebner, Dwayne. "Toward a Remaking of Curricular Language." In *Heightened Consciousness, Cultural Revolution, and Curriculum Theory*. Edited by William Pinar. Berkeley, Calif.: McCutchen, 1974.

Idinopulos, Thomas A. "Christianity and the Holocaust." *Cross Currents* 28:3 (Fall 1978):257–267.

Inhelder, Bärbel, and Piaget, Jean. *The Growth of Logical Thinking*. New York: Basic Books, 1958.

International Encyclopedia of the Social Sciences. 17 vols. Edited by David L. Sills. New York: Macmillan and The Free Press, 1968.

The Interpreters Dictionary of the Bible. 4 vols. Edited by George Aurther Buttrick et al. Nashville: Abingdon Press, 1962.

James, William. *The Principles of Psychology*. 2 vols. New York: Henry Holt, 1893.

Jay, Martin. *The Dialectical Imagination*. Boston: Little, Brown, 1973.

The Jerome Biblical Commentary. 2 vols. Edited by Raymond E. Brown et al. Englewood Cliffs, N.J.: Prentice-Hall, 1968.

Joyce, Bruce, and Weil, Marsha. *Models of Teaching*. Englewood Cliffs, N.J.: Prentice-Hall, 1972.

Jungmann, Josef A. *The Good News: Yesterday and Today*. New York: Sadlier, 1962.

Jungmann, Josef A. *Handing on the Faith: A Manual of Catechetics*. Edited and translated by A. W. Feuerst. New York: Herder and Herder, 1959.

Jungmann, Josef A. "Religious Education in Late Middle Times." In *Shaping the Christian Message*. Edited by Gerard S. Slogan. New York: Macmillan, 1958.

Kamii, C., and DeVries, R. *Physical Knowledge in Preschool Education: Implications of Piaget's Theory*. Englewood Cliffs, N.J.: Prentice-Hall, 1978.

Kant, Immanuel. "What Is Enlightenment." In *On History*. Edited by Lewis Beck. Translated by Lewis Beck, Robert Anchor, and Emil Fackenheim. Indianapolis: Bobbs-Merrill, 1975.

Käsemann, Ernst. *Jesus Means Freedom*. Philadelphia: Fortress Press, 1969.

Käsemann, Ernst. *The Testament of Jesus*. Philadelphia: Fortress Press, 1968.

Kasper, Walter. *Jesus the Christ*. New York: Paulist Press, 1977.

Kauchak, Don. "T.V. Ads: What Are Youngsters Buying?" *Educational Leadership* 35:7 (April 1978):530–532.

Kegan, Robert G. "Ego and Truth: Personality and the Piaget Paradigm." Ph.D. dissertation, Harvard University, 1977.

Kennedy, David R. "Young Adults Confront a Bishop." *Today's Parish* 10:1 (January 1978):30–32.

Koyama, Kosuke. *Waterbuffalo Theology*. Maryknoll, N.Y.: Orbis Books, 1974.

Kuhn, Deanna. "Application of Piaget's Theory of Cognitive Development to Education." *Harvard Educational Review* 49:3 (August 1979):340–360.

Küng, Hans. *On Being a Christian*. Translated by Edward Quinn. Garden City, N.Y.: Doubleday, 1976.

Lamm, Norman. *Faith and Doubt: Studies in Traditional Jewish Thought*. New York: KTAV Publishing House, 1971.

Lee, James Michael. *The Flow of Religious Instruction*. Dayton, Ohio: Pflaum, 1973.

Lee, James Michael. *The Shape of Religious Instruction*. Dayton, Ohio: Pflaum, 1971.

Liddell, Henry George, and Scott, Robert, compilers. *A Greek-English Lexicon*. Oxford: Clarendon Press, 1968.

Lobkowicz, Nicholas. *Theory and Practice*. Notre Dame, Ind.: University of Notre Dame Press, 1967.

Locke, John. *Two Treatises on Government*. New York: Dutton, Everyman's Library, 1970.

Lonergan, Bernard. "Theology and Praxis." In *Proceedings of the Thirty Second Annual Convention, C.T.S.A.* Edited by Luke Salm. New York: Catholic Theological Society of America, 1977.

Lonergan, Bernard. *The Way to Nicaea*. Philadelphia: Westminster Press, 1976.

McBride, Alfred. "Reaction to Fowler: Fears About Procedure." In *Values and Moral Development*. Edited by Thomas C. Hennessy. New York: Paulist Press, 1976.

McBrien, Richard P. *Basic Questions for Christian Educators*. Winona, Minn.: St. Mary's College Press, 1977.

McBrien, Richard P. *Church: The Continuing Quest*. New York: Newman Press, 1970.

McBrien, Richard P. *Do We Need the Church?* New York: Harper & Row, 1969.

McBrien, Richard P. *The Remaking of the Church*. New York: Harper & Row, 1973.

McBrien, Richard. "Toward an American Catechesis." *The Living Light* 13:2 (Summer 1976):167–181.

McKenzie, John L. *Dictionary of the Bible*. London: Geoffrey Chapman, 1968.

Macquarrie, John. *Principles of Christian Theology*. 2nd ed. New York: Charles Scribner's Sons, 1977.

Mahowald, Mary B. "Feminism, Socialism and Christianity." *Cross Currents* 15:1 (Spring 1975):31–49.

Marthaler, Berard L. *Catechetics in Context*. Huntington, Ind.: Our Sunday Visitor, 1973.

Marthaler, Berard L. "Toward a Revisionist Model in Catechetics." *The Living Light* 13:3 (Fall 1976):458–469.

Marx, Karl. *Capital*. Edited by Frederich Engels. Translated by Samuel Moore and Edward Aveling. New York: International Publishers, 1967.

Marx, Karl. *A Contribution to the Critique of Political Economy*. Edited by M. Dobb. Translated by S. W. Ryazanskaya. New York: International Publishers, 1970.

Marx, Karl. "The Critique of Hegelian Philosophy." In *Critical Sociology*. Edited by Paul Connerton. New York: Penguin Books, 1976.

Marx, Karl. *Economic and Philosophic Manuscripts of 1844*. Translated by Martin Milligan. Moscow: Foreign Languages Publishing House, 1961.

Marx, Karl. "Theses on Feuerbach." In *The German Ideology*. New York: International Publishers, 1947.

Marx, Karl, and Engels, Friedrich. *Marx and Engels on Religion*. Introduction by
    Reinhold Niebuhr. New York: Schocken Books, 1964

Mause, Lloyd de, ed. *The History of Childhood*. New York: The Psychohistory Press,
    1974.

Mead, G. H. *Mind, Self and Society*. Chicago: University of Chicago Press, 1934.

Miller, Randolph Crump. *Christian Nurture and the Church*. New York: Charles
    Scribner's Sons, 1961.

Miller, Randolph Crump. *The Clue to Christian Education*. New York: Charles
    Scribner's Sons, 1952.

Moltmann, Jürgen. *The Church in the Power of the Spirit*. New York: Harper & Row,
    1977.

Moltmann, Jürgen. *The Crucified God*. New York: Paulist Press, 1977.

Moran, Gabriel. *Design for Religion*. New York: Herder and Herder, 1970.

Moran, Gabriel. *Education Toward Adulthood: Religion and Lifelong Learning*. New
    York: Paulist Press, 1979.

Moran, Gabriel. *The Present Revelation*. New York: Herder and Herder, 1972.

Moran, Gabriel. *Religious Body*. New York: Seabury Press, 1974.

Moran, Gabriel. "Religious Education Toward America." *Religious Education* 72:5
    (Sept./Oct. 1977):473–483.

Moran, Gabriel. "Two Languages of Religious Education." *The Living Light* 14:1
    (Spring 1977):7–15.

Nelson, C. Ellis. *Where Faith Begins*. Richmond: John Knox Press, 1971.

Neville, Gwen Kennedy, and Westerhoff, John H. *Learning Through Liturgy*. New
    York: Seabury Press, 1978.

The New Catholic Encyclopedia. 16 vols. New York: McGraw-Hill, 1967.

Newman, John Henry Cardinal. *An Essay on the Development of Christian Doctrine*.
    Westminster, Md.: Christian Classics, 1968.

Niebuhr, H. Richard. *Christ and Culture*. New York: Harper and Brothers, 1951.

Niebuhr, H. Richard. *The Meaning of Revelation*. New York: Macmillan, 1974.

Nietzsche, F. "Thus Spoke Zarathustra." *The Portable Nietzsche*. Compiled and trans-
    lated by Walter Kaufmann. New York: Viking Press, 1954.

O'Collins, Gerald. *What Are They Saying About Jesus?* New York: Paulist Press, 1977.

Ogden, Schubert M. *Faith and Freedom*. Nashville, Tenn.: Abingdon Press, 1979.

O'Hare, Padraic, ed. *Foundations of Religious Education*. New York: Paulist Press,
    1978.

O'Hare, Padraic, ed. *Tradition and Transformation in Religious Education*. Birming-
    ham, Ala.: Religious Education Press, 1979.

Palermo, James. "Pedagogy as a Critical Hermeneutic." *Cultural Hermeneutics* 3:2
    (August 1975):135–146.

Palmer, Richard E. *Hermeneutics*. Evanston, Ill.: Northwestern University Press, 1969.

Pannenberg, Wolfhart. *Jesus—God and Man*. Translated by Lewis L. Wilkins. Phila-
    delphia: Westminster Press, 1968.

Pannenberg, Wolfhart. *Theology and the Kingdom of God*. Philadelphia: Westminster
    Press, 1969.

Parks, Sharon. "Communities as Ministry: An Exploration of the Role of Community in
    Undergraduate Faith Development." *NICM Journal* 2:1 (Winter 1977):73–87.

Paton, David M., ed. *Breaking Barriers: Nairobi 1975*. Grand Rapids, Mich.: Wm. B.
    Eerdmans, 1976.

Perrin, Norman. *Jesus and the Language of the Kingdom.* Philadelphia: Fortress Press, 1976.

Pestalozzi, J. H. *How Gertrude Teaches Her Children.* Translated by L. E. Holland and F. C. Turner. Syracuse, N.Y.: Bardeen, 1894.

Phenix, Philip H. *Education and the Worship of God.* Philadelphia: Westminster Press, 1966.

Piaget, Jean. *Genetic Epistemology.* Translated by Eleanor Duckworth. New York: W. W. Norton, 1970.

Piaget, Jean. *Science of Education and the Psychology of the Child.* New York: Viking Press, 1971.

Piaget, Jean. *Six Psychological Studies.* Translated by David Elkind. New York: Random House, Vintage Books, 1967.

Piaget, Jean. *To Understand Is to Invent: The Future of Education.* New York: Penguin Books, 1973.

Piaget, Jean, and Inhelder, Bärbel. *The Psychology of the Child.* New York: Basic Books, 1969.

Pindar. *The Works of Pindar.* Translated by Lewis R. Farnell. London: MacMillan, 1930.

Plato. *The Republic.* In *Great Dialogues of Plato.* Translated by W. H. D. Rouse. New York: The New American Library, 1956.

Polanyi, Michael. *The Tacit Dimension.* Garden City, N.Y.: Doubleday, 1967.

Powers, Edward A. "On Keeping One's Balance." In *A Colloquy on Christian Education.* Philadelphia: United Church Press, 1972.

Quinton, Anthony. "Critical Theory: On the Frankfurt School." *Encounter* 43:4 (October 1974):43–53.

Radtke, Barbara Anne. "The State of Catechetics in U.S. Catholic Seminaries." *The Living Light* 12:3 (Fall 1975):373–391.

Rahner, Karl. "Christianity and the New Earth." *Theology Digest* 15 (Winter 1967):257–282.

Rahner, Karl. *Foundations of Christian Faith.* Translated by William V. Dych. New York: Seabury Press, 1978.

Rahner, Karl. *The Shape of the Church to Come.* New York: Seabury Press, 1974.

Rahner, Karl. *Theological Investigations.* 12 vols. Baltimore, Md.: Helicon Press, 1961.

Rauschenbusch, Walter. *Christianity and the Social Crisis.* New York: Macmillan, 1907.

Ricoeur, Paul. *Freud and Philosophy.* New Haven, Conn.: Yale University Press, 1970.

Ricoeur, Paul. *Interpretation Theory.* Fort Worth, Tex.: The Texas Christian University Press, 1976.

"The Rights of Children." Parts I & II. *Harvard Educational Review* 43:4 (Nov. 1973) and 44:1 (Feb. 1974).

Rite of Christian Initiation of Adults. Washington, D.C.: U.S.C.C., 1974.

Rite of Penance. Washington, D.C.: U.S.C.C., 1975.

Robinson, John A. T. *Honest to God.* Philadelphia: Westminster Press, 1963.

Rousseau, Jean Jacques. *Emile: Selections.* Translated and edited by William Boyd. Classics in Education, No. 10. New York: Teachers College Press, 1963.

Russell, Letty M. *Human Liberation in a Feminist Perspective: A Theology.* Philadelphia: Westminster Press, 1974.

Sacramentum Mundi. 6 vols. Edited by Karl Rahner. New York: Herder and Herder, 1968.

Sand, Ole. "Curriculum Change." *The Curriculum: Retrospect and Prospect.* In *The Seventieth Yearbook of the National Society for the Study of Education,* part 1. Edited by Robert M. McClure. Chicago: University of Chicago Press, 1971.

Sartre, Jean-Paul. *Being and Nothingness.* Translated by Hazel E. Barnes. New York: Philosophical Library, 1956.

Schillebeeckx, Edward. *Jesus.* New York: Seabury Press, 1979.

Schillebeeckx, Edward. *The Understanding of Faith.* New York: Seabury Press, 1974.

Schnackenburg, Rudolf. *God's Rule and Kingdom.* New York: Herder and Herder, 1963.

Schoof, Mark. *A Survey of Catholic Theology 1800-1970.* New York: Paulist Press, 1970.

Schoonenberg, Piet. *The Christ.* New York: Herder and Herder, 1971.

Schottroff, Luise. "Non-Violence and the Love of One's Enemies." In *Essays on the Love Commandment.* Edited by Luise Schottroff et al. Translated by Reginald H. Fuller and Ilse Fuller. Philadelphia: Fortress Press, 1978.

Schroyer, Trent. *The Critique of Domination.* New York: George Braziller, 1973.

Segundo, Juan. *The Liberation of Theology.* Maryknoll, N.Y.: Orbis Books, 1976.

Sharing the Light of Faith. National Catechetical Directory for Catholics of the United States. Washington, D.C.: U.S.C.C., 1979.

Sherrill, Lewis Joseph. *The Gift of Power.* New York: Macmillan, 1955.

Skinner, B. F. *Beyond Freedom and Dignity.* New York: Alfred A. Knopf, 1971.

Smart, James D. *The Teaching Ministry of the Church.* Philadelphia: Westminster Press, 1954.

Smith, H. Shelton. *Faith and Nurture.* New York: Charles Scribner's Sons, 1941.

Smith, Wilfred Cantwell. *Belief and History.* Charlottesville, Va.: University Press of Virginia, 1977.

Smith, Wilfred Cantwell. *The Meaning and End of Religion.* New York: Harper & Row, 1978.

Sobrino, Jon. *Christology at the Crossroads.* Translated by John Drury. Maryknoll, N.Y.: Orbis Books, 1978.

Sölle, Dorothee. *Christ the Representative.* Philadelphia: Fortress Press, 1967.

Sölle, Dorothee. *Political Theology.* Philadelphia: Fortress Press, 1974.

Steeman, Theodore M. "Durkheim's Professional Ethics." *Journal for The Scientific Study of Religion* 2:2 (Spring 1963):163-181.

Steere, Douglas V. *On Listening to Another.* New York: Harper & Row, 1961.

Stewart, J. A. *Notes on the Nicomachean Ethics of Aristotle.* Oxford: Clarendon Press, 1892.

Theological Dictionary of the New Testament. 10 vols. Edited by Gerhard Kittel. Edited and Translated by Geoffrey W. Bromiley. Grand Rapids, Mich.: Wm. B. Eerdmans, 1967.

Tillich, Paul. *Biblical Religion and the Search for Ultimate Reality.* Chicago: University of Chicago Press, 1955.

Tillich, Paul. *Systematic Theology.* Chicago: University of Chicago Press, 1957.

To Teach as Jesus Did. Washington, D.C.: U.S.C.C., 1973.

Tracy, David. *Blessed Rage for Order.* New York: Seabury Press, 1975.

Vygotsky, L. S. *Mind in Society.* Edited by Michael Cole et al. Cambridge, Mass.: Harvard University Press, 1978.

Wade, Stephen H. "Epistemology and the Matching of Intentions with Models in Religious Education." *Religious Education* 70:3 (May–June 1975):227–234.

Warford, Malcolm. "Between the Plumbing and the Saving: Education, Theology and Liberation." *Living Light* 11:1 (Spring 1974):60–76.

Warford, Malcolm L. *The Necessary Illusion.* Philadelphia: Pilgrim Press, 1976.

Weber, Max. *From Max Weber: Essays in Sociology.* Edited by H. H. Gerth and C. W. Mills. New York: Oxford University Press, 1976.

Weber, Max. *The Sociology of Religion.* Boston: Beacon Press, 1963.

Weil, Marsha, and Joyce, Bruce. *Information Processing Models of Teaching.* Englewood Cliffs, N.J.: Prentice-Hall, 1978.

Weil, Marsha, and Joyce, Bruce. *Social Models of Teaching.* Englewood Cliffs, N.J.: Prentice-Hall, 1978.

Weil, Marsha, Joyce, Bruce, and Kluwin, Bridget. *Personal Models of Teaching.* Englewood Cliffs, N.J.: Prentice-Hall, 1978.

Wellmer, Albrecht. *The Critical Theory of Society.* New York: Herder and Herder, 1971.

Westerhoff, John H. "A Call to Catechesis." *The Living Light* 14:3 (Fall 1977):354–358.

Westerhoff, John H., ed. *A Colloquy on Christian Education.* Philadelphia: United Church Press, 1972.

Westerhoff, John H., ed. *Who Are We?* Birmingham, Ala.: Religious Education Press, 1978.

Westerhoff, John H. *Will Our Children Have Faith?* New York: Seabury Press, 1976.

Westerhoff, John H., and Neville, Gwen K. *Generation to Generation.* Philadelphia: United Church Press, 1974.

Westerhoff, John H., and Neville, Gwen K. *Learning Through Liturgy.* New York: Seabury Press, 1978.

Whitehead, Alfred North. *The Aims of Education and Other Essays.* New York: The Free Press, 1929.

Wiesel, Elie. *Messengers of God.* New York: Pocket Books, 1977.

Wink, Walter. *The Bible in Human Transformation.* Philadelphia: Fortress Press, 1973.

Wyckoff, D. Campbell. *Theory and Design of the Christian Education Curriculum.* Philadelphia: Westminster Press, 1961.

Wyckoff, D. Campbell. "Understanding Your Church Curriculum." *The Princeton Seminary Bulletin* 63:1 (1970):77–84.

Yeats, William Butler. *The Collected Poems of W. B. Yeats.* New York: Macmillan, 1972.

Index